Advanced Investigation Strategies for IoT Forensics

Advanced Investigation Strategies for IoT Forensics: Technical Approaches to Encrypting, Security, and Investigation Strategies in IoT Forensics is an edited book that explores the crossroads of digital forensics and the Internet of Things. The book offers a one-stop solution to understanding forensic mechanisms, security weaknesses, and privacy issues in IoT ecosystems. Spanning core theories, applied case studies, and new approaches—such as AI, blockchain, and memory forensics—the book is an essential handbook for researchers, practitioners, and students. From the international subject matter expert community, it presents a visionary summary of the future trends and ethical issues in IoT forensic analysis.

Features:

- Examines forensic investigation techniques focused on IoT devices and IoT systems.
- Examines identification, data gathering, preservation, and evidence analysis tools and techniques in IoT systems.
- Examines encryption algorithms, covert channel discovery, and privacy-preserving mechanisms.
- Addresses the ethical, legal, and compliance perspective of IoT forensics from a worldwide viewpoint.
- Emphasizes trends such as AI, blockchain adoption, and edge computing, introducing a model for the development of forensic procedures.

The book is especially useful for academic researchers, undergraduate students, postgraduate students, and industry researchers and professionals.

Advanced Investigation Strategies for IoT Forensics

Technical Approaches to Encrypting, Security, and Investigation Strategies in IoT Forensics

Edited by
Shreyas J, Keshav Kaushik, Gururaj H L,
Tanupriya Choudhury, and Udayaprasad P K

CRC Press
Taylor & Francis Group
Boca Raton London New York

CRC Press is an imprint of the
Taylor & Francis Group, an **informa** business

Designed cover image: Shutterstock ID: 2553944355

First edition published 2027
by CRC Press
2385 NW Executive Center Drive, Suite 320, Boca Raton FL 33431

and by CRC Press
4 Park Square, Milton Park, Abingdon, Oxon, OX14 4RN

CRC Press is an imprint of Taylor & Francis Group, LLC

Library of Congress Cataloging-in-Publication Data
Names: J., Shreyas editor | Kaushik, Keshav editor | Gururaj, H. L., 1988- editor | Choudhury, Tanupriya editor | Udayaprasad P. K. editor
Title: Advanced investigation strategies for IoT forensics : technical approaches to encrypting, security, and investigation strategies in iot forensics / edited by Shreyas J, Keshav Kaushik, Gururaj H L, Tanupriya Choudhury, and Udayaprasad P K.
Description: First edition. | Boca Raton : CRC Press, 2026. | Includes bibliographical references and index. |
Identifiers: LCCN 2026002739 (print) | LCCN 2026002740 (ebook) | ISBN 9781032823546 hardback | ISBN 9781032845722 paperback | ISBN 9781003513896 ebook
Subjects: LCSH: Digital forensic science | Internet of things
Classification: LCC HV8078.7 .A37 2026 (print) | LCC HV8078.7 (ebook)
LC record available at https://lccn.loc.gov/2026002739
LC ebook record available at https://lccn.loc.gov/2026002740

ISBN: 9781032823546 (hbk)
ISBN: 9781032845722 (pbk)
ISBN: 9781003513896 (ebk)

DOI: 10.1201/9781003513896

Typeset in Sabon
by KnowledgeWorks Global Ltd.

Contents

Preface

The almost explosive expansion of the Internet of Things (IoT) has transformed the technological frontiers of our times, rendering devices smart and pervasive connectivity a way of life across segments and individual environments. But with this goes a very serious challenge—fostering digital trust, forensic traceability, and robust security in ever more complicated and heterogenous networks. This book, *Advanced Investigation Strategies for IoT Forensics: Technical Approaches to Encrypting, Security, and Investigation Strategies in IoT Forensics*, attempts to solve this same issue by creating a comprehensive analysis of forensic strategies, privacy protection, and future-proof technology within the paradigm of the IoT ecosystem.

For digital forensics, the book is similarly interested in not only the technical level at which it is possible to analyze IoT systems but also the interdisciplinary nature of working with actual cyber threats in actuality. Spanning from foundational knowledge in IoT architecture to data safeguarding and advanced forensic methods, legal infrastructure, and AI-convergence blockchain, each chapter is part of a larger story that readies professionals and researchers to address emerging security challenges.

This book aims to bridge the practice–theory gap in the field of IoT forensic science. It outlines an interdisciplinary approach toward IoT system security and investigation, ranging from device-level forensics and latest encryption technologies to legal and ethical considerations and the incorporation of emerging technologies such as blockchain and artificial intelligence. By its systematic presentation, the book allows readers to gain a clear understanding of the conceptual models and real methods needed to carry out proper forensic investigation in IoT environments.

In a time when digital evidence is most critical for cybersecurity, regulation compliance, and forensic analysis, the book is a definitive handbook for experts in academics, forensic science, security, and lawmaking. The book provides the readers with the information and instruments required to comprehend and react to the intricate security dynamics that IoT technologies bring.

The contributing authors—who are leading researchers, educators, and practitioners from industry, providing multidisciplinary expertise akin to this multidisciplinary field—provide collective knowledge so that the book is not just a technology guide but a thoughtful handbook that determines rising trends, open problems, and directions for future research in IoT forensics.

As you proceed through the next chapters, we encourage you to venture into the complex interdependence among dependent systems and forensic science. Let the book inspire more inquiry, collaborative ingenuity, and the development of secure, open, and robust digital infrastructure.

Shreyas J
Keshav Kaushik
Gururaj H L
Tanupriya Choudhury
Udayaprasad P K

About the authors

Dr. Shreyas J holds B.E., M.Tech., and Ph.D. degrees in computer science and engineering from Visvesvaraya Technological University and Bangalore University. He earned his doctorate in 2021 from UVCE, Bangalore University, specializing in Artificial Intelligence of Things, supported by a National Doctoral Fellowship. Currently, he serves as Assistant Professor in the Department of Information Technology at Manipal Institute of Technology, MAHE, Bengaluru. With over nine years of combined academic, research, and industry experience, he has published 100+ papers in top-tier journals and conferences indexed in SCI and Scopus. Dr. Shreyas has received Best Paper Awards in international conferences held in Hong Kong, Dubai, and NIT Delhi. He has authored a Springer book, edited volumes with Elsevier and Taylor & Francis, and filed multiple patents and copyrights. He is a reviewer for prestigious journals, including *Nature*, *IEEE*, and *Elsevier*, and serves on editorial and technical committees globally. Currently guiding three research scholars at MAHE, he has received an IBM research grant worth ₹8.5 lakhs and collaborates with global universities like USC, MSU, and King Saud University. His research interests include AIoT, sensor networks, swarm intelligence, and AI in agriculture. He is an active member of ACM, IEEE, ISTE, and IAENG.

Keshav Kaushik is a globally acclaimed cybersecurity and digital forensics expert, featured in the Stanford University–Elsevier World's Top 2% Scientists list for consecutive years. His work spans IoT security, AI-driven threat intelligence, blockchain-based trust systems, and cyber-physical forensics. Currently Associate Professor at Sharda University, Dr. Kaushik has authored 40 books, published 200+ scholarly works, and secured 15 patents across the U.K., India, and Australia. He serves as Guest Editor for the *IEEE Journal of Biomedical and Health Informatics* and as Associate Editor for *Springer Nature Scientific Reports*, shaping the global research landscape through his innovation, scholarship, and leadership.

Dr. Gururaj H L (Senior Member, IEEE) received a Ph.D. degree in computer science and engineering from Visvesvaraya Technological University, India in 2019. He has published more than 200 research articles in peer-reviewed and reputed international journals. He has authored 15 edited books in Springer, IET, IGI Global, and Taylor & Francis. He has presented more than 70 papers at various international conferences. He is Senior Member of ACM. He received a Young Scientist International Travel Support (ITS-SERB), Department of Science and Technology, Government of India, in December 2016. He was a recipient of best paper awards at various national and international conferences. He was appointed as ACM Distinguish Speaker (2018–2021) by the ACM U.S. Council. He has been honored as Keynote Speaker, Session chair, TPC member, advisory committee member at International Seminars, Workshops and Conferences across Globe. Prof. Gururaj's research interests are applications in machine and federated learning, data mining, blockchain, and cybersecurity.

Tanupriya Choudhury (Senior Member, IEEE) received the bachelor's degree in computer science and engineering from West Bengal University of Technology, Kolkata, India, in 2008, the master's degree in computer science and engineering from Dr. M.G.R. University, Chennai, India, in 2010, and the Ph.D. degree from Jagannath University, Jaipur, in 2016. With 15 years of experience in teaching and research, he holds the position of Visiting Professor with Daffodil International University, Bangladesh. Currently, he is Professor with UPES, Dehradun, India. Before this role, he was with Symbiosis International Deemed University, Pune, and Graphic Era Hill University, Dehradun, as Research Professor; Amity University Noida as Assistant Professor (Grade 3) and International Department Head; and other prestigious academic institutions, such as the Dronacharya College of Engineering, Gurgaon, Lingaya's University, Faridabad, Babu Banarsi Das Institute of Technology, Ghaziabad, and Syscon Solutions Pvt. Ltd., Kolkata. His areas of expertise encompass human computing, soft computing, cloud computing, and data mining. Notably accomplished within his field thus far is filing 25 patents and securing copyrights for 16 software programs from the Ministry of Human Resource Development (MHRD). He has actively participated as an attendee or speaker at several national and international conferences across India and abroad. He holds lifetime membership with the International Engineering and Technology Association (IETA), the Institute of Electrical and Electronics Engineers (IEEE), the Institution of Engineering and Technology, U.K. [IET (U.K.)], and other reputable technical societies. Additionally, he is associated with corporate entities and serves as Technical Adviser for Deetya Soft Pvt. Ltd., Noida, IVR GURU, and MyDigital360. He serves as Honorary Secretary for Indian Engineering Teacher's Association (IETA), India, alongside his role as the Senior Advisor Position in Indo-U.K. Confederation of Science, Technology and Research Ltd., London, U.K., and a fellow of International Association of Professional Engineers-Delaware-U.S.A.

Udayaprasad P. K. received the B.E. degree from Visvesvaraya Technological University, in 2018, and the M.Tech. degree from the Department of Computer Science and Engineering, University Visvesvaraya College of Engineering (UVCE, IIT Model College), Bangalore University, Bengaluru, in 2021. He is currently Assistant Professor with the Department of Computer Science and Business Systems, BMS Institute of Technology and Management, Yelahanka, Bengaluru, India. He is involved in research, and teaching B.E. and M.Tech. students of computer science and engineering and he has more than four years of research, academia, and industrial experience. He has published more than 15 papers in international journals, including *Elsevier*, *Springer*, and *Inderscience*, and international conferences. He has worked as a reviewer for various reputed journals, including *Nature*, *IEEE*, *Springer*, and *Johnny Wiley* publishers and international conferences. His current research interests include the Internet of Things, machine learning, artificial intelligence, sensor networks, and image processing.

List of Contributors

Mohamed Abouhawwash, Department of Computational Mathematics, Science and Engineering (CMSE), College of Engineering, Michigan State University, East Lansing, MI, USA; Department of Mathematics, Faculty of Science, Mansoura University, Mansoura, Egypt

Archana R A, BMS Institute of Technology and Managements, VTU, Bengaluru, India

Ayush Kumar Agrawal, Assistant Professor, Department of Information Technology and Computer Science, Dr. C. V. Raman University, Kargi Road, Kota, Bilaspur, C.G., India

S S Askar, Department of Statistics and Operations Research, College of Science, King Saud University, Riyadh, Saudi Arabia

Korhan Cengiz, Associate Research Professor, Department of Electrical Engineering, Prince Mohammad, Bin Fahd University, Al Khobar, Saudi Arabia

Renuka N D, Department of Computer Science and Engineering, Atria Institute of Technology, Bengaluru, India

Anita Devare, Amity University, Mumbai, India

Manoj H Devare, Professor & HOI AIIT-AUM, Mumbai, India

Sathishkumar V E, School of Computing and Artificial Intelligence, Faculty of Engineering and Technology, Sunway University, Jalan Universiti, Bandar Sunway, Selangor Darul Ehsan, Malaysia

Pooja Ekbote, Director, K2NP One Boat Solutions, Belagavi, Karnataka, India

Shreyas J, Manipal Institute of Technology, Bengaluru, Manipal Academy of Higher Education, Manipal, India

Abhilasha Jayakanavar, Assistant Professor, Department of Computer Science and Engineering, Jain College of Engineering and Research, Belagavi, India

Dhanalakshmi B K, BMS Institute of Technology and Managements, VTU, Bengaluru, India

Pankaja K, Nagarjuna College of Engineering and Technology, Bengaluru, India

Udayaprasad P K, BMS Institute of Technology and Managements, VTU, Bengaluru, India

Jiwanjot Kaur, Assistant Professor, Chandigarh Group of Colleges, Jhanjeri, Mohali, Punjab, India

Keshav Kaushik, Center for Cyber Security and Cryptology, Sharda School of Computer Science & Engineering, Sharda University, Greater Noida, India

Keerthi, Dayananda Sagar College of Engineering, Bengaluru, India

Ahmed A Khalifa, Department of Networking and Security, College of Information Technology, University of Fujairah, Fujairah, UAE, Switching and Traffic Department, National Telecommunication Institute, Cairo, Egypt

Mudassir Khan, Department of Computer Science, College of Computer Science, Applied College Tanumah, King Khalid University, Abha, Saudi Arabia

Anil Khatak, Assistant Professor, Department of Allied Health Sciences, Guru Jambheshwar University of Science & Technology, Hisar, Haryana, India

Vijaylaxmi Kochari, Department of Computer Science and Engineering, K. L. S Gogte Institute of Technology, Belagavi, Visvesvaraya Technological University, Belagavi, Karnataka, India

Anuj Kumar, Head of Research and Associate Professor, Rushford Business School, Valencia, Spain

Gururaj H L, Manipal Institute of Technology, Bengaluru, Manipal Academy of Higher Education, Manipal, India

Pradeep Kumar G M, BMS Institute of Technology and Managements, VTU, Bengaluru, India

Shanthi M, Department of Information Science & Engineering EAST Point College of Engineering & Technology, Bengaluru, Karnataka, India

Yash Mulay, Department of Computer Science and Engineering (AIML), KIT's College of Engineering (Autonomous), Shivaji University, Kolhapur, India

Shreelakshmi Yadav N, Manipal Institute of Technology, Bengaluru, Manipal Academy of Higher Education, Manipal, India, Karnataka, India

Amulya P, BMS Institute of Technology and Managements, VTU, Bengaluru, India

Arpitha P, Dayananda Sagar College of Engineering, Bengaluru, India

Dayananda P, Manipal Institute of Technology, Bengaluru, Manipal Academy of Higher Education, Manipal, India

Rutuja Pakhare, Department of Computer Science and Engineering (AIML), Jain College of Engineering and Research, Udyambag, Belagavi, India

Nandakumar R, Scientist, National Institute of Electronics & Information Technology (NIELIT), Calicut, India

Roja R, Department of Computer Science and Engineering, New Horizon College of Engineering, Bengaluru, India

Sowmya T Rao, Manipal Institute of Technology, Bengaluru, Manipal Academy of Higher Education, Manipal, India

VinayKumar Ravi, Center for Artificial Intelligence, Prince Mohammad Bin Fahd University, Khobar, Saudi Arabia

Darshan Revankar, Department of Computer Science and Engineering, Jain College of Engineering and Research, Belagavi, India

Roopa S, Professor, Dept. of Artificial Intelligence and Machine learning, Global Academy of Technology, Bengaluru, India

Sanjeev S Sannakki, Department of Computer Science and Engineering, K. L. S Gogte Institute of Technology, Belagavi, Visvesvaraya Technological University, Belagavi, Karnataka, India

Farhan Shaikh, Associate Professor, Rizvi College of Engineering, Mumbai, India

C Christlin Shanuja, Assistant Professor, Dept. of Artificial Intelligence and Machine learning, Global Academy of Technology, Bengaluru, India

Kunaal Shirish Shindagi, Managing Director, K2NP One Boat Solutions, Belagavi, Karnataka, India

Prakash Sonwalkar, Professor and HOD, Department of Computer Science and Engineering (AIML), Jain College of Engineering and Research, Visvesvaraya Technological University, Belagavi, India

Prakesh Sonwalkar, Department of Computer Science and Engineering, Jain College of Engineering and Research, Belagavi, India

Manish Thakral, Senior Consultant, EY, Mumbai IN, India

Vishwakiran S, BMS Institute of Technology and Managements, VTU, Bengaluru, India

P William, School of Engineering and Technology, Sanjivani University, Kopargaon, Maharashtra, India

Malathi S Y, Department of Computer Science and Engineering, KLE Institute of Technology, Hubballi, India

Chapter 1

Introduction to IoT forensics

Arpitha P, Keerthi, C Christlin Shanuja, Roopa S, and Korhan Cengiz

1.1 INTRODUCTION

The Internet offers instant information across cultural, linguistic, temporal, and geographical boundaries. This is a strong tool for worldwide communication (Hou et al., 2014). The Internet is a global network of billions of networks that are interconnected to a vast range of digital, electronic, and wireless technology from the local to the global network, including academic, scientific, government, and commercial networks. The Internet brought amazing changes into our everyday lives, without ignoring any field such as school life, healthcare, entertainment, science, civilization, education, tourism, technology, art, administration, commerce, communication, services, and manufacturing. The interchange of data, information, news, and ideas takes place in more than 180 countries. Internet World Stats shows that there are 3.26 billion Internet users worldwide. This is nearly 42.7% of the people in the globe.

The Internet of Things (IoT) will become the next revolution in the field of the Internet. In the IoT network, most of the devices around us will be on the Internet and interconnected. A massive change and the ever-greater engagement of IoT technologies can be seen in our everyday lives. The idea of smart home systems (SHS) and devices comprising Internet-based gadgets, the automation system for houses, and sustainable energy management systems are huge advancements toward IoT (Zhou et al., 2017). In addition, smart health sensing is another big accomplishment of IoT. SHS includes tiny smart gadgets and equipment that assist human health. Indoors as well as outdoors, these gadgets may be used to monitor various health problems and fitness levels or the number of calories burnt in the fitness center, etc. It is also utilized in hospitals and medical facilities to monitor severe health situations. Thus, the complete medical picture has altered, making it easier with high-tech and smart gadgets (Riahi Sfar et al., 2018). In addition, IoT researchers are actively engaged in enhancing the living style of individuals with disabilities and aging.

IoT has demonstrated a dramatic performance and given a new path for such people's everyday lives. Since these gadgets and equipment are cost-effective and widely available at standard prices, the majority of people make use of them (Gaona-García et al., 2017), as shown in Figure 1.1.

Transportation is also another vital part of everyday life. To improve efficiency, convenience, and safety, IoT has developed a few remarkable developments. Smart sensors and drone equipment now regulate traffic across large cities at different, signalized points. Vehicles are also being equipped with pre-installed sensor systems that can detect impending traffic congestion and suggest alternate routes with lower traffic (Behrendt, 2019). That is why IoT has a lot to do with numerous life and technological elements. We may infer that IoT has a great deal of opportunity both to improve technology and to make life easier for humans.

DOI: 10.1201/9781003513896-1

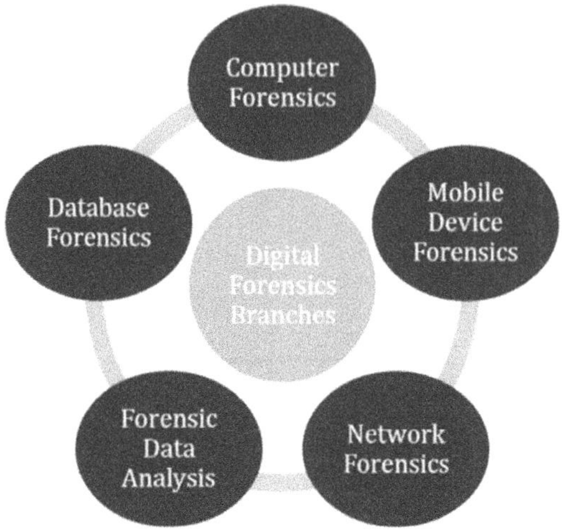

Figure 1.1 Main branches of forensics.

IoT forensics (IoTF) is a specialized field within electronic forensics that focuses on exploring protection violations, incidents, and abnormalities within the IoT environment using expert systems such as artificial intelligence (AI) (Alam & Kabir, 2023). Leveraging electronic forensic devices and IoT-specific methods, forensic investigators can discover insights into cyber-attacks, strengthen the security stance of IoT deployments, and alleviate risks related to the interconnected nature of IoT gadgets and systems (Grispos et al., 2024).

1.2 LITERATURE REVIEW

In the technology industry, politics, and engineering, the IoT is an important concern and has become the leading topic in the professional media and public media. The technology is being used in applications of a broad set of interconnected systems, devices, and sensors through enhancements in computer capabilities, electronic nanotechnology, and connectivity to provide new opportunities. The IoT revolution's impact from new marketplace opportunity and business models to security, privacy, and technology interoperability is discussed and made at various conferences, journals, and newspapers (Riahi Sfar et al., 2018).

The mass deployment of IoT devices holds in store some aspect of our lives to be transformed. Consumer IoT products like Internet-based products, home automation devices, and energy management products lead us toward a vision of 'smart home' that provides greater security and power saving (Al-Hamadi & Chen, 2017). Certain other consumer IoT products like fitness products and networked monitoring products transform medicine. This technology has the potential to assist disabled people and the elderly, offering better health and wellbeing at a reasonable cost from Figure 1.2.

The concept of 'smart cities,' which minimizes overcrowding and power usage, is brought closer by IoT technologies such as networked cars, intelligent transport systems, and sensors embedded in highways and bridges (Al-Rousan, 2015). By increasing the availability of data in the value production chain through a networked sensor, IoT has the potential to modify agriculture, industrial, and energy production and distribution. However, IoT presents various problems and obstacles to be handled and evaluated to achieve potential advantages.

The smart city is among the current IoT applications that also include smart houses. Smart home comprises IoT-enabled household appliances, air-conditioning systems, TVs, audio/

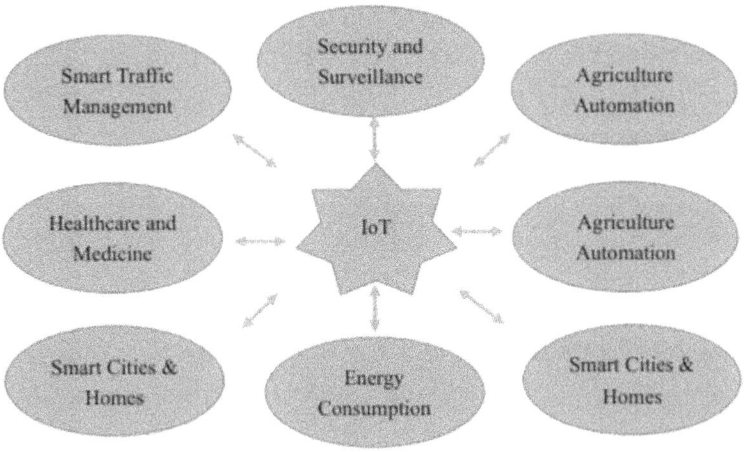

Figure 1.2 Major applications of IoT.

video streamers, and interconnected security systems that provide maximum comfort, security, and energy usage. This whole communication is carried out via an Internet-based IoT centralized device (Zanella et al., 2014). In addition to providing in-house comfort, a smart home helps the house owner in cost cuts in various ways; i.e. reduced power consumption will result in relatively smaller energy bills.

In addition to smart homes, smart cars are another category under the smart city. Intelligent gadgets and sensors that regulate most elements from the car's headlights to engines are installed in modern automobiles (Gershenfeld et al., 2004). The IoT aims to build new smart automobile systems that include a wireless connection between car-to-car and driver to provide preventive modeling with comfortable and secure driving (Kumar et al., 2012).

Khajenasiri et al. (2017) conducted an IoT solutions study to regulate smart power applications for the sake of smart cities. They said that IoT has been implemented for technology and personnel in very few applications. The IoT scope is quite large, and IoT can cover nearly every application area soon. They said that conserving energy is one of the key aspects of society and that IoT can help build an intelligent energy control system, which would save money and energy. The authors also talked about the immaturity of IoT operating systems as one of the challenges in achieving this. They proposed solutions to these problems so that a dependable, effective, and user-friendly IoT system could be provided.

Alavi et al. (2018) discussed the problem of urbanization in populated cities. The transfer of individuals from rural to urban environments leads to an increase in the urban population. Smart transportation, energy, medical treatment, and infrastructure solutions are therefore needed. Smart city is one of IoT developers' main fields of application. They said that IoT strives hard to address these difficult challenges. The demand for more intelligent city infrastructure and the requirement for more urban development has created possibilities for businesses in the development of smart city technology. The authors found that technology provided by IoT is highly essential for sustainable cities' growth. Privacy and security is also a significant topic for IoT, and more research is needed.

Weber (2010) emphasized the above issues and proposed that a private IoT-enabled company should include access control, network security, attack resistance, and clients' privacy, which would be a substantial advantage.

Later, on the IP-based IoT system, Heer et al. (2011) identified a security problem. They said that the Internet is the foundation of communication between devices in an IoT system.

Security problems are also a major concern in IP-based IoT devices. The network security should also be built to consider the lifespan and capabilities of each IoT device.

1.3 OPPORTUNITIES FOR IoT FORENSICS

This section illustrates how IoTF opportunities can adapt to the evolving threat landscape, enhance their investigative capabilities, and effectively address emerging challenges within IoT ecosystems.

1.3.1 Leveraging big data analytics for IoT forensics

By using complex analytic methods, such as predictive analytics and AI-driven algorithms, forensic examiners can detect hidden trends, anomalies, and correlations in IoT data flows, hence triggering security and safety rule breaches, suspicious behavior, and possible danger being exposed in real time. Anomaly detection formulas can detect variations from standard IoT device performance that could signal potential security risks or unauthorized attempts to access (Musa et al., 2022). Apart from that, predictive analytics can also forecast potential fads and probable weakness from previous IoT data, and the application of prudent hazard mitigation and risk management measures comes into the picture. IoTF can further enhance its ability to identify, analyze, and neutralize security attacks in IoT ecological environments, hence keeping confidential information safe and upholding the integrity of connected devices (Rizal et al., 2023).

1.3.2 Integration of artificial intelligence and machine learning

There is yet another field for IoTF to capitalize on in using AI and machine learning (ML) equations for automating and improving forensic analysis processes. AI and ML methods can be used across all areas of IoTF, like data analysis, outlier identification, and pattern detection, to facilitate forensic examiners to process and analyze vast volumes of IoT data effortlessly (Shakeel et al., 2021). AI-driven data category algorithms are able to categorize IoT data streams based on their forensic analysis suitability for enabling higher-quality task prioritization of information evaluation. Second, ML-driven abnormality detection systems can identify strange trends or patterns in IoT networks and mark them as potential safety and security breaches or problems (Brotsis et al., 2023). IoTF also promotes investigative processes, minimizes the extent of manual labor, speeds up forensic analysis and effectiveness, and therefore enables much more reliable event response and threat mitigation practices in IoT networks; a good illustration of the forensic environment is shown in Figure 1.3 (Khanpara et al., 2023).

1.3.3 Utilizing blockchain for data integrity in IoT forensics

Blockchain technology offers a suitable method of information stability and tampering prevention in IoT forensic analysis. Leverage of decentralized and immutable characteristics of blockchain ledgers allows private investigators to securely timestamp and record electronic evidence extracted from IoT devices to provide proof of authenticity and reliability in the investigation process (Conti et al., 2018). Cryptographic hashing of forensic information such as device logs, sensor data, and shopping history can be maintained on a blockchain to establish an immutable, traceable audit trail for forensic processing. Smart contracts also allow data handling procedures and chain of custody protocols to be automated and executed in a

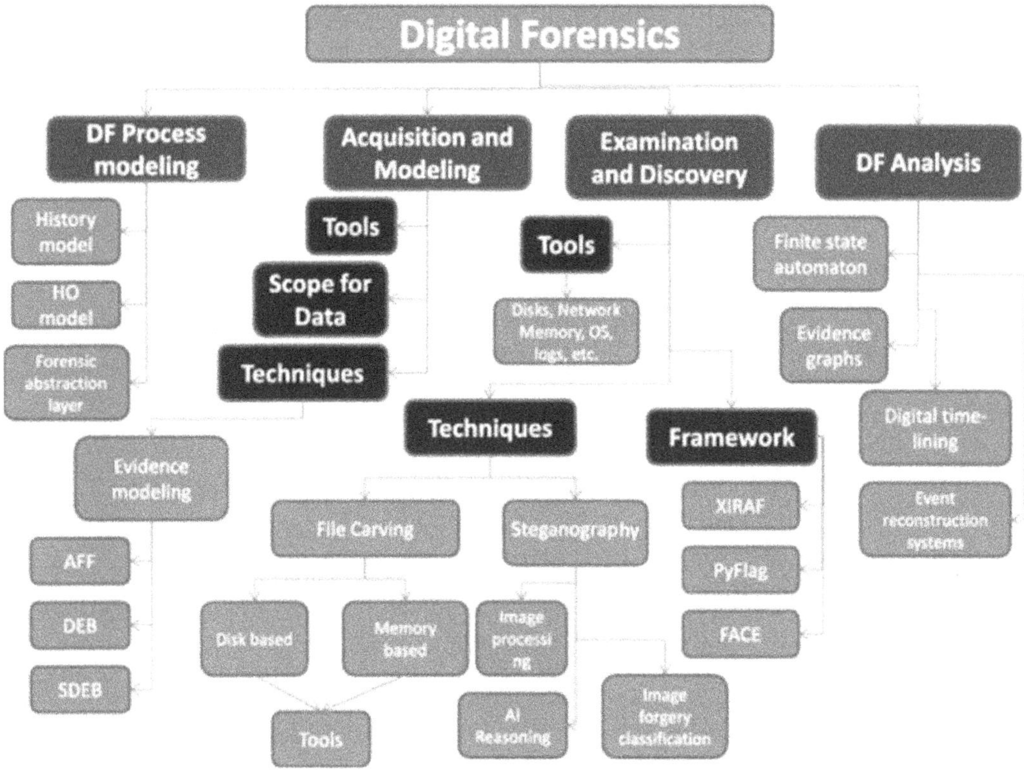

Figure 1.3 Digital forensics landscape.

way that provides legal and regulatory compliance for forensic analysis (Sadineni et al., 2022). With blockchain technology, IoTF have the potential to deliver greater trust and transparency for forensic procedures, increase the admissibility value of electronic evidence, and offer a tamper-proof way of maintaining the integrity of forensic information within IoT systems (Alabdulsalam et al., 2018).

1.3.4 Interdisciplinary collaboration for comprehensive forensic solutions

Interoperation between different self-controls, such as cybersecurity, digital forensics, information scientific research, and law enforcement, has the potential for building integrated and efficient services for IoTF. Through the intelligence and resources of many stakeholders, IoTF can benefit from various visions, approaches, and tools so that more sustainable and more natural ways of forensic examination and case action are facilitated (Lutta et al., 2021). Cybersecurity experts can provide insights into arising threats and assault vectors targeting IoT gadgets. Yet, digital forensics professionals can contribute knowledge in information procurement, evaluation, and conservation techniques (Ahmed et al., 2021). Information researchers can develop innovative analytics models and algorithms for processing and analyzing IoT information, while police can offer lawful and regulative advice for forensic investigations. IoTF can improve its abilities in dealing with complex challenges and progressing threats within IoT ecological communities, ultimately improving the safety, security, and strength of linked systems (Saleh et al., 2023).

1.3.5 Advancements in forensic tools and methodologies

Constant improvements in forensic devices and methodologies customized particularly for IoT environments offer a chance to boost the efficiency of IoTF investigations. As the complexity and diversity of IoT ecosystems continue to evolve, the development of specialized forensic devices and strategies ends up being vital for attending to the distinct obstacles presented by IoT gadgets, networks, and data (Alam & Kabir, 2023). IoT-centric forensic models, like IoTPOT, provide personalized facilities for IoT data gathering, examination, and visualization, which enable forensic specialists to rebuild occurrences, recognize vulnerabilities, and attribute malignant behavior to individual units or actors (Grispos et al., 2024). The developments in AI methods and expert system approaches make possible automation and enrichment of forensic assessment processes, speeding up the tempo and predictability of forensic examination procedures in IoT setups. Through harnessing such innovations within forensic tools and techniques, IoTF is able to remain informed about the new threat landscape, augment its detective strength, and effectively counter the current challenges of IoT ecosystems (Al-Hussaeni et al., 2023).

1.3.6 Privacy-preserving forensic techniques

Since IoT devices primarily capture sensitive personal data such as health data or location data, forensic examiners must comply with stringent personal privacy procedures and practices throughout the investigative process. Privacy-revoking forensic techniques try to limit the public disclosure of sensitive information throughout forensic analysis without compromising meaningful evidence relevant to the investigation (Sharma et al., 2020). Such differential confidentiality methods, homomorphic safeguarding, and secure multi-party computation are applicable to anonymize or encrypt the IoT data prior to analysis so that directly identifiable data is protected. Furthermore, pseudonymization strategies can be utilized to replace determining information with pseudonyms, permitting detectives to carry out analysis while protecting the privacy of individuals entailed (Renold, 2023). By including privacy-preserving forensic methods in IoT examinations, forensic detectives can maintain privacy principles, follow legal and regulatory needs, and construct a count on stakeholders, eventually boosting the honesty and integrity of forensic analysis in IoT environments (Bindrwish et al., 2023).

1.4 IoT APPLICATIONS

1.4.1 IoT in healthcare, business, and industry

IoT is totally committed to bringing greater financial and public benefits to society and humanity. IoT encompasses a wide variety of public infrastructures, including economic growth, water purity maintenance, health, and industrialization. Overall, IoT works hard to achieve the social, health, and economic goals of the United Nations. Environmental sustainability is another big concern. In a bid to counter the negative effect, developers of IoT have to be concerned with the environmental impact of IoT devices and systems (Colakovic & Hadzialic, 2018). Energy consumption by IoT devices is one of the problems of environmental concern.

There has to be a study in this regard in a bid to develop quality materials for constructing new IoT devices that use less energy. Green technology can also be employed in the future for use to develop low-energy-consuming appliances. Not only is it eco-friendly but also human-friendly. The development of IoT devices for engineers and researchers is based on numerous health conditions, including diabetes, obesity, or stress (Hou et al., 2014).

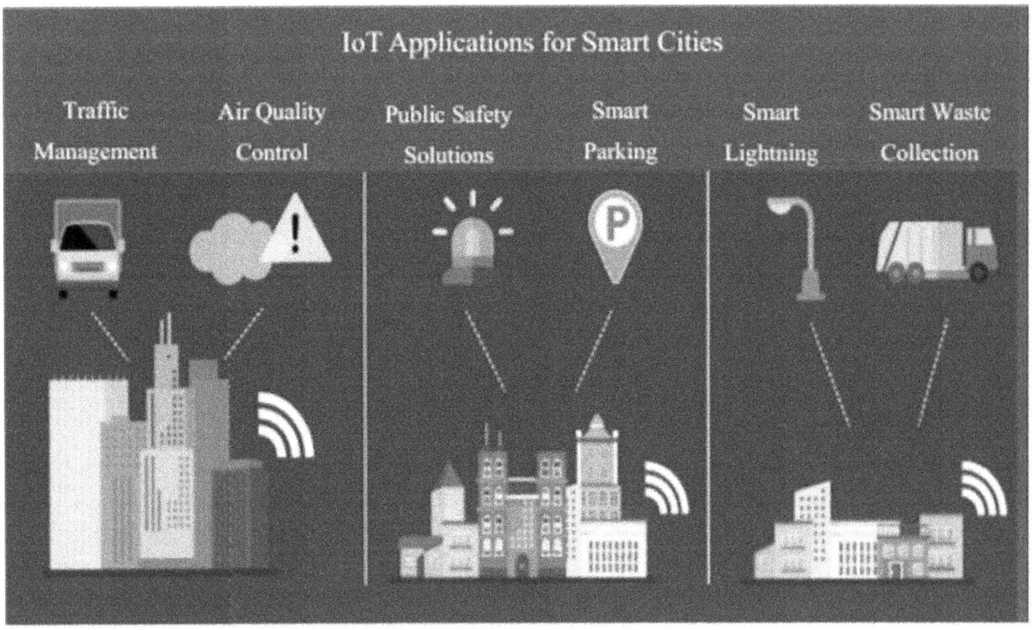

Figure 1.4 IoT applications for smart cities.

1.4.2 Smart city, smart things, and smart vehicles

By applying a vision to an intelligent home, city, transport, and vehicles, IoT converts the traditional city civil infrastructure into a high-tech infrastructure. Techniques such as ML and deep learning are applied to improve in a grand scale in understanding technical needs and utilization at home (Park et al., 2018). There are various technologies like cloud servers and wireless sensor networks required to construct a smart city with optimized IoT server usage. There also needs to be consideration of the green side of the smart city, as shown in Figure 1.4.

In addition, smart sensors included in recently launched vehicles can detect congested road traffic and may therefore advise the driver of an optimal alternative route. The traffic in the city can be lowered. In addition, intelligent sensors with optimal costs should be created to monitor engine activity in all cars. In keeping the health of the car, IoT is also extremely useful. Self-driving automobiles can interact via intelligent sensors with other self-driving vehicles. It would improve the flow of traffic more than automobiles driven by people. It will take time to execute this method throughout the world. Until then, IoT devices can assist and can take the necessary action by monitoring the traffic congestion ahead. A transport manufacturer should thus include IoT devices in its manufactured vehicles to benefit society.

1.4.3 Industrial and agricultural automation

Agriculture is vital in our daily lives. We must push the present agriculture techniques to feed such a huge population. Hence, agriculture and technology must be combined so that productivity may be efficiently enhanced. One possible way to do this is greenhouse technology. It offers a means of controlling the environmental conditions to enhance output. Manual control of this technology is nevertheless less effective and requires manual effort and cost, leading to energy waste and reduced productivity (Kumar et al., 2012).

With the development of IoT, smart devices enable controlling the temperature within the chamber and controlling the process that saves energy and increases productivity easier. Another IoT advantage is the automation of industries. To digitalize factories, stock management, quality control, logistics, and supply chain management, IoT has been delivering innovative solutions.

1.5 IoT CHALLENGES

The IoT presents big challenges which might prevent its possible advantages from being implemented. Some of the challenges are explained in the following sections.

1.5.1 Security

Many IoT applications bring new and distinct problems to security. A major goal must be to address these problems and to ensure safety for IoT goods and services. Users must be confident that IoT and associated data services are safe from vulnerabilities, particularly as this technology is more prevalent and is embedded into our everyday lives. Weakly secured IoT devices and applications might act as possible cyber-attack points of entry and expose users to theft by poorly protecting datasets (Singh et al., 2014).

1.5.2 Privacy

The true potential of IoT systems relies on policies that meet a wide range of expectations for personal privacy rights. IoT devices may provide an extraordinary unique value for IoT users due to the data streams and individual particularities (Zhou et al., 2017). However, privacy concerns and possible damage can prevent the Internet from being adopted completely. This implies that privacy and user protection rights are essential to guaranteeing user confidence and trust in the Internet-linked devices and associated services.

1.5.3 Interoperability

The capability of two or more devices to communicate information and utilize modified information is described as interoperability. IoT is essential in terms of interoperability, because it contains many heterogeneous devices, networks, and systems that have to operate together to build an IoT (Gaona-García et al., 2017).

1.5.4 Rights and legal issues

The usage of IoT equipment generates several new legal and regulatory concerns and intensifies current legal problems surrounding the Internet (Singh et al., 2014). The issues are broad, and the fast rate of development in IoT technology sometimes exceeds the capacity of the legislative, regulatory, and legal system to adapt.

1.5.5 Development and economic issues

The IoT offers great promises for developing nations to achieve economic and social advantages. This comprises sustainable farming, water quality and utilization, healthcare, industrialization, and environment protection. As a means of attaining the UN sustainable development objectives, IoT holds great possibility (Kumar et al., 2012).

In developed countries, the vast range of IoT issues will not be unique. To achieve the potential benefits of IoT, developing countries must also respond. Furthermore, specific implementing demands and problems in less-developed regions, such as infrastructural preparedness, trade and investment encouragement, technical competence requirements, and political resources, must be addressed.

1.6 IoT FORENSICS CASE STUDIES

These case studies emphasize the importance of IoTF in detecting and mitigating cyber threats targeting IoT-enabled vehicles.

1.6.1 Smart home intrusion investigation

In this case study, forensic private investigators were charged with investigating a security breach in a smart home environment. The owner was complaining about malicious activity, such as unauthorized access to door locks, security cam, and thermostat management. Forensic examination revealed traces of an advanced cyber-attack on vulnerable IoT devices throughout the home network. Examining network web traffic logs, device firmware, and protocols for interaction, private investigators determined the breach vector and linked the attack to a hacked IoT device (Chung & Choo, 2020). With the help of digital forensic tools and techniques, including disk imaging and memory analysis, the researchers can recreate the chain of events that resulted in the security incident, trace the intruder, and document electronic evidence for court proceedings. The case study illustrates the significance of IoTF in revealing safety violations and assigning fault in smart home settings, raising the security standing of IoT rollouts and safeguarding sensitive data against exploitation.

1.6.2 Industrial IoT system compromise

Forensic consultants were utilized in this research to analyze a suspected IIoT system violation in a production plant. Production errors, equipment errors, and sensing unit analysis deviance were being encountered by the factory, which is characteristic of cyberattacks against vital infrastructure. Forensic analysis of IIoT solutions, business control systems, and network infrastructures yielded malware infections, unauthorized access, and data exfiltration attempts. Tests of network traffic behavior, configuration settings, and log file operations by the researchers confirmed vulnerabilities that have been used by cyberattackers to gain entry into IIoT devices and disrupt functioning. In addition, forensic evidence provided compromise indicators, Indicators of Compromise (IoCs) and malware traces related to identified risk stars, allowing for anticipatory mitigation measures for risks and promoting the resilience of the IIoT system against expected attacks. This case study demonstrates the use of proactive risk discovery and case response to safeguard commercial IoT deployments against cyberattacks and ensure the integrity and reliability of critical framework processes.

1.6.3 Vehicle IoT forensics investigation

Unauthorized access to motor vehicle control systems, general practitioner spoofing, and On-Board Diagnostics (OBD) system tampering violated the security and safety of the fleet operation. Telemetry information from automobiles, automotive systems, and networks forensic analysis indicated proof of a sophisticated cyberattack that exploited vulnerabilities in auto IoT systems and cellular connectivity (Lutta et al., 2021). Through data log retrieval,

GPS location, and data communication streams, the researchers pieced together the history of cyberattacks. They found how cyberattackers remotely accessed car systems without permission and altered sensing unit data (Alam & Kabir, 2023).

Besides, forensic examination indicated evidence of data exfiltration activity footprints and remote-control commands issued to hijacked trucks, which illustrate the implied effect of cyber-attacks on transport infrastructure and public safety and security. The case study illustrates the significance of IoTF in their ability to identify and neutralize cyber threats to IoT-based vehicles, consequently enhancing the security and resilience of transport fleets and safeguarding passengers against potential injury (AlShaer et al., 2023).

1.6.4 Healthcare IoT breach investigation

There were cases of misuse of client monitoring devices, healthcare devices, and electronic health records (EHR) that caused a concern regarding confidentiality of patients and safety and security of information. Forensic examination of IoT devices, network logs, and EHR systems revealed evidence of an advanced cyber-attack that focused on unauthorized access to confidential patient data and interference with healthcare processes (Saleh et al., 2023). Through monitoring network traffic, tool logs, and access-control event logs, the attack vector was identified and the breach traced to a compromised and hacked IoT gateway device. There was also evidence of data exfiltration and unauthorized access attempts uncovered through forensic analysis that validated the extent of the breach and its potential effect on patient safety and the provision of healthcare (Renold, 2023). This study focuses on the contribution of IoTF to securing healthcare systems from cyber-attacks, patient privacy defense, and compliance with healthcare legislation and private privacy law.

1.6.5 Smart city IoT infrastructure compromise

Civil service disruption logs and web traffic management offices raised issues of concern to national security and stable deployment of the smart city. Forensic examination of IoT devices, sensing unit records, and network infrastructures reported evidence of a coordinated cyber-attack on crushing top framework operations and sowing pandemonium (Musa et al., 2022). By examining network site traffic logs, system configuration, and sensor data, vulnerabilities of attackers used to exploit IoT devices and power city-wide solutions were discovered. Forensic analysis produced evidence of ransomware malware artifacts, data corruption, and command-and-control communication, testifying to the sophistication and perseverance of cyberattackers. This study sheds light on the necessity of IoTF in securing smart city deployments against cyber-attacks, enhancing resilience of city infrastructure, and guaranteeing safety and quality of life for citizens of urban areas (Rizal et al., 2023).

1.7 CONCLUSION

In real life, the IoT is a working participant, and its uses are phenomenal and vast. There are incredible statistics for the impact of IoT on the Internet and economy, with others projecting up to 100 billion IoT devices to be connected and the economic value to the world of over 11 billion dollars by 2025. The best part of the IoT is that they give the quality of life, operating efficiencies, and control conditions that do not allow human intervention.

Researchers and engineers worldwide have made new developments in the domain of IoT. Researchers and developers work together to develop the technology as much as possible and make it relevant to society. But simultaneously, the IoT also creates enormous challenges that can delay its positive virtues. In the future, the IoT has to be more innovative, implementation-oriented, architecture-oriented, standardization-oriented, and problem-oriented in nature in order to address ethical issues. We need to prioritize challenges of IoT to turn possible benefits into reality for individuals, organizations, and industries.

IoT provides not just services, but it creates a lot of data as well. There is thus also a discussion on the relevance of big data analytics which may deliver accurate and enhanced IoT systems.

REFERENCES

Ahmed, H., Yousef, S., & Mohammad, A. (2021). An Internet of Things (IoT) Forensics Model Using Third-Party Logs-Vault. ACM International Conference Proceeding Series. https://doi.org/10.1145/3460620.3460746

Alabdulsalam, S., Schaefer, K., Kechadi, T., & Le-Khac, N. A. (2018). Internet of Things Forensics – Challenges and a Case Study. IFIP Advances in Information and Communication Technology, 532. https://doi.org/10.1007/978-3-319-99277-8_3

Alam, M. N., & Kabir, M. S. (2023). Forensics in the Internet of Things: Application Specific Investigation Model, Challenges and Future Directions. 2023 4th International Conference for Emerging Technology, INCET 2023.

Alavi, A., Jiao, P., Buttlar, W., & Lajnef, N. (2018). Internet of Things-Enabled Smart Cities: State-of-the-Art and Future Trends. Measurement, 129, 589–606. https://doi.org/10.1016/j.measurement.2018.07.067

Al-Hamadi, H., & Chen, I. (2017). Trust-Based Decision Making for Health IoT Systems. IEEE Internet of Things Journal, 4(5), 1408–1419. https://doi.org/10.1109/jiot.2017.2736446

Al-Hussaeni, K., Brits, J., Praveen, M., Yaqoob, A., & Karamitsos, I. (2023). A Review of Internet of Things (IoT) Forensics Frameworks and Models. Lecture Notes in Business Information Processing, 464 LNBIP. https://doi.org/10.1007/978-3-031-30694-5_37

Al-Rousan, T. (2015). Cloud Computing for Global Software Development. International Journal of Cloud Applications And Computing, 5(1), 58–68. https://doi.org/10.4018/ijcac.2015010105

AlShaer, M., AlShehhi, K., & Abdulla, S. (2023). The Internet of Things (IoT) Forensic Investigation Process. Journal of Information Security and Cybercrimes Research, 6(2). https://doi.org/10.26735/dbeu2801

Behrendt, F. (2019). Cycling the Smart and Sustainable City: Analyzing EC Policy Documents on Internet of Things, Mobility and Transport, and Smart Cities. Sustainability, 11(3), 763. https://doi.org/10.3390/su11030763

Bindrwish, F. B., Ali, A. N. A., Ghabban, W. H., Alrowwad, A., Fallatah, N. A., Ameerbakhsh, O., & Alfadli, I. M. (2023). Internet of Things for Digital Forensics Application in Saudi Arabia. Advances in Internet of Things, 13(01). https://doi.org/10.4236/ait.2023.131001

Brotsis, S., Grammatikakis, K. P., Kavallieros, D., Mazilu, A. I., Kolokotronis, N., Limniotis, K., & Vassilakis, C. (2023). Blockchain Meets Internet of Things (IoT) Forensics: A Unified Framework for IoT Ecosystems. Internet of Things (Netherlands), 24. https://doi.org/10.1016/j.iot.2023.100968

Chung, H., & Choo, K. R. (2020). The Need for Internet of Things Digital Forensic Black-Boxes. WIREs Forensic Science, 2(6). https://doi.org/10.1002/wfs2.1385

Colakovic, A., & Hadzialic, M. (2018). Internet of Things (IoT): A Review of Enabling Technologies, Challenges, and Open Research Issues. Computer Networks, 144, 17–39. https://doi.org/10.1016/j.comnet.2018.07.017

Conti, M., Dehghantanha, A., Franke, K., & Watson, S. (2018). Internet of Things security and forensics: Challenges and opportunities. In Future Generation Computer Systems (Vol. 78). https://doi.org/10.1016/j.future.2017.07.060

Gaona-García, P., Montenegro-Marin, C., Prieto, J., & Nieto, Y. (2017). Analysis of Security Mechanisms Based on Clusters IoT Environments. International Journal of Interactive Multimedia and Artificial Intelligence, 4(3), 55. https://doi.org/10.9781/ijimai.2017.438

Gershenfeld, N., Krikorian, R., & Cohen, D. (2004). The Internet of Things. Scientific American, 291(4), 76–81. https://doi.org/10.1038/scientificamerican1004-76

Grispos, G., Studiawan, H., & Alrabaee, S. (2024). Internet of Things (IoT) forensics and incident response: The good, the bad, and the unaddressed. In Forensic Science International: Digital Investigation (Vol. 48). https://doi.org/10.1016/j.fsidi.2023.301671

Heer, T., Garcia-Morchon, O., Hummen, R., Keoh, S., Kumar, S., & Wehrle, K. (2011). Security Challenges in the IP-Based Internet of Things. Wireless Personal Communications, 61(3), 527–542. https://doi.org/10.1007/s11277-011-0385-5

Hou, S., Charlery, S., & Roberson, K. (2014). Systematic Literature Review of Internet Interventions across Health Behaviors. Health Psychology and Behavioral Medicine, 2(1), 455–481. https://doi.org/10.1080/21642850.2014.895368

Khajenasiri, I., Estebsari, A., Verhelst, M., & Gielen, G. (2017). A Review on Internet of Things Solutions for Intelligent Energy Control in Buildings for Smart City Applications. Energy Procedia, 111, 770–779. https://doi.org/10.1016/j.egypro.2017.03.239

Khanpara, P., Shah, I., Tanwar, S., Verma, A., & Sharma, R. (2023). Toward the Internet of Things Forensics: A Data Analytics Perspective. Security and Privacy, 6(5). https://doi.org/10.1002/spy2.306

Kumar, S., Tiwari, P., & Zymbler, M. (2012). Internet of Things Is a Revolutionary Approach for Future Technology Enhancement: A Review. Journal of Big Data, 6, 111. https://doi.org/10.1186/s40537-019-0268-2

Lutta, P., Sedky, M., Hassan, M., Jayawickrama, U., & Bakhtiari Bastaki, B. (2021). The complexity of Internet of Things forensics: A state-of-the-art review. In Forensic Science International: Digital Investigation (Vol. 38). https://doi.org/10.1016/j.fsidi.2021.301210

Musa, N. S., Mirza, N. M., & Ali, A. (2022). Current Trends in Internet of Things Forensics. Proceedings – 2022 23rd International Arab Conference on Information Technology, ACIT 2022. https://doi.org/10.1109/ACIT57182.2022.9994213

Park, E., del Pobil, A., & Kwon, S. (2018). The Role of Internet of Things (IoT) in Smart Cities: Technology Roadmap-Oriented Approaches. Sustainability, 10(5), 1388. https://doi.org/10.3390/su10051388

Renold, A. P. (2023). Survey of Evidence Collection Methods for Internet of Things Forensics. Proceedings of the 1st IEEE International Conference on Networking and Communications 2023, ICNWC 2023. https://doi.org/10.1109/ICNWC57852.2023.10127407

Riahi Sfar, A., Natalizio, E., Challal, Y., & Chtourou, Z. (2018). A Roadmap for Security Challenges in the Internet of Things. Digital Communications And Networks, 4(2), 118–137. https://doi.org/10.1016/j.dcan.2017.04.003

Rizal, R., Selamat, S. R., & Mas'ud, M. Z. (2023). An Overview Diversity Framework for Internet of Things (IoT) Forensic Investigation. International Journal on Informatics Visualization, 7(2). https://doi.org/10.30630/joiv.7.2.1520

Sadineni, L., Pilli, E. S., & Battula, R. B. (2022). ProvNet-IoT: Provenance Based Network Layer Forensics in Internet of Things. Forensic Science International: Digital Investigation, 43. https://doi.org/10.1016/j.fsidi.2022.301441

Saleh, M., Othman, S. H., Driss, M., Al-dhaqm, A., Ali, A., Yafooz, W. M. S., & Emara, A. H. M. (2023). A Metamodeling Approach for IoT Forensic Investigation. Electronics (Switzerland), 12(3). https://doi.org/10.3390/electronics12030524

Shakeel, P. M., Baskar, S., Fouad, H., Manogaran, G., Saravanan, V., & Montenegro-Marin, C. E. (2021). Internet of Things Forensic Data Analysis Using Machine Learning to Identify Roots of Data Scavenging. Future Generation Computer Systems, 115. https://doi.org/10.1016/j.future.2020.10.001

Sharma, B. K., Hachem, M., Mishra, V. P., & Kaur, M. J. (2020). Internet of things in forensics investigation in comparison to digital forensics. In Advances in Intelligent Systems and Computing (Vol. 1132). https://doi.org/10.1007/978-3-030-40305-8_32

Singh, D., Tripathi, G., & Jara, A. J. (2014). A survey of Internet-of-Things: Future vision, architecture, challenges and services, *2014 IEEE World Forum on Internet of Things (WF-IoT)*, Seoul, Korea (South), 2014, pp. 287-292, doi: 10.1109/WF-IoT.2014.6803174.

Weber, R. (2010). Internet of Things – New Security and Privacy Challenges. Computer Law & Security Review, 26(1), 23–30. https://doi.org/10.1016/j.clsr.2009.11.008

Zanella, A., Bui, N., Castellani, A., Vangelista, L., & Zorzi, M. (2014). Internet of Things for Smart Cities. IEEE Internet Of Things Journal, 1(1), 22–32. https://doi.org/10.1109/jiot.2014.2306328

Zhou, J., Cao, Z., Dong, X., & Vasilakos, A. (2017). Security and Privacy for Cloud-Based IoT: Challenges. IEEE Communications Magazine, 55(1), 26–33. https://doi.org/10.1109/mcom.2017.1600363cm

Chapter 2

Foundation of IoT forensics

Udayaprasad P K, Archana R A, Dhanalakshmi B K, Shreyas J, Mohamed Abouhawwash, and S S Askar

2.1 INTRODUCTION

The introductory section is, thus, the beginning of this critical field of Internet of Things (IoT) Forensics. It puts into context, defines the motivation of the research, outlines its scope and objectives, and maps out the structure of the chapter for the reader.

2.1.1 Background and motivation

The IoT has revolutionized the digital landscape, now interconnecting billions of devices across homes, industries, healthcare, and public infrastructure. By 2030, the world will have over 500 billion connected IoT devices online, ushering in unparalleled levels of automation, efficiency, and connectivity. On the other hand, this growth is accompanied by vulnerabilities that cybercriminals leverage for different forms of malicious purposes [1–3].

The dynamic nature of IoT devices, from wearables and smart home appliances to autonomous vehicles and industrial sensors, attracts cyberattacks. As such, digital forensics in the IoT scenario has devolved several unique challenges: volatile data collection, cross-jurisdictional litigations, and privacy preservation. These present special challenges that go beyond the conventional digital forensics and thus need tailored IoT forensic platforms to address such challenges [4,5] as from its ecosystem (Figure 2.1).

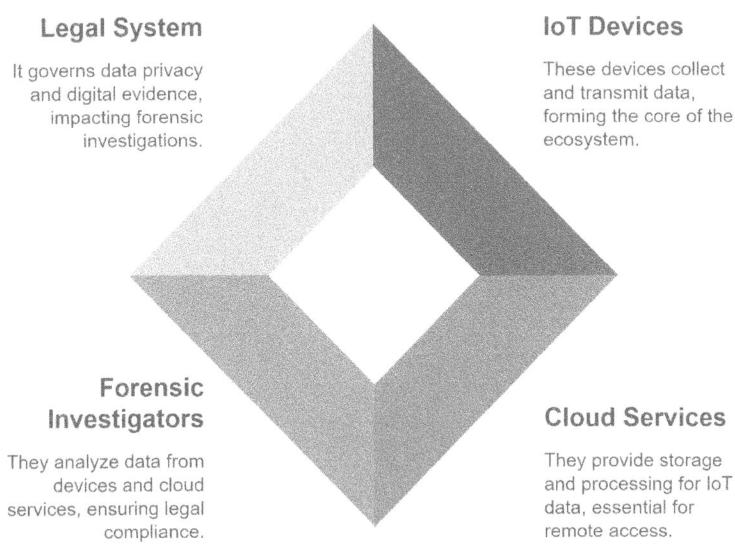

Figure 2.1 IoT forensics ecosystem overview.

DOI: 10.1201/9781003513896-2

2.1.2 Scope and objectives

This work will be based on the background of IoT forensics and address the technical and procedural challenges involved in investigating IoT security incidents. The purpose of this work is as follows:

- **Define IoT Forensics:** Strongly differentiate between classical and IoT forensics by emphasizing the unorthodox nature of IoT environments.
- **Examine Current Frameworks:** Evaluate the current forensic practices in order to determine what shortcomings are in their adequacy in IoT investigations.
- **Resolve Open Challenges:** Describe a few of the challenges involved in evidence acquisition, legal disputes, integrity of data, and ethics in IoT forensics.
- **Recommend Future Directions:** Recommend directions toward standardizing IoT forensic practices, such as privacy-preserving practices, and utilizing decentralized architectures such as blockchain.

2.1.3 Contributions of the study

This study adds to the expanding pool of literature on IoT forensics through:

1. **Full-Featured Review:** Performing a full review of the available frameworks and methodologies committed to IoT forensics.
2. **Taxonomy Development:** Creating a taxonomy for the categorization of IoT forensic processes, tools, and challenges.
3. **Exploring Emerging Trends:** Discovering emerging trends like blockchain-based forensics, AI-based analytics, and the Forensics-as-a-Service (FaaS) framework, as shown in Figure 2.2.
4. **Research Gaps and Future Directions:** Suggesting the research gaps and giving recommendations about how the procedural, legal, and technological limitations can be met as shown in Figure 2.3.

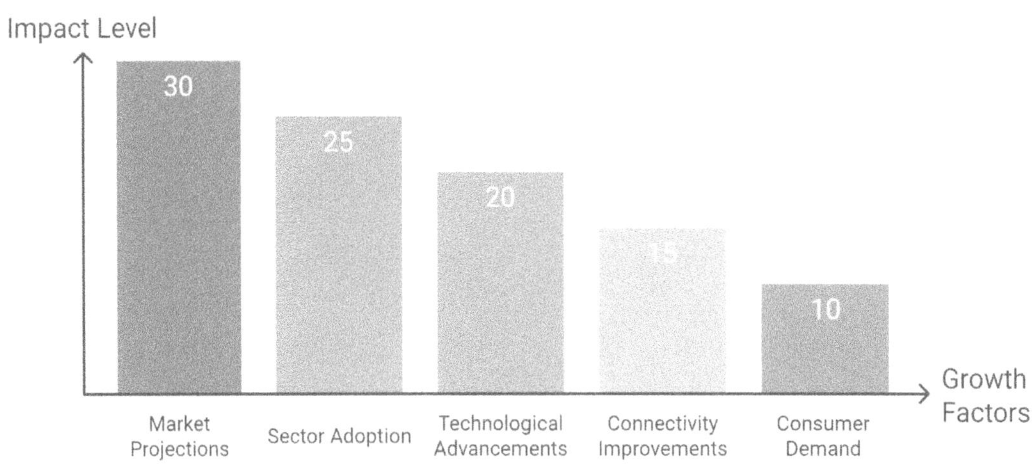

Figure 2.2 Growth of IoT devices (2020–2030).

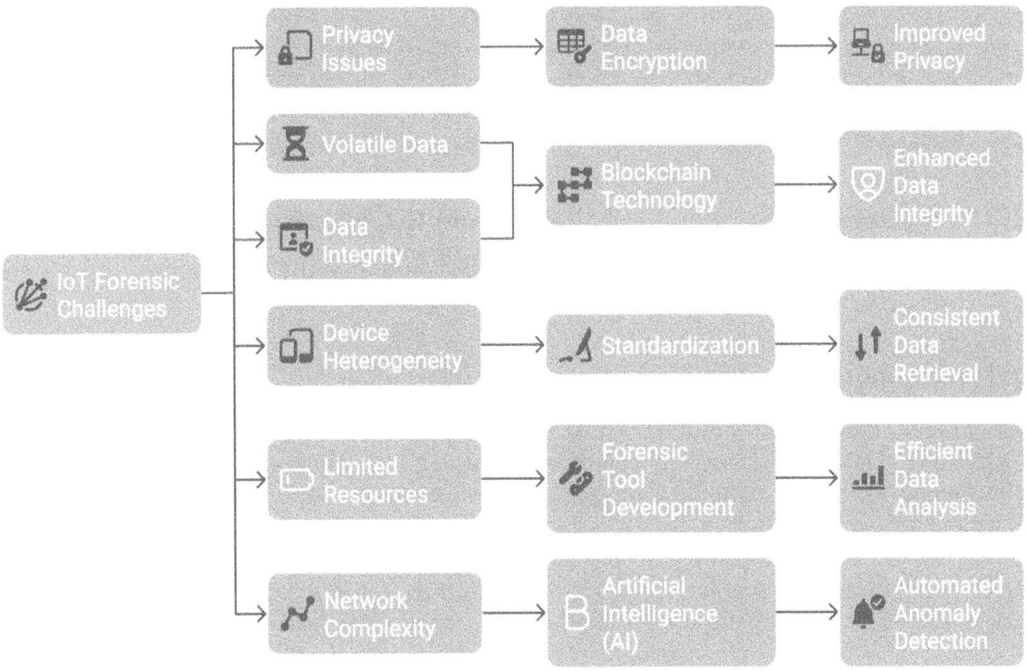

Figure 2.3 IoT forensic challenges and solutions map.

2.1.4 Structure of the chapter

The structure of the chapter is designed to offer a sequential and logical examination of IoT forensics:

Section 2.2 explores definitions, importance, and distinctions between traditional and IoT forensics. Section 2.3 discusses IoT components, evidence sources, and challenges associated with volatile and sensitive data. Section 2.4 analyzes key forensic frameworks and emerging paradigms like blockchain-enabled investigations. Section 2.5 deals with challenges in IoT forensics and emerging trends and innovations in Section 2.6. Section 2.7 shows future directions. Section 2.8 summarizes the study's findings and emphasizes its implications for research and practice.

2.2 LITERATURE REVIEW

IoT Forensics is a subfield of digital forensics that deals with identifying, collecting, preserving, analyzing, and presenting electronic evidence from IoT environments. This discipline has to address the special complexities of IoT devices: their heterogeneity, dependence on different communication protocols, and pervasiveness in connectivity [6].

The rapid growth of IoT devices in critical domains such as healthcare, smart homes, transportation, and industrial automation has escalated their role in digital ecosystems. Consequently, IoT forensics has become very critical for the following reasons:

Investigation of Cybercrimes: IoT devices can be a source of evidence or tools used to execute other cyberattacks, like Distributed Denial of Service (DDoS).

Support Cases in Court: Evidence from IoT devices is increasingly used to support litigation, especially in civil and criminal cases [7,8].

Secure the Integrity of Data and Environment: IoT forensics helps ensure data integrity and secure environments by exposing vulnerabilities.

Proactive Forensic Readiness: By adopting IoT forensic principles, organizations can prepare for potential incidents, reducing response times and ensuring compliance with legal standards [9].

2.2.1 Differences between traditional and IoT forensics

IoT forensics considerably deviates from the traditional digital forensics area due to the nature of devices and ecosystems as shown in Table 2.1.

2.2.2 Challenges in IoT forensics

The unique characteristics of IoT ecosystems introduce several challenges in forensic investigations, (i) Data Collection and Volatility: IoT devices mostly have low storage capacities and therefore tend to overwrite data quickly, as shown in Table 2.2. Evidence is dispersed across cloud servers, edge nodes, and local devices, hence making data retrieval complicated. (ii) Device Heterogeneity: The wide variety of IoT devices, from sensors and wearables to vehicles, makes it very difficult to standardize forensic tools and techniques. (iii) Encryption and Privacy Concerns: End-to-end encryption poses significant hurdles in accessing evidence without violating user privacy. Legal constraints around data access further complicate investigations. (iv) Legal and Jurisdictional Issues: IoT evidence often spans

Table 2.1 Difference between traditional forensics and IoT forensics

Aspect	*Traditional forensics*	*IoT forensics*
Evidence source	Computers, smartphones, servers	IoT devices (sensors, wearables, vehicles)
Data volume	Moderate	Massive (Big Data from IoT ecosystems)
Data volatility	Low	High (real-time operations, limited storage)
Device heterogeneity	Homogeneous (similar device types)	Heterogeneous (diverse devices and standards)
Data storage	Local or centralized (hard drives, servers)	Distributed (cloud, edge, on-device)
Jurisdictional issues	Often single jurisdiction	Cross-border and multi-jurisdictional complexities
Encryption	Standard cryptographic techniques	End-to-end encryption, often proprietary
Tools availability	Mature and well-documented tools	Emerging tools, often experimental
Legal frameworks	Established frameworks	Limited or inconsistent globally

Table 2.2 Different IoT forensics challenges and their potential solutions

Challenge	*Description*	*Potential solutions*
Data volatility	IoT devices overwrite data quickly due to limited storage.	Proactive evidence collection and cloud backups.
Device heterogeneity	Diverse protocols and standards among IoT devices.	Development of universal forensic frameworks and adaptable tools.
Encryption and privacy	End-to-end encryption hinders evidence access.	Use of privacy-preserving forensics models like PRoFIT.
Legal frameworks	Inconsistent laws across jurisdictions.	Global standardization of IoT forensic guidelines.
Chain of custody	Maintaining data integrity in distributed environments.	Blockchain-based chain of custody for immutable evidence tracking.

multiple jurisdictions, resulting in conflicts in laws and procedural frameworks. The lack of standardized legal guidelines for IoT forensics hinders cross-border collaboration. (v) Technical Limitations: IoT forensics lacks robust tools for evidence extraction, especially from resource-constrained devices. Existing tools often do not consider proprietary protocols and formats that IoT manufacturers use. (vi) Chain of Custody Maintenance: The integrity of evidence in distributed environments, such as the cloud, remains a continuing challenge. The immaterial nature of digital evidence increases the risk of its manipulation or tampering [10–12] as shown in Figures 2.4 and 2.5.

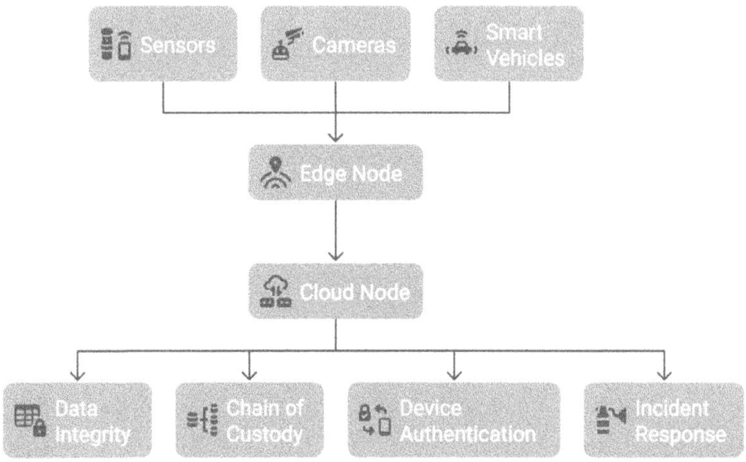

Figure 2.4 IoT forensics ecosystem.

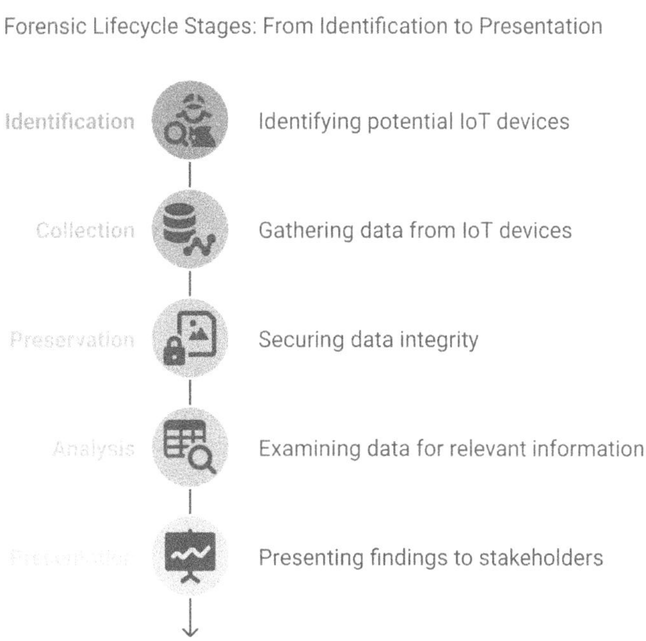

Figure 2.5 IoT forensic process flow.

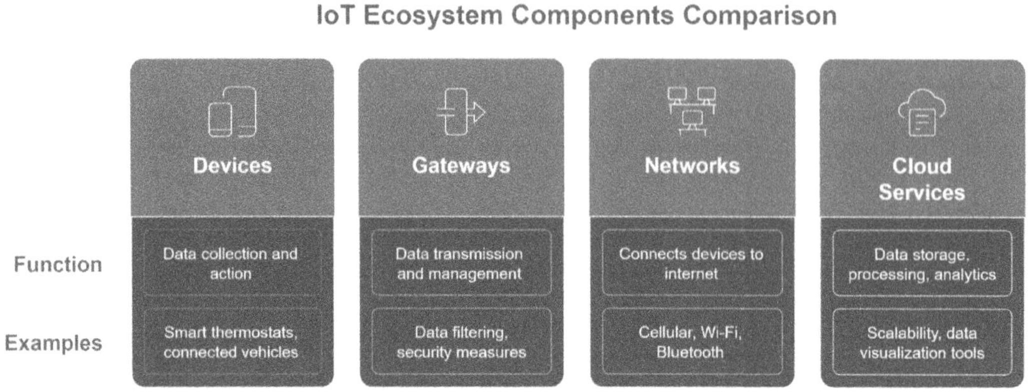

Figure 2.6 The interconnected components of the IoT ecosystem, such as devices, gateways, networks, and cloud services.

2.3 IoT ECOSYSTEM AND FORENSIC EVIDENCE

The IoT ecosystem is a complex network of interconnected devices, communication protocols, and supporting infrastructure that provides seamless data exchange and automation [11–14]. The key components are shown in Figure 2.6.

1. IoT Devices:
   - Examples: Sensors, wearables, smart appliances, autonomous vehicles, and industrial equipment.
   - Function: Collect and transmit data to other devices or central servers for processing.
2. Gateways:
   - Role: Bridge communication between IoT devices and the network (e.g., Wi-Fi routers, edge devices).
   - Function: Perform protocol translation, data aggregation, and preliminary processing.
3. Networks:
   - Types: Wireless technologies like Wi-Fi, Bluetooth, Zigbee, 5G, and LPWAN (LoRa, Sigfox).
   - Role: Enable communication between IoT devices, gateways, and cloud platforms.
4. Cloud Platforms:
   - Function: Provide storage, computation, and analytics for IoT-generated data.
   - Examples: Amazon Web Services (AWS) IoT Core, Microsoft Azure IoT, Google Cloud IoT.
5. Edge Computing Devices:
   - Role: Perform local data processing to reduce latency and bandwidth usage.
   - Examples: IoT edge gateways and edge servers.
6. Application Interfaces:
   - Types: Web and mobile applications that interact with IoT devices.
   - Function: Enable users to control and monitor IoT systems.

2.3.1 Sources of digital evidence

IoT environments produce diverse and voluminous data, which can be critical evidence in forensic investigations as shown in Table 2.3. (i) Device Logs: Activity logs from smart

Table 2.3 Different data sources with their examples and forensics challenges

Source	*Examples*	*Forensic challenges*
Device logs [3]	Activity logs, error logs	Data volatility, proprietary formats
Cloud storage [5]	Data logs, backups	Cross-border legal issues, encryption
Communication logs [8]	Network packets, protocol messages	High data volume, protocol diversity
Edge devices [12]	Cached data, local logs	Limited memory, accessibility issues
Mobile/web applications [14]	Session logs, user activity	Privacy concerns, inconsistent logging formats
Environmental data [15]	Sensor readings	Limited availability, sensor tampering possibilities

devices, wearables, and home automation systems. Importance: Activity timelines of users and device interactions. (ii) Cloud Storage: Data logs, configurations, and user settings stored in AWS or Google Cloud. Challenges: Cross-jurisdictional issues of a legal nature and possible access restrictions. (iii) Communication Logs: Network traffic data, message queues, and alerts exchanged between IoT devices. Importance: Traces the origin of malicious activities and pinpoints vulnerabilities in the network. (iv) Edge Devices: Logs and data caches on edge servers or gateways. Role: Offer localized evidence for quick analysis. (v) Mobile and Web Applications: User interaction logs, session data, and authentication records. Relevance: Can validate user actions or device misuse. (vi) Environmental Data: Data from sensors (temperature, motion, sound). Usage: Validate physical events, such as door openings or temperature changes [15,16] as shown in Figure 2.7.

2.3.2 Data sensitivity and volatility

Characteristics of IoT data are usually sensitive and very volatile, posing unique problems for forensic investigations as shown in Figure 2.8.

1. **Data Sensitivity:**
   - Private information stored on wearables and smart home devices includes location information, health metrics, and behavioral patterns.

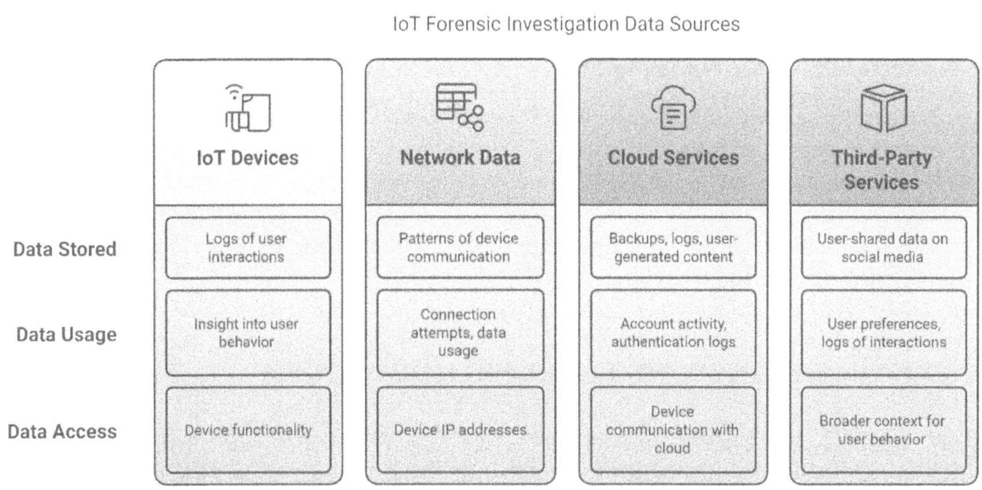

Figure 2.7 The various sources of evidence in IoT, from devices to cloud services.

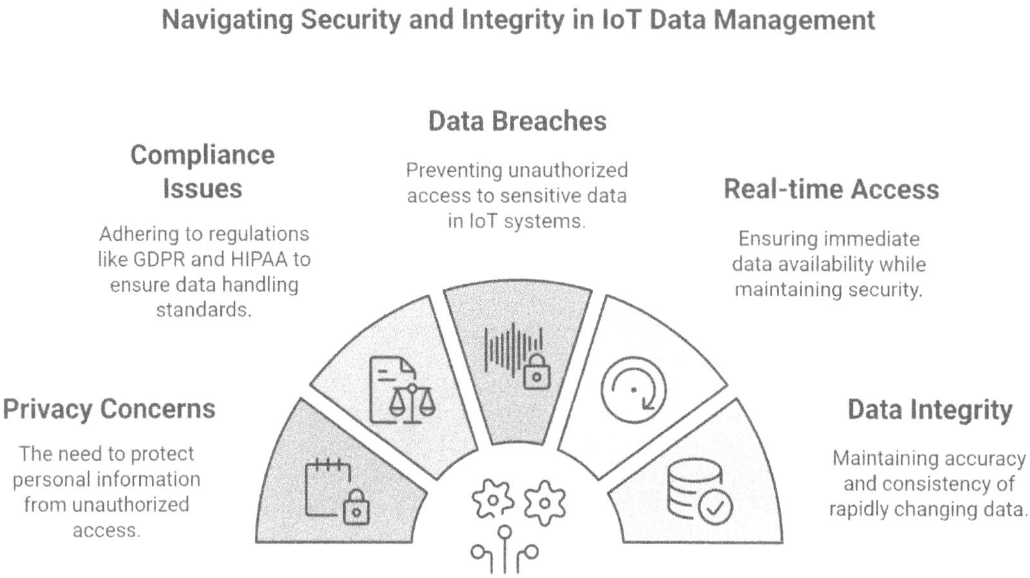

Figure 2.8 IoT data sensitivity and volatility: Challenges of sensitive and volatile data in IoT.

- Similarly, industrial IoT devices may contain operation-sensitive data crucial for business continuity.
- Legal and Ethical Concerns: Such data requires privacy laws like GDPR and HIPAA to be applied while processing it.

2. **Data Volatility:**
   - Short Retention Periods: IoT devices usually have constrained storage and tend to overwrite data in short intervals.
   - Dynamic Operations: The real-time data flow makes it very difficult to take snapshots of evidence.
   - Network Dependencies: Devices often depend on cloud and network services that may result in the loss of evidence during outages or attacks.

Proposed Solutions for Handling Sensitivity and Volatility:

- Privacy-Preserving Techniques: Use frameworks like PRoFIT to protect sensitive data during forensic analysis.
- Real-Time Evidence Collection: Employ continuous logging mechanisms to capture data before it is overwritten.
- Blockchain-Based Solutions: Leverage blockchain for immutable evidence storage and integrity verification.

2.4 EXISTING FRAMEWORKS AND METHODOLOGIES

Digital forensics investigation frameworks model a structured approach to identifying, collecting, analyzing, and presenting evidence for use in court or organizational contexts. Initially developed for traditional computing environments, these frameworks evolved to meet the complexities of IoT systems.

Key Features of Digital Forensic Frameworks:

1. Phases of Investigation:
   - Identification: Recognizing potential evidence sources.
   - Preservation: Ensuring data integrity.
   - Analysis: Interpreting the data.
   - Presentation: Reporting findings in a legal context.
2. Standardization: Global consistency in frameworks like NIST SP 800-86 and ISO/IEC 27037.
3. Tools and Techniques: Regularly use data recovery, timeline analysis, and evidence integrity verification tools.

Challenges in Traditional Frameworks for IoT:

- Lack of compatibility with IoT-specific protocols.
- Inability to handle data diversity and distributed environments.

2.4.1 IoT-specific forensic models

Specialized forensic models have been developed to address IoT ecosystems' unique challenges.

a. DFIF-IoT proposed by Kebande and Ray is a detailed framework for IoT forensics. Evidence collection from device, network, and cloud layers. Incorporates real-time monitoring and analysis to address data volatility. Emphasizes privacy-preserving mechanisms during evidence acquisition. Effective for handling heterogeneous IoT environments. Focuses on end-to-end evidence chain validation [17] as shown in Figure 2.9.
b. IoTDOTS is a forensic framework tailored for intelligent environments, focusing on minimal disruption during investigations, as shown in Figure 2.10. Automated evidence collection through device scanning. Compatibility with diverse IoT protocols like ZigBee, MQTT, and Bluetooth. Supports real-time alerts for suspicious activities. High dependence on device compatibility and firmware support. Limited scalability for larger IoT environments [18].

2.4.2 Blockchain-based solutions in forensics

New integrity and traceability solutions are offered by blockchain technology in digital forensics. Immutable Storage of Proof: Tamper-evident storage of proof on a blockchain-based decentralized ledger. (i) Transparency and Accountability: All transactions can be traced back, enabling a trusted chain of custody. (ii) Distributed Forensics: This allows

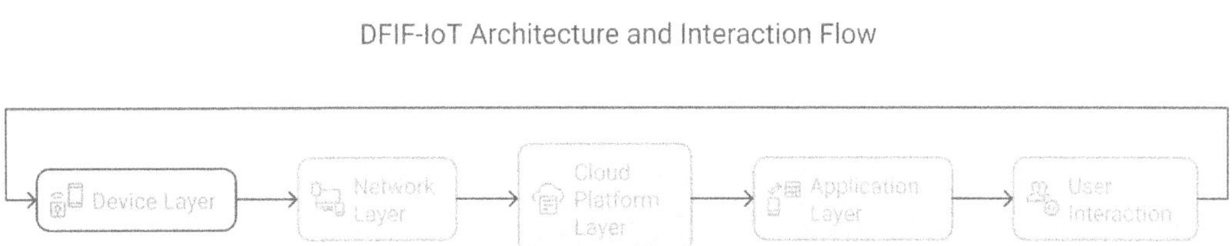

Figure 2.9 A multi-layer diagram illustrating DFIF-IoT, showing interactions between devices, networks, and cloud platforms.

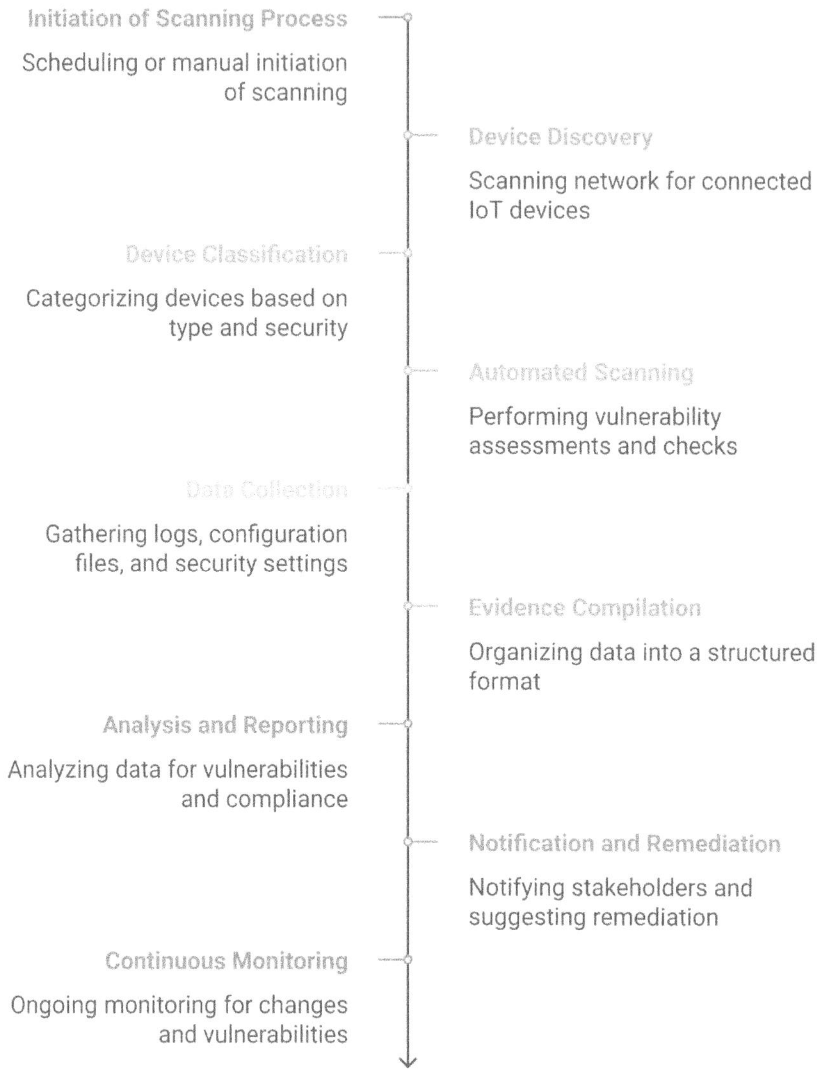

Figure 2.10 Workflow diagram depicting IoTDOTS' automated scanning and evidence collection process.

collaborative cross-border investigations. IoT Forensics Applications: (i) Chain of Custody Management: An application used for real-time evidence collection and storage tracking. (ii) Privacy Preservation: Access control layers and encryption protect data. Examples of Blockchain-Based Tools: FSAIoT (Forensic State Acquisition from IoT) focuses on acquiring and preserving volatile IoT data using blockchain for validation. Chainkit: Ensures the integrity of evidence through blockchain-based logging, as shown in Figure 2.11.

2.4.3 Forensics-as-a-Service (FaaS) paradigm

The FaaS paradigm leverages cloud computing to deliver on-demand forensic capabilities while reducing the need for dedicated infrastructure as shown in Table 2.4.

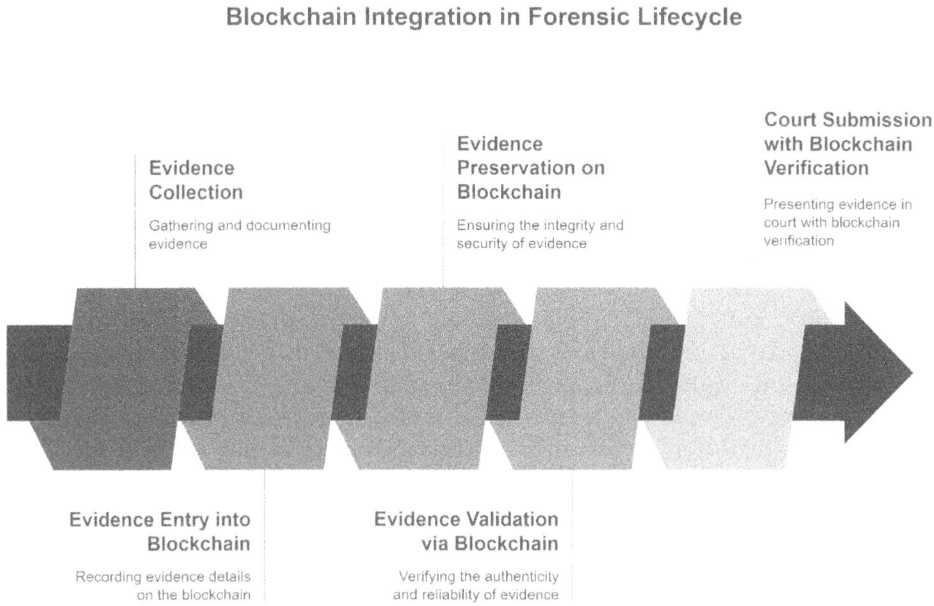

Figure 2.11 Flowchart showing blockchain integration in the forensic lifecycle.

Table 2.4 Various IoT forensics frameworks and their focus area with limitations

Framework/paradigm	*Focus area*	*Strengths*	*Limitations*
DFIF-IoT [19]	End-to-end IoT forensic lifecycle	Handles heterogeneity; privacy focus	Implementation complexity
IoT DOTS [20]	Smart environment forensics	Automated collection; protocol support	Limited scalability
Blockchain solutions [21]	Evidence integrity	Tamper-proof; decentralized storage	High computational requirements
FaaS [22]	Cloud-based forensic services	Scalability; accessibility	Dependency on cloud providers

Core Principles:

1. Scalability: The resources provided are tailored to the size and complexity of the investigation.
2. Accessibility: Allows investigators to access tools and evidence from remote locations.
3. Cost Efficiency: Eliminates the need for specialized hardware and maintenance.

Workflow:

4. Data acquisition from IoT devices and networks.
5. Secure upload to a cloud-based forensic platform.
6. Use of Forensic Tools to Analyze Pattern Recognition, Metadata Extraction
7. Evidence Sharing and Collaborative Reporting

Challenges:

- Privacy concerns in storing evidence on third-party platforms.
- Dependency on cloud service providers for infrastructure security.

2.5 CHALLENGES IN IoT FORENSICS

The very nature of IoT forensics is complex, given the distributed nature of IoT systems and the new challenges they present. The next section covers the big challenges in IoT forensics and how these impact the effectiveness of investigations, as shown in Figure 2.12.

2.5.1 Data collection and preservation

One of the biggest challenges in IoT forensics is that of collecting and preserving evidence.

Data Volatility: IoT devices mostly have low storage capacity and tend to overwrite data rapidly. This can be very ephemeral, hence making evidence collection difficult since crucial information might not be gathered on time. Distributed Data: Evidence in IoT systems is scattered across the devices, edge nodes, and cloud services. The logistical and technical challenges in accessing and consolidating the data are an issue. Device Heterogeneity: The great heterogeneity of IoT devices with diverse operating systems and communication protocols makes evidence acquisition a complex task. **Proposed Solutions: (i) Implement continuous logging mechanisms. (ii) Use edge computing for preliminary evidence preservation. (iii) Standardize evidence extraction protocols across device manufacturers** [23].

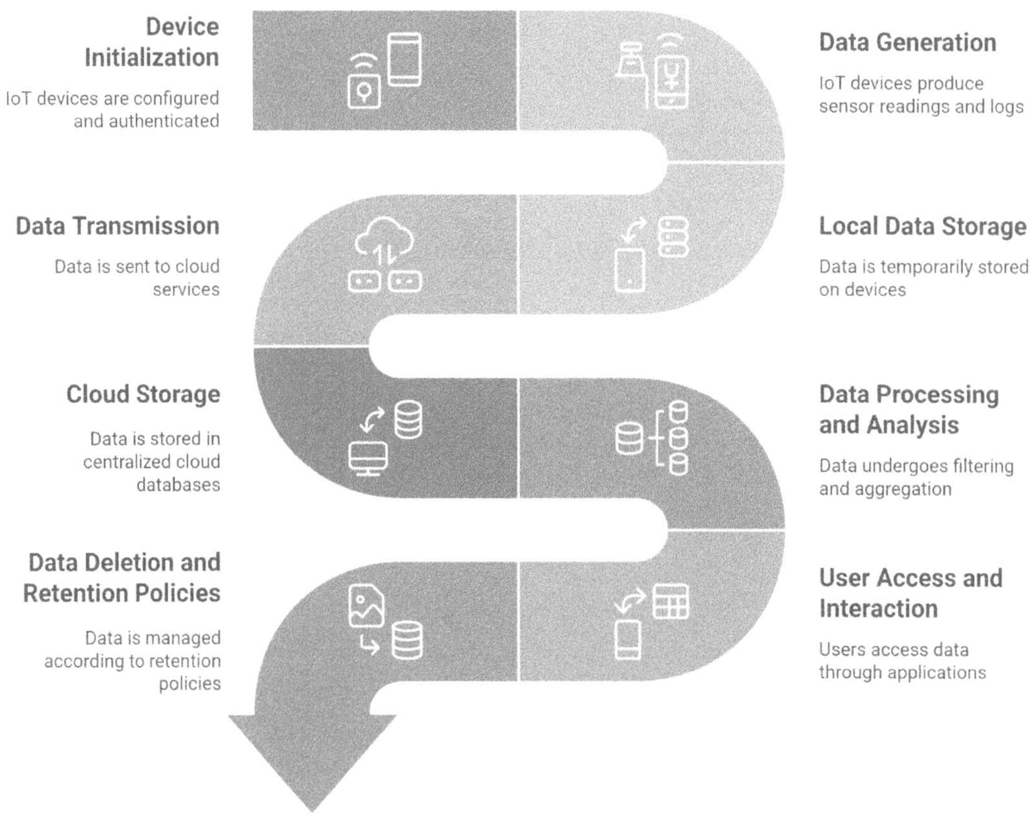

Figure 2.12 Data collection process in IoT forensics.

2.5.2 Privacy and ethical concerns

IoT devices will continue to gather sensitive personal and corporate data, raising concerns around privacy and ethics. User Privacy: Forensic investigations often require access to personal data (e.g., health metrics, location). Unauthorized access could breach privacy laws like GDPR or HIPAA. Data Sharing: Cross-jurisdictional investigations may involve data sharing between organizations and countries, increasing the risk of misuse. Ethical Considerations: The use of IoT device data, specifically wearables and smart home devices, may give rise to ethical issues, especially where such data concerns bystanders or people unrelated to the case. Proposed Solutions: (i) Use privacy-preserving frameworks like PRoFIT. (ii) Encrypt sensitive data during collection and transmission. (iii) Seek appropriate legal authorization before accessing private data, as shown in Figure 2.13.

2.5.3 Legal and jurisdictional issues

IoT forensics involves a field that is as intricate as it is to traverse labyrinthine legal and jurisdictional territories. (i) Cross-Border Investigations: Data of IoT devices can be located in different countries that have varied legal jurisdictions, and there may be a dispute as to whose right it is to obtain the data. (ii) Inconsistent Regulations: Laws regarding the collection of digital evidence are multifaceted, even within the same nation, leaving a nebulous scenario for forensic experts. (iii) Admissibility of Evidence: Evidence gathered by IoT devices will be admissible in court only if the process of gathering such evidence has complied with local laws. **Proposed Solutions:** Develop international standards for IoT evidence handling. Foster cross-border collaboration through mutual legal assistance treaties (MLATs). Use blockchain to ensure evidence authenticity and admissibility as shown in Table 2.5.

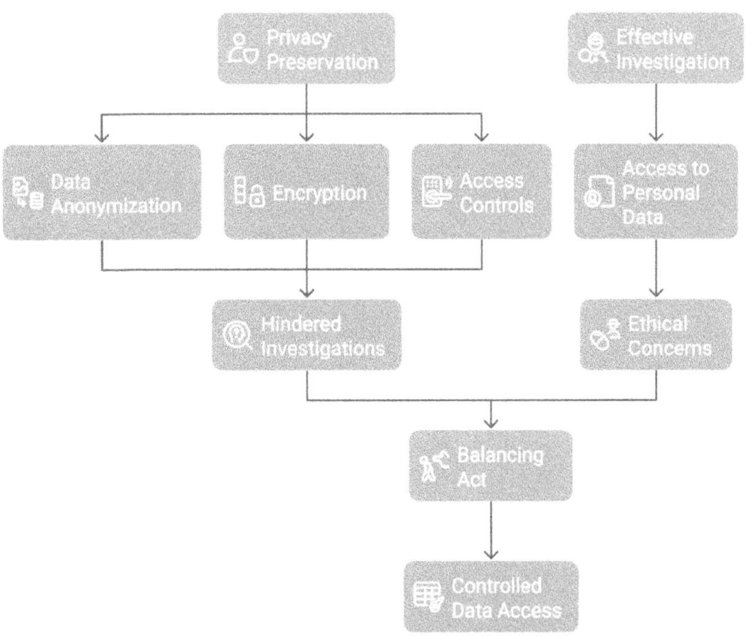

Figure 2.13 Balancing privacy and forensics.

Table 2.5 Different IoT forensics challenges

Challenge	*Description*	*Impact*	*Proposed solution*
Data localization	Data stored in foreign servers	Access restrictions	Mutual legal agreements
Contradictory laws	Conflicts in privacy and evidence handling	Evidence inadmissibility	Global standardization efforts
Time delays	Cross-border data requests are slow	Delayed investigations	Automate data-sharing protocols

2.5.4 Evidence integrity and chain of custody

This would be very primitive in proving the authenticity of the evidence before the court. Volatility of Digital Evidence: IoT data is volatile and easily susceptible to modification or destruction, as it is dynamic in nature; this would be an issue in court. Chain of Custody Challenges: Creating a visible and tamper-evident chain of custody in IoT environments, particularly distributed ones involving many actors dealing with data processing, is inherently difficult, as shown in Figure 2.14. **Proposed Solutions:** (i) Implement blockchain-based digital chain of custody systems to ensure immutability. (ii) Use tamper-evident storage for forensic data. (iii) Standardize documentation and audit trails for evidence handling.

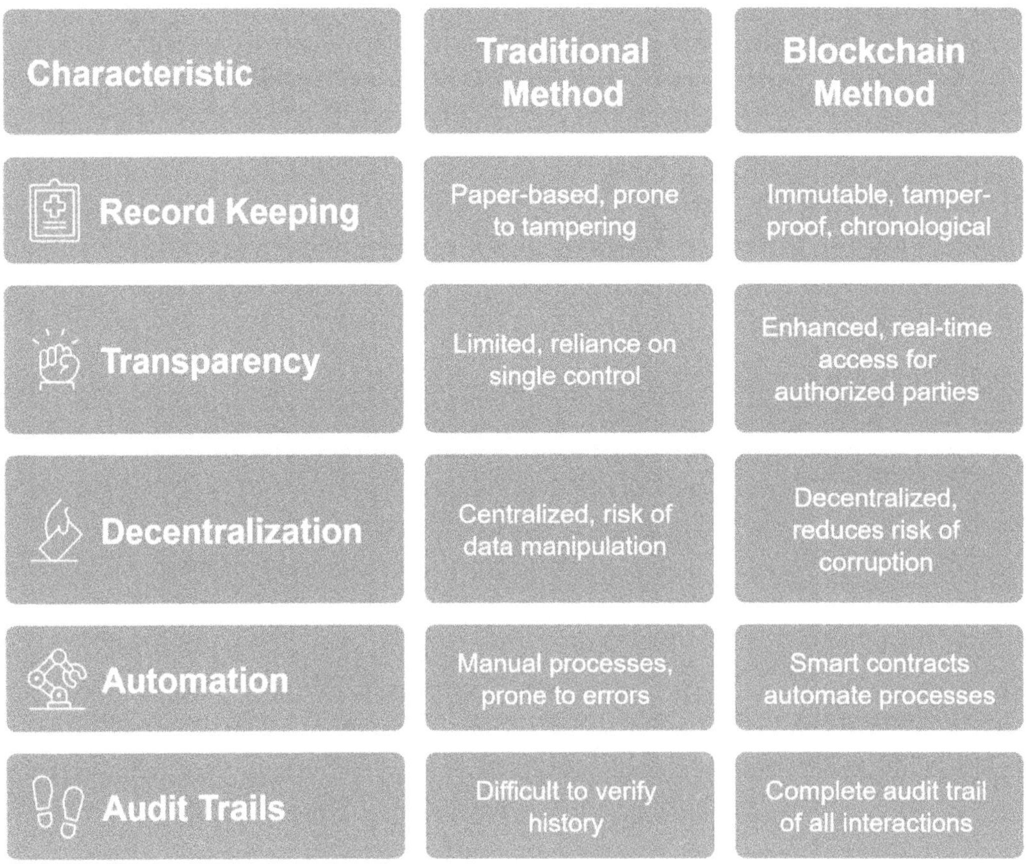

Figure 2.14 Blockchain-based chain of custody.

Table 2.6 Different IoT forensics challenges with their impact and solutions

Challenge	*Description*	*Impact*	*Proposed solution*
Device diversity [24]	Varied hardware and protocols	Inconsistent tool compatibility	Develop adaptable forensic frameworks
Encryption [25]	Secure communication protocols	Evidence inaccessible	Collaborate with manufacturers
Real-time data [26]	High data volume and velocity	Delayed analysis	AI-driven real-time data processing

2.5.5 Technical limitations in tools and techniques

The very dynamic nature of the IoT ecosystem poses significant technical challenges to forensic analysts as shown in Table 2.6.

- **Lack of Standardization:** IoT devices employ varied hardware, firmware, and protocols, making it difficult to construct generic forensic tools.
- **Encryption and Security Measures:** Although they are critical for users' security, end-to-end encryption poses obstacles to forensic analysis.
- **Tool Limitations:** Most available tools are based on traditional digital forensics and not IoT-specific friendly.

Proposed Solutions:

- Develop adaptive forensic mechanisms that can handle the various IoT protocols.
- Implement artificial intelligence (AI) and machine learning (ML) for automatic evidence analysis.
- Create cooperation between industry, academia, and law enforcement to standardize IoT-specific forensic processes.

2.6 EMERGING TRENDS AND INNOVATIONS

The IoT forensic field is evolving, with challenges introduced by emerging technology and growing complexities in the IoT environment still emerging. Recent trends and innovations discussed herein tackle issues in IoT forensic investigation.

2.6.1 Privacy-preserving forensics

IoT appliances collect sensitive user and business data; hence, protecting user privacy in a forensic analysis becomes imperative. Key Approaches: (i) Data Minimization: Collecting pertinent evidence, not exposing the user to unnecessary private data. (ii) Homomorphic Encryption: Enables me to conduct computations on encrypted data without decrypting it, thus maintaining privacy. (iii) Anonymization Methods: Stripping of identifying information preserves user identity while preserving the analytical worth of content, as shown in Figure 2.15. Frameworks and Tools: (i) PRoFIT (Privacy-Preserving Forensics in IoT): Ensures the integrity of the evidence and preserves user privacy. (ii) Differential Privacy: Introduces noise into information, which is statistically indiscriminate and therefore does not compromise privacy during analysis.

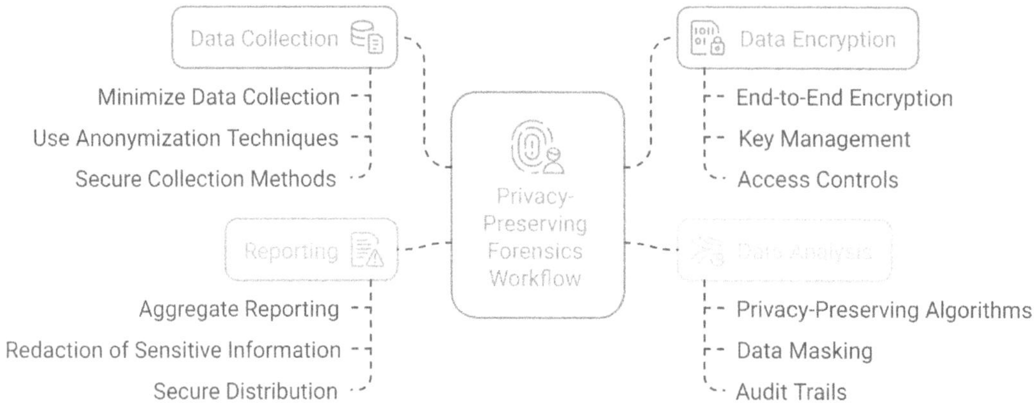

Figure 2.15 Privacy-preserving forensics workflow.

Benefits:

- Builds trust between users and investigators.
- Compliant with regulatory requirements such as GDPR and HIPAA.

Challenges:

- Balancing end-to-end evidence with the requirement for privacy.
- Steep computational cost of privacy-preserving solutions.

2.6.2 AI and machine learning in evidence analysis

The face of IoT-based forensic evidence analysis is being transformed with AI and ML, as shown in Figure 2.16. Applications: (i) Anomaly Detection: Unusual patterns in the behavior

Figure 2.16 AI in evidence analysis.

of IoT devices that can indicate tampering or malicious activity are identified. (ii) Pattern Recognition: Analyze large volumes of data from IoT networks to uncover hidden timelines and correlations. (iii) Natural Language Processing: Extraction of matter-of-fact content-related information from logs, messages, and reports produced by IoT systems. Key Tools and Techniques: (i) Supervised Learning: For training models to classify evidence or detect anomalies. (ii) Unsupervised Learning: This is used to identify new threats or attack vectors without labeled data. (c) Reinforcement Learning: Simulation and optimization of forensic strategies.

Benefits:

- Reduces analysis time by automating repetitive tasks.
- Increases accuracy in identifying and correlating evidence.

Challenges:

- Dependence on quality training data.
- Potential biases in AI models affecting investigation outcomes.

2.6.3 Decentralized frameworks using blockchain

Blockchain technology offers a firm foundation for chain of custody, traceability, and evidence integrity. Applications in Forensics: (i) Immutable Evidence Storage: Ensures evidence is tamper-proof through the blockchain's decentralized ledger. (ii) Chain of Custody Management: Provides transparent and verifiable records of evidence handling. (iii) Smart Contracts: Automate forensic workflows, ensuring that legal and procedural requirements are met as shown in Figure 2.17. Examples of Blockchain-Based Forensic Systems: (i) IoT-FSA—FSAIoT: IoForensics will work on volatile data preservation utilizing blockchain in IoT devices. (ii) Chainkit: Blockchain-secured logging platform for validation of evidence.

Benefits:

- Enhances trust and transparency in forensic investigations.
- Facilitates cross-border collaboration by standardizing evidence-handling processes.

Challenges:

- High computational and storage demands.
- Legal recognition of blockchain-based evidence in courts.

2.6.4 Role of edge and cloud computing

Edge and cloud computing have been the cornerstones of modern IoT forensics, since this technology enables the efficient collection, storage, and analysis of evidence as shown in Table 2.7.

- Edge Computing in Forensics:
  - Processes data locally, reducing latency and bandwidth usage.
  - Allows for real-time evidence acquisition and preliminary analysis.
  - Ideal for environments where immediate action is critical, such as industrial IoT.

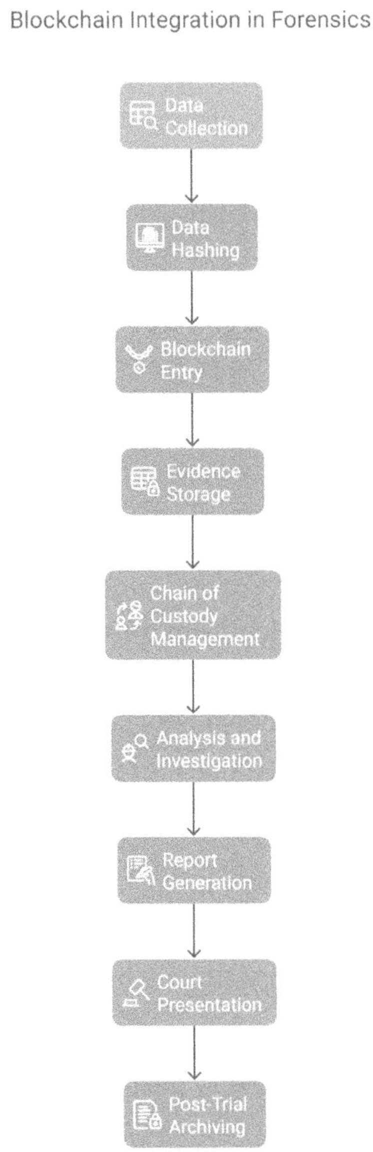

Figure 2.17 Blockchain in forensics.

Table 2.7 IoT forensics futuristic trends with benefits and challenges

Trend	*Key features*	*Benefits*	*Challenges*
Privacy-preserving forensics	Encryption, anonymization, data minimization	Enhances trust, complies with regulations	High computational overhead
AI/Ml in forensics	Anomaly detection, pattern recognition, NLP	Faster, more accurate analysis	Data dependency, potential biases
Blockchain frameworks	Immutable records, smart contracts, chain of custody	Ensures evidence integrity and transparency	High resource consumption
Edge-cloud computing	Local processing, scalable storage, SaaS tools	Real-time analysis, reduced data loss	Privacy risks, network dependency

- Cloud Computing in Forensics:
  - Offers scalable storage for large volumes of IoT-generated data.
  - Provides access to advanced forensic tools and platforms through Software-as-a-Service (SaaS).
  - Facilitates collaboration between investigators by centralizing data access.

Hybrid Edge-Cloud Models:

Combining edge and cloud computing allows for efficient data handling by processing time-sensitive data at the edge and storing and analyzing comprehensive datasets in the cloud.

Benefits:

- Reduces data loss during transmission.
- Enhances scalability and accessibility for forensic investigations.

Challenges:

- Privacy concerns over storing sensitive data in the cloud.
- Dependence on reliable network connectivity for seamless operation.

2.7 FUTURE DIRECTIONS

IoT forensics is an evolving field due to the increasing adoption of IoT devices and ecosystem complexity. Future research and development in IoT forensics should address issues related to standardization, cross-border collaboration, proactivity in preparation, and resolution of unsolved challenges that have already been brought forth to improve effectiveness and efficiency in investigations.

2.7.1 Standardization and guidelines

Importance of Standardization: IoT ecosystems contain a large variety of devices, communication protocols, and data formats; hence, standardization will be very instrumental in forensic investigations.

Key Areas for Standardization:

1. Evidence Collection Protocols: to ensure homogeneous data acquisition from devices with heterogeneous architectures.
2. Forensic Tools and Techniques: Developing global tools to serve various IoT settings.
3. Legal Admissibility Standards: Establishment of evidence handling procedures to conform to international legal norms.

Proposed Initiatives:

- Collaboration among ISO, NIST, and INTERPOL in an attempt to establish universally accepted standards for IoT.
- Development of certification programs for IoT device manufacturers that guarantee forensic support capability.

2.7.2 Cross-border collaboration in forensics

Challenges in Cross-Border Investigations:

1. Jurisdictional Conflicts: Different legal systems and regulations impede the sharing of evidence.
2. Data Sovereignty Issues: Laws of countries strictly control data storage and transfer.
3. Lack of Unified Frameworks: There is a lack of standardized procedures for international cooperation.

Proposed Solutions:

- MLATs: Clear agreements between countries on accessing and sharing evidence.
- International Forensic Networks: Real-time collaboration by investigators across borders on a single platform.
- Blockchain for Evidence Sharing: Blockchain could be used to create an open, immutable record of cross-border evidence transactions.

Benefits:

- **Accelerates investigation timelines by simplifying evidence sharing.**
- **Promotes trust and cooperation between nations.**

2.7.3 Integration of proactive forensic readiness

Concept of Forensic Readiness: Proactive forensic readiness is the preparation of systems and organizations for the efficient collection and analysis of evidence before incidents occur.

Key Elements of Proactive Forensic Readiness:

1. Incident Logging: Maintaining an uninterrupted device activity log for real-time evidence capture.
2. Forensic Policies: Organization policies on incident response and data preservation.
3. Automated Evidence Collection: Use of tools in the automatic identification of relevant data in events.

Proposed Approaches:

- Embedding forensic readiness features in IoT device firmware.
- Deploying edge computing for local evidence preservation in real-time.
- Integrating ML to predict potential threats and gather preemptive evidence.

Benefits:

- Reduces investigation costs and time.
- Enhances compliance with legal and regulatory frameworks.

2.7.4 Addressing open issues

Critical Open Issues in IoT Forensics as Shown in Table 2.8:

1. Heterogeneity of Devices: Development of forensic tools should function seamlessly on different devices.
2. Encryption: Synchronization of encryption with the security advantage through the provision of forensic data.

Table 2.8 IoT forensics open issues and their impact

Open issue	*Description*	*Proposed solution*	*Impact*
Device heterogeneity	Diverse devices with unique protocols	Development of universal forensic APIs	Streamlines forensic investigations
Data encryption	Challenges in accessing encrypted data	Privacy-preserving forensic models	Balances privacy with forensic needs
Volatile data	Difficulty in capturing real-time data	Continuous logging and edge preservation	Minimizes data loss
Ethical concerns	Privacy violations during investigations	Establishing forensic ethical guidelines	Enhances public trust

3. Volatile Data: Mitigating issues of recording and storing temporary data on IoT devices.
4. Ethical Concerns: Ensuring forensic processes respect user privacy and reduce ethical barriers.

Potential Research Directions:

- Development of universal Application Programming Interfaces (APIs) for IoT forensics tools.
- Privacy-preserving forensics using differential privacy and homomorphic encryption.
- Enhanced techniques for recovering data from volatile environments using AI and ML.
- Ethical guidelines for IoT forensics investigations.

Benefits of Resolving Open Issues:

- Increases reliability and scalability of forensic investigations.
- Promotes user trust in IoT technologies by ensuring privacy and security.

2.8 CONCLUSION

This chapter gives an overview of all the results in the context of IoT forensics research, describing the research and application implications as well as future directions in this field of pressing concern. This research study of IoT forensics also discovered a number of key issues and corresponding advancements in this field: (i) unique challenges in IoT forensics volatility and heterogeneity of information are major hindrances; to these has been appended the decentralized nature of IoT environments. Jurisdictional, ethical, and legal complexity is a hindrance to unimpeded investigations. (ii) Emerging Technologies and Frameworks: Privacy-preserving platforms, blockchain integration, and AI-powered evidence analysis are revolutionizing IoT forensic processes. FaaS offers forensic services that are scalable and on-demand. (iii) Future Trends and Directions: Preemptive forensic preparedness and standardization are the optimal ways of addressing growing complexity in IoT investigations. International cooperation is necessary to resolve jurisdictional disputes and enhance international forensic standards.

2.8.1 Implications for research and practice

The findings have a lot of implications in academia and industry as shown in Table 2.9.

Table 2.9 IoT forensics domain phases

Domain	*Implications*	*Outcome*
Research	Development of IoT-specific forensic frameworks and tools	Advanced forensic methodologies
Practice	Adoption of proactive forensic readiness strategies	Reduced response time in investigations
Policy	Global collaboration on legal and jurisdictional standards	Streamlined cross-border investigations

For Research:

- Forensic Technique Enhancement: The next research must emphasize creating tools and methods that are capable of bypassing issues characteristic of IoT, like encryption, device heterogeneity, and data fluidity.
- Interdisciplinary Approaches: Combining expertise from law, ethics, computer science, and data analytics is crucial to creating holistic forensic solutions.
- Ethical Frameworks: Developing robust ethical guidelines for handling sensitive IoT data is a pressing need.

For Practice:

- Increased Forensic Preparedness: Organizations need to implement proactive solutions such as real-time logging and edge storage to facilitate proper investigations.
- Capacity Building and Training: Police and forensic experts need to be trained to deal with IoT-specific devices and situations.
- Policy Formulation: Policymakers need to give top priority to developing legal frameworks that take into account the specific needs of IoT forensics, such as cross-border data-sharing procedures.

2.8.2 Final remarks and recommendations

With the growth in the number of IoT devices, the role of efficient forensic processes cannot be overstated. Overcoming the present challenges and using future technologies can go a long way toward improving the effectiveness and reliability of IoT forensic analysis as shown in Table 2.10. (i) **Standardization Efforts:** Collaborate globally to create unified guidelines for IoT forensic practices. Establish certification programs to ensure device compatibility with forensic tools. (ii) **Investment in Technology:** Develop advanced tools for IoT evidence collection and analysis. Integrate AI and blockchain technologies into forensic workflows for improved accuracy and transparency. (iii) **Ethical and Legal Reforms:** Prioritize privacy-preserving techniques in forensic investigations. Advocate for global treaties to resolve

Table 2.10 IoT forensics recommendations

Recommendation	*Actionable steps*	*Expected impact*
Standardization	Develop global IoT forensic standards	Consistency and reliability in investigations
Technology investment	Integrate AI and blockchain into forensic processes	Improved accuracy and transparency
Ethical reforms	Establish privacy-preserving forensic frameworks	Enhanced trust and compliance
Education and training	Create IoT-focused forensic training programs	Better preparedness of forensic professionals

jurisdictional conflicts in IoT evidence handling. (iv) **Focus on Education and Training:** Create training programs for forensic experts in IoT issues. Foster inter-disciplinary collaboration to drive innovation in forensic science.

REFERENCES

1. Stoyanova, M., Nikoloudakis, Y., Panagiotakis, S., Pallis, E., & Markakis, E. K. (2020). A survey on the Internet of Things (IoT) forensics: Challenges, approaches, and open issues. *IEEE Communications Surveys & Tutorials*, *22*(2), 1191–1221.
2. Janarthanan, T., Bagheri, M., & Zargari, S. (2021). IoT forensics: An overview of the current issues and challenges. In: Montasari, R., Jahankhani, H., Hill, R., Parkinson, S. (eds) *Digital forensic investigation of Internet of Things (IoT) devices. Advanced sciences and technologies for security applications*. Springer. https://doi.org/10.1007/978-3-030-60425-7_10
3. Hou, J., Li, Y., Yu, J., & Shi, W. (2019). A survey on digital forensics in Internet of Things. *IEEE Internet of Things Journal*, *7*(1), 1–15.
4. Udayaprasad, P. K., Shreyas, J., Srinidhi, N. N., Kumar, S. D., Dayananda, P., Askar, S. S., & Abouhawwash, M. (2024). Energy efficient optimized routing technique with distributed SDN-AI to large scale I-IoT networks. *IEEE Access*, *12*, 2742–2759.
5. Kumar, G., Saha, R., Lal, C., & Conti, M. (2021). Internet-of-Forensic (IoF): A blockchain based digital forensics framework for IoT applications. *Future Generation Computer Systems*, *120*, 13–25.
6. Atlam, H. F., Hemdan, E. E. D., Alenezi, A., Alassafi, M. O., & Wills, G. B. (2020). Internet of Things forensics: A review. *Internet of Things*, *11*, 100220.
7. Yaqoob, I., Hashem, I. A. T., Ahmed, A., Kazmi, S. A., & Hong, C. S. (2019). Internet of Things forensics: Recent advances, taxonomy, requirements, and open challenges. *Future Generation Computer Systems*, *92*, 265–275.
8. Reddy, C. S., Chouhan, D., Udayaprasad, P. K., Srinidhi, N. N., & Dilipkumar, S. M. (2022). Geographic routing scheme for resource and communication efficiency in the IoT ecosystem using swarm-intelligence based BFO algorithm. *Journal of Information Technology Management*, *14*(1), 41–64.
9. Ahmed, S. F., Shawon, S. S., Bhuyian, A., Afrin, S., Mehjabin, A., Kuldeep, S. A., Alam, S. B., & Gandomi, A. H. (2025). Forensics and security issues in the Internet of Things. *Wireless Networks*, *31*(4), 3431–3466.
10. Zulkipli, N. H. N., & Wills, G. B. (2021). An exploratory study on readiness framework in IoT forensics. *Procedia Computer Science*, *179*, 966–973.
11. Kebande, V. R., & Awad, A. I. (2024). Industrial Internet of Things ecosystems security and digital forensics: Achievements, open challenges, and future directions. *ACM Computing Surveys*, *56*(5), 1–37.
12. Shreyas, J., Chouhan, D., Rao, S. T., Udayaprasad, P. K., Srinidhi, N. N., & Kumar, S. D. (2021). An energy efficient optimal path selection technique for IoT using genetic algorithm. *International Journal of Intelligent Internet of Things Computing*, *1*(3), 230–248.
13. Castelo Gómez, J. M., Carrillo Mondéjar, J., Roldán Gómez, J., & Martínez Martínez, J. L. (2021). A context-centered methodology for IoT forensic investigations. *International Journal of Information Security*, *20*, 647–673.
14. Rondeau, C. M., Temple, M. A., & Lopez, J. (2019). Industrial IoT cross-layer forensic investigation. *Wiley Interdisciplinary Reviews: Forensic Science*, *1*(1), e1322.
15. Garg, A., & Singh, A. K. (2022). Internet of Things (IoT): Security, cybercrimes, and digital forensics. In *Internet of Things and cyber physical systems* (pp. 23–50). CRC Press.
16. Chernyshev, M., Zeadally, S., Baig, Z., & Woodward, A. (2018). Internet of Things forensics: The need, process models, and open issues. *IT Professional*, *20*(3), 40–49.
17. Yaacoub, J. P. A., Noura, H. N., Salman, O., & Chehab, A. (2022). Advanced digital forensics and anti-digital forensics for IoT systems: Techniques, limitations and recommendations. *Internet of Things*, *19*, 100544.
18. Montasari, R., Carroll, F., Mitchell, I., Hara, S., & Bolton-King, R. (Eds.). (2022). *Privacy, security and forensics in the Internet of Things (IoT)*. Springer.
19. Zhang, X., Choo, K. K. R., & Beebe, N. L. (2019). How do I share my IoT forensic experience with the broader community? An automated knowledge sharing IoT forensic platform. *IEEE Internet of Things Journal*, *6*(4), 6850–6861.

20. Shreyas, J., Chouhan, D., Harshitha, M., Udayaprasad, P. K., & Kumar, S. D. (2022). Network lifetime enhancement routing algorithm for IoT enabled software defined wireless sensor network. In *Sustainable advanced computing: Select proceedings of ICSAC 2021* (pp. 499–508). Singapore: Springer Singapore.
21. Kebande, V. R. (2022). Industrial Internet of Things (IIoT) forensics: The forgotten concept in the race towards industry 4.0. *Forensic Science International: Reports*, *5*, 100257.
22. Li, S., Choo, K. K. R., Sun, Q., Buchanan, W. J., & Cao, J. (2019). IoT forensics: Amazon echo as a use case. *IEEE Internet of Things Journal*, *6*(4), 6487–6497.
23. Hossain, M., Karim, Y., & Hasan, R. (2018, July). FIF-IoT: A forensic investigation framework for IoT using a public digital ledger. In *2018 IEEE International Congress on Internet of Things (ICIOT)* (pp. 33–40). IEEE.
24. Koroniotis, N., Moustafa, N., & Sitnikova, E. (2019). Forensics and deep learning mechanisms for botnets in Internet of Things: A survey of challenges and solutions. *IEEE Access*, *7*, 61764–61785.
25. Chhabra, G. S., Singh, V. P., & Singh, M. (2020). Cyber forensics framework for big data analytics in IoT environment using machine learning. *Multimedia Tools and Applications*, *79*, 15881–15900.
26. Kamal, R., Hemdan, E. E. D., & El-Fishway, N. (2021). A review study on blockchain-based IoT security and forensics. *Multimedia Tools and Applications*, *80*(30), 36183–36214.

Chapter 3

Security challenges in large-scale IoT systems

Sowmya T Rao, Shreyas J, Gururaj H L, and Anuj Kumar

3.1 INTRODUCTION

The Internet of Things (IoT) is revolutionizing the digital world by connecting a wide and expanding variety of smart devices—spanning sensors and actuators to embedded systems—into sophisticated networks. Through their function of gathering, transmitting, and processing information, the devices initiate automation, real-time decision-making, and smart control across a wide range of fields spanning healthcare and transport to manufacturing and critical infrastructure. The appeal of IoT depends on its potential to provide greater operational efficiency, cost savings, and better user experience. But the same qualities of IoT systems that make them appealing—their pervasiveness, heterogeneity, and interconnectivity—also give rise to a vast array of security weaknesses.

Most IoT devices differ from more mature computing environments in that they run with reduced computing capabilities, tiny memories, and limited security configurations. They tend to have limited update processes, which expose them to long-term vulnerabilities and zero-day attacks. Second, physical installation of IoT devices in vulnerable or inaccessible points adds to the risk since attackers may use physical access to exploit system integrity. In large-scale IoT installations, such vulnerabilities are not isolated incidents; instead, they aggregate and spread, leading to extensive reach, such as failure of critical infrastructure, extensive service disruption, data leakage, and loss of user trust.

IoT security threats cut across network structure layers—ranging from the perception (sensors and actuators) to network, middleware, and application levels. All these layers have unique vulnerabilities that call for customized countermeasures. For the given example, the perception layer can be vulnerable to physical attacks and data injection attacks, the network layer can be targeted by routing and man-in-the-middle (MITM) attacks, and the application layer can be targeted by data exposure and unauthorized access. So a one-size-fits-all approach to security does not apply to IoT.

This chapter examines those challenges and suggests an end-to-end, layer-by-layer security system prepared to meet them. Solutions range from lightweight encryption and authentication schemes for resource-constrained devices, intrusion detection systems (IDS) specifically tailored to IoT traffic patterns, secure boot schemes, periodic firmware updates, and policy-based access. With a defense-in-depth approach, stakeholders can establish robust IoT ecosystems that are well-equipped to resist existing and emerging cyberattacks.

3.2 IoT ARCHITECTURE OVERVIEW

Knowledge of IoT system layered architecture is critical for security risk detection and prevention. The perception layer consists of physical devices such as sensors and actuators

DOI: 10.1201/9781003513896-3

that communicate with the world. The network layer sends gathered data wirelessly or over wire via protocols like Wi-Fi, Zigbee, or 5G. The middleware layer offers storage of data, analytics, and device management services using cloud or edge infrastructure. Lastly, the application layer is tasked with serving users through interfaces such as dashboards or mobile applications.

Figure 3.1 depicts this four-layered architecture, and data moves from physical worlds to user applications with the different attack surfaces in between three key security challenges.

With IoT installations going up to millions or even billions of devices that are networked, the security environment becomes all the more challenging and harder to control. There are some key security issues that arise that need to be addressed to ensure these mass installations are robust and reliable:

Device Authentication: Possibly the biggest challenge is creating a scalable and reliable means of authenticating each individual device within the network. Unlike the traditional IT infrastructures, where a handful of devices and users can be centrally managed, IoT networks are made up of huge numbers of heterogeneous devices, commonly manufactured by multiple vendors with different security profiles. Most IoT devices come preconfigured with default or compromised credentials—like factory-installed passwords or hardcoded keys—that, barring exceptional circumstances, are never changed by end users or system administrators. This exposure invites the attackers to easily take over devices, pretend to be them, and have unauthorized access to

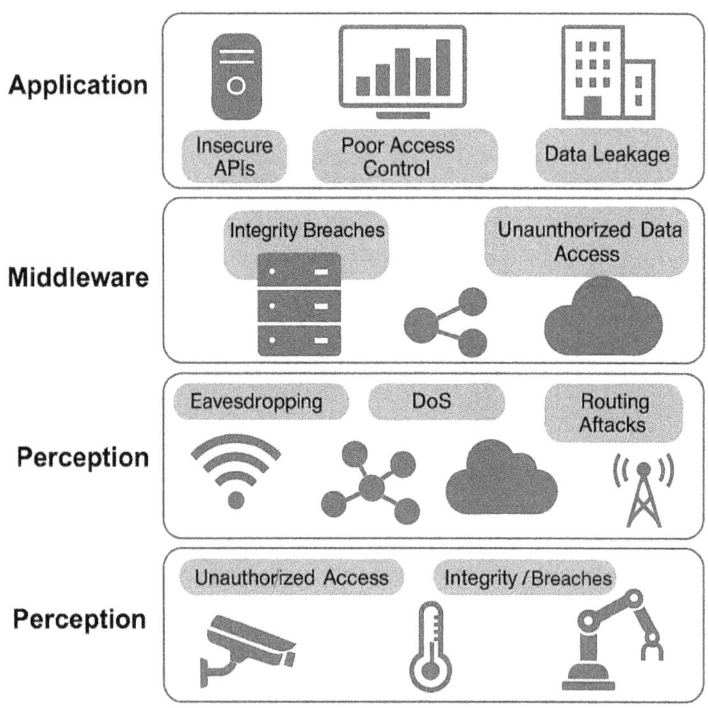

Figure 3.1 Architecture of a large-scale IoT system.

the network. Second, the absence of universally standardized identity management systems across various devices makes it challenging to have uniform authentication procedures that are secure but light enough for resource-constrained hardware.

Data Integrity and Confidentiality: Maintaining the confidentiality and integrity of data being transferred and stored over the IoT systems is another major challenge. Most IoT devices lack a lot of computational power, memory, and energy supply, which limits their capacity to carry out computationally intensive cryptographic processes that are usually adopted in conventional cybersecurity. Consequently, information—whether sensor measurements, commands, or confidential information—could be sent with weak encryption and integrity verification susceptible to interception, tampering, or replay attack by unauthorized parties. This weakness impacts not just unauthorized revelation of confidential information but can even compromise the authenticity and reliability of data used in critical decisions in smart infrastructure or industrial control systems.

Secure Firmware Updates: Secure device firmware updates are one of the most important features for remediation of vulnerabilities, as well as the addition of capabilities in the future. But most IoT devices have insecure or intermittent update mechanisms. Others don't have automated updates at all; instead, they use manual updates that are mostly forgotten. Others will not set up secure channels for updates, and this allows the attack to install malicious firmware that will hijack the device or install backdoors into the network. This is much harder in mass deployments as it needs tremendous, fail-safe, and scalable distribution systems that can distribute the updates to millions of devices at the same time that verify the authenticity and integrity of the firmware before installation.

Privacy Infringements: Most IoT devices tend to harvest and process extremely private personal data such as GPS location, biometric data, health records, and behavior patterns. In the absence of effective privacy-protection technologies, such information is liable to leak or be misused and lead to serious infringements of users' privacy and trust. The problem is aggravated in mass-scale contexts in which information passes through many stakeholders-third-party apps, cloud service providers, network operators, and device makers-so it might be difficult to implement uniform access controls and privacy policies. Furthermore, people usually are opaque and lack control over how their information is gathered, distributed, and stored, and this is a regulatory and ethical concern.

Scalability of Security Mechanisms: Legacy security designs rely heavily on centralized control mechanisms such as centralized identity providers, security information and event management (SIEM) systems, and access control lists. While satisfactory for smaller networks, these solutions can't scale well as the number of IoT devices scales to millions. Centralized systems are the bottleneck, causing single points of failure and performance degradation. Additionally, managing security policies, credentials, and logs over a huge number of devices places a gigantic overhead. Scalable IoT systems demand decentralized or hierarchical security models that can distribute trust and automate security management with low latency and high availability. These demands continue to be an old problem for both researchers and practitioners.

Figure 3.2 maps these challenges across each layer of the IoT architecture, helping visualize where vulnerabilities are most likely to occur.

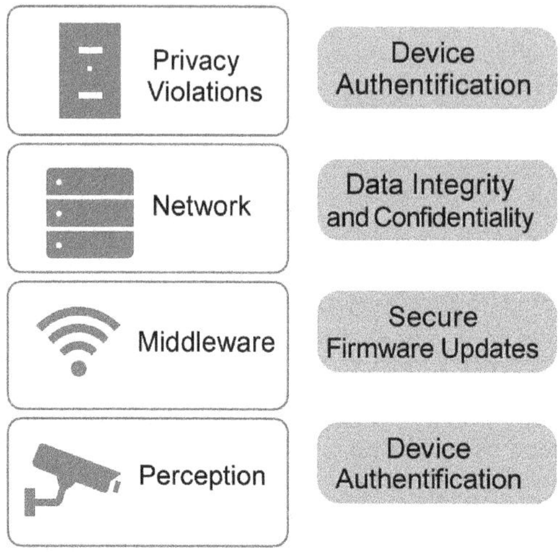

Figure 3.2 Security challenges in IoT systems.

3.3 COMMON ATTACK VECTORS

IoT networks, particularly large-scale implementations, are extremely attractive targets for attackers because they are so pervasive, typically have minimal security controls, and are mission-critical applications. Heterogeneity of devices, communication protocols, and sometimes minimal security awareness among end-users and manufacturers render them vulnerable. Below are some of the most common attack vectors against IoT environments:

Botnets: Perhaps the most visible threat to IoT networks is the creation of botnets—mass armies of compromised devices under remote control by attackers. Infected with default or weak passwords, unpatched exploits, or insecure communication protocols, these devices are coerced into orchestrating synchronized cyberattacks. Distributed Denial-of-Service (DDoS) attacks are the main tool used by IoT botnets, flooding targeted networks or servers with colossal amounts of traffic that bring services to a crawl or disable them entirely. A classic example is the Mirai botnet, in which attackers used default usernames and passwords on thousands of IoT devices like IP cameras and routers to illustrate how poor security hygiene could wreak havoc on internet infrastructure. Botnets not only initiate attacks on the availability of the victim service but also are used for spam campaigns, credential stuffing, or the distribution of malware.

MITM Attacks: MITM attacks are instances when an attacker secretly intercepts communication between two honest parties—like an IoT device and its cloud server—and is able to eavesdrop, alter, or inject malicious data without both parties realizing it. As encryption or authentication supported through IoT communication protocols tends to be ineffective, attackers may exploit network weaknesses to place themselves between devices and control servers. This attack vector has data confidentiality and integrity implications wherein hackers can redirect personal data or command and control instructions or interfere with the data streams such that devices act in an uncontrollable manner or carry out malicious instructions.

Replay Attacks: Replay attacks exploit genuine message exchange by intercepting and then resending the messages to trick an IoT system into performing unauthorized actions. An example is that an attacker can intercept a valid control command or authentication token and resend it to acquire unlawful access or control device functions. Since IoT devices are not highly capable and do not support efficient nonce or timestamp-based authentication schemes, such devices are highly susceptible to such attacks. Replay attacks lower the trust level in the communication of the system and can lead to unauthorized control, data corruption, or false alerts.

Side-Channel Attacks: Contrary to classic software vulnerability attacks, side-channel attacks attempt to exploit physical characteristics and unexpected side-channels of IoT devices for breaking sensitive cryptographic keys or data. For instance, the observation of electromagnetic emanations, power consumption patterns, timing variation, or acoustics along the length of an encryption process. These attacks are especially undesirable in IoT because the majority of devices are not properly protected or shielded against them, and the attackers are even able to perform side-channel attacks with little or no physical presence or remotely. Efficient side-channel attacks are even able to completely disregard encryption so that attackers are able to decrypt sensitive messages or impersonate legitimate devices.

Routing Attacks: The majority of IoT networks, particularly mesh, ad hoc, and wireless sensor network-based networks, make significant use of dynamic routing protocols to facilitate devices' communication. Routing attacks attack the network layer by distorting or impersonating routing information that eventually causes misrouted, dropped, or intercepted traffic. These attacks encompass the likes of sybil attacks, in which an attacker assumes multiple identities for purposes of affecting routing decisions, and wormhole attacks, in which attackers tunnel packets between two distant locations in the network for purposes of creating shortcuts that degrade topology and routing trust. They may have the ability to inflict high loss in network performance, node splitting, or enable other attacks like data eavesdropping or selective forwarding.

3.4 SECURITY STANDARDS AND FRAMEWORKS

Some organizations have set standards to ensure IoT systems:

- **NIST IR 8259** outlines foundational security capabilities such as secure boot, cryptographic operations, and secure communication.
- **ETSI EN 303 645** sets baseline security requirements for consumer IoT, emphasizing secure passwords and vulnerability disclosure.

Figure 3.3 depicts an MITM scenario where a hidden attacker relays and potentially modifies data between a smart device and the cloud.

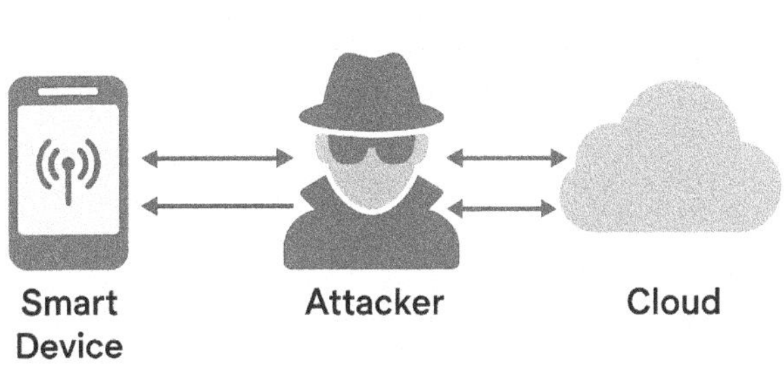

Figure 3.3 MITM attack.

- OWASP IoT Top 10 is a publicly developed list of the top security challenges to the IoT, such as insecure data storage, absence of hardening, and weak encryption practices.

  These frameworks give direction to manufacturers and developers, urging the use of secure protocols such as DTLS or light encryption algorithms like TinyECC for resource-limited devices.

3.5 SECURITY-BY-DESIGN PRINCIPLES

As the IoT grows more widespread across infrastructures and industries, security has also grown to become one of its biggest challenges. One of the biggest weaknesses in most deployments of IoT is the reactive deployment of post-deployment security after systems are up and running. Post-deployment patching is not only technically difficult and cost-ineffective, but it is extremely ineffective at eliminating root security flaws. Rather, a paradigm shift—security needs to be incorporated upfront, from the very initial stages of system architecture and development. Security-by-design, this initial effort, guarantees security not as an afterthought but as a fundamental design requirement.

Security-by-design involves integrating security factors into every aspect of the IoT ecosystem—hardware, firmware, communication protocols, software applications, and lifecycle management processes. It emphasizes more prevention than remediation, and it greatly improves trustworthiness, reliability, and compliance. There are several key principles enabling the construction of secure IoT systems with this methodology:

3.5.1 Least privilege access

This is a rule that states that every process, device, or user runs with the least amount of privilege necessary to carry out its function—nothing more, nothing less. This limitation cuts down on damage incurred by compromised pieces and limits off-budget access to sensitive portions of the system. For instance, a smart facility temperature sensor only needs access to the temperature data, and no other system controls like lighting or door locks. Least privilege in action is enforced through rigorous role-based access control (RBAC) and highly specific permission settings on each and every entity in the system. By cutting off unnecessary permissions, the system attack surface is minimized, and lateral movement by attackers is restricted.

3.5.2 Defense-in-depth

Realizing that any one security control is imperfect, defense-in-depth uses various layers of defense to provide redundancies and resiliency. Layers ranging from hardware to firmware, operating systems, networks, and applications work together to detect, block, and suppress threats. For example, in the case of a device being compromised, defense-in-depth assures that encryption, IDS, and network segmentation can still intercept data exfiltration or system compromise. Critical implementations are secure communications (e.g., TLS/SSL), firewalls, behavioral analysis, multi-factor authentication (MFA), and policy enforcement in the cloud. This multi-layer strategy causes an IoT network to do everything in its power to catch and recover from cyberattacks without catastrophic collapse.

3.5.3 Secure boot and trusted hardware

Since IoT devices typically run in open, unattended environments, the integrity of their hardware and firmware needs to be guaranteed. Secure boot operations check the digital signature of firmware when the system is booting and only execute trusted and unmodified code.

It relies on a hardware root of trust, which is the key security component of the device as a whole. The root of trust safely stores cryptographic keys and serves as the first checkpoint to ensure system integrity. This fusion substantially lowers the threat of persistent malware, firmware hijacking, and supply chain attacks—attacks that prove to be highly contagious in distributed IoT settings.

3.5.4 Anomaly detection

Security models based on predefined rules or signature-based detection don't fare well in identifying novel or advanced threats. AI and machine learning (ML)-based anomaly detection solutions provide a more dynamic defense. Through ongoing surveillance of IoT devices and the creation of behavior baselines, the devices can track anomalies that indicate likely threats—such as anomalous data rate of transmission, anomalous device interactions, or communications with unknown domains. Static defenses differ from anomaly detection systems because they improve only through time by acquiring knowledge on the quirks of device behavior and becoming more sensitive to novel forms of attacks. Implemented at the device, network, and application levels, anomaly detection provides elevated situational awareness and facilitates near-instant incident response.

Through the adoption of these security-by-design best practices, IoT infrastructures can be designed to be resilient, private, and trustworthy from day one. Not only does this make it easier to achieve long-term security maintenance and lower operating costs, but it also supports compliance with increasingly stringent regulatory requirements. Finally, the security-by-design ethic drives public and institutional trust in the security, dependability, and moral integrity of IoT technology and offers a basis for safe, sustainable innovation in networked surroundings.

Figure 3.4 demonstrates a defense-in-depth model, layering security measures from physical devices up to cloud platforms.

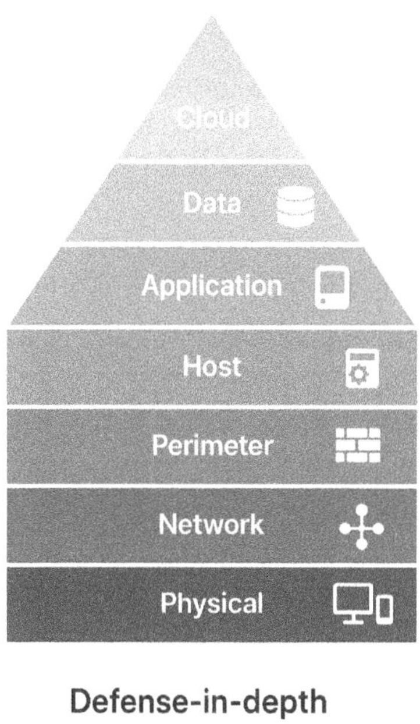

Figure 3.4 Defense-in-depth model.

3.6 LAYERED SECURITY MODEL

A layered approach addresses specific threats at each stage of the IoT architecture:

3.6.1 Perception layer (physical layer)

This is the foundational layer of the IoT architecture, consisting of physical devices like sensors, actuators, RFID tags, embedded systems, and edge nodes that directly interact with the physical environment. As these devices often operate in uncontrolled or vulnerable environments, they are particularly exposed to physical and low-level cyber threats.

Key Security Threats:

- Physical tampering or theft
- Data spoofing or injection
- Unauthorized device access
- Cloning or counterfeit devices

Security Measures:

- Tamper-resistant and tamper-evident hardware to detect or prevent physical interference
- Hardware-based security modules (e.g., TPM, Secure Elements) to store cryptographic keys
- Local data encryption before transmission to ensure confidentiality
- Unique device identifiers to prevent spoofing and impersonation
- Secure boot to ensure only verified firmware runs on the device

3.6.2 Network layer

This layer is responsible for the transmission of data between IoT devices and backend systems via wired or wireless communication technologies (e.g., Wi-Fi, LTE, 5G, Zigbee, LoRaWAN). As data travels across networks, it becomes vulnerable to interception, disruption, or rerouting.

Key Security Threats:

- Eavesdropping and MITM attacks
- Routing manipulation (e.g., sybil or wormhole attacks)
- Denial-of-Service (DoS) attacks
- Replay attacks

Security Measures:

- Virtual private networks (VPNs) for encrypted tunnels between edge devices and servers
- Secure routing protocols such as RPL with DTLS or IPsec integration
- Network segmentation and firewalls to isolate critical devices or zones
- IDS tailored for IoT protocols
- Rate-limiting and packet filtering to reduce the impact of DoS attacks

3.6.3 Middleware layer (service layer)

This intermediate layer manages IoT services, device coordination, data processing, and integration with external applications. It acts as the "brain" of the IoT ecosystem, interpreting and processing data for actionable outcomes.

Key Security Threats:

- Unauthorized service access
- Malicious code execution
- Application Programming Interface (API) abuse and injection attacks
- Compromised data processing modules

Security Measures:

- Secure APIs with authentication and authorization controls (e.g., OAuth 2.0, JWT)
- Run-time monitoring and anomaly detection using AI/ML techniques
- Policy-based access control systems for dynamic security rule enforcement
- Code signing and integrity checks for middleware components
- Containerization and sandboxing of microservices to limit the blast radius of an attack

3.6.4 Application layer

This is the topmost layer and the main interface for end users, administrators, and third-party applications. It facilitates user interactions, visualizations, and control over IoT devices and services.

Key Security Threats:

- Credential theft and account hijacking
- Unauthorized access to sensitive information
- Data leakage via poorly secured interfaces
- Application-level DoS and injection attacks

Security Measures:

- MFA to strengthen user identity verification
- RBAC to restrict access to sensitive functions and data
- Secure user interfaces with input validation and protection against XSS/SQLi attacks
- End-to-end encryption for data exchanged between users and backend systems
- Audit logs and activity tracking for user actions and access history

This model promotes extensive coverage so that no single weakness would render the system insecure.

3.7 CASE STUDY: SMART CITY IoT SECURITY

In an IoT implementation of a smart city, waste management, traffic lights, utilities, and surveillance are all controlled by IoT devices. Each of these sub-systems has its own specific security vulnerabilities. A hacked traffic control sensor can cause accidents, and a fake

Figure 3.5 Unified smart city map.

surveillance system will breach privacy or allow criminals to travel freely. To secure such a sophisticated infrastructure:

- Blockchain is used to authenticate the integrity of data that is being sent.
- Public key infrastructure (PKI) authenticates devices before communication.
- Edge AI processes traffic or video streams at the edge, minimizing exposure of raw data and allowing real-time anomaly detection.

Figure 3.5 shows an integrated smart city map where secure layers guard numerous services like streetlights, street cameras, and public transportation systems.

3.8 FUTURE DIRECTIONS

Future technologies have promising avenues to improving IoT security:

- **Quantum-Resistant Cryptography:** Guards encrypted data from being accessed even for future-generation quantum computers.
- **Federated Learning:** Allows ML models to be trained locally on devices, preserving data privacy.
- **Blockchain and Smart Contracts:** Create decentralized trust models, automating and securing IoT interactions.
- **Edge AI:** By moving computation closer to the source, edge AI enables faster response and reduces reliance on centralized data centers.

Constant research and development in such fields target developing more robust and smart IoT Ecosystems.

3.9 CONCLUSION

Mass-scale IoT networks pose an enormous, large-scale, and dynamic attack surface from their distributed, heterogeneous device signatures and pervasive adoption into critical sectors such as healthcare, smart cities, transportation, energy, and manufacturing. As these networks get further embedded into the infrastructure and fabric of modern life, they are no longer merely a technology challenge but a social imperative to secure. This end-to-end, multi-layered security-by-design model is essential in establishing a solid foundation. This involves bringing in security across all phases of the system lifecycle—device production and software programming, all the way through to deployment, updating, and ultimate decommissioning. All of this must be accompanied by strict adherence to global security standards and regulatory policies with the aim of bringing about consistency, interoperability, and accountability to the ecosystem. Besides, the incorporation of best practices such as frequent firmware updates, encryption, access control, threat modeling, and supply chain security greatly boosts system integrity. Beyond these fundamental considerations, deployment of newer technologies such as AI-enabled threat detection, blockchain-enabled trust management, and quantum-resistant cryptography offers promising paths toward safeguarding against extremely sophisticated attacks. However, the ever-changing nature of cyber threats necessitates continuous innovation and vigilance. The future of IoT security depends on watchful, collective action by device manufacturers, software writers, network operators, policymakers, and university researchers. Cooperation alone will allow us to build future-proof, adaptive, and scalable models of security capable of protecting the networked IoT world that continues to grow.

BIBLIOGRAPHY

1. National Institute of Standards and Technology. (2020). *Recommendations for IoT Device Manufacturers: Foundational Activities and Core Device Cybersecurity Capability Baseline* (NIST IR 8259). https://doi.org/10.6028/NIST.IR.8259
2. European Telecommunications Standards Institute. (2020). *Cyber Security for Consumer Internet of Things: Baseline Requirements* (ETSI EN 303 645 V2.1.1). https://www.etsi.org/deliver/etsi_en/303600_303699/303645/02.01.01_60/en_303645v020101p.pdf
3. Open Web Application Security Project. (2021). *OWASP Internet of Things Project.* https://owasp.org/www-project-internet-of-things/
4. Sicari, S., Rizzardi, A., Grieco, L. A., & Coen-Porisini, A. (2015). Security, privacy and trust in Internet of Things: The road ahead. *Computer Networks*, *76*, 146–164. https://doi.org/10.1016/j.comnet.2014.11.008
5. Roman, R., Najera, P., & Lopez, J. (2011). Securing the Internet of Things. *Computer*, *44*(9), 51–58. https://doi.org/10.1109/MC.2011.291
6. Alrawais, A., Alhothaily, A., Hu, C., & Cheng, X. (2017). Fog computing for the Internet of Things: Security and privacy issues. *IEEE Internet Computing*, *21*(2), 34–42. https://doi.org/10.1109/MIC.2017.37
7. Lee, I., & Lee, K. (2015). The Internet of Things (IoT): Applications, investments, and challenges for enterprises. *Business Horizons*, *58*(4), 431–440. https://doi.org/10.1016/j.bushor.2015.03.008
8. Lin, J., Yu, W., Zhang, N., Yang, X., Zhang, H., & Zhao, W. (2017). A survey on Internet of Things: Architecture, enabling technologies, security and privacy, and applications. *IEEE Internet of Things Journal*, *4*(5), 1125–1142. https://doi.org/10.1109/JIOT.2017.2683200
9. Kolias, C., Kambourakis, G., Stavrou, A., & Gritzalis, S. (2017). DDoS in the IoT: Mirai and other botnets. *Computer*, *50*(7), 80–84. https://doi.org/10.1109/MC.2017.201
10. Mosenia, A., & Jha, N. K. (2017). A comprehensive study of security of Internet-of-Things. *IEEE Transactions on Emerging Topics in Computing*, *5*(4), 586–602. https://doi.org/10.1109/TETC.2016.2606384

11. Ammar, M., Russello, G., & Crispo, B. (2018). Internet of Things: A survey on the security of IoT frameworks. *Journal of Information Security and Applications*, *38*, 8–27. https://doi.org/10.1016/j.jisa.2017.11.002
12. Fernandes, E., Jung, J., & Prakash, A. (2016). Security analysis of emerging smart home applications. *IEEE Symposium on Security and Privacy*, 636–654. https://doi.org/10.1109/SP.2016.44
13. Weber, R. H. (2010). Internet of Things – New security and privacy challenges. *Computer Law & Security Review*, *26*(1), 23–30. https://doi.org/10.1016/j.clsr.2009.11.008
14. Zhao, K., & Ge, L. (2013). A Survey on the Internet of Things Security. *2013 Ninth International Conference on Computational Intelligence and Security*, 663–667. https://doi.org/10.1109/CIS.2013.145
15. Khan, R., Khan, S. U., Zaheer, R., & Khan, S. (2012). Future Internet: The Internet of Things Architecture, Possible Applications and Key Challenges. *2012 10th International Conference on Frontiers of Information Technology*, 257–260. https://doi.org/10.1109/FIT.2012.53
16. Granjal, J., Monteiro, E., & Silva, J. S. (2015). Security for the Internet of Things: A survey of existing protocols and open research issues. *IEEE Communications Surveys & Tutorials*, *17*(3), 1294–1312. https://doi.org/10.1109/COMST.2015.2388550
17. Hossain, M. S., & Muhammad, G. (2016). Cloud-assisted industrial internet of things (IIoT) – Enabled framework for health monitoring. *Computer Networks*, *101*, 192–202. https://doi.org/10.1016/j.comnet.2016.01.009
18. Suo, H., Wan, J., Zou, C., & Liu, J. (2012). Security in the Internet of Things: A Review. *2012 International Conference on Computer Science and Electronics Engineering*, 648–651. https://doi.org/10.1109/ICCSEE.2012.193
19. Babar, S., Mahalle, P., Stango, A., Prasad, N., & Prasad, R. (2011). Proposed Security Model and Threat Taxonomy for the Internet of Things (IoT). *International Conference on Network Security and Applications (CNSA)*, 420–429.
20. Porambage, P., Ylianttila, M., & Gurtov, A. (2016). Lightweight security protocols for machine-type communication in 5G: A survey. *IEEE Communications Surveys & Tutorials*, *20*(3), 2292–2320.
21. Shreyas, J., Chouhan, D., Rao, S. T., Udayaprasad, P. K., Srinidhi, N. N., & Kumar, S. D. (2021). An energy efficient optimal path selection technique for IoT using genetic algorithm. *International Journal of Intelligent Internet of Things Computing*, *1*(3), 230–248.
22. Shreyas, J., Chouhan, D., Rao, S. T., Udayaprasad, P. K., Srinidhi, N. N., & Dilip Kumar, S. M. (2021). EERO: Energy Efficient Route Optimization Technique for IoT Network. *Futuristic Trends in Network and Communication Technologies: Third International Conference, FTNCT 2020, Taganrog, Russia, October 14–16, 2020, Revised Selected Papers, Part II 3*, 207–218. Springer Singapore.
23. Álvarez Casado, C., & Bordallo López, M. (2021). Real-time face alignment: Evaluation methods, training strategies and implementation optimization. *Journal of Real-Time Image Processing, 18*, 2239–2267. https://doi.org/10.1007/s11554-021-01107-w
24. N, S. Y., R, A., S, S. U., Z, S. Z. T., Mathew, A., & V T, M. A. (2024). Smart Headband with a Mobile Application to Predict and Monitor Seizures Using EEG Spring Technology an Ultimate Effective Model for Seizure Free Life. *2024 Second International Conference on Advances in Information Technology (ICAIT)*, 1–7, Chikkamagaluru, Karnataka, India. http://dx.doi.org/10.1109/ICAIT61638.2024.10690375

Chapter 4

Tracing devices and privacy concerns

Shreelakshmi Yadav N, Shreyas J, Gururaj H L, Dayananda P, and Korhan Cengiz

4.1 INTRODUCTION

Rapid technological evolution has also introduced a plethora of innovations that raise convenience, security, and efficiency levels in daily life. One such innovation is tracing technology—technology used in devices for real-time tracking and surveillance of people, goods, and vehicles. As increasing numbers of devices are being installed, the issue of invasion of privacy and eavesdropping has emerged as a cause of increasing concern. As societies continue to become more interconnected and data-based, the balance between the usefulness of tracing devices and protecting privacy rights must be more strongly emphasized. This chapter examines different kinds of tracing devices, how and why they are used, the risks they pose, as well as the law and ethics that have evolved to restrict their ambit over privacy.

People use tracking devices that enable real-time monitoring of individuals and their possessions and vehicles throughout their daily activities because these devices provide them with practical benefits, secure their operations, and improve their work efficiency. As the number of deployed devices increases, so do the public concerns regarding their potential to invade personal privacy, conduct surveillance, and misuse collected information. This chapter investigates multiple tracing technologies that exist in different forms and serve various purposes, while it assesses their potential dangers and evaluates legal and ethical systems that exist to safeguard personal privacy rights.

Location and movement trackers—technology-based devices that gather and report location or movement information—have become ubiquitous in contemporary life. From the phone in your pocket to global positioning system (GPS) trackers on cars and Internet of Things (IoT) sensors in smart cities, they support compelling use cases that make life more convenient, secure, and efficient. But they also raise thorny privacy issues. The high-granularity location information that is being collected can expose intimate aspects of people's lives, including home and workplace locations, social relationships, and daily routines.

In this chapter we discuss the technology underlying tracking devices, look at what they make possible, examine the privacy threat that they pose, and look at how existing privacy-protection methods and regulatory regimes try to counter it. We end by turning our attention to what the future might hold. Figure 4.1 depicts the architecture of the tracing devices.

4.2 UNDERSTANDING TRACING DEVICES

Tracking devices are technological equipment that can be used to track and monitor people's and objects' movement or positioning. The devices range in variety, including GPS trackers, RFID (Radio Frequency Identification) tags, Bluetooth beacons, Wi-Fi

DOI: 10.1201/9781003513896-4

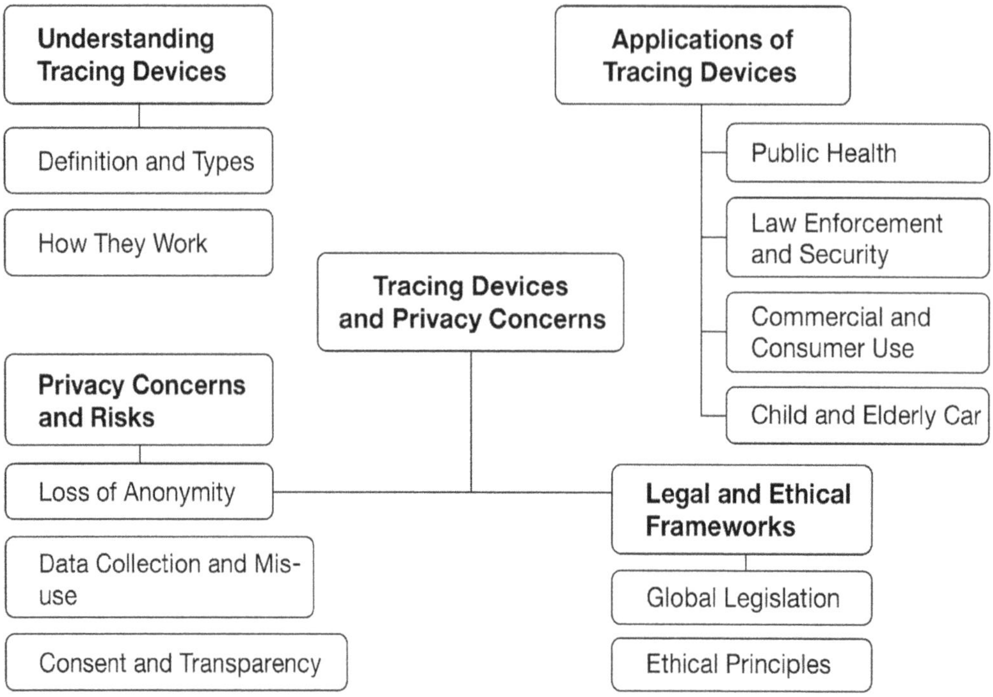

Figure 4.1 Architecture of tracing devices and privacy.

tracking systems, and biometric monitoring devices. GPS trackers are installed in smartphones, vehicles, and wearable gadgets to offer real-time positioning information. RFID tags can be used in logistics, retail, and access control systems, whereas Bluetooth beacons are used for short-distance communication requirements, like proximity marketing or medical tracking.

The devices function through the capture of data through sensors and communication modules, which are sent to centralized servers to be analyzed and processed. For instance, GPS relies on satellite signals for position location, whereas RFID uses radio waves in an attempt to pass information across readers and tags. In many cases, the data collected is stored or shared over networks, making it essential to understand the underlying mechanisms and potential vulnerabilities of such systems.

4.3 TECHNOLOGIES OF TRACING DEVICES

4.3.1 Global positioning system (GPS)

GPS operates through a constellation of at least 24 satellites orbiting Earth. A GPS receiver calculates its position by measuring the time delay of signals from multiple satellites, using trilateration. GPS provides accuracy typically within 5–10 meters for civilian use.

- Use Case: Smartphones use GPS for navigation apps like Google Maps or fitness tracking.
- Limitation: GPS signals can be weak or unavailable indoors, underground, or in dense urban areas (urban canyons).

4.3.2 Cellular network-based tracking

Mobile devices communicate with multiple cell towers, and triangulation or multilateration techniques estimate device location based on signal strength, time delay, or angle of arrival.

- Use Case: Telecom providers use this data for network optimization and emergency services.
- Accuracy: Typically 100–500 meters, but can be less precise than GPS.

4.3.3 Wi-Fi and Bluetooth tracking

Wi-Fi access points and Bluetooth beacons detect nearby devices by monitoring MAC addresses and signal strength. Retailers use this for foot traffic analysis.

- Example: Shopping malls use Wi-Fi tracking to study customer movement patterns.
- Privacy Concern: MAC addresses, if not randomized, can be linked to specific users.

4.3.4 RFID and NFC

RFID tags broadcast identifiers when scanned by a reader. Common in supply chain management, asset tracking, and contactless payments.

- Example: RFID in passports or employee ID badges.
- Range: Typically short (up to a few meters).

4.3.5 IoT sensors and edge devices

IoT ecosystems integrate multiple sensors (GPS, cameras, accelerometers) feeding data to edge devices for local processing.

- Example: Smart city sensors track traffic flows in real-time.
- Advantage: Edge computing reduces latency and limits data exposure.

4.4 APPLICATIONS OF TRACING DEVICES

Tracing devices have found diverse applications across multiple sectors, enhancing both functionality and safety. In public health, these devices play a crucial role in contact tracing during disease outbreaks, such as the COVID-19 pandemic. Mobile apps leveraging Bluetooth or GPS were deployed globally to track individuals' interactions and limit the virus's spread. Additionally, wearable health monitors are used to track patient vitals remotely, enabling better management of chronic conditions and emergency responses.

In law enforcement and security, tracking technology facilitates surveillance work, electronic monitoring of parolees, and live crime tracking. Governments and authorities employ these technologies to respond to emergencies, track criminal suspects, and improve public safety. In business, tracking technology is employed in fleet management, tracking inventory, and tracking customer behavior. Smartwatches and fitness trackers track users' activity levels, but consumers use location data to enhance service and optimize store layouts.

In addition, tracking devices are becoming more commonly used in elderly care, particularly for sensitive groups like children and aging individuals. GPS and geofencing-capable devices assist caregivers in monitoring people with cognitive disorders to avoid accidents and enhance quality of life. Tracking devices facilitate a variety of applications, which identify their usefulness to society:

- Navigation and Fitness: Wearables track steps, heart rate, and location for health insights.
- Fleet Management: Logistics companies optimize routes, monitor vehicle conditions, and enhance security.
- Healthcare Monitoring: Remote patient monitoring includes tracking movement to detect falls or inactivity.
- Retail Analytics: Understanding customer behavior to optimize store layouts and promotions.
- Law Enforcement: Location tracking supports investigations and emergency response.
- Smart Cities: Integration of sensors enhances urban planning and public safety.

4.5 PRIVACY CONCERNS AND RISKS

Although useful, tracking devices pose grave privacy issues. One of the largest issues is the elimination of anonymity. Since devices gather and send data constantly, people can be tracked in public areas as much as in their own homes, eliminating the idea of private lives. In sensor- and camera-filled cities, it is difficult to walk down the street without being tracked. The second legitimate problem is information collection and abuse. Data acquired from tracking devices may contain extremely personal details, including health status, location histories, social contacts, and behavioral habits. Without robust data governance, this information can end up in the hands of hackers, corporations, or even oppressive governments. Abuse can be identity theft, stalking, manipulation, or surveillance capitalism, whereby corporations profit on individual data in the absence of explicit consent.

In addition, there is the issue of openness and consent. The vast majority of users are not aware of the amount of information being collected and why. Terms and conditions are usually long, complicated, or hidden, making it extremely hard to provide informed consent. The issue of function creep, where information collected for one reason is used for another, contributes to the risk. For instance, location information originally collected for mapping purposes can be resold to advertisers or transferred on the sly to police. Figure 4.2 provides a flowchart for the location data lifecycle.

4.5.1 Data collection and consent

Location information is normally gathered continuously or by default, with no sign of awareness from users on the scope or size of retention practice. For instance, mobile applications do request location permission just for one thing, but gather data expansively beyond it.

Case Study: In 2018, the fact that most smartphone applications share location information with third-party vendors without direct user consent was reported in *The Wall Street Journal* report.

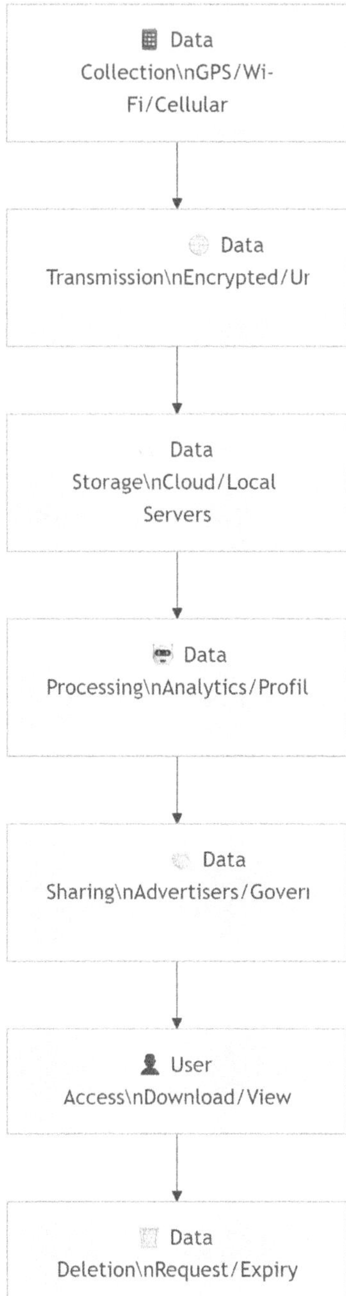

Figure 4.2 Flowchart of location data lifecycle from collection to deletion.

4.5.2 Data security and breaches

Location leaks can put vulnerable groups at risk of harassment or stalking.

Example: The 2018 Strava heat map leak exposed military base locations by tracing anonymous fitness activity.

4.5.3 Profiling and behavioral analysis

Ongoing location tracking enables unprecedented profiling. Advertisers, for example, target users based on histories of visits to sensitive places like medical clinics, religious temples, or political protests.

Risk: Discrimination or manipulation based on location-based profiles.

4.5.4 Government surveillance and misuse

Surveillance proposals can utilize tracking devices with insufficient controls.

Example: Reports about the National Security Agency (NSA)'s mass surveillance programs showed how location data can be collected at scale.

4.5.5 Data retention and sharing

Data often persists beyond its original purpose and can be shared or sold, raising concerns about loss of control.

Transparency Issue: Users are often unaware of secondary data uses.

4.6 PRIVACY-PRESERVING TECHNIQUES AND BEST PRACTICES

4.6.1 Data minimization

Collect only necessary data. For instance, an app for weather updates doesn't need continuous GPS tracking.

4.6.2 User consent and transparency

Implement granular permission controls and clear privacy policies.

Suggested Illustration: Flowchart illustrating user consent acquisition and data access controls.

4.6.3 Anonymization and pseudonymization

Removing direct identifiers or replacing them with pseudonyms can reduce re-identification risks, though location data can often be re-identified through patterns.

Example: Differential privacy techniques add noise to location data to obscure individual traces.

4.6.4 Secure data storage and transmission

Use end-to-end encryption (e.g., Transport Layer Security (TLS) for data in transit) and encrypted databases for storage.

4.6.5 User control and data portability

Provide users with dashboards to review, export, or delete their location data.

4.6.6 Privacy by design

Embed privacy considerations at every stage of development, from hardware to software.

4.7 LEGAL AND ETHICAL FRAMEWORKS

To mitigate these concerns, numerous legal and ethical frameworks have been established worldwide. The **General Data Protection Regulation (GDPR)** in the European Union is among the most comprehensive data privacy laws, mandating that organizations collect data transparently and with user consent. It mandates the right to view, alter, or erase personal data and levies punishment for default. The California Consumer Privacy Act (CCPA) also grants consumers the right to control the gathering and sharing of personal information by businesses.

India's Digital Personal Data Protection (DPDP) Act is a giant leap toward data protection, which will oversee the processing of digital personal information while providing individual rights and legal use. Such laws are indicative of increasing calls for accountability and ethical use of technology.

Ethically, such values as proportionality, responsibility, and data minimization are stressed. Technologies must be proportionately used to the purpose that they serve, and organizations must take responsibility for the data collected. Only necessary amounts of data being collected make the possibility of violation and abuse less.

4.8 REGULATORY FRAMEWORKS AND STANDARDS

4.8.1 General Data Protection Regulation (GDPR)

- Scope: Personal information of EU citizens.
- Significant Provisions: Clarity of consent, right of access and erasure, data protection impact analysis.
- Relevance: Geolocation data is regarded as personal data under GDPR from Table 4.1.

4.8.2 California Consumer Privacy Act (CCPA)

- Rights: Users can know, delete, and opt out of the sale of personal data.
- Challenges: Enforcement is evolving.

4.8.3 Location Privacy Protection Act (LPPA)

- Status: Proposed US legislation aiming to regulate the commercial use of location data.

4.8.4 Industry standards

- IEEE P7012: Standard for artificial intelligence (AI) transparency, which applies to location-based services.
- ISO/IEC 27701: Privacy Information Management Systems.

Table 4.1 Comparative table of privacy laws (GDPR vs. CCPA vs. LPPA)

Aspect	*GDPR (EU)*	*CCPA (California)*	*LPPA (Proposed US)*
Scope	All personal data of EU citizens	Personal data of California residents	Commercial use of location data in US
Consent required	Explicit and informed consent	Opt-out of sale required	Consent required for location data collection
User rights	Access, erasure, portability, objection	Know, delete, opt-out	Similar to GDPR, focus on location data
Penalties	Up to 4% of global turnover	Fines up to $7,500 per violation	Proposed civil penalties
Data minimization	Required	Encouraged	Proposed

4.9 ETHICAL CONSIDERATIONS

Ethical use of tracing devices calls for moving beyond compliance to include:

- Informed Consent: Respect for autonomy.
- Non-Discrimination: Avoid biased profiling.
- Proportionality: Limit data collection to what is necessary.
- Accountability: Clear responsibility for data misuse.

4.10 TECHNOLOGICAL SAFEGUARDS AND BEST PRACTICES

Apart from legal controls, various technological tools can ensure user privacy. Privacy by design allows for the integration of privacy aspects in hardware and software systems during the design stage and not as an afterthought. Encrypted data ensures the protection of information while being sent over the internet and while saved. Data anonymization and data aggregation also provide scope for the creation of meaningful insights without the disclosure of individual identity. Best practices also encompass providing opt-in models where users opt in willingly.

To allow them to exchange their data, and ensure openness through transparent and clear privacy policies. Providing users with control over their data guarantees trust and secure use of technology.

4.11 BALANCING UTILITY AND PRIVACY

Achieving the proper balance among the utility of tracking technologies and the protection of privacy remains a challenge. As valuable as they are, their misuse can cause harm. All stakeholders—governments, technology companies, and civil society—need to work together to develop guidelines, standards, and practices that ensure responsible innovation.

Pioneering projects like the Apple-Google Exposure Notification API (Application Programming Interface) try offer a privacy-friendly contact tracing model. Or, experiences such as China's social credit system show the possibility of unregulated surveillance, in which intense tracking and aggregation of information can result in a diminution of civil liberties.

4.12 CASE STUDIES

4.12.1 Case study 1: The Strava heat map incident (2018)

Popular fitness app Strava published an international heat map of user exercise using GPS data. Anonymous as it was, the map uncovered sensitive spots, like patrol stations and military installations, due to users running or cycling through those. This gave rise to alarms over unintended location disclosures undermining national security. Figure 4.3 represents the GPS network for the location sharing.

Privacy Concerns:

- Location data, even anonymized, can expose sensitive sites.
- Aggregated data can lead to unintended surveillance.
- Lack of user awareness about data aggregation consequences.

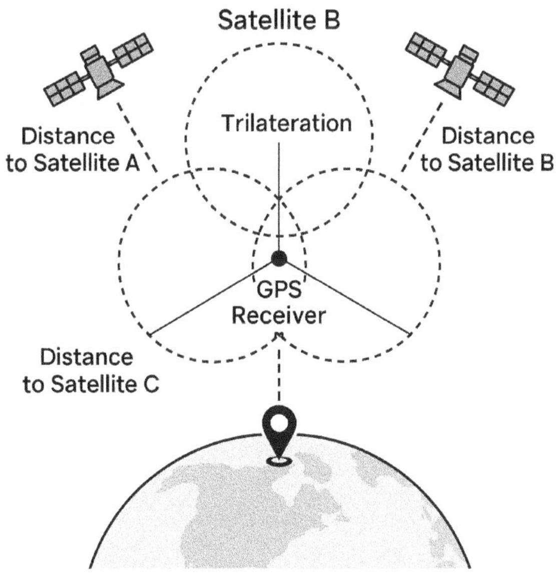

Figure 4.3 GPS trilateration.

Lesson:

There needs to be diligent consideration before posting aggregated location data, such methods as differential privacy must be employed.

4.12.2 Case study 2: Facebook's location data sharing scandal (2019)

It was discovered that Facebook collected users' location data—even when location services were switched off—and third parties were made aware of this fact without explicit consent.

Privacy Concerns:

- Violation of user consent and transparency principles.
- Potential for profiling and misuse by advertisers or malicious actors.

Lesson:

Unwavering commitment to openness and consent is absolutely necessary for trust.

4.12.3 Case study 3: Google location tracking default settings (2018)

A study showed that Google gathered users' locations by default even when they disabled 'Location History,' due to other location services still being enabled.

Privacy Concerns:

- Complex settings confuse users, leading to unintentional data collection.
- Highlights the importance of clear, granular control over location data.

4.13 FUTURE DIRECTIONS

The merging of AI and tracing technologies should be anticipated to boost predictive power but also raise privacy issues. AI is capable of digitizing large volumes of data, interpreting behavior, and arriving at independent choices—raising further the question of regulation. Cross-border flows of data also raise the specter of jurisdiction and enforcement, particularly when multinational corporations are operating in countries with different privacy legislations.

Public awareness of digital rights and protection of privacy is also required. Enhancing digital literacy can enable people to make more informed choices regarding their data and hold organizations to account.

Privacy-Protecting Technologies: Technologies such as federated learning enable models to learn on-device without exposing raw location information.

More Capable User Tools: More capable user interfaces for dynamic permission control.

Regulatory Transformation: Regulation will have to evolve to accommodate new modalities of tracking, like drone surveillance.

Inter-Disciplinary Strategies: Inter-disciplinary collaboration between technologists, policymakers, and ethicists.

4.14 CONCLUSION

Trace technologies are a double-edged sword in contemporary society. They offer undeniable benefits to public security, health, and business, but carry high risks to individual privacy. As they continue to expand, it is crucial to craft strong legal barriers, ethical norms, and technical safeguards that respect human rights. By creating a culture of transparency, accountability, and informed consent, society may utilize the advantage of tracking devices without invading privacy.

BIBLIOGRAPHY

1. J. Zang, et al., "Privacy Risks of Location Data: A Systematic Review," *ACM Computing Surveys*, vol. 52, no. 6, pp. 1–34, 2019.
2. A. Rieke, et al., "Data Protection and Privacy Challenges in the Internet of Things," *IEEE Internet of Things Journal*, vol. 7, no. 3, pp. 2559–2570, Mar. 2020.
3. R. Shokri and C. Troncoso, "Privacy and Security for Location-Based Services," *Foundations and Trends® in Privacy and Security*, vol. 2, no. 2–3, pp. 157–255, 2018.
4. European Parliament and Council of the European Union, "Regulation (EU) 2016/679 (General Data Protection Regulation)," *Official Journal of the European Union*, Apr. 27, 2016.
5. California Legislature, "California Consumer Privacy Act (CCPA)," *California Civil Code §§ 1798.100 et seq.*, 2018.
6. Wall Street Journal, "How Your Phone Tracks You," *The Wall Street Journal*, 2018.
7. Electronic Frontier Foundation, "Location Privacy," 2024.
8. National Institute of Standards and Technology (NIST), "Privacy Framework: A Tool for Improving Privacy through Enterprise Risk Management," *National Institute of Standards and Technology*, Jan. 2020.
9. A. Solanas, C. Patsakis, M. Conti, I. Vlachos, V. Ramos, F. Falcone, O. Martin, S. Azizi, and R. Martinez-Balleste, "Smart Health: A Context-Aware Health Paradigm within Smart Cities," *IEEE Communications Magazine*, vol. 52, no. 8, pp. 74–81, Aug. 2014, doi: 10.1109/MCOM.2014.6871673.
10. A. Ghosh, V. Aggarwal, and M. Singh, "A Comprehensive Review on Location Privacy Protection Techniques in Mobile and Sensor Networks," *IEEE Communications Surveys & Tutorials*, vol. 20, no. 1, pp. 421–454, 1st Quart. 2018.

11. R. Shokri, G. Theodorakopoulos, C. Troncoso, J. P. Hubaux, and J. Le Boudec, "Protecting Location Privacy: Optimal Strategy against Localization Attacks," *Proceedings of the 2012 ACM Conference on Computer and Communications Security (CCS '12)*, pp. 617–627, 2012, doi: 10.1145/2382196.2382261.
12. A. R. Beresford and F. Stajano, "Location Privacy in Pervasive Computing," *IEEE Pervasive Computing*, vol. 2, no. 1, pp. 46–55, Jan.–Mar. 2003, doi: 10.1109/MPRV.2003.1186725.
13. M. E. Peck, "Strava Heat Map and the Unintended Consequences of Location Sharing," *IEEESpectrum*, Feb. 2018. [Online].
14. J. Krumm, "A Survey of Computational Location Privacy," *Personal and Ubiquitous Computing*, vol. 13, no. 6, pp. 391–399, 2009, doi: 10.1007/s00779-008-0212-5.
15. S. Ziegeldorf, F. Morchon, and K. Wehrle, "Privacy in the Internet of Things: Threats and Challenges," *Security and Communication Networks*, vol. 7, no. 12, pp. 2728–2742, Dec. 2014, doi: 10.1002/sec.795.
16. P. Voigt and A. von dem Bussche, *The EU General Data Protection Regulation (GDPR): A Practical Guide*, Springer International Publishing, 2017. [Online], doi: 10.1007/978-3-319-57959-7.
17. B. Liu, C. Y. Chow, and L. Wang, "Privacy-Preserving Point-of-Interest Recommendation Using Geosocial Data," *IEEE Transactions on Services Computing*, vol. 11, no. 3, pp. 549–561, May–Jun. 2018.
18. C. Zhang, H. Zhao, and J. Guan, "A Privacy-Preserving Location Sharing Scheme in Vehicular Social Networks Based on Hierarchical Encryption," *IEEE Access*, vol. 6, pp. 38490–38500, 2018.
19. R. Shokri, C. Troncoso, and P. Hubaux, "Privacy Games Along Location Traces: A Game-Theoretic Framework for Optimizing Location Privacy," *ACM Transactions on Privacy and Security (TOPS)*, vol. 19, no. 4, pp. 1–31, Jan. 2017.
20. L. Sweeney, "k-Anonymity: A Model for Protecting Privacy," *International Journal of Uncertainty, Fuzziness and Knowledge-Based Systems*, vol. 10, no. 5, pp. 557–570, 2002, doi: 10.1142/S0218488502001648.
21. C. Dwork, "Differential Privacy," *33rd International Colloquium on Automata, Languages and Programming (ICALP)*, Springer, pp. 1–12, 2006, doi: 10.1007/11787006_1.
22. Shreelakshmi Yadav N., Abhishek R., Sajith Umar S., Syeda Zobia Tazeen Z., Mathew A., and Muzammil Ahmed V. T. Smart Headband with a Mobile Application to Predict and Monitor Seizures Using EEG Spring Technology an Ultimate Effective Model for Seizure Free Life. In *2024 Second International Conference on Advances in Information Technology (ICAIT)*, Chikkamagaluru, Karnataka, India, 2024, pp. 1–7, doi: 10.1109/ICAIT61638.2024.10690375.
23. R. S. Ramya, S. Yadav N, V. K R, S. S. Iyengar, and Patnaik L. M. "Real-Time Multi-View Face Recognition using Alignment-RMFRA (April 25, 2021)," *Proceedings of the International Conference on Innovative Computing & Communication (ICICC)*, 2021, Available at SSRN: https://ssrn.com/abstract=3833799 or http://dx.doi.org/10.2139/ssrn.3833799
24. J. Shreyas, D. Chouhan, S. T. Rao, P. K. Udayaprasad, N. N. Srinidhi, and S. D. Kumar. (2021). "An Energy Efficient Optimal Path Selection Technique for IoT Using Genetic Algorithm," *International Journal of Intelligent Internet of Things Computing*, vol. 1, no. 3, pp. 230–248.
25. J. Shreyas, D. Chouhan, S. T. Rao, P. K. Udayaprasad, N. N. Srinidhi, and S. M. Dilip Kumar, EERO: Energy Efficient Route Optimization Technique for IoT Network. In *Futuristic Trends in Network and Communication Technologies: Third International Conference, FTNCT 2020*, Taganrog, Russia, October 14–16, 2020, Revised Selected Papers, Part II 3, 2021, pp. 207–218, Springer Singapore.

Chapter 5

IoT forensics

Opportunities and challenges

Udayaprasad P K, Dhanalakshmi B K, Pradeep Kumar G M, Shreyas J, and Ahmed A Khalifa

5.1 INTRODUCTION

The Internet of Things (IoT) has become one of the most revolutionary technological advancements of the 21st century, transforming industries and affecting daily life. This section introduces IoT and its development, highlights the importance of digital forensics in IoT, summarizes the objectives and scope of this research study, and delineates the paper structure.

5.1.1 Background of IoT and its evolution

Technologies that enable them to gather and share information. Since its birth in the early 2000s to becoming widespread today, IoT has grown with lightning speed and impacted major sectors like healthcare, agriculture, smart cities, and manufacturing (Figure 5.1).

Key Milestones in the Evolution of IoT Include the Following:

- **1999**: Kevin Ashton used the term "Internet of Things" for the first time.
- **2008 and 2009**: IoT was a profound concept when the number of connected devices exceeded the planet Earth's population.
- **2010–onward:** Increased smart devices, edge computing, and 5G technologies spurred IoT further.

5.1.2 Importance of digital forensics in IoT

With the increasing integration of IoT devices into critical systems, these devices produce vast amounts of data that can prove significant evidence in forensic and investigative cases. IoT forensics involves finding, preserving, analyzing, and presenting digital evidence (Figure 5.2).

Key Aspects of IoT Forensics Include the Following:

- **Data Heterogeneity**: The large variety of data types produced from these devices, including logs, sensor readings, and multimedia (Table 5.1).
- **Security Challenges:** The vulnerability of IoT systems to cyberattacks calls for forensic capabilities, given potential data breaches.
- **Legal and Regulatory Compliance**: Forensics helps address any legal disputes and is critical in ensuring regulation compliance, such as General Data Protection Regulation (GDPR).

 DOI: 10.1201/9781003513896-5

IoT Evolution Timeline

Time Period	Key Events	Developments
1999	Term coined	Kevin Ashton's vision
2000-2005	First IoT device	ITU report published
2008-2009	Connected devices surpass people	First IoT Conference
2010-2013	IPv6 protocol introduced	Google's Nest Thermostat launch
2014-2016	IoT devices reach 10 billion	Mirai botnet attack
2017-2019	AI integration	5G networks launch
2020-Present	COVID-19 pandemic	New regulations and standards

Figure 5.1 A timeline showcasing the evolution of IoT from 1999 to the present.

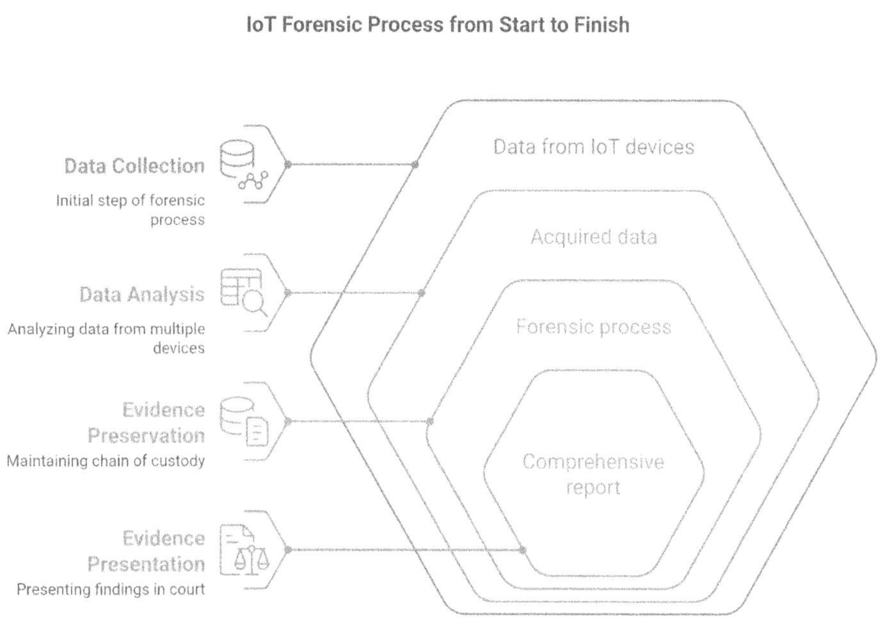

Figure 5.2 An illustration of the IoT forensic process, from data collection to evidence presentation.

Table 5.1 IoT devices and their data source with key challenges

Aspect	*Challenge*	*Example*
Data volume	High data generated by IoT	Smart cities generating terabytes daily
Device diversity	Heterogeneous device types	Smartphones, wearables, home devices
Real-time analysis	Immediate need for insights	Cyberattack incident response
Legal complexity	Cross-jurisdiction issues	Data privacy laws

5.1.3 Objectives and scope of the study

The main objective of the research will be to discover challenges and opportunities in IoT forensics. Such a goal in this work will focus on technological, legal, and procedural issues. Specific goals of the chapter will be the following:

- Identifying the unique characteristics of IoT data relevant to forensic investigations.
- Highlighting existing gaps in forensic tools and methodologies for IoT environments.
- Proposing solutions and frameworks to enhance forensic capabilities.

IoT forensics' overview, practical challenges, emerging opportunities, and future directions are under discussion in the chapter. The work will therefore benefit researchers, law enforcement agencies, and practitioners who deal with IoT security and forensic investigations as (Table 5.2).

5.1.4 Structure of the chapter

This chapter is organized into seven sections:

Section 5.1: Introduction, providing the background, importance, objectives, and structure of the chapter.
Section 5.2: Fundamentals of IoT and forensics, discussing their core principles and integration.
Section 5.3: Challenges in IoT forensics, focusing on technical and legal issues.
Section 5.4: Opportunities in IoT forensics, exploring emerging technologies and use cases.
Section 5.5: Methodologies and frameworks, presenting state-of-the-art forensic approaches
Section 5.6: Open research directions, highlighting areas requiring further investigation.
Section 5.7: Conclusion, summarizing insights, and suggesting future work.

Table 5.2 Framed objectives with expected outcomes

Objective	*Expected outcome*
Analyze IoT forensics challenges	Comprehensive understanding of key issues
Explore forensic frameworks and tools	Identification of effective methodologies and practices
Recommend future research directions	Strategic insights for stakeholders

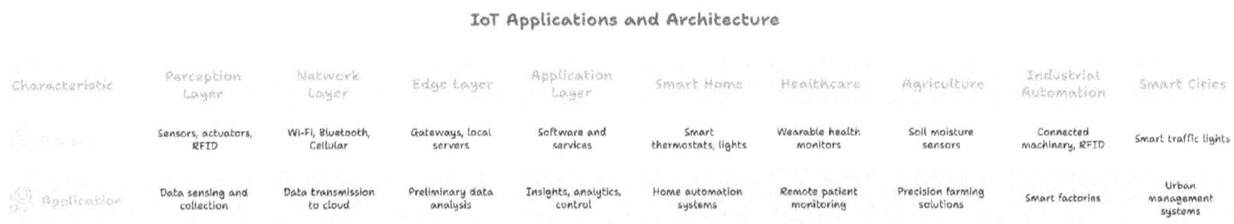

Figure 5.3 A diagram of IoT architecture showcasing the four layers.

5.2 FUNDAMENTALS OF IoT AND FORENSICS

5.2.1 Overview of IoT architecture and applications

The IoT is a transformative technology that enables the interconnectivity of physical devices, sensors, and systems and allows them to exchange data seamlessly with each other for automation. The architecture in IoT does not always have four layers as shown in Figure 5.3.

- **Perception Layer:** This layer consists of physical sensors and devices that collect environmental data (e.g., temperature, motion, or location).
- **Network Layer:** This layer transmits the collected data to other systems via Wi-Fi, ZigBee, or Bluetooth.
- **Processing Layer:** Data processing occurs at this layer, typically involving cloud servers, edge devices, or gateways.
- **Application Layer:** The end-user interfaces and applications that provide actionable insights and enable decision-making.

Applications of IoT:

- **Smart Homes and Cities:** Smart thermostats, lighting, and surveillance systems increase comfort and efficiency.
- **Healthcare:** Wearable devices monitor patient vitals in real time.
- **Industrial IoT (IIoT):** Automation and predictive maintenance in manufacturing processes.
- **Transportation:** Fleet management and autonomous vehicles.
- **Agriculture:** Precision farming and livestock monitoring.

5.2.2 Digital forensics: Key concepts and processes

Digital forensics deals with the collection, analysis, and preservation of digital evidence in the investigation of a crime or for the resolution of disputes. The key concepts and steps are mentioned below (Figure 5.4):

- **Identification:** Possible sources of evidence include IoT devices such as smart cameras, sensors, and gateways.
- **Preservation:** Ensuring the integrity of evidence using methods like write-blockers and cryptographic hashing.
- **Analysis:** Extracting and interpreting data to reconstruct events or identify anomalies.
- **Documentation:** Maintaining a detailed record of findings to ensure transparency.
- **Presentation:** Delivering evidence and analysis in a court-admissible format.

Forensics frameworks emphasize maintaining the **chain of custody** and minimizing data tampering risks.

Figure 5.4 Illustration of data flow from an IoT device to a forensic investigator.

5.2.3 The intersection of IoT and forensics

IoT presents specific opportunities and challenges to digital forensics. Devices create vast amounts of data, frequently in real time, from diverse sources such as smart locks, fitness trackers, and vehicle sensors. The data streams offer rich context to an investigation (Figure 5.5). Major challenges are the following: (i) Data Volatility: IoT data tends to be transient and needs to be collected in real time. (ii) Proprietary Protocols: Companies employ distinct standards, which are difficult to interoperate. (iii) Distributed Evidence: Data can be on the device, edge servers, and the cloud. Opportunities are the following: (i) Behavioral Analysis: IoT logs exhibit usage patterns and abnormalities. (ii) Cross-Device Correlation: Collecting data from devices gives end-to-end information.

5.2.4 Relevance of IoT data as evidence

IoT devices produce varied types of data, such as sensor logs, audio/video recordings, and environmental metadata. This data can prove to be useful evidence in different contexts: Criminal Investigations: Home appliances can give timelines and context data in the course of an event. Civil Disputes: Fitness tracker information was used to deny claims of injury before a court. Compliance and Auditing: IoT systems keep track of regulatory compliance. Major IoT Evidence Features: Volume: Amounts of data produced can be too large for conventional forensic tools to handle. Variety: Formatted, half-formatted, and unformatted data. Velocity: Rapid data production demands real-time collection techniques (Table 5.3).

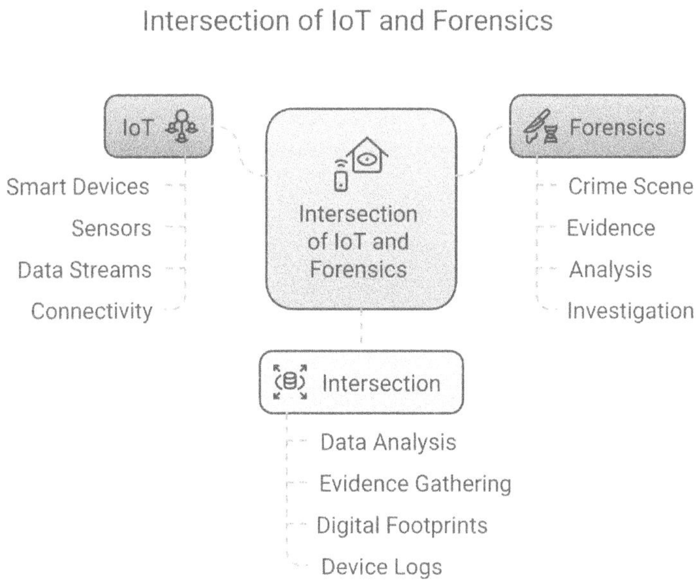

Figure 5.5 The framework of IoT and forensics.

Table 5.3 IoT device evidence types with key challenges

IoT evidence type	*Source device*	*Forensic use case*	*Challenges*
Location data	GPS-enabled devices	Tracking suspect movement	Data accuracy and spoofing
Environmental sensor logs	Smart thermostats	Determining activity timelines	Volatility of data
Communication logs	Smart speakers	Voice recognition and incident analysis	Privacy concerns
Video surveillance	Smart cameras	Visual evidence of incidents	Tampering and storage issues

5.3 CHALLENGES IN IoT FORENSICS

The increasing population of IoT devices poses dark threats to digital forensics. The following section emphasizes the prevailing challenges that stall successful IoT forensic investigations.

5.3.1 Heterogeneity and scalability issues

IoT ecosystems are inherently diverse, comprising devices with varying hardware, software, protocols, and communication standards. This heterogeneity complicates data extraction and analysis, as no single forensic tool can handle all device types effectively. Moreover, the scalability issue arises due to the sheer number of IoT devices interconnected in modern systems (Figure 5.6 and Table 5.4).

5.3.2 Data acquisition and preservation challenges

IoT devices generate vast volumes of data most often dispersed over cloud storage, edge devices, and local storage. Acquiring this data without altering its integrity is one of the biggest challenges. Real-time data generation increases the difficulties in preserving volatile evidence and makes traditional forensic methods inappropriate (Table 5.5).

IoT Devices and Protocols

Characteristic	Smart Thermostats	Security Cameras	Wearables	Smart Home Hubs	Smart Appliances	Smart Lighting
Wi-Fi	Yes	Yes	Yes	Yes	Yes	Yes
ZigBee	Yes	Yes	No	Yes	Yes	Yes
Z-Wave	Yes	No	No	Yes	No	No
Ethernet	No	Yes	No	No	No	No
Bluetooth	No	No	Yes	No	Yes	Yes
NFC	No	No	Yes	No	No	No

Figure 5.6 Different IoT device types with their communication protocols.

Table 5.4 IoT device types with their protocols and forensics challenges

Device type	*Protocol*	*Forensic challenge*
Smart home devices	ZigBee	Lack of protocol-specific forensic tools
Wearables	Bluetooth	Limited storage for forensic artifacts
Industrial IoT (IIoT)	Ethernet	The high volume of real-time data

Table 5.5 IoT data sources and their preservation challenges with possible solutions

Data source	*Preservation challenge*	*Possible solution*
Cloud storage	Access restrictions, jurisdiction issues	Blockchain-based audit trails
Local device storage	Limited memory, data overwrite	Real-time forensic acquisition
Network traffic	High volume, encryption	AI-based packet analysis

5.3.3 Privacy and security concerns

IoT Forensics Investigation has to balance the line between privacy and evidence collection. Any investigation into IoT systems usually involves access to sensitive user data, whether it be health metrics or location history. Further, IoT devices are frequent targets of cyberattacks, which also complicates the collection of uncompromised evidence (Table 5.6 and Figure 5.7).

5.3.4 Legal and ethical constraints

IoT forensics faces different legal frameworks in jurisdictions, which makes cross-border investigations very complicated. Ethical issues arise when keeping users' trust and handling

Table 5.6 IoT devices' privacy concerns and their mitigation strategies

Privacy concern	*Impact on forensics*	*Mitigation strategy*
Sensitive user data	Legal restrictions on data access	Data anonymization techniques
Device encryption	Inaccessible evidence	Collaboration with manufacturers
Network attacks	Compromised forensic integrity	End-to-end data validation

Figure 5.7 The overlap between IoT security, user privacy, and forensic access needs.

Table 5.7 IoT devices' ethical constraints with their forensics impact

Legal/ethical constraint	*Region*	*Forensic impact*
GDPR compliance	European Union	Limits on data collection
Lack of standardization	Global	Inconsistent forensic procedures
Ethical data handling	Global	Erosion of user trust

sensitive data responsibly. Compliance with regulations such as GDPR is essential to avoid legal consequences (Table 5.7).

5.3.5 Limitations of current forensic tools

Traditional forensic tools are designed for conventional computing environments and thus incompatible with IoT-specific architectures. Most tools cannot address dynamic IPs, encrypted communication, and device-specific file systems (Table 5.8).

Table 5.8 Limitations of current forensic tools

Forensic tool	*Limitation*	*IoT-specific requirement*
Traditional disk analyzers	Cannot access real-time data	Support for volatile memory analysis
Network analyzers	Inadequate encrypted traffic	Decryption capability
Cloud forensic tools	Limited scalability for IoT ecosystems	Distributed data analysis

5.4 OPPORTUNITIES IN IoT FORENSICS

5.4.1 Emerging trends in forensic technologies

The high-growth IoT networks have spurred immense innovation in forensic technology. This innovation meets the specific challenges that arise from the distributed, heterogeneous nature of IoT ecosystems (Figure 5.8).

Some of the key trends are the following:

1. **Cloud Forensic Tools:** Because IoT devices tend to save data in cloud services, cloud-based forensic tools are beginning to emerge to simplify data acquisition and analysis.
2. **Edge Forensics:** This would enable data processing at the edge devices, minimizing latency and greatly minimizing data loss during transit.
3. **AI-Driven Analysis:** Forensic software more and more are making use of machine learning (ML) algorithms to extract patterns, outliers, and correlations in large datasets.
4. **Big Data Analytics:** New-generation big data architectures enable processing and visualization of IoT forensic evidence at an actionable level of granularity.

5.4.2 Leveraging AI and machine learning for IoT forensics

ML and artificial intelligence (AI) lead the revolution of IoT forensics by making complex processes easier and offering real-time analysis (Table 5.9). (i) Data Analysis: ML processes vast data from IoT devices to derive forensic evidence with minimal human interaction and reduced error rates. (ii) Anomaly Detection: AI is capable of identifying unusual patterns or activities in IoT networks that could be a sign of security breaches or unauthorized access. (iii) Predictive Modeling: Past experience, supported by ML models, can also predict likely forensic data, allowing investigators to target the most pertinent areas. (iv) Natural Language Processing (NLP): NLP tools facilitate processing of log and text data produced by IoT devices, allowing enhanced comprehension.

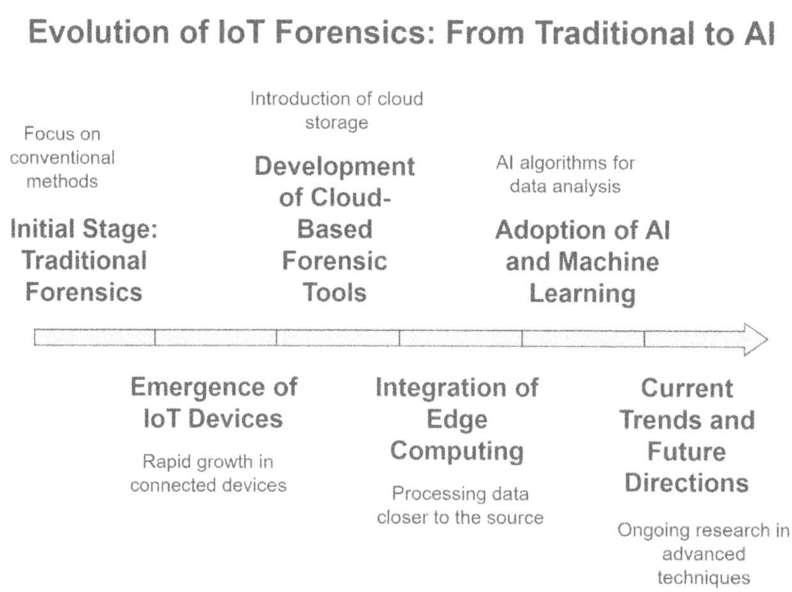

Figure 5.8 A development of IoT forensic technologies, with emphasis on innovations such as cloud-based tools, edge computing, and AI integration.

Table 5.9 AI and machine techniques for IoT forensics

AI/ML technique	*Application in IoT forensics*	*Benefits*
Anomaly detection models	Intrusion detection	Identifies suspicious activities
Predictive analytics	Prioritizing evidence	Improves investigation efficiency
NLP	Log and data analysis	Extracts meaningful insights
Deep learning algorithms	Device behavior analysis	Recognizes complex patterns

5.4.3 Role of blockchain in ensuring data integrity

The advantages of applying blockchain technology to ensure and maintain forensic data integrity for IoT applications are unparalleled (Figure 5.9).

1. **Tamper-Proof Data Storage:** A permanent blockchain ledger provides forensic data in tamper-proof form, and consequently, any type of tampering will always be traceable.
2. **Decentralized Evidence Management:** Decentralized ledger architecture can store evidence on different nodes to limit the chances of data tampering.

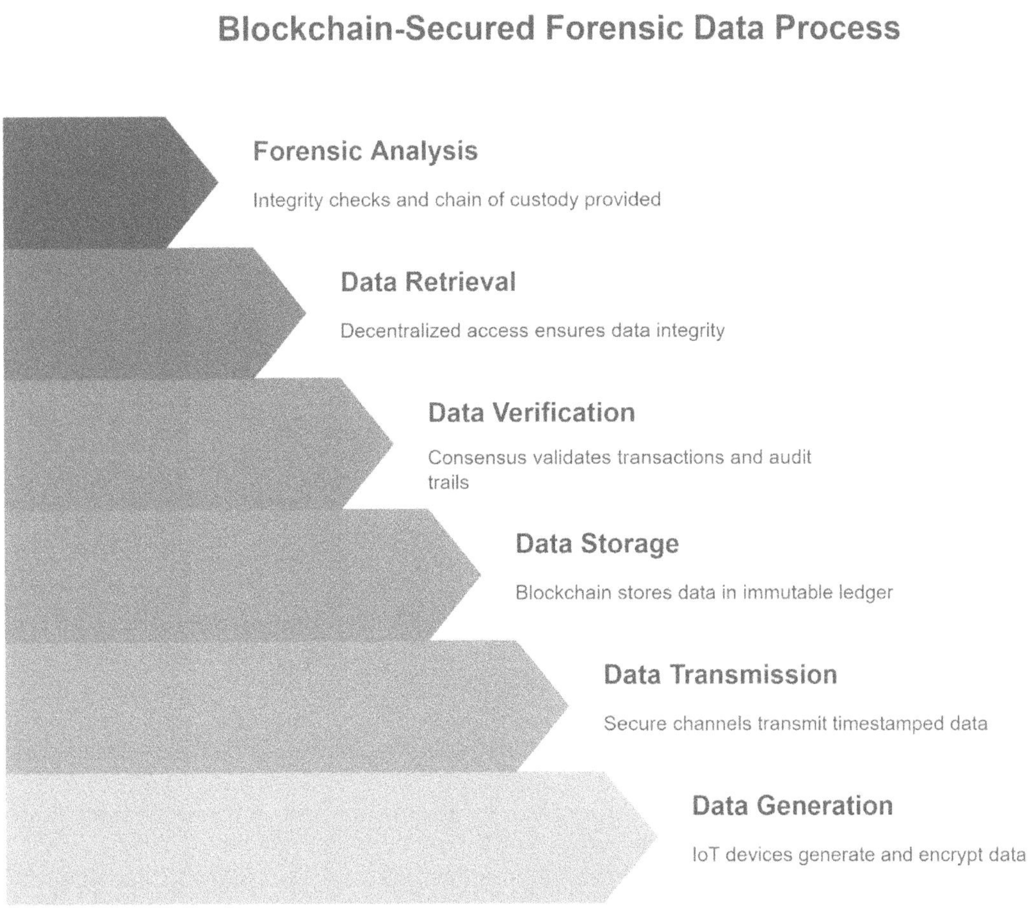

Figure 5.9 A layered diagram illustrating how blockchain secures forensic data in IoT systems, from data generation to storage and verification.

Table 5.10 IoT forensics critical infrastructure and its outcomes

Critical infrastructure	*Forensic application*	*Outcome*
Smart grids	Detecting intrusions in energy systems	Enhanced grid security
Healthcare IoT	Investigating breaches in medical devices	Improved patient safety
Transportation	Securing IoT-enabled vehicles and systems	Reduced cyber risks in transport
Industrial IoT	Identifying anomalies in production devices	Increased operational reliability

3. **Transparency and Auditability:** Blockchain makes tracing feasible and hence it becomes simple to ascertain the chain of custody of forensic evidence.
4. **Automation through Smart Contracts:** The sharing and saving of forensic data can be automated by the smart contract between the stakeholders.

5.4.4 IoT forensics in critical infrastructure: Use cases

IoT forensics will secure critical infrastructure, including energy grids, health systems, and transportation networks (Table 5.10).

1. **Smart Grids:** IoT forensic tools identify and mitigate cyber threats against smart meters and grid devices for a consistent energy supply.
2. **Healthcare IoT:** Forensics assists in investigating breaches in medical IoT devices to safeguard patients' sensitive data and the devices' reliability.
3. **Transportation Systems:** Forensic techniques in the transportation sector find vulnerabilities in IoT-connected vehicles and traffic systems for the prevention of accidents and misuse of data.
4. **IIoT:** IoT forensics helps to detect cyber incidents at the level of automated manufacturing.

5.5 METHODOLOGIES AND FRAMEWORKS FOR IoT FORENSICS

5.5.1 Taxonomy of IoT forensic frameworks

IoT forensics is a multidisciplinary field requiring specially developed frameworks to address the new challenges IoT environments pose. Frameworks could be viewed under the following broad categories (Figure 5.10):

1. **Device-Centric Frameworks:** Collect evidence from individual IoT devices like sensors, actuators, and gateways.
2. **Network-Centric Frameworks:** Emphasize monitoring and analysis of data flows between devices within IoT networks.
3. **Cloud-Centric Frameworks:** Target forensic analysis of data stored in cloud environments, where IoT devices often offload their data.
4. **Hybrid Frameworks:** Combine device, network, and cloud-centric approaches to create a comprehensive forensic strategy.

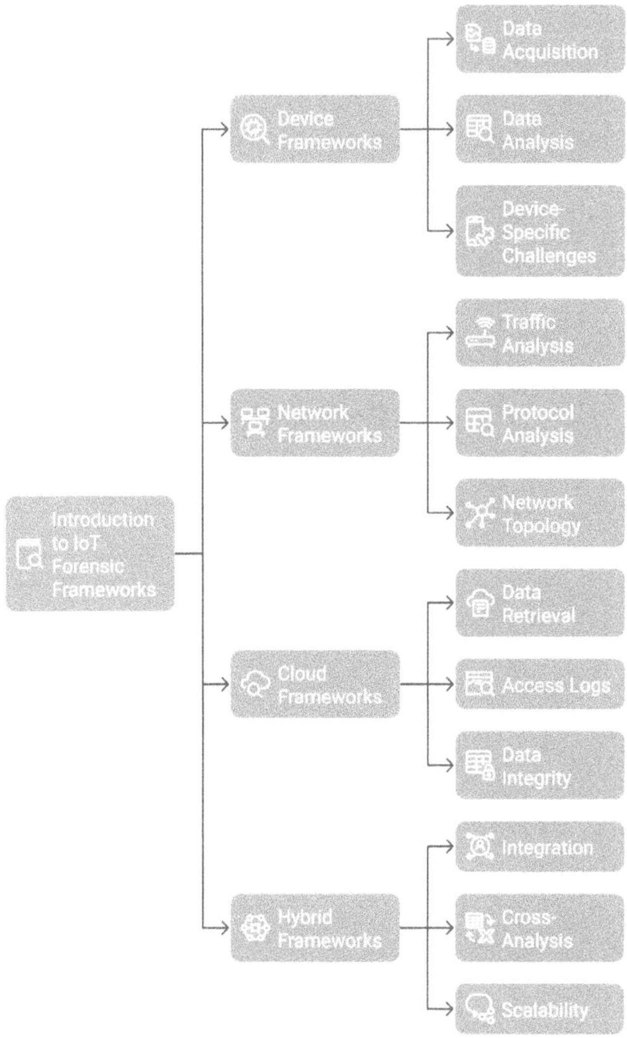

Figure 5.10 A IoT forensic frameworks' taxonomy shows the interconnections between device, network, cloud, and hybrid frameworks.

5.5.2 State-of-the-art approaches

Recent advancements in IoT forensics leverage cutting-edge technologies to improve data collection, analysis, and preservation (Figure 5.11). These approaches include the following:

1. **AI and ML for Anomaly Detection:** Use supervised and unsupervised learning algorithms to detect unusual activities indicative of security breaches.
2. **Blockchain for Data Integrity:** Employing blockchain technology to ensure the immutability and transparency of forensic data records.
3. **Edge Computing for Localized Evidence Processing:** Processing forensic data near the source to minimize latency and enhance efficiency.
4. **Cross-Layer Forensic Models:** Data integration across different layers of IoT architecture (e.g., physical, application, and network layers) for a holistic analysis.

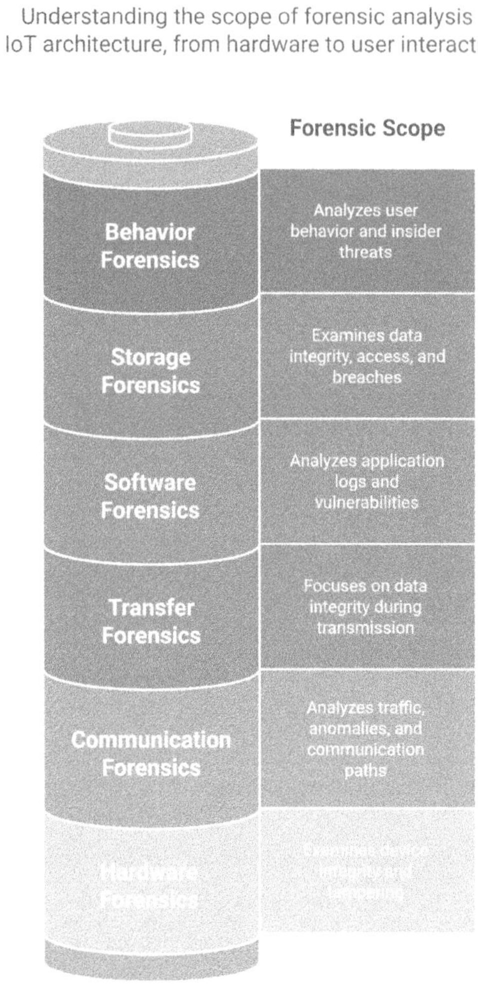

Figure 5.11 A layered diagram of cross-layer forensic models in IoT architecture.

5.5.3 Integration of existing forensic tools with IoT-specific needs

Adapting traditional forensic tools for IoT environments involves addressing the following features (Table 5.11):

1. **Scalability:** Tools must handle massive volumes of data generated by IoT devices.
2. **Device Diversity:** IoT ecosystems consist of heterogeneous devices with varying communication protocols and storage formats.
3. **Real-Time Analysis:** Enhanced capabilities to analyze data streams in real time for timely incident response.

Table 5.11 Comparison of traditional and IoT-specific forensic tool features

Feature	*Traditional tools*	*IoT-specific requirements*
Scalability	Limited	High (big data handling)
Device diversity	Standardized	Heterogeneous devices
Real-time analysis	Rarely supported	Essential
Interoperability	Limited	Extensive support needed

4. **Interoperability:** Tools should support many file systems, network protocols, and cloud storage formats.

5.5.4 Case studies: Successful IoT forensic investigations

1. **Smart Home Device Compromise:** Analysis of evidence from compromised IoT cameras and voice assistants revealed malicious firmware updates as the attack vector (Figure 5.12).
2. **IIoT Breach:** Forensic analysis of a manufacturing plant's IoT sensors revealed a cyberattack exploiting unpatched vulnerabilities in network protocols.
3. **Healthcare IoT Security Incident:** Further investigation into the hack of an IoT medical device revealed unauthorized data access through insecure authentication mechanisms of the IoT devices.
4. **Connected Car Intrusion:** Forensic investigation of data logs of an infotainment system of an autonomous vehicle identified unauthorized remote access, exploiting communication protocols as referred from Table 5.12.

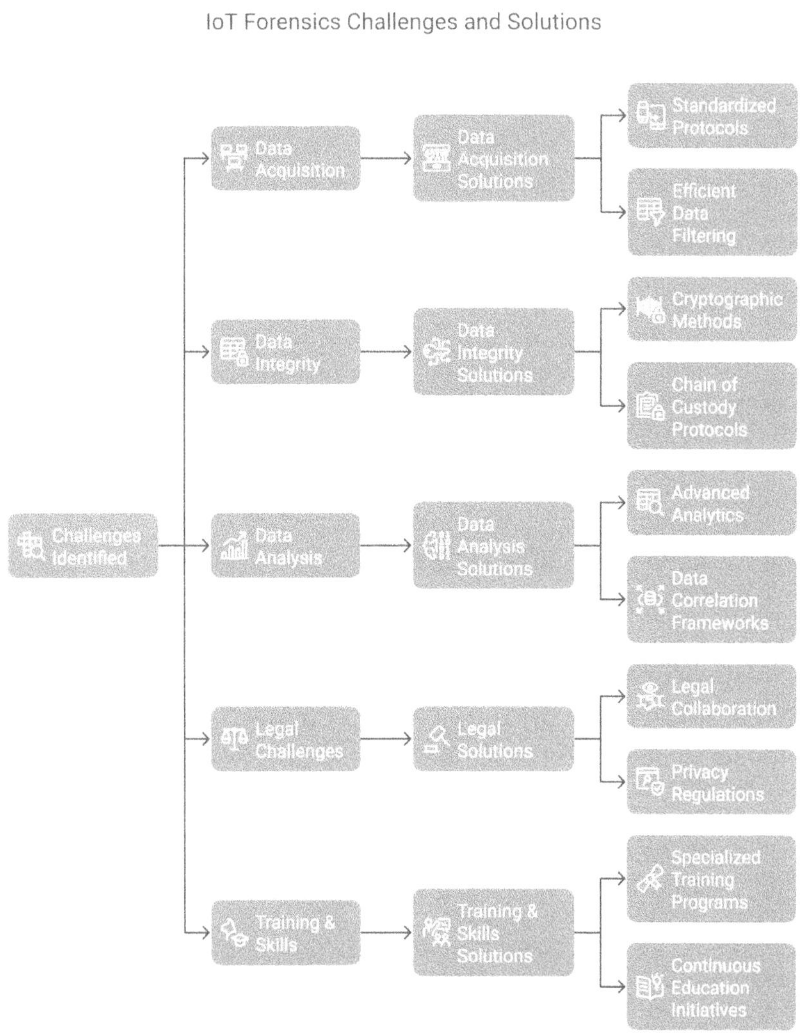

Figure 5.12 A flowchart illustrating the practical challenges and potential solutions in IoT forensics.

Table 5.12 Summary of IoT forensic case studies

Case study	*Device(s) analyzed*	*Attack vector*	*Key findings*	*Outcome*
Smart home compromise	IoT cameras, assistants	Malicious firmware updates	Vulnerable firmware protocol	Device update policies
Industrial IoT breach	IoT sensors	Unpatched network protocols	Protocol exploitation	Protocol patching
Healthcare device hack	IoT medical devices	Unauthorized access	Weak authentication	Enforced device security
Connected car intrusion	Autonomous vehicles	Exploited communication	Unencrypted protocol	Protocol hardening

5.6 OPEN RESEARCH DIRECTIONS

IoT forensics is a highly infancy-stage field with boundless expansion opportunities. Some areas of activity have been placed in this chapter where more research and communication between the experts is needed to address the existing demands and lay down the foundation toward establishing appropriate forensic techniques for IoT domains.

5.6.1 Addressing practical challenges in IoT forensics

The significant technical challenges in IoT forensics are device heterogeneity, evidence collection, and reliability. New approaches and technological advancements must be developed to address such challenges, which are the following (Figure 5.12).

1. **Device Heterogeneity:** The IoT environment includes heterogeneous devices with different protocols and standards, and therefore the challenge of designing standard forensic procedures. Researchers have to create frameworks that are extremely flexible in accommodating different devices.
2. **Data Acquisition:** IoT sensors generate massive amounts of data in a distributed setting. This necessitates effective means of detecting, extracting, and maintaining valuable evidence.
3. **Evidence Reliability:** IoT forensics requires techniques to verify evidence integrity and authenticity. Anti-tampering methods must be implemented, and blockchain technologies will be critical.

5.6.2 Improving forensic tool development

Most of the available forensic tools are useless in IoT devices, and their usage is affected by this. There should be more effort to develop tailor-made tools that account for the special requirements imposed on IoT forensics (Table 5.13).

1. **Tool Compatibility:** Tools should be compatible with IoT protocols like Message Queuing Telemetry Transport (MQTT), Constrained Application Protocol (CoAP), and ZigBee so as to extract evidence seamlessly.
2. **Automation:** AI and ML can be used to extract evidence automatically and detect anomalies; patterns can be identified in the IoT environment.
3. **Cloud Integration:** The majority of IoT devices rely on cloud services, and forensic tools are required to review the data and logs in the cloud.

Table 5.13 Forensic tool features

Forensic tool feature	*Traditional tools*	*IoT-specific tools*
Protocol support	Limited	Extensive (MQTT, CoAP)
Data volume handling	Moderate	High
Cloud data analysis	Minimal	Advanced
Automation	Basic	AI/ML-enabled

5.6.3 Improving collaboration among researchers, practitioners, and law enforcement officials

Practical IoT forensics involves cross-disciplinary cooperation to resolve technological, legal, and operational problems (Figure 5.13).

1. Knowledge Sharing: Creating platforms for experience sharing, tools, and best practices can enable speeding up progress in IoT forensics.
2. Collaborative Training Workshops: Joint training workshops of researchers, practitioners, and law enforcement can fill knowledge gaps and bring efforts together.
3. Case Study Reviews: Reviews of actual IoT forensic case studies in a collaborative manner can also prove beneficial for creating better methodologies.

5.6.4 Developing standards and policies for IoT forensics

Standardization will provide an international and reliable jurisdictive forensic investigation (Table 5.14).

1. **Standards for Evidence Handling:** Establishing worldwide data collection, storage, and examination standards can make IoT forensic investigation more authentic.
2. **Privacy and Security Policy:** Forensic requirements must be weighed against privacy needs. Policies must provide users' rights and ensure that rights are protected according to law.
3. **Interoperability Standards:** Standardization of interfacing IoT devices will simplify forensic data collection and analysis.

Figure 5.13 Intersection of roles and responsibilities between researchers, practitioners, and law enforcement.

Table 5.14 Forensic policy areas and their proposed standards

Policy area	*Current gaps*	*Proposed standards*
Evidence handling	Lack of global protocols	Unified evidence collection standards
Privacy and security	Limited privacy-compliant methods	Privacy-preserving data acquisition
Device interoperability	Inconsistent interfaces	Standardized communication protocols

5.7 CONCLUSION

The IoT ecosystem has increased manyfold and has revolutionized numerous industries. Some gigantic, humongous digital forensics issues are also arising before us. In this chapter, some of the most significant IoT device issues, i.e., heterogeneity, scalability, and data acquisition issues, are being considered. It stresses heavily that there is a requirement for forensics so that the IoT world becomes accountable and secure.

Heterogeneity and Complexity of Data: The IoT devices produce heterogeneous and extensive data, which is hard to collect and proof. Challenges Regarding Privacy and Security: IoT forensics has to deal with privacy issues and secure sensitive information. Technological Enhancement: AI, ML, and blockchain integration hold potential to advance forensic analysis beyond the current boundaries. Legal and Ethical Issues: Standardization of IoT forensics practice through harmonization of global policies and resolution of ethical issues is essential.

This review highlights the promise of IoT forensics in core areas such as healthcare, smart cities, and industrial systems while considering areas to work on.

5.7.1 Future prospects in IoT forensics

This review emphasizes the potential of IoT forensics in some of the prominent areas like healthcare, smart cities, and industrial systems and taking into consideration areas to improve:

- **AI and ML for Automated Analysis:** Developing intelligent systems for anomaly detection, evidence extraction, and pattern recognition in IoT networks.
- **Blockchain for Immutable Evidence:** Utilizing decentralized ledger technology to enhance the integrity and traceability of forensic data.
- **Edge and Fog Computing:** Leveraging distributed computing models to process forensic data closer to the source, reducing latency and preserving data authenticity.
- **Cross-Disciplinary Collaboration:** Encouraging cooperation among technologists, legal experts, and policymakers to address technical, legal, and ethical aspects.
- **IoT-Specific Forensic Tools:** Designing tools tailored to IoT environments, including lightweight software for resource-constrained devices.
- **Global Standards and Protocols:** Establishing universally accepted guidelines for IoT forensic practices to ensure consistency and legal admissibility.

5.7.2 Call to action for researchers and stakeholders

Overcoming the hurdles of IoT forensics requires an end-to-end effort by policymakers, industry, and academia. A few of the following are recommended responses (Table 5.15):

- **For Researchers:**
  - Explore novel forensic methodologies leveraging AI and blockchain technologies.
  - Investigate solutions to overcome device heterogeneity and scalability challenges.
  - Conduct interdisciplinary research to bridge the gap between technology and law.

Table 5.15 Summarization of IoT forensics key areas and their impact

Key area	*Current challenges*	*Future solutions*	*Impact*
Data acquisition	Device diversity, large volume	AI-driven anomaly detection, edge computing	Faster and more accurate evidence collection
Evidence integrity	Risk of tampering	Blockchain-based immutable logs	Enhanced trust and reliability
Forensic tools	Incompatibility with IoT devices	IoT-specific lightweight forensic tools	Better resource efficiency
Legal standards	Lack of uniform policies	Global standardization and harmonization	Improved legal admissibility
Privacy and security	Balancing forensic needs and privacy	Privacy-preserving cryptographic techniques	Ethical and secure investigations

- **For Industry Stakeholders:**
  - Invest in the development of IoT-specific forensic tools and platforms.
  - Establish clear protocols for data collection and preservation in IoT networks.
  - Collaborate with academia to test and refine new forensic frameworks.
- **For Policymakers:**
  - Develop all-inclusive laws that are IoT-forensic-specific.
  - Promote international cooperation to harmonize standards and practices.
  - Facilitate ethical forensic investigations, a balance between privacy and security.

The public needs to unite in bringing IoT forensic practices to the point of being reliable, accurate, and acceptable to reveal the potential of a safe and moral IoT future.

BIBLIOGRAPHY

1. Stoyanova, M., Nikoloudakis, Y., Panagiotakis, S., Pallis, E., & Markakis, E. K. (2020). A survey on the internet of things (IoT) forensics: Challenges, approaches, and open issues. *IEEE Communications Surveys & Tutorials*, *22*(2), 1191–1221.
2. Servida, F., & Casey, E. (2019). IoT forensic challenges and opportunities for digital traces. *Digital Investigation*, *28*, S22–S29.
3. Janarthanan, T., Bagheri, M., & Zargari, S. (2020). IoT forensics: An overview of the current issues and challenges. *Digital forensic investigation of Internet of Things (IoT) devices*, 1st Edition, 223–254.
4. Conti, M., Dehghantanha, A., Franke, K., & Watson, S. (2018). Internet of Things security and forensics: Challenges and opportunities. *Future Generation Computer Systems*, *78*, 544–546.
5. Shreyas, J., Chouhan, D., Harshitha, M., Udayaprasad, P. K., & Kumar, S. D. (2022). Network lifetime enhancement routing algorithm for IoT enabled software defined wireless sensor network. In *Sustainable Advanced Computing: Select Proceedings of ICSAC 2021* (pp. 499–508). Singapore: Springer Singapore.
6. MacDermott, A., Baker, T., & Shi, Q. (2018, February). IoT forensics: Challenges for the IoA era. In *2018 9th IFIP International Conference on New Technologies, Mobility and Security (NTMS)* (pp. 1–5). IEEE.
7. Yaqoob, I., Hashem, I. A. T., Ahmed, A., Kazmi, S. A., & Hong, C. S. (2019). Internet of things forensics: Recent advances, taxonomy, requirements, and open challenges. *Future Generation Computer Systems*, *92*, 265–275.
8. Choo, K. K. R. (2021, November). Internet of Things (IoT) security and forensics: Challenges and opportunities. In *Proceedings of the 2th Workshop on CPS&IoT Security and Privacy* (pp. 27–28).
9. Dawson, L., & Akinbi, A. (2021). Challenges and opportunities for wearable IoT forensics: TomTom Spark 3 as a case study. *Forensic Science International: Reports*, *3*, 100198.

10. Reddy, C. S., Chouhan, D., Udayaprasad, P. K., Srinidhi, N. N., & Dilipkumar, S. M. (2022). Geographic routing scheme for resource and communication efficiency in the IoT ecosystem using swarm-intelligence based BFO algorithm. *Journal of Information Technology Management*, *14*(1), 41–64.
11. Alabdulsalam, S., Schaefer, K., Kechadi, T., & Le-Khac, N. A. (2018). Internet of things forensics–challenges and a case study. In *Advances in Digital Forensics XIV: 14th IFIP WG 11.9 International Conference, New Delhi, India, January 3-5, 2018, Revised Selected Papers 14* (pp. 35–48). Springer International Publishing.
12. Kebande, V. R., & Awad, A. I. (2024). Industrial internet of things ecosystems security and digital forensics: Achievements, open challenges, and future directions. *ACM Computing Surveys*, *56*(5), 1–37.
13. Azmoodeh, A., Dehghantanha, A., & Choo, K. K. R. (2019). Big data and internet of things security and forensics: Challenges and opportunities. *Handbook of big data and IoT security*, 1–4. Springer International Publishing.
14. Wu, T., Breitinger, F., & Niemann, S. (2021). IoT network traffic analysis: Opportunities and challenges for forensic investigators?. *Forensic Science International: Digital Investigation*, *38*, 301123.
15. Wu, T., Breitinger, F., & Baggili, I. (2019, August). IoT ignorance is digital forensics research bliss: A survey to understand IoT forensics definitions, challenges and future research directions. In *Proceedings of the 14th International Conference on Availability, Reliability and Security* (pp. 1–15).
16. Aal, S. I. A., Shreyas, J., & Udayaprasad, P. K. (2024). Selecting optimal charcoal company using multi-criteria decision making methodology. *Multicriteria algorithms with applications*, *3*, 15–22.
17. Montasari, R., Hill, R., Parkinson, S., Peltola, P., Hosseinian-Far, A., & Daneshkhah, A. (2020). Digital forensics: Challenges and opportunities for future studies. *International Journal of Organizational and Collective Intelligence (IJOCI)*, *10*(2), 37–53.
18. Yang, W., Johnstone, M. N., Sikos, L. F., & Wang, S. (2020, April). Security and forensics in the internet of things: Research advances and challenges. In *2020 Workshop on Emerging Technologies for Security in IoT (ETSecIoT)* (pp. 12–17). IEEE.
19. Montasari, R., & Hill, R. (2019, January). Next-generation digital forensics: Challenges and future paradigms. In *2019 IEEE 12th International Conference on Global Security, Safety and Sustainability (ICGS3)* (pp. 205–212). IEEE.
20. Zawoad, S., & Hasan, R. (2015, August). Digital forensics in the age of big data: Challenges, approaches, and opportunities. In *2015 IEEE 17th International Conference on High Performance Computing and Communications, 2015 IEEE 7th International Symposium on Cyberspace Safety and Security, and 2015 IEEE 12th International Conference on Embedded Software and Systems* (pp. 1320–1325). IEEE.
21. Hou, J., Li, Y., Yu, J., & Shi, W. (2019). A survey on digital forensics in Internet of Things. *IEEE Internet of Things Journal*, *7*(1), 1–15.
22. Udayaprasad, P. K., Shreyas, J., Srinidhi, N. N., Kumar, S. D., Dayananda, P., Askar, S. S., & Abouhawwash, M. (2024). Energy efficient optimized routing technique with distributed SDN-AI to large scale I-IoT networks. *IEEE Access*, *12*, 2742–2759.
23. Koroniotis, N., Moustafa, N., & Sitnikova, E. (2019). Forensics and deep learning mechanisms for botnets in internet of things: A survey of challenges and solutions. *IEEE Access*, *7*, 61764–61785.
24. Lutta, P., Sedky, M., Hassan, M., Jayawickrama, U., & Bastaki, B. B. (2021). The complexity of internet of things forensics: A state-of-the-art review. *Forensic Science International: Digital Investigation*, *38*, 301210.
25. Sayakkara, A. P., & Le-Khac, N. A. (2021). Electromagnetic side-channel analysis for IoT forensics: Challenges, framework, and datasets. *IEEE Access*, *9*, 113585–113598.

Chapter 6

Innovative approaches and techniques in digital forensics

Manish Thakral, Keshav Kaushik, Farhan Shaikh, Anita Devare, and Manoj H Devare

6.1 INTRODUCTION

Digital forensics is an expanding discipline of significant significance in analyzing cybercrime, investigating digital evidence, and preserving digital information. Due to the development and advancement in technology, the approaches adopted by the criminals are also on the increase. As a result, the methods used in digital forensics must be constantly on the lookout for new threats because they are ever evolving. This chapter highlights new and current methodologies, together with the current tools that have been developed to support forensic investigation.

6.1.1 The evolution of digital forensics

Digital forensics has come a long way since its early development. At first, it specialized in computer forensics, which involved the recovery and examination of data from individual computing devices. Although it has started with web applications, it has grown over time, and it also covers mobile devices, network, cloud, and Internet of Things (IoT) devices. This has been occasioned by the growing use of technological devices in everyday life and the increased cases of cybercrimes.

Even in the early stages of digital investigations and digital forensics, basic methods like disk imaging or file retrieval were used. However, with increasing complexity in encryption techniques, storage technologies, and network distribution structures in modern networks, the mentioned traditional methods are no longer satisfactory. The modern digital forensics has used different methods and tools to solve these challenges, such as memory forensics, network forensics, and the use of artificial intelligence (AI) and machine learning (ML), as shown in Figure 6.1.

6.1.2 Memory forensics

Memory analysis, also known as RAM dump analysis, is one of the breaking branches of digital forensics. While disk forensics concerns its data lying within disks and typically deals with hard drives, memory forensics is concerned with volatile memory located in the system RAM. This data is temporary in nature, and it reflects the current state of the system and includes running processes, established network connections, and present user sessions.

Another benefit that stands out in memory forensics is that the evidence may be obtained from the memory when it is not from the hard disk. For instance, there are memory-resident viruses/malware that cannot be detected by disk-based forensics. Tools like, for example, Volatility or Recall allow the investigator to have the possession of memory dump files and gather information about the system activity including virus presence, as shown in Figure 6.2.

DOI: 10.1201/9781003513896-6

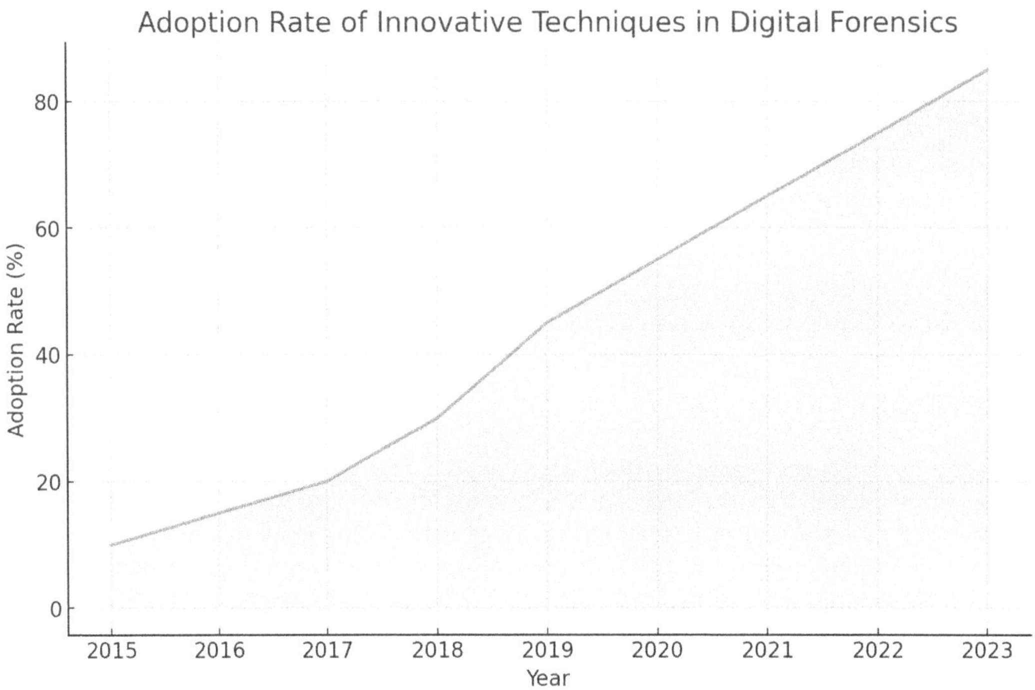

Figure 6.1 Depiction of adoption rate (%) in accordance with the year.

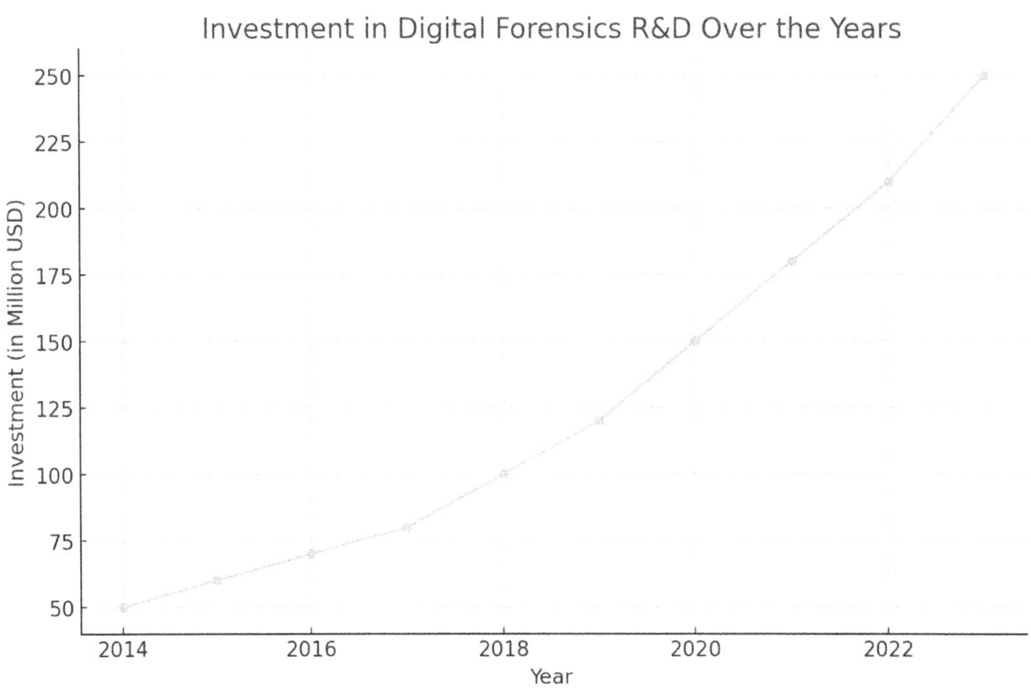

Figure 6.2 Depiction of investment (in million USD) in accordance with the year.

Memory analysis also has implementation in computer incident handling. When the copy of a compromised system's memory is analyzed, it is possible to immediately determine what kind of attack occurred, how the attackers infiltrated the system, and how deep the intrusion went. The data presented herein is crucial to forming an adequate response plan and minimizing the consequences of the attack.

6.1.3 Live forensics

Live forensics refers to a situation whereby an analyst investigates a live system with the aim of collecting data. This approach is a departure from a post-mortem examination, where the machine is shut down with the analysis conducted elsewhere. Live forensics is really essential when it is not desirable to stop the system, like critical servers or any type of system that cannot be turned off.

The first of the significant problems of the Live Forensics concept has to do with the data collected from the running system: how can you guarantee that this data has not been tampered with? Since the system is in operation, there is the ability for data to be written over or changed in any way. Regarding this, the forensic investigators employ certain tools and methods that are less intrusive when compared to the original normal methods of acquiring volatile data, such as running processes, network connections, and open files.

Implementing live forensics is crucial when dealing with APTs (Advanced Persistent Threats) when the attackers physically reside on the targeted network. Through the analysis of live data, one is able to identify the existence of an APT group, recognize the tactics used by the group in control, and how the group moves around the network. This information is very useful to eliminate the threat and ensure a solid protection of the organization, as shown in Figure 6.3.

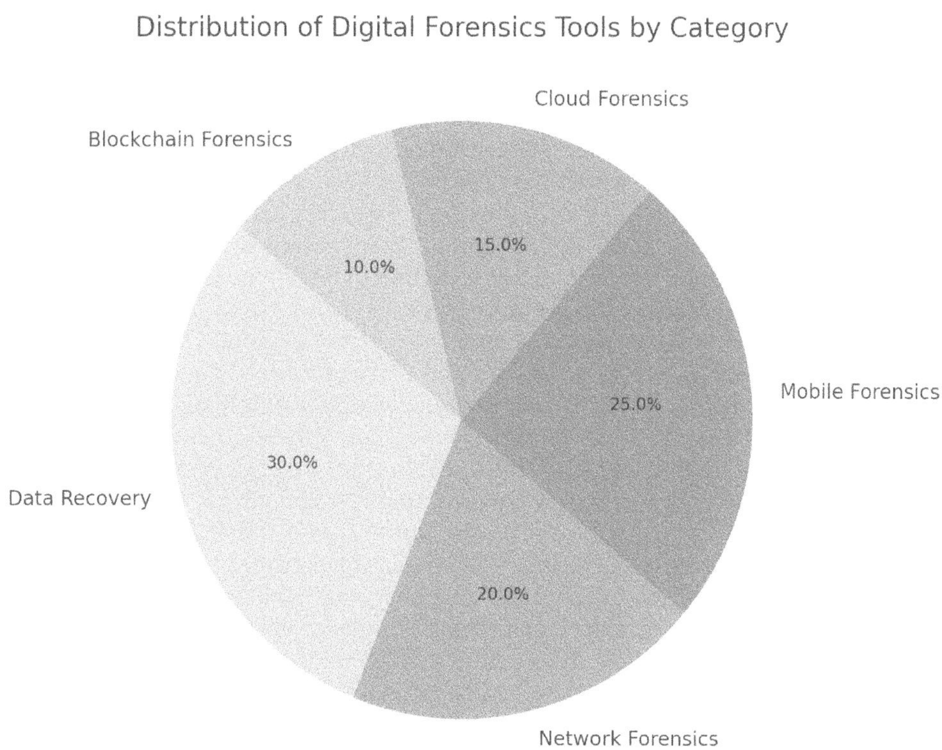

Figure 6.3 Illustration of various forensics in the distribution of digital forensics.

6.1.4 Network forensics

Forensics operating in the network environment involves the analysis of the flow of traffic in a network with the aim of solving a crime. This becomes important given that organizations have adopted the use of advanced network structures, making network forensics a key aspect of IT investigations. Several sophisticated strategies in network forensics are deep packet inspection (DPI), network flow analysis, and intrusion detection systems (IDS).

DPI is the process of analyzing the content of a packet along with its instructions when it passes through a specific checkpoint along the network. DPI can classify and analyze network traffic and recognize counterfeit activities, including data leakage or unauthorized connections. Packet content analysis enables the recovery of communication sessions and the collection of evidence of cyber-attacks.

While network flow analysis is closely related to analyzing data flow on the network, the important parameters of network traffic, such as source and destination IP addresses, ports, and time stamps, should reveal characteristics of the Internet traffic that can indicate the existence of an attack. Security-oriented gatherers, known as NetFlow and Argus, turn out to be highly efficient instruments for analyzing the interaction between the network nodes and help to draw the origin of the attack.

IDS are one more essential aspect of network forensics as tools. IDS solutions like Snort and Suricata continually analyze network traffic looking for anomalies. When it recognizes an anomaly, the IDS triggers an alert for forensic investigators who may ascertain the threat's existence. Thus, by comparing IDS alerts with the other body of forensic information, the body of knowledge about the attack, its origins, and authors can be reconstructed.

6.1.5 Cloud forensics

Due to the popularity of using clouds to store information, there are new concerns about obtaining and analyzing digital evidence. Cloud forensics is a form of digital forensics that focuses on cloud environments, which encompass distributed data storage over several servers and are provided by third parties. The nature of digital evidence acquisition in a cloud computing environment is complex, mainly due to the flexibility of the cloud model, which is quite different from traditional models, making it difficult to carry out forensic investigation, hence the call for techniques and solutions to these problems.

Despite cloud computing being a popular technology today, one of the main challenges facing the field of cloud forensics is the data acquisition process. Existing forms of computer forensics like disk imaging are impossible to perform in cloud computing scenarios. However, forensic investigators have very limited means to directly access those artifacts as they need to rely on cloud-specific tools and application programming interfaces (APIs) offered by the cloud service providers (CSPs). These tools let you capture virtual computer screenshots, extract log files, and receive information from cloud storage.

Another apparent difficulty is the question of how to maintain the genuineness of evidence stored in cloud computing environments. In the case of off-site storage of the data and with third-party management, there is a possibility to alter the information. In order to counter this, the forensic investigators make use of cryptographic processes of hashing and digital signatures to confirm the admissibility of the evidence obtained.

Cloud forensics also involves communication with CSP since they own the cloud environment and can avail themselves of the necessary data. Record keeping and getting all legal work formalities right are critical in this process. CSPs should be engaged, meaning that a good rapport is developed to ensure that cloud-based evidence is dealt with comprehensively and legally, as shown in Figure 6.4.

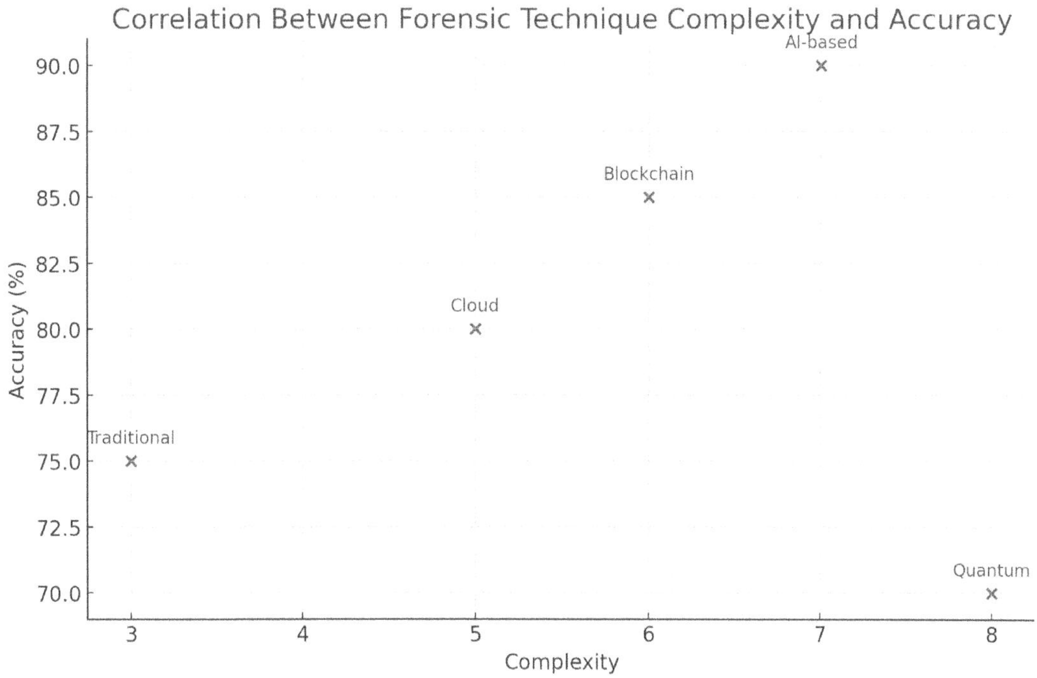

Figure 6.4 Depiction of accuracy (%) in alignment with complexity for the correlation function between forensic and accuracy.

6.1.6 Mobile device forensics

Smartphones and tablets are today an integral part of people's lives as they can be used everywhere and at any time. They retain a lot of users' information, including personal and sensitive data, which makes these devices indispensable to hackers. Mobile device forensics involves the investigation and identification of data within the devices, and more so in trying to get evidence of a crime.

A major factor that has made mobile device forensics complex is the numerous types of devices and OS currently in the market. The manufacturers and models of the devices have different file systems, different encryption, and different levels of security, which further complicates the forensic work. In response to this, forensic investigators rely on tools like Cellebrite and Oxygen Forensic Suite since they work perfectly with different devices with diverse operating systems.

Another concern is getting past such controls as Passcode and encryption methods. Chip off and JTAG, which is short for Joint Test Action Group, enable the investigators to extract data from the device's memory chips through injection. While these techniques call for sophisticated tools and knowledge, they are pretty efficient in data extraction from confined or impaired apparatus.

It also includes examination of data, such as those stored on applications of the Mobile device. While many applications take and harbor very important details, including messages, call details, or location, among others, these prove very useful in trials. By examining app data, forensic investigators can reconstruct user activity, identify contacts, and uncover evidence of criminal behavior, as shown in Figure 6.5.

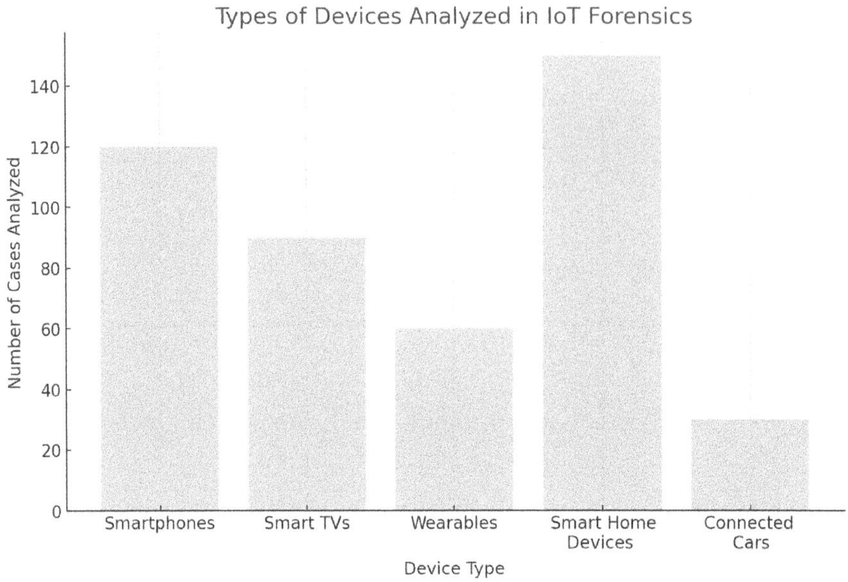

Figure 6.5 Depiction of types of devices analyzed in IoT forensics vs. the number of cases analyzed.

6.1.7 Internet of Things (IoT) forensics

The use of IoT devices has brought out a new problem for digital forensics. IoT forensics refers to the solution of offense-related cases using electronic resources from IoT devices, smart home systems, wearable technology, and industrial systems. These devices produce tremendous amounts of information, and the majority of them can process information in real-time; they are utilized in cybercrimes.

Precise identification of what happened and at what time is still one of the most significant problems in IoT forensics due to the communication heterogeneity of the devices and protocols involved. For example, IoT devices engage numerous communications protocols, data formats, and storage, which bring additional complexities to the forensic task. In response to this, forensic investigators employ unique tools and methods to examine forensic data from IoT devices by analyzing their traffic data and even their firmware.

Another is the problems with the restricted memory and computational power of smart units in IoT. Some connected objects can only locally store a small amount of information, and it is challenging to acquire pertinent evidence from them. To overcome this, forensic investigators may have little choice but to redirect their focus toward data stored within actual cloud services or the centralized IoT platforms and may have to enlist the help of service providers, employing cloud forensics techniques in a process.

IoT forensics also involves the analysis of sensor data. IoT devices are equipped with various sensors, such as cameras, microphones, and environmental sensors, which can provide valuable evidence. By analyzing sensor data, forensic investigators can reconstruct events, identify perpetrators, and uncover evidence of cyber-attacks.

6.1.8 Artificial intelligence and machine learning in digital forensics

AI and ML concepts are becoming increasingly popular in space as a means of transforming digital forensics. The use of AI and ML also means that computer-aided pattern matching is

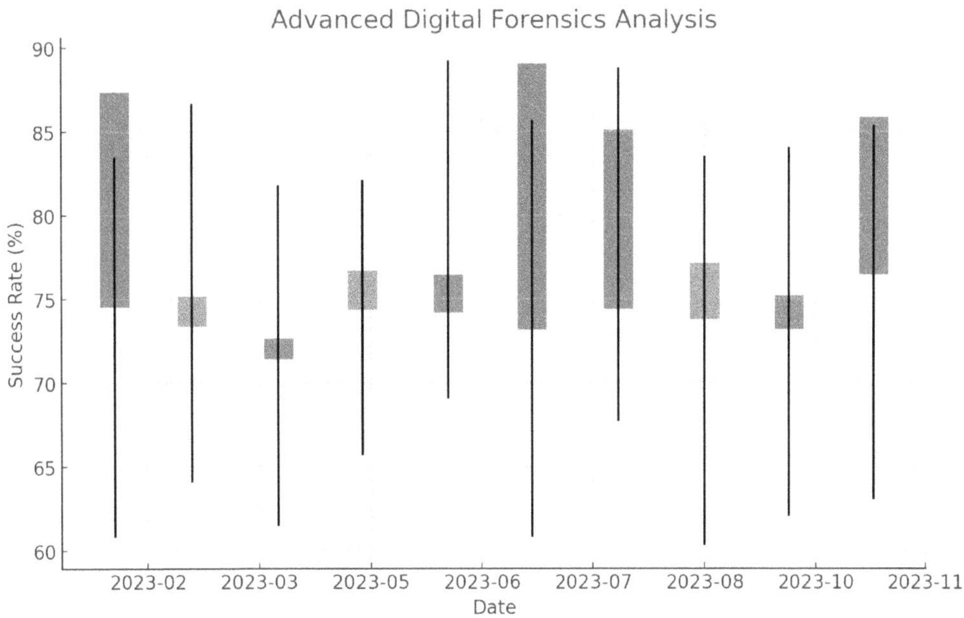

Figure 6.6 Depiction of advanced digital forensic analysis in alignment with the success rate (%).

faster and more accurate than traditional methods of investigation. These technologies are most useful to wade through large volumes of data, identify anomalous behavior, and detect the emergence of security threats.

The two main provinces of applying AI and ML in DF are explained below: an initial and major area of AI and ML in the DF field is data analytics. Computer-assisted techniques can help detect known indicators of compromise (including malware signatures and malicious URLs) directly on digital evidence, and this will save much time. ML algorithms about new threats can also be learnt to make proactive defense against cyber-attacks, as shown in Figure 6.6.

One of the other applications is anomaly detonation. A threat can be learned by ML algorithms to scour through NL, SLs, and USL to detect anomalous traffic.

6.2 SOURCE OF DATA

A major requirement for digital forensic investigation and analysis is that all possible sources of data need to be identified and explained. Digital evidence can be obtained from a wide range of sources, principally different in terms of nature and difficulties. In this chapter, the author will focus on describing the primary sources of digital data, to wit: laptops and PCs, mobile devices, networks, clouds, IoT devices, and other advanced technologies, such as blockchain. Through the analysis of the options explored in this paper, it is possible to conclude that a greater understanding of these data sources will assist forensic investigators in addressing the challenges of digital evidence collection and analysis.

6.2.1 Computers and laptops

Thus, computers and laptops continue to serve as major reservoirs of cyber evidence. These devices consist of a huge amount of information data on their storage media, which include hard disk drives (HDDs), solid state drives (SSDs), and transportable storage devices, which include the USB and external disk drives.

6.2.1.1 *Hard drives and SSDs*

HDDs and SSDs are used to store an infinite amount of information, including system, application, users' documents, and even browser history. These drives are usually seized by forensic investigators, who may have to copy these drives to another for case analysis, hence having original evidence that has not been tampered with. Key areas of interest include

File Systems: Forensic analysis of file systems (e.g., NTFS, FAT32, ext4) can reveal file creation, modification, and access times, helping to establish timelines of user activity.

Deleted Files: They also noted that even when files are deleted, there will always be some residual data on the storage media. These deleted files can be recovered using techniques like File carving and Slack Space analysis.

Operating System Artifacts: It has been known for years that various system logs, registry entries, and other OS artifacts contain information about system usage, installed apps, and user activity.

6.2.1.1.1 Removable storage devices

Some of the most frequently used types of storage devices are portable storage devices such as USBs and memory cards used in transferring data and data backup. They can store copies of files, portable applications, and residual evidence of activities performed by the user. Forensic analysis of these devices can uncover:

File Transfers: Any modifications to file-relevant attributes, such as the time of the files copied to or from the device, will be disclosed.

Portable Applications: Some users start executable programs from removable storage, thereby not installing them to the main system. Therefore, analyzing these applications can be useful when trying to obtain other types of evidence of the user's activities.

Device Usage Logs: BIOs also have records of connected portable media with times and identification numbers to construct usage histories.

6.2.2 Mobile devices

Smartphones and tablets, particularly, are almost in every hand, and they hold lots of data – personal and often sensitive. Mobile forensics is the process of forensically acquiring data from a mobile device or recovering data from different areas of the device.

6.2.2.1 *Internal storage*

Different types of internal storage are utilized to store system files, actual or resident applications, and the users' data in the mobile devices. Key areas of focus for forensic investigators include:

Contacts and Call Logs: Contact lists may be analyzed to identify the frequency of communication with friends and family or to reveal that the user has no contacts at all.

App Data: Most apps contain data at the local level, such as chat histories, shared, media contents and interactions, logs and histories specific to the apps. Sometimes, by looking at this data, one might be able to identify user activity as well as interactions.

Multimedia Files: Images, videos, voice, text, and call records usually store temporal and spatial information that can help to model timelines and show the sequence of activities.

6.2.2.2 Cloud synchronization

Most of the mobile perform sync data with cloud services that provide further evidence, corroborating sources. Forensic investigators can obtain data from these cloud services, including:

Backups: Cloud backups often contain comprehensive snapshots of the device's data, including contacts, messages, app data, and multimedia files.
Synchronization Logs: synchronization logs can show what was synchronized, when, and where, from and to which devices, thus pinpointing activity of the user across multiple devices.

6.2.3 Network systems

Network systems are an important component in digital investigations, especially where such things as cyber crusades and other network-related events are in question. Key sources of network data include:

6.2.3.1 Network traffic

Network traffic analysis can be defined as the process of gathering and analyzing data packets that are circulating over the network. Important aspects of network traffic analysis include:

Packet Captures: Applications such as Wireshark enable the forensic investigators to capture packets on the network and analyze them to get a broad view and understanding of the network's communication, the protocols in use, and the data exchanged between the nodes of the network.
Deep Packet Inspection (DPI): Unlike typical protocols used in packet sniffers, DPI focuses not only on the content of data packets that transport the data but on the data in itself. This technique will be useful in identifying application-level data, supplementing an anomaly detection system, and also pointing out malicious activities.
Network Flow Data: NetFlow or IPFIX records are the type of flow data that condenses the network's traffic characteristics like source and destination addresses and volumes, as well as the ports. This way of analyzing flow data enables the revelation apocalyptic traffic increases and security threats.

6.2.3.1.1 Logs and event data

Routers, switches, firewalls, and other network devices, as well as IDS instruments, produce logs and event data that are important for forensic investigations. Key log sources include:

Firewall Logs: Firewall logs store information on the incoming and outgoing network traffic allowed or barred. It means that the examination of these logs can identify unauthorized attempts at accessing the site and possible security violations.
IDS/IPS Logs: Intrusion detection and prevention systems produce data sets of threats or anomalies that are detected. When compared with other log information, IDS/IPS logs can show possible attack patterns and affected computers.
Syslog Servers: Centralized syslog servers collect logs from multiple network devices, providing a comprehensive view of network activity and facilitating correlation and analysis of events across the network.

6.2.4 Cloud environments

Now, cloud computing is a significant part of every modern IT organization and provides variously scalable services. However, it creates its own set of problems in Digital forensics. Key sources of data in cloud environments include:

6.2.4.1 *Virtual machine and containers*

IT infrastructures of cloud sites commonly employ virtual machines or VMs and containers to deliver isolated and elastic resources. Forensic analysis of these environments involves:

VM Snapshots: Currently, to work with VMs, CSPs provide options for the creation of VM snapshots to capture the exact picture of memory, storage, and processes running through the system. These snapshots can be analyzed for signs of malicious activity and evidence of a compromise of the system.

Container Logs: Containers produce logs of activity of an application, such as error, access logs, and resource usage logs. It is found that some valuable information about application logs, such as their behavior and security concerns, can be traced in the container logs.

6.2.4.1.1 *Cloud storage*

Large-distributed data storage services, including Amazon S3, Google Cloud Storage, and Microsoft Azure Blob Storage, are employed to store data. Key aspects of cloud storage forensics include:

Data Access Logs: Log information kept by CSPs contains information on who accessed the data and files and at what time. This kind of log should be analyzed to detect unauthorized access and data exfiltration.

File Metadata: File save locations, such as other clouds usually, follow each file with metadata such as timestamps, permissions, and versions. This paper postulates that information regarding a file that is not the content of the file itself is useful in forensic investigation processes.

6.2.4.2 *Cloud services and APIs*

Cloud services and APIs are available to produce logs and information useful in a forensic probe. Key sources include:

Audit Logs: Most of the current cloud services come with audit trails, which capture the activities performed by users, configurations made, and access attempts made. By reviewing audit logs, it is possible to set time frames and consider possible cyber threats.

API Logs: Cloud APIs produce API logs of request and response data during information interaction, such as access to an account, stored data, and configuration. API activity logs can be useful to determine how resources within the cloud are being consumed and even exploited.

6.2.5 Internet of Things (IoT) devices

This emerging technology has brought new challenges and possibilities for the digital forensics processes in its wake. The IoT device is one of the most prolific producers of data, which can be real-time, and can be used in smart home automation, industrial automation, and more.

6.2.5.1 Device logs and data

Smart devices in particular produce logs and data, which are highly useful in forensic use. Key sources of data from IoT devices include:

Sensor Data: IoT devices contain many different sensors, beginning from cameras and microphones to environmental sensors. This information can be used as proof that something has happened, an activity has taken place, or the condition of the environment around the sensor.

Device Logs: IoT devices record system transactions such as firmware upgrades, configuration modifications, and data connections. When looking closely at the device logs, possible problems regarding security and attempts at unauthorized access can be found.

Network Traffic: IoT devices interact through various networks, which leads to network traffic on which one may choose to capture data. Having access to information from IoT devices allows us to analyze the traffic patterns on the network and notice potentially malicious behavior.

6.2.5.2 Centralized IoT platforms

A large number of implementations of IoT are based on platforms that control and monitor various devices. These platforms provide additional sources of data, including:

Platform Logs: Centralized IoT platforms create records of the device operations, users, and other activities as well as system events. Monitoring logs offers an excellent way of not only tracking IoT device activity and possible security problems that may arise in the future.

Configuration Data: Usually, IoT platforms contain configuration data where settings, firmware versions, and network configurations of connected devices are stored. Specifically, potential exposures to threats that can be obtained from configuration data encompass vulnerabilities and misconfigurations.

6.2.6 Emerging technologies: Blockchain

Considering that Blockchain is generally applied for decentralization and enhanced security of records, this technology can be beneficial for Digital forensics. Key sources of data in blockchain forensics include:

6.2.6.1 Blockchain transactions

Blockchain transactions include all the transactions in the blockchain, creating an open and secure digital record. Forensic analysis of blockchain transactions involves:

Transaction Histories: Records of transactions can be analyzed to identify transactions as usage of cryptocurrency, interactions with smart contracts, as well as changes in ownership of assets.

Address Analysis: By analyzing the properties of blockchain addresses and their transactions, scientists can potentially evaluate participants in blockchain operations and the flow of assets.

6.3 LITERATURE REVIEW

Digital forensics as a discipline has rapidly developed over the last two decades because of the constant growth of technologies and the development of cybercrimes. This paper conducts a literature review of the most important achievements in the field of digital forensics, presenting methods, tools, and theoretical research. Foundational variables, memory forensics, live forensics, network forensics, cloud forensics, mobile forensics, IoT forensics, blockchain forensics, and AI and ML in digital forensics are the categories of the review.

6.3.1 Foundational aspects of digital forensics

The essential beginnings of digital forensics set the basis for learning about the principles and methodologies that are required for solving computer crimes. Several key works have shaped the field:

Carrier and Spafford [28]: In their groundbreaking paper titled "An Event-Based Digital Forensic Investigation Framework," they proposed a model for conducting digital forensics crime scene investigation. This framework focused on the preservation of digital evidence, and it provided a recommended approach to the collection, analysis, and documentation of this digital evidence.

Casey [29]: In the article "Digital Evidence and Computer Crime," the author Casey gives general information about the principles and practices of digital forensics. This work also established the distinction between cyber forensic science and cyber law, as well as presented different methods of examining e-forensic.

Pollitt [30]: The area's one of the earliest papers is Pollitt's, in which he presented the topic "Computer Forensics: An Approach to Evidence in Cyberspace." Work procedures should be carried out in consistent channels and procedures with regard to training and certification of the forensic investigators, as supported by Pollitt.

6.3.2 Memory forensics

Memory forensics has become an important subdiscipline in digital forensics – the study of volatile memory (RAM) and possible evidence that may not be available on disks. Key contributions to this field include:

Dolan-Gavitt et al. [31]: Their work, *Virtual Machine Introspection Forensics: Exploring Memory Dumps, Virtuoso*, specifically focused on what they called VM introspection and its similarities to the process of forensics. Memory forensics in virtual environments was a focus area discussed in this research, including method refinements for memory analysis accuracy and efficiency.

Schatz [32]: For "Digital Evidence: Representation and Assurance," Schatz observed that memory forensics could capture real-time pictures of system activity. In his work, Schatz has enumerated the directions for the increase of reliability of the memory contents, which is critical to keep volatile data evidence admissible.

Ligh et al. [33]: In the Art of Memory Forensics, Ligh et al. have presented complete knowledge of memory analysis, including methods to acquire the memory image. This work brought Volatility – and later Recall again – into the field that is indispensable for memory forensic examinations.

6.3.3 Live forensics

As with any real-time activity analysis, live forensics entails analysis of the system while it is in operation, leading to the extraction of data significant to ongoing scenarios. Significant contributions to this field include:

Carvey [34]: Carvey has been one of the pioneers in Live forensics, and in his book "Windows Forensic Analysis Toolkit," he offered an insight into knowing more about Live forensics in Windows environments. Carvey also explained the characteristics of live systems and mentioned such tools and techniques for capturing live data.

Vömel and Freiling [35]: Their paper titled "A Survey of Main Memory Acquisition and Analysis Techniques for the Windows Operating System" included a detailed survey of techniques for memory captures from live and volatile Windows systems. The difficulties and impossibilities of live forensics were discussed in this work, and ways to address them are defined here.

Adelstein [36]: Adelstein's article "Live Forensics: Diagnosing Your System Without Killing It First" was focused on the practical side of conducting a live forensics investigation. Adelstein stressed the least effect to be shown on the running system and presented rules for maintaining the unaltered state of real-time evidence.

6.3.4 Network forensics

While network flow analysis is used to observe, capture, and study crimes in cyberspace, network forensics is thus developed from flow. Key contributions to this field include:

Jiang et al. [37]: In the paper with the foregoing title, Wei Ji made an explanation of dry packet inspection, which is also known as DPI. To assess the effectiveness of DPI for identifying and characterizing malicious network traffic, Jiang and his co-authors have proposed a new concept in which useful information on the behavior of attackers in a network is provided.

Pilli et al. [38]: The survey "Network Forensics: Current Approaches, Challenges and Research Directions" proposed by Pilli and his collaborators presents a state-of-the-art description of methodologies and tools in the field of network forensics. This work brought into focus the need to perform network forensics in an attempt to counter cyber threats and presented future research directions.

Bejtlich [39]: Network security monitoring and forensics were described in Bejtlich's book titled, *The Practice of Network Security Monitoring*, on how to practice the concept. Bejtlich focused on the persistent and systematic view, stating several tools and techniques for sniffing and analysis of traffic.

6.3.5 Cloud forensics

Cloud computing offers new sets of challenges to digital forensics, with all the methodologies and tools being required to work with cloud-based applications. Significant contributions to this field include:

Ruan et al. [40]: In their paper "Cloud Forensics: An Overview," the authors discussed major challenges and prospects of cloud forensics. Still, Ruan and his co-authors pointed out specific characteristics of cloud computing environments and outlined an approach to the forensic examination of the cloud environment.

Dykstra and Sherman [41]: Dykstra and Sherman are the authors of the study that looked at the matter of issues in cloud forensics through the prism of two hypothetical cases: Understanding Issues in Cloud Forensics: Two Hypothetical Case Studies. Their case studies covered secular aspects of data acquisition, data quality, as well as legal concerns.

Quick and Choo [42]: Their paper titled "Cloud Storage Forensics: Analyzing Data Remnants on Deleted User Accounts" investigated the subject of remnants in cloud storage services. Quick and Choo showed that it is possible for forensic investigators to retrieve meaningful data from cloud storage if the user's account has been deactivated.

6.3.6 Mobile forensics

Smartphones and tablets are now a treasure trove of digital evidence. These kinds of devices are referred to as mobile forensics. Key contributions to this field include:

Jansen and Ayers [43]: Their suggested publication of "Guidelines on cell phone forensics" contains precise details on the execution of the forensic investigations on the cell phones. Jansen and Ayers' chapter focused on approaches to collecting data, processing it, and archiving it, with stress on the fact that all activities should be done systematically.

Zdziarski [44]: In his book titled "Hacking and Securing iOS Applications," Zdziarski looked at ways of obtaining information from iOS devices. This work described the security measures available on iOS and suggested ways of getting around these measures to get to forensic data.

Marrington et al. [45]: In their paper titled "A Model for Computer Forensics Investigation Process," Marrington and his colleagues presented a framework for investigating mobile devices. This model gave a clean and organized process to follow in mobile forensics, data collection and analysis, and lastly, the report.

6.3.7 The Internet of Things (IoT) is a new research terrain with growing prominence in the field of digital forensics

The IoT era has presented new issues and possibilities for a discipline called Digital Forensics. Key contributions to this field include:

Oriwoh et al. [46]: They entitled their paper "Internet of Things Forensics: Challenges and Approaches," in which they described the challenges and approaches to IoT forensics. Oriwoh and his co-authors provided a detailed analysis of IoT devices and suggested how to investigate IoT crime scenes.

Perumal et al. [47]: In their paper titled "IoT Forensic Framework: Smart Home System," Perumal and his team have put forward a forensic model. This framework dealt with the collection, processing, and documentation of IoT data with a focus on the admissibility of IoT evidence.

Zawoad and Hasan [48]: Their paper "Faiot: Towards Building a Forensics Aware Eco System for the Internet of Things" looked into the environment, or what they referred to as the Faiot. Zawoad and Hasan discussed approaches that can be used to incorporate forensic features into IoT devices and platforms for forensic purposes.

6.3.8 Blockchain forensics

The paradigm that was brought about by blockchain technology reverses the normal concepts of digital forensics, where data are distributed and once written, cannot be altered. Key contributions to this field include:

Fung et al. [49]: In their paper, they discussed "Blockchain and Trustworthy Systems: Challenges and Opportunities." Fung and his co-authors described the potential of blockchain technology in forensic applications and suggested approaches for using blockchain for evidence management.

Huang et al. [50]: Huang and his co-authors prescribed a blockchain-based framework for auditing cloud storage systems in their work, "Blockchain-Based Auditing Framework for Cloud Storage Systems." This framework exploited the use of blockchain to make cloud storage evidence easily reversible, but at the same time, the properties of the blockchain guarantee the integrity and authenticity of the information stored.

Zheng et al. [51]: From their paper titled "An Overview of Blockchain Technology: Architecture, Consensus, and Future Trends," I managed to gain knowledge on what blockchain is and its uses. Zheng and his co-authors also described the forensic perspective of blockchain and suggested potential research avenues.

6.4 EXPERIMENTAL SETUP

Thus, an elaborate experimental framework is required to assess and verify sophisticated approaches in the area of digital forensics. This setup should cover the collection, processing, and understanding of digital evidence in respect to the various standards, contexts, and or situations. This chapter will explain the parts and phases of a good experimental paradigm for digital forensics, in terms of required and recommended computer hardware and software, how to prepare appropriate test data, which specific tools should be employed, and what kind of scenarios are most appropriate for systematically learning and validating more sophisticated, real-world digital forensic techniques.

6.4.1 Hardware requirements

The hardware demands for an experimental setup in digital forensics depend on the category of the investigations. Key components include:

6.4.1.1 Workstations

Unlike regular workstations, high-performance forensic workstations are required by the large amounts of data that need to be processed. These workstations should include:

High-Performance CPUs: Many-core processors, with an example being Intel Xeon or AMD Ryzen, to manage complicated computational processes.

Ample RAM: Recommended to be not less than 32 GB, with higher capacity recommended for memory forensics as well as big data analysis.

Storage: Fast access capabilities are an important attribute of high-capacity SSDs alongside additional conventional HDDs for data storage. Another type of RAID is designed to give redundancy and enhance the performance of the storage system.

Graphics Processing Units (GPUs): For boosting operations that can be conducted in parallel, where data patterns are recognized at speed, for instance, AI and ML operations in computer forensics.

6.4.1.2 *Servers*

Indeed, for network and cloud forensics, specially designed servers replicate an enterprise environment. These servers should include:

Network Interface Cards (NICs): Multiple NICs for the purpose of arranging networks and testing the traffic on different networks.
Virtualization Capabilities: Capabilities for simulated environments involving VMs as well as containers.
High Storage Capacity: For the purpose of archiving large logs and forensic images.

6.4.1.3 *Mobile forensic devices*

For mobile forensics, specialized hardware tools are required:

Forensic Mobile Devices: Tools such as Cellebrite UFED or MSAB XRY, for instance, for retrieving data from mobile devices.
Faraday Bags: To eliminate any possibility of mobile devices being wiped remotely or any attempts at tampering while analysis is going on.

6.4.1.4 *IoT devices*

For IoT forensics, a variety of IoT devices should be included in the setup:

Smart Home Devices: Of smart devices such as thermostats, cameras, and voice assistants.
Wearable Devices: Like wristbands and wearables for health and fitness, smartwatches and the like.
Industrial IoT Devices: In the case of ICS-related scenarios.

6.4.2 Software requirements

The software environment in an experimental setup for digital forensics should include a variety of tools for data acquisition, analysis, and reporting. Key software components include:

6.4.2.1 *Operating systems*

Multiple operating systems are required to cover different forensic scenarios:

Windows: Various versions (e.g., Windows 10, Server 2019) for standard desktop and server environments.
Linux: Distributions like Ubuntu, CentOS, and Kali Linux for open-source forensic tools and server environments.
MacOS: For forensic scenarios involving Apple devices.

6.4.2.2 *Forensic software*

A range of forensic software tools is necessary to cover different aspects of digital forensics:

Disk Imaging Tools: Tools like FTK Imager, EnCase, and DD for creating forensic images of storage devices.
Memory Forensics Tools: Volatility and Rekall for analyzing memory dumps.

Network Forensics Tools: Wireshark, Zeek (formerly Bro), and NetworkMiner for capturing and analyzing network traffic.
Mobile Forensics Tools: Cellebrite UFED, MSAB XRY, and Oxygen Forensic Detective for extracting and analyzing data from mobile devices.
IoT Forensics Tools: Tools tailored for IoT data extraction and analysis, such as IoT Inspector and Binwalk for firmware analysis.

6.4.2.3 *Data analysis and visualization tools*

For analyzing and visualizing forensic data, the following tools are essential:

Database Management Systems: Hadoop file system, Map Reduce, MongoDB, and Cassandra for data storage and retrieval.
Data Visualization Tools: Some of the visualization software include: Tableau, Grafana, and Kibana for the purpose of drawing a representation of forensic data.
AI and ML Frameworks: TensorFlow, PyTorch, and Scikit-Learn as tools to incorporate AI and ML into forensic data processing.

6.4.2.4 *Log management and SIEM tools*

For network and cloud forensics, log management and security information and event management (SIEM) tools are necessary:

Log Aggregation Tools: Software such as the ELK Stack, a combination of Elasticsearch, Logstash, and Kibana for collation and analysis of logs.
SIEM Platforms: Splunk, QRadar, ArcSight as products used and configured in detecting and analyzing security incidents in real time.

6.4.3 Test data preparation

Thus, test data needs to be as realistic as possible in order to provide credible, valuable feedback on the effectiveness of given forensic procedures. This includes generating various types of data that forensic investigators may encounter:

6.4.3.1 *Synthetic data generation*

Creating synthetic data helps simulate different forensic scenarios:

File System Data: Grouping files and directories with certain date and time marks on creation, modification, or last access to test file system analysis tools.
Network Traffic: The objective of using tools such as tcpreplay and Ostinato on traffic generators is to simulate network traffic behavior of normal, DDoS attacks, and data exfiltration.
Memory Dumps: The researchers have made memory dumps with activities and specific items that can be detected by some memory tools.

6.4.3.1.1 Real-world data sets

Using real-world data sets adds authenticity to the experimental setup:

Public Data Sets: Utilizing publicly available data sets from sources like the Digital Corpora project or the M57-Patents scenario.
Captured Data: Collecting data from actual systems, ensuring compliance with privacy and ethical guidelines.

6.4.3.1.2 Scenarios and case studies

Developing detailed scenarios and case studies to test forensic techniques:

Insider Threat: Simulating scenarios where an insider exfiltrates sensitive data, testing the ability to detect and analyze such activities.
Malware Infection: Creating scenarios involving malware infections, including ransomware and APTs, to evaluate malware detection and analysis techniques.
IoT Attacks: Simulating attacks on IoT devices, such as unauthorized access and data tampering, to assess IoT forensic capabilities.

6.4.4 Forensic tools and techniques

The configuration of the tools as a major part of the experiment is also achievable and important. This section outlines the setup and usage of key forensic tools for different scenarios:

6.4.4.1 Disk imaging and analysis

Setting up disk imaging and analysis tools:

FTK Imager: This paper explains the process of installing and configuring FTK Imager specifically for the purpose of capturing and later comparing the hash values of the forensic images.
EnCase: Configuration of the EnCase for deep disk scanning: file system analysis and keyword search.

6.4.4.2 Memory forensics

Configuring memory forensics tools:

Volatility: It is configured for the analysis of the memory dump, with a plugin list for specific tasks, like process listing, or DLL injection detection.
Rekall: Installing Rekall and setting up Rekall for memory analysis for the purposes of detection of malware and rootkits.

6.4.4.3 Network forensics

Deploying network forensics tools:

Wireshark: Configuring the program for capturing packets and filters for suspicious traffic identification on the network.
Zeek: Zeek for Network Analysis and Logging. It is to use Zeek for network monitoring and collect more information to look for security breaches.

6.4.4.4 Mobile forensics

Configuring mobile forensics tools:

Cellebrite UFED: Configuration of the Cellebrite UFED interface for the acquisition of data from mobile devices, Apple devices being one example.

MSAB XRY: It should be noted that in their current state, MSAB XRY lacks a separate, clearly explained section dedicated to mobile data analysis to which I devoted considerable time setting up for the execution of the Relevance of Deleted Data and Analysis of Application Usage hypotheses.

6.4.4.5 IoT forensics

Deploying IoT forensics tools:

IoT Inspector: Configuring IoT Inspector for the purpose of examining the traffic of IoT devices to find threats.
Binwalk: Setting up Binwalk for firmware analysis: Emphasizing firmware images extraction and analysis of IoT devices' firmware.

6.4.4.6 Cloud forensics

Configuring cloud forensics tools:

AWS CloudTrail: Configuring AWS CloudTrail for logging and analyzing activity in an AWS account; primarily for identifying unauthorized access and changes in configuration.
Google Cloud Logging: Google Cloud Logging is a service that is used for capturing and analyzing logs originating from Google Cloud Platform services, which is configured in the following way.

6.4.5 Experimental scenarios

Developing comprehensive experimental scenarios to validate forensic techniques across different environments:

Scenario 1: Insider Threat
Objective: I find out how to detect and analyze exfiltration of data by an insider.
Setup: Set up a network handling data which should not be leaked, have someone within the network acting as an insider transferring files, and then run network analytical tools to diagnose and determine what the within-network transfer activity was.
Scenario 2: Malware Infection
Objective: Detect the vulnerable and infected systems on the network.
Setup: Set up a Windows environment, put in different samples of malware, and use memory and disk forensic utilities to try to identify and analyze the malware.
Scenario 3: IoT Device Compromise
Objective: Students are to study unauthorized access to an IoT device.
Setup: Set up an IoT home, attack one of the smart home devices, and use IoT forensics tools in the investigation process.
Scenario 4: Cloud Data Breach
Objective: Simulate an event of data leak and intrusion of the cloud system.
Setup: Build infrastructure in the AWS or Google Cloud, conduct an attack and collect information from it, and use cloud forensics tools.
Scenario 5: Analysis of the Blockchain of Transactions
Objective: Survey the ledger of a blockchain for traces of fraud.
Setup: Create a blockchain network, perform the fake transactions, and of course, solve the problem by using the tools of blockchain forensics.

6.5 LEGAL CONSIDERATIONS

Digital forensics is a vital part of criminal investigation and prosecution where computer-generated evidence is required. However, the industry is governed by a web of legal issues that forensic investigators have to observe in order to provide evidence that will be considered in a court of law. This chapter attempts to answer those questions, focusing on the specific issues of evidence handling, as well as the scope and importance of digital forensics, issues of privacy rights, jurisdiction, admissibility, and the use of expert testimony.

6.5.1 Specific guidelines for submitting documents

Technological accuracy of the digital evidence is especially important for it to be received by the Court. Compliance with generally accepted rules of handling the evidence is critical to preserving the probative value of digital assets.

6.5.1.1 Chain of custody

Definition: The term chain of custody on the other hand is the recorded sequence of the movement, possession, and analysis of the evidence and its eventual disposal.

Importance: Avoiding contamination is specific because it seeks to ensure that there is continuity from the scene of the crime, through the evidence collection process, to prosecution and trial.

Best Practices: Recording all the evidence handling activities in chronological order in order to know who touched the evidence, at which time, and why the transfer was made. This is enhanced by the use of tamper-proof labels and appropriate storage facilities to avoid damage to the samples.

6.5.1.2 Evidence preservation

Definition: Preservation basically means ensuring that the electronic evidence to be used in a case is protected from being either deleted, changed, or lost.

Importance: Maintenance of such evidence in its original state can however, be a major challenge, a factor that counts against them in the court of law.

Best Practices: Forensic imaging of the storage media, utilizing write lockers to eradicate changes to the information assets, and preserving original evidence in appropriate containment.

6.5.1.3 Documentation and reporting

Definition: C sheer documentation and reporting implies the documentation of all the activities, equipment, and procedures used throughout the forensic investigation.

Importance: Integration of documentation enhances the credibility of forensic analysis since it eases the process of reproducing the results.

Best Practices: Documenting all activities performed by the forensic tools and documenting configurations of all tools to be used in the process. Preparing syntactical and accurate reports that give a description of forensic processes and conclusions.

6.5.2 Privacy concerns

Conservation of individual credit privacy and forensic scrutiny imposes enormous legal dilemmas.

6.5.2.1 Legal frameworks for privacy

General Data Protection Regulation (GDPR): In the European Union, the General Data Protection Regulation in the EU sets high standards of protection of personal data, especially the data that is collected from forensic investigations. Law enforcement authorities have to meet GDPR challenges like data minimization, purpose limitation, and the subject's rights.

Electronic Communications Privacy Act (ECPA): In the United States, the ECPA regulates the interception and access of electronic communication and stored electronic information. Investigators and specialists engaged in the examination of digital evidence have to operate under such regulations.

Health Insurance Portability and Accountability Act (HIPAA): In any probe that comes into contact with medical data, HIPAA provides a guide on how to handle patients' information. It means forensic analysts need to satisfy HIPAA privacy and security rules in the course of their operations.

6.5.2.2 Minimizing privacy invasions

Data Minimization: The focused information collection, which means to collect only the necessary data that will be required for the investigation, avoids the collection of large amounts of personal data.

Anonymization and Pseudonymization: Measures like anonymization and pseudonymization are useful techniques for preserving personal data from identification.

Informed Consent: Where possible, getting informed consent from the people who may be involved in the data that is to be subjected to forensic analysis.

6.5.3 Jurisdictional challenges

As a subdiscipline, cyber forensics tends to encompass information that may be stored across multiple jurisdictions, thus giving rise to several related legal concerns of jurisdictions and cross-border investigations.

6.5.3.1 Jurisdictional authority

Definition: Jurisdiction means the power of a court or any law-enforcing agency to investigate any case or prosecute any offense in a particular region.

Challenges: Digital evidence can move to another country and even another state at the blink of an eye, which causes difficulty in identifying which court has jurisdiction over the case.

Resolution: International treaties and agreements, such as the Budapest Convention on Cybercrime, facilitate cross-border cooperation and mutual legal assistance. Investigators must be aware of the relevant treaties and legal frameworks that govern international cooperation.

6.5.3.1.1 Mutual legal assistance treaties (MLATs)

Definition: It is an interstate treaty aimed at providing cooperation in the field of Criminal Justice between countries.

Importance: Anticipated MLATs give a lawful procedure for gathering evidence situated in another country.

Best Practices: Using MLATs to make the request for cooperation with the foreign authority in accordance with ensuring that the request meets the formalities set out in the treaty and engaging in strict coordination with the counterparts.

6.5.3.2 *Extradition and cross-border enforcement*

Definition: Extradition is the actual transfer of a criminal suspect from one country to another for the purposes of prosecution and or being punished.

Challenges: The legal systems, evidentiary requirements, and data protection laws of the countries involved may pose challenges to extradition and cross-jurisdictional enforcement efforts.

Best Practices: Knowledge of the legal situation and practice of extradition in some jurisdictions, and cooperation with countries' law enforcement bodies.

6.5.4 Chak's admissibility is compared to the general legal standards for admissibility

Before electronic evidence can be presented in court, it has to be in compliance with legal requirements. Such standards make certain that the evidence is the right kind, credible, and has been procured lawfully.

6.5.4.1 *Relevance*

Definition: Relevant evidence means evidence that has any rational probability or tendency to affect the admissibility of a fact or the issues other than merely suggesting the possibility that its existence could be a coincidence.

Application: Courts also demand that forensic investigators explain precisely how the data discovered links to the case being mediated.

6.5.4.2 *Reliability*

Definition: It might mean that the evidence is genuine, and that it is as accurate as possible, or that one has not been able to judge its accuracy.

Application: Each method and instrument employed in the course of forensic analysis needs to be as scientifically sound as it should be embraced by the majority of forensic practitioners. Some of the features increase the reliability of the evidence, such as the application of standard and well-reproducible procedures.

6.5.4.3 *Authentication*

Definition: In this case, the process of authentication checks if the presented evidence is actually genuine or not.

Application: It needs to undergo a process of proving its originality, and that is by proving the data has not been tampered with. There exist methods that can confirm the integrity of digital evidence, such as hashing.

6.5.4.4 *Hearsay and exceptions*

Definition: A hearsay statement is one made outside of court, and which is tendered for the purpose of proving the truth of the content of the statement, and is inadmissible unless the exception pertains to the case.

Application: Computer printouts, emails, and text messages may also be classified as hearsay. Nevertheless, there are occasional exceptions to the hearsay rule, like the business records or electronic records, where the mentioned sort of evidence may be allowed.

6.5.5 Role of expert witnesses

Another function of expert witnesses is to offer specialist knowledge and opinion that the court requires to comprehend when conducting a digital forensic investigation.

6.5.5.1 The expert witnesses are entitled to certain qualifications

Education and Training: The expert in digital evidence should possess an academic background and professional training in digital investigation or information technology and security, computer science.

Certifications: Some of the certifications that improve the credibility of expert witnesses include Certified Information Systems Security Professional (CISSP), Certified Forensic Computer Examiner (CFCE), and the EnCase Certified Examiner (EnCE).

Experience: First-hand experience in conducting a digital forensic investigation, and then using such experience as actual experience in testifying in court is important in the establishment of the witness's credibility.

6.5.5.2 Testimony of expert witnesses

Preparation: Several rules apply to expert witnesses in connection with witness testimony, namely preparing for the case by studying the materials of the case as to the forensic evidence, methodologies that were used, and the findings. There should be a willingness to also discuss technical issues in simple ways that one without this knowledge will understand.

Presentation: Expert witnesses in a court case offer their opinion and evidence to the side that hired them, often during direct questioning. It is mandatory for them to express their procedures, analysis, and their conclusion without bias.

Cross-Examination: The authors were forced to pick cross-examination as the stage when the expert witnesses must be ready to defend their results and methods under overt pressure from the attorney for the other party.

6.5.5.3 Ethical considerations

Impartiality: In order to deliver their testimonies, expert witnesses must not be aligned with any of the parties and should not express any bias at all.

Confidentiality: To protect the specifics, it is necessary in most cases. Experts should only provide information about the case and should not disclose information of any other nature or area of specialization.

6.5.6 New legal developments in digital investigation

Given that technology advances, it is observed that new legal problems persist in the digital forensics domain. This accords with the fact that it is important for forensic practitioners to keep abreast with such developments.

6.5.6.1 Encryption and decryption

Challenges: They also know that encryption is getting used much more frequently, creating problems for forensic investigators. Litigation around the compelled decryption of a device and the content of the encrypted data is increasingly seen.

Legal Landscape: Jurisdictions have provided a mix of decisions on compelled decryption, ranging from considerations of necessity in cases as a violation of a citizen's right against self-incrimination. One area of concern is that great attention should be paid to new legal requirements and changes throughout the investigators' work.

6.5.6.2 Data privacy laws

Challenges: Outcomes of the California Consumer Privacy Act (CCPA) and GDPR are challenging guidelines for handling and processing personal data. The latter defines how digital evidence can be collected and used through those laws.

Compliance: People working in forensic practice should always be very careful to see whether they are violating the privacy of data subjects or not, or whether they require the consent of the data subjects concerned or not, and, in general, should endeavor to minimize the data being processed from data subjects as much as possible.

6.5.6.3 Artificial intelligence and machine learning

Challenges: AI and ML implementation in digital forensics displayed application-level legal issues concerning the credibility and legitimacy of the algorithm in decision-making.

Best Practices: Making AI and ML models in forensics transparent, explainable to auditors, and validated can help allay legal issues and improve the believability of forensic results.

6.6 LIMITATION AND CONCLUSION

6.6.1 Limitations

More efficient and detailed methods for the digital forensic examination are the following: Although the techniques applied in this area are very effective, there are some limitations. It is crucial for forensic investigators to comprehend such constraints in viewed findings to endorse recommended studies and improve the consistency of their professional investigations.

6.6.1.1 Technical limitations

Encryption and Data Obfuscation: While digital forensics is a complex field even in its basic forms, one of the most important difficulties is working with encrypted and disguised data. AES and modern-day code-hiding mechanisms can effectively deny you access to data you need without the right decryption key or method. This can easily compromise the chances that forensic investigators have of gathering and analyzing the evidence that they seek.

Anti-Forensic Techniques: Today, computer criminals employ more and more anti-forensic methodologies, which allow them to avoid being easily identified and then cease their activity. These are data wiping techniques, steganography, and rootkits that change the system's functionality in order to disguise mischievous processes. It is sometimes not possible to effectively detect or counter these techniques, as this needs insight and equipment, which requires expertise.

Evolving Technology: Digital forensics is under constant pressure due to the fact that new technologies are being developed at a fast rate. New devices, OSs, and apps are being developed daily, and all of them may have different features and susceptibilities. These developments and innovations may generally require significant resources, effort, and time in their consistent application to forensic tools and methodologies.

6.6.1.2 Legal and ethical limitations

Jurisdictional Issues: Digital evidence can often be spread across many jurisdictions, having different legislation and often contradictory requirements. The factors increasing difficulty in evidence investigations arising from these jurisdictional considerations include: An MLA necessitates the assistance of treaties and international collaboration, which while indispensable can at times be time-consuming and cumbersome.

Privacy Concerns: A primary legal and ethical issue that arises when conducting forensic investigations is how to meet clients' exigencies based on forensic investigation while maintaining the dignity of individuals' rights to privacy. The analysis of evidence involves acting consistently with data protection legislation such as GDPR, HIPAA, CCPA, or any other legislation of the Member State where data is processed. Noncompliance with these regulations draws legal implications and puts the credibility of the investigation into question.

Admissibility of Evidence: There are several factors that should be met to make the e–evidence admissible in the system and courts. In a car, evidence must be not only credible, but also admissible in court and reliable as well as being proven to be authentic. Such variations make the admissibility of digital evidence in the court, especially in cross-border cases, a very sensitive area of concern.

6.6.1.3 Practical limitations

Resource Constraints: Proper digital forensic investigations entail the use of a lot of resources such as hardware, software, and skilled labor. Larger cases may take longer to be solved than the smaller ones, and small organizations or underfunded agencies would not be able to resource appropriately, meaning valid cases may not get the attention they deserve.

Skill and Expertise: It is therefore hardly surprising that digital forensics, in terms of the extent of sophistication, employs highly trained and skilled personnel. The lack of enough qualified forensic professionals poses a threat since it would hamper the investigations being conducted. Therefore, continuing education is a must in order to be able to achieve and sustain the required professionally developed staff.

Volume of Data: In the current complex environments, forensic investigators may be overwhelmed by the avalanche of data that is produced in digital form. The analysis of massive amounts of data needs reliable means and approaches; however, crucial information might go unnoticed or incorrectly interpreted.

6.6.2 Conclusion

There has been progressive growth in the existing practices concerning digital investigations in recent years due to the emergence of innovative technologies as a method of digital forensics. These have helped in dealing with the higher level of volume of digital crimes and have assisted forensic investigators in their efforts to find very relevant pieces of evidence in support of the legal prosecution of cyber criminals.

6.6.2.1 Summary of key advancements

Memory Forensics: Modern advances in memory analysis tools like Volatility and Rekall have allowed investigators to analyze volatile memory (RAM), which is often difficult, if not impossible, to capture on a traditional image. This is used in the detection of malware, getting the list of running processes, and real-time analysis of activities on the memory.

Live Forensics: Methods for performing live analysis on active systems have increased the possibility of collecting information in parallel with work processes. This is particularly important when it comes to analyzing APTs and other similar ongoing cyber threats.

Network Forensics: Recent developments in network analysis such as DPI and network flows have improved the capacity to study traffic streams for signs of trouble. This is something that is used in enabling analysts detect data exfiltration, the trends of the attacker, and the attacking tactics, among others.

Cloud Forensics: The rapid espousal of cloud computing has led to the birth of several cloud-specific forensic procedures and instruments. Cloud forensics is the process of copying data from virtual machines, storage devices, and cloud services and usually involves coordination with CSPs.

Mobile Forensics: In particular, mobile device usage, which has grown explicitly, has produced tremendous improvement in mobile forensics. Cellebrite UFED and MSAB XRY are two examples of applications that can be used to collect and review material found on people's smartphones and tablets, as well as app history, messages, and media files.

IoT Forensics: This review has found that IoT has brought new challenges and possibilities for digital forensics in the following ways. IoT forensics can be defined as the process of investigating an enormous number of connected devices, including smart homes, smart city components, and Industrial IoT.

Blockchain Forensics: The implementation of blockchain technology poses a set of opportunities in the context of credibility and the safeguarding of digital evidence. Blockchain can also be used for forensic purposes, mainly for tracing back the activities of users in the blockchain, as well as the authenticity of contracts and other decentralized applications.

AI and ML Integration: AI and ML can be said to have transformed digital forensics since the two technologies are used in the field. Algorithms for AI and ML can analyze something like insights using greater numbers than humans, which they can filter and examine for patterns and irregularities that investigators might overlook.

6.6.2.2 Future directions

As digital forensics continues to evolve, several areas hold promise for further advancement:

Enhanced Collaboration: Enhanced cooperation of the police with organizations of the private sector, as well as universities, may result in the enhancement of the existing and the creation of new and efficient forensics tools and techniques.

Standardization and Certification: It can be therefore concluded that the cause of reliability and credibility of digital forensic investigation can be improved by following standardized methods and introducing certification programs in this sphere.

Legal and Regulatory Frameworks: If the legal and regulatory systems are to remain relevant, the law must be dynamic in its ability to accept new evidence and changing technology, while citizens' privacy must be protected.

Continuous Learning and Training: This is a clear implication that there is vital importance in the continuous updating of knowledge and skills in carrying out sophisticated digital investigations.

BIBLIOGRAPHY

1. Kaushik, K. (2022). A Novel Approach to Secure Files Using Color Code Authentication. In: Sugumaran, V., Upadhyay, D., Sharma, S. (eds) Advancements in Interdisciplinary Research. AIR 2022. Communications in Computer and Information Science, vol. 1738. Springer, Cham. https://doi.org/10.1007/978-3-031-23724-9_4
2. Kaushik, K., Singh, V., Manikandan, V. P. (2022). A Novel Approach for an Automated Advanced MITM Attack on IoT Networks. In: Sugumaran, V., Upadhyay, D., Sharma, S. (eds) Advancements in Interdisciplinary Research. AIR 2022. Communications in Computer and Information Science, vol. 1738. Springer, Cham. https://doi.org/10.1007/978-3-031-23724-9_6
3. Kaushik, K., Naik, V. (2023). Making Ductless-Split Cooling Systems Energy Efficient Using IoT. In: 2023 15th International Conference on Communication Systems & Networks (COMSNETS), Bangalore, India, pp. 471–473. https://doi.org/10.1109/COMSNETS56262.2023.10041408
4. Porwal, P., Devare, M. (2024, August 1). Scientific Impact Analysis: Unraveling the Link between Linguistic Properties and Citations. Journal of Informetrics. https://doi.org/10.1016/j.joi.2024.101526
5. Porwal, P., Devare, M. (2023, September 20). Citation Count Prediction Using Weighted Latent Semantic Analysis (wlsa) and Three-Layer-Deep-Learning Paradigm: A Meta-Heuristic Approach. Multimedia Tools and Applications. https://doi.org/10.1007/s11042-023-16957-8
6. Porwal, P., Devare, M. (2021). "Citation Classification Prediction Implying Text Features Using Natural Language Processing and Supervised Machine Learning Algorithms," Communications in Computer and Information Science, Jan. 01, 2021. https://doi.org/10.1007/978-981-16-0507-9_46
7. Tatkare, K. A., Devare, M. (2019). "A Novel Region Duplication Detection Algorithm Based on Hybrid Approach," Social Science Research Network, Jan. 01, 2019. https://dx.doi.org/10.2139/ssrn.3425340
8. Mohurle, S., Devare, M. "Fuzzy Probability Model for Quantifying the Effectiveness of the MSW Compost," IEEE Conference Publication, IEEE Xplore, Jan. 01, 2019. https://ieeexplore.ieee.org/document/8945830
9. Shitole, A., Devare, M., "Machine Learning Supported Statistical Analysis of IoT Enabled Physical Location Monitoring Data," Springer eBooks, Jan. 01, 2020. https://doi.org/10.1007/978-3-030-41862-5_13
10. Devare, M., Thakral, M. (2023). Enhancing Automatic Speech Recognition System Performance for Punjabi Language Through Feature Extraction and Model Optimization. International Journal of Intelligent Systems and Applications in Engineering, vol. 12, no. 8s, pp. 307–313.
11. Devare, M., Thakral, M. "Designing an Automatic Speech Recognition System for the Minor Age Group," IEEE Conference Publication, IEEE Xplore, Dec. 15, 2023. https://ieeexplore.ieee.org/abstract/document/10431311
12. Thakral, M., Singh, R. K., Kaushik, K. (2022). Integration of Blockchain Technology and Intelligent System for Potential Technologies. Chapman and Hall/CRC eBooks, Aug. 23, 2022. https://www.taylorfrancis.com/chapters/edit/10.1201/9781003193425-6/integration-blockchain-technology-intelligent-system-potential-technologies-manish-thakral-rishi-raj-singh-keshav-kaushi
13. Thakral, M., Singh, S. (2022). "A Secure Bank Transaction Using Blockchain Computing and Forest Oddity," Blockchain Technologies, Jan. 01, 2022. https://link.springer.com/chapter/10.1007/978-981-19-1960-2_6
14. Thakral, M., Singh, R. R., Singh, S. P. (2022). An Extensive Framework Focused on Smart Agriculture Based Out of IoT. In: Choudhury, A., Singh, T.P., Biswas, A., Anand, M. (eds) Evolution of Digitized Societies Through Advanced Technologies. Advanced Technologies and Societal Change. Springer, Singapore. https://doi.org/10.1007/978-981-19-2984-7_12
15. Thakral, M., Singh, R. K., Kalghatgi, B. V. (2022). "Cybersecurity and Ethics for IoT System: A Massive Analysis," Transactions on Computer Systems and Networks, Jan. 01, 2022. https://link.springer.com/chapter/10.1007/978-981-19-1585-7_10
16. Singh, R. R., Thakral, M., Kaushik, S., Jain, A., Chhabra, G. (2022). A Blockchain-Based Expectation Solution for the Internet of Bogus Media. In: Hemanth, D.J., Pelusi, D., Vuppalapati, C. (eds) Intelligent Data Communication Technologies and Internet of Things. Lecture Notes on Data Engineering and Communications Technologies, vol. 101. Springer, Singapore. https://doi.org/10.1007/978-981-16-7610-9_28

17. Thakral, M., Jain, A., Kadyan, V., Jain, A. (2021). An Innovative Intelligent Solution Incorporating Artificial Neural Networks for Medical Diagnostic Application. In: 2021 Sixth International Conference on Image Information Processing (ICIIP), Shimla, India, pp. 529–532. https://doi.org/10.1109/ICIIP53038.2021.9702631
18. Thakral, M., Singh, R. R., Jain, A., Chhabra, G. (2021). Rigid Wrap ATM Debit Card Fraud Detection Using Multistage Detection. In: 2021 6th International Conference on Signal Processing, Computing and Control (ISPCC), Solan, India, pp. 774–778. https://doi.org/10.1109/ISPCC53510.2021.9609521
19. Girish, I., Kumar, A., Kumar, A., M., A. (2020). Driver Fatigue Detection. In: 2020 IEEE 17th India Council International Conference (INDICON), New Delhi, India, pp. 1–6. https://doi.org/10.1109/INDICON49873.2020.9342456
20. Prajeesha, M., A. (2021). EDGE Computing Application in SMART GRID – A Review. In: 2021 Second International Conference on Electronics and Sustainable Communication Systems (ICESC), pp. 1–6. https://doi.org/10.1109/ICESC51422.2021.9532792
21. Udeshi, D. M., Divakarla, S. G. L., Rajdev, N. C., M., A. (2022). Wind Speed Forecasting Using Hybrid Model. In: 2022 IEEE 7th International Conference for Convergence in Technology (I2CT), Mumbai, India, pp. 1–5. https://doi.org/10.1109/I2CT54291.2022.9823995
22. Tammana, A., Amogh, M. P., Gagan, B., Anuradha, M., Vanamala, H. R. (2021). Thermal Image Processing and Analysis for Surveillance UAVs. In: Kaiser, M.S., Xie, J., Rathore, V.S. (eds) Information and Communication Technology for Competitive Strategies (ICTCS 2020). Lecture Notes in Networks and Systems, vol. 190. Springer, Singapore. https://doi.org/10.1007/978-981-16-0882-7_50
23. Balasubramanian, S., Kashyap, R., Cvn, S. T., Anuradha, M. (2020). Hybrid Prediction Model for Type-2 Diabetes with Class Imbalance. In: 2020 IEEE International Conference on Machine Learning and Applied Network Technologies (ICMLANT), Hyderabad, India, pp. 1–6. https://doi.org/10.1109/ICMLANT50963.2020.9355975
24. Yakasiri, M., M, A., B. K., K. (2020). Comparative Analysis of Markov Chain and Polynomial Regression for the Prognostic Evaluation of Wind Power. In: 2020 IEEE International Conference for Innovation in Technology (INOCON), Bangluru, India, pp. 1–5. https://doi.org/10.1109/INOCON50539.2020.9298374
25. J., P., M., V., Pai, V. G., M., A. (2020). Comparative Analysis of Marker and Marker-Less Augmented Reality in Education. In: 2020 IEEE International Conference for Innovation in Technology (INOCON), Bangluru, India, pp. 1–4. https://doi.org/10.1109/INOCON50539.2020.9298303
26. Yakasiri, M., Avrel, J., Sharma, S., Anuradha, M., Keshavan, B. K. (2019). A Stochastic Approach for the State-Wise Forecast of Wind Speed Using Discrete-Time Markov Chain. In: TENCON 2019 – 2019 IEEE Region 10 Conference (TENCON), Kochi, India, pp. 575–580. https://doi.org/10.1109/TENCON.2019.8929529
27. Chhabra, G., Prasad, A., Marrabenta, V. (2022). Comparison and Performance Evaluation of Human Bio-Field Visualization Algorithm. Archives of Physiology and Biochemistry, vol. 128, no. 2, pp. 321–332. https://doi.org/10.1080/13813455.2019.1680699
28. Brian D. Carrier and Eugene H. Spafford, An Event-Based Digital Forensic Investigation Framework, Digital Investigation, 2004, https://api.semanticscholar.org/CorpusID:2912997
29. Casey, E. (2011). Digital Evidence and Computer Crime: Forensic Science, Computers, and the Internet (3rd ed.). Academic Press/Elsevier, Waltham, MA.
30. Pollitt, M. M. (1995). Computer Forensics: An Approach to Evidence in Cyberspace. In: Proceedings of the 18th National Information Systems Security Conference, National Institute of Standards and Technology and National Computer Security Center, Baltimore, MD, pp. 487–491.
31. Dolan-Gavitt, B., Srivastava, A., Traynor, P., Giffin, J. (2009). Robust Signatures for Kernel Data Structures. In: Proceedings of the 16th ACM Conference on Computer and Communications Security (CCS '09), ACM Digital Library, Chicago, Illinois, USA, pp. 566–577.
32. Schatz, B. L. (2007). Digital Evidence: Representation and Assurance (Doctoral dissertation). Queensland University of Technology, Brisbane, Australia. https://eprints.qut.edu.au/16507/
33. Ligh, M. H., Case, A., Levy, J., Walters, B. (2014). The Art of Memory Forensics: Detecting Malware and Threats in Windows, Linux, and Mac Memory. John Wiley & Sons, Indianapolis, IN.
34. Carvey, H. (2009). Windows Forensic Analysis DVD Toolkit (2nd ed.). Syngress Publishing, Burlington, MA.

35. Vömel, S., Freiling, F. C. (2011). A Survey of Main Memory Acquisition and Analysis Techniques for the Windows Operating System. Digital Investigation, vol. 8, no. 1, pp. 3–22.
36. Adelstein, F. (2006). Live Forensics: Diagnosing Your System Without Killing it First. Communications of the ACM, vol. 49, no. 2, pp. 63–66. https://doi.org/10.1145/1113034.1113070
37. Jiang, F., Fu, Y., Gupta, B. B., Loukas, G., Liang, K., Ricci, J. (2017). Deep Learning Based Multi-channel Intelligent Attack Detection for Social Networks. IEEE Access, vol. 5, pp. 24757–24767.
38. Pilli, E. S., Joshi, R. C., Niyogi, R. (2010). Network Forensic Frameworks: Survey and Research Challenges. Digital Investigation, vol. 7, no. 1–2, pp. 14–27.
39. Bejtlich, R. (2013). The Practice of Network Security Monitoring: Understanding Incident Detection and Response. No Starch Press, San Francisco, CA.
40. Ruan, K., Carthy, J., Kechadi, T., Crosbie, M. (2011). Cloud Forensics: An Overview. In Advances in Digital Forensics VII. IFIP Advances in Information and Communication Technology, vol 361, pp. 35–46. Springer, Berlin, Heidelberg.
41. Dykstra, J., Sherman, A. T. (2012). Understanding Issues in Cloud Forensics: Two Hypothetical Case Studies. Journal of Network Forensics, vol. 4, no. 1, pp. 19–31.
42. Quick, D., Martini, B., Choo, K.-K. R. (2014). Cloud Storage Forensics. Syngress/Elsevier, Amsterdam.
43. Jansen, W., Ayers, R. (2007). Guidelines on Cell Phone Forensics (NIST Special Publication 800-101). National Institute of Standards and Technology (NIST), Gaithersburg, MD.
44. Zdziarski, J. (2012). Hacking and Securing iOS Applications: Stealing Data, Hijacking Software, and How to Prevent It. O'Reilly Media, Sebastopol, CA.
45. Marrington, A., Mohay, G., Clark, A., Morarji, H. (2011). A Model for Digital Forensics Investigation Process and its Application to Mobile Devices. International Journal of Digital Evidence, vol. 1, no. 1, pp. 1–15.
46. Oriwoh, E., Jazani, D., Epiphaniou, G., Sant, P. (2013). Internet of Things Forensics: Challenges and approaches. In: Proceedings of the 9th IEEE International Conference on Collaborative Computing: Networking, Applications and Worksharing (Collaboratecom), IEEE, Austin, TX, USA, pp. 608–615.
47. Perumal, S., Norwawi, N. M., Raman, V. (2015). Internet of Things (IoT) Digital Forensic Investigation Model: Top-Down Forensic Approach Methodology. In: Proceedings of the 2015 Fifth International Conference on Digital Information Processing and Communications *(ICDIPC)*, IEEE, Sierre, Switzerland, pp. 19–23.
48. Zawoad, S., Hasan, R. (2015). FAIoT: Towards Building a Forensics Aware Eco System for the Internet of Things. In: Proceedings of the 2015 IEEE International Conference on Services Computing (SCC), IEEE, New York, NY, pp. 279–284. https://doi.org/10.1109/SCC.2015.46
49. Fung, S. G., K. Y. Kwok, and S. M. Cheng. "Blockchain and Trustworthy Systems: Challenges and Opportunities." In Proceedings of the 2018 International Conference on Blockchain and Trustworthy Systems (BlockSys 2018). Berlin, Heidelberg: Springer, 2018.
50. Huang, J., Hu, J., Gu, L., Yu, J., Li, C. (2018). Blockchain-Based Auditing Framework for Cloud Storage Systems. In: Proceedings of the 2018 27th International Conference on Computer Communications and Networks (ICCCN), IEEE, Hangzhou, China, pp. 1–9.
51. Zheng, Z., Xie, S., Dai, H., Chen, X., Wang, H. (2017). An Overview of Blockchain Technology: Architecture, Consensus, and Future Trends. In: Proceedings of the 2017 IEEE International Congress on Big Data (BigData Congress), IEEE, Honolulu, HI, USA, pp. 557–564.

Chapter 7

Navigating the legal and ethical maze

IoT forensics

Manish Thakral, Keshav Kaushik, Farhan Shaikh, Anita Devare, and Manoj H Devare

7.1 INTRODUCTION

The Internet of Things (IoT) as a concept marks a new form of connection, changing the ways through which humans engage with technology and everything else. Today, there is almost nothing in the world that does not relate to the world of IoT – from homes and wearables to industrial sensors and automobiles by automobile giants. Nevertheless, it is important to understand that along with these possibilities, an entanglement of legal and ethical factors has been born, the solutions for which cannot be a simple yes-or-no issue and have to solve, which requires successful passing system from Figure 7.1.

"Navigating the Legal and Ethical Maze: IoT Forensics" can be considered as a versatile analysis of the diverse nature of IoT technologies, and legal and ethical aspects of forensic investigation in this topic. Written by a team of legal and computer science and cybersecurity and ethics professionals, this work provides a comprehensive guide and unique perspective

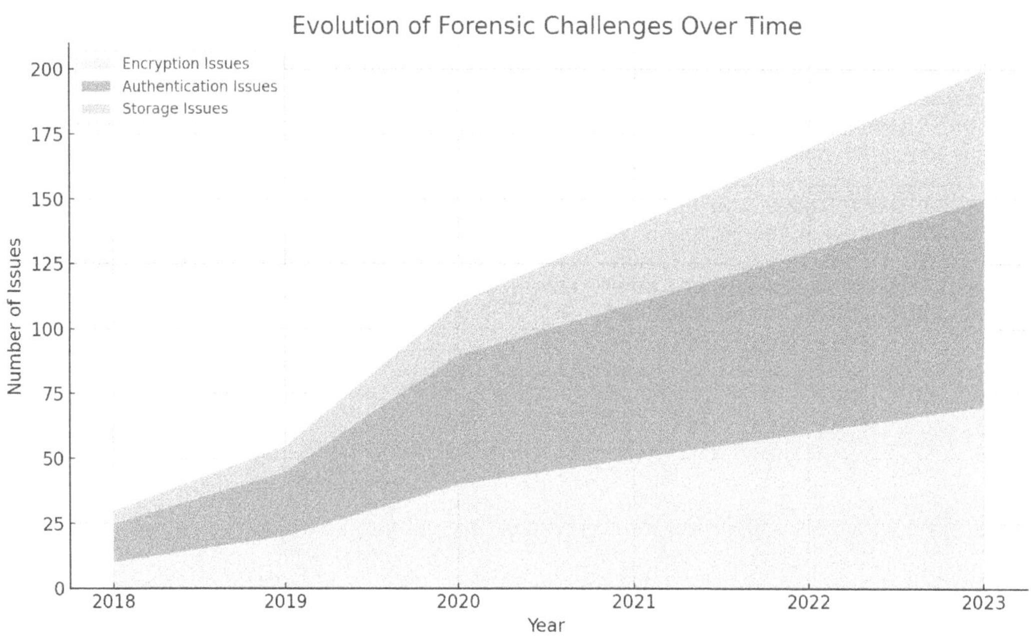

Figure 7.1 Representation of number of issues between 2018–2023.

 DOI: 10.1201/9781003513896-7

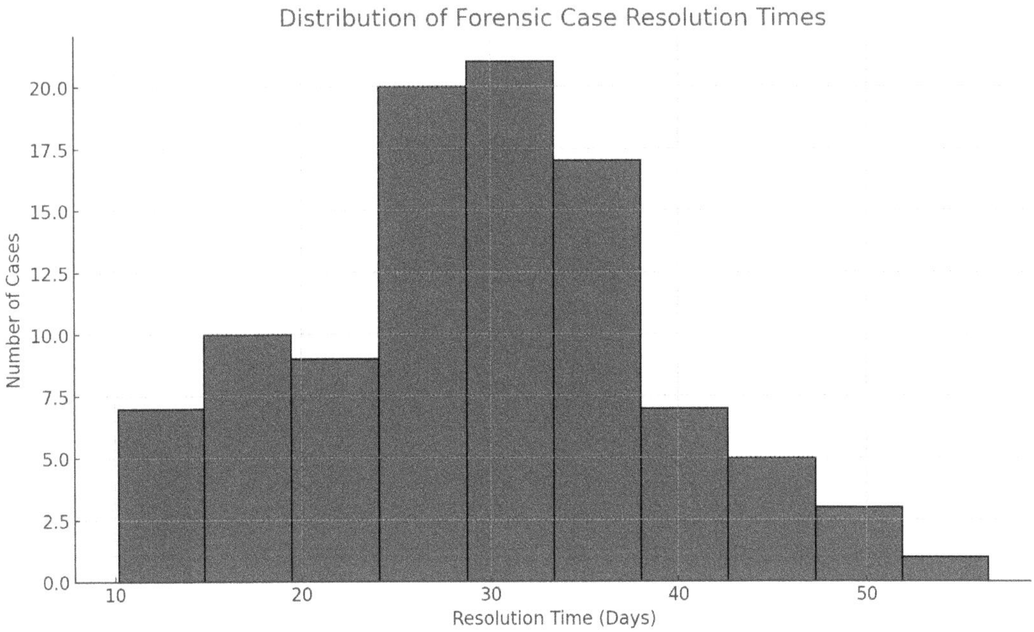

Figure 7.2 Representation of resolution time vs number of cases in distribution of forensics case resolution times.

of IoT forensics for those in this fast-growing career stream while also serving as a reference for independent researchers and scholars.

The IoT devices prevailing nowadays have only been rising at an exponential rate; the global estimate of connected IoT devices has been pegged to billions and the numbers are expected to rise at an enthusiastic rate in the future years. These devices gather vast amounts and details about the behaviors, preferences, and interactions and thus create a huge volume of data that can have excellent potential for revolutionizing such aspects of life as healthcare, transportation, energy consumption, and environmental control from Figure 7.2.

However, this has given rise to many IoT devices, which in turn poses many questions on the security, privacy, and accountability questions. While IoT devices are smart interconnected devices which create new opportunities of influencing infrastructure and even the objects we use, they open new opportunities for hackers to introduce malicious software and perform cyber operations. From distributed denial-of-service (DDoS) attacks to ransomware campaigns, data breaches, and everything in between, IoT-based threats are vast and only continue to get worse – putting the safety of the individual, business, and society at large in jeopardy.

As a result of these threats, the concept of IoT forensics has become an important tenet of IoT cybersecurity, based on identification, analysis, and attribution of IT cyber incidents. Investigation also has a central, crucial part, needed to determine the causes of security incidents, and the users responsible for them, as well as to gather information for legal procedures. However, performing efficient forensic executions concerning IoT has its limitations because of the decentralized IoT architecture, the exponential data generation in IoT systems, and the heterogeneity of different IoT devices and communication protocols.

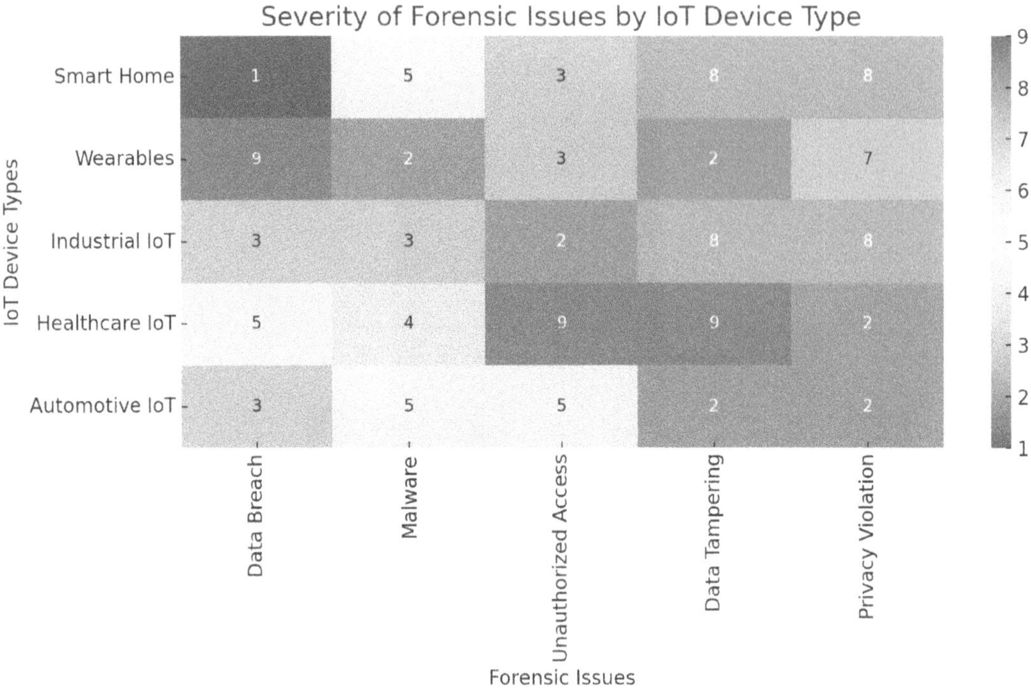

Figure 7.3 Depiction of forensic issues vs IoT device types.

However, IoT forensics significantly brings out legal and ethical issues, hence require some consideration. This means that the process of getting, storing, and analyzing the IoT data for the purpose of forensic increases the concerns of privacy and right to consent and protection of individual rights. With more and more IoT devices being deployed in everyday life and closely interacting with their users, the problem of unwanted spying and intrusion arises, together with questions of permissible behavior and both device makers' and users' duties (Figure 7.3).

In addition, assigning responsibilities for cyber incidents involving IoT devices is problematic because IoT environments are complex and uncontrolled, and IoT devices can be easily infected by malicious actors and redesigned for more nefarious goals. Data custody of IoT data and certainty and genuineness of evidence are crucial steps in the analysis, which demands scrupulous compliance with research principles and procedures.

Against this backdrop, "Navigating the Legal and Ethical Maze: IoT Forensics" aims at presenting an exhaustive list of legal and ethical issues for forensic investigators in the IoT domain. The book takes a socio-legal, computational, and ethical approach to analyzing the issues relevant to IoT forensics, including data protection, and individual's rights and consent, responsibility, and reasons for the practice of such forensic activities, among others.

This way, the book also seeks to open a debate among professionals from different fields related to IoT forensics, search for ideas, recommendations, and experiences that can be shared among relevant professionals in the respective fields. This book is a wealth of information using case studies, real-life scenarios, and examples to equip the readers with the knowledge required to do IoT forensics legally and safely from Figure 7.4.

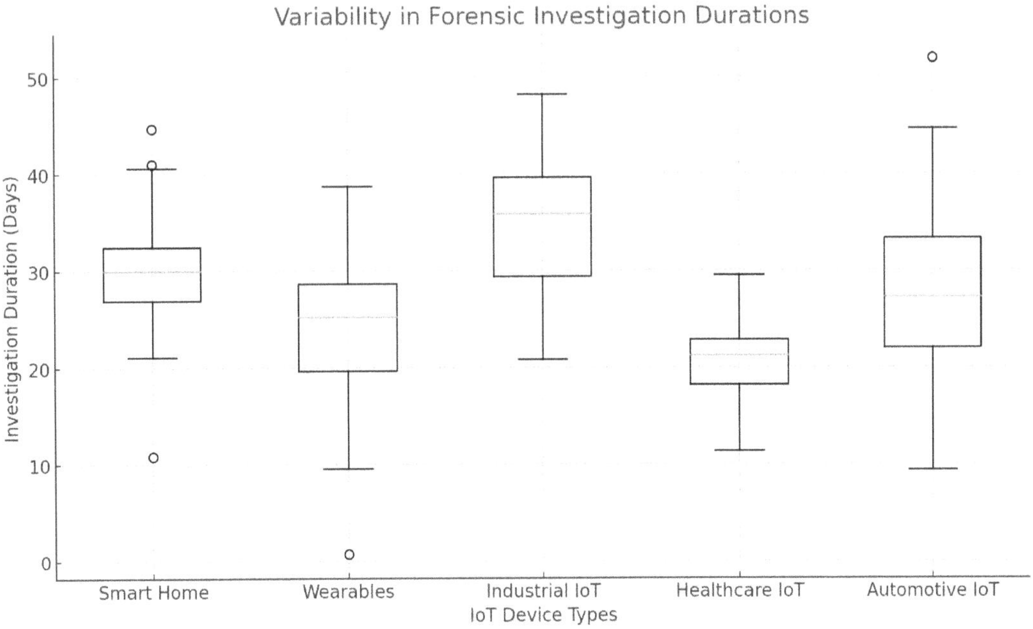

Figure 7.4 Depiction of IoT device types vs investigation duration (days).

7.2 SOURCE OF DATA

For those involved in the practice of IoT forensics, it's basic to consider the source of data. Therefore, when IoT ecosystems develop, the number of interconnected objects and the type of data create a colossal amount of diverse data. This chapter is focused to establish the nature of data in IoT context in terms of data origin, data attributes, and its relevance to forensics. Through a better understanding of the challenges that data sourcing entails within IoT, forensic professionals can better identify them, manage them, and abide by legal and ethical benchmarks.

7.2.1 The diverse sources of data

IoT signifies a spectrum of devices, sensors, including systems of various primary industries, including health, transport, homes, and industry. All these gadgets create data fusiform which constantly gathers data about the environment, the user, and how the gadget is being operated and used. The data in IoT can be of a traditional data type like structured numerical data, frequency data, and ratios or more of a multimedia and metadata type.

This type of data is well-ordered and part of defined IoT datasets, straightforward formats, such as databases, logs, and spreadsheets. Data examples include sensor telemetry, configuration settings of devices, and event logs that help in understanding the performance and status of the devices as well as environmental conditions were indicated. For instance, temperature sensors that are attached to at least one smart thermostat to create structured data on increases and decreases in room temperatures over time to encourage insights into energy and occupancy rates.

On the other hand, unstructured data is characterized by its inability to conform to a prescribed format and may incorporate textual, visual, or audible data that is collected by IoT instruments. Closed-circuit television videos and recordings from smart speakers and voice assistants, security camera feeds are among the examples of unstructured data which pose many difficulties for further forensic processing due to the type and variety of the data it consists of. Analyzing text data still involves specialized tools and methods on factors that are useful in distilling the results arising from unstructured data forms.

Metadata works together with structured and unstructured data as an augmenting framework that effectively delivers information about the content of data, time of creation, the identification number of the device constructing it, geographical coordinates, and data origin. Metadata itself is instrumental to the reconstruction of events, the definition of timelines, and the identification of data flows in favor of the IoT networks under investigation. When working within the scope of IoT investigation, forensic metadata helps the professionals to better understand the context of the artifacts and determine the relations between them in order to gain insights from the data.

7.2.2 Legal and ethical dimensions

Broad and populous issues surrounding law and ethics come into play when dealing with the collection, storage, and usage of data in IoT environments, thus requiring a complex method toward sourcing and analyzing of data. Based on a legal standpoint, data privacy as well as security is highly important especially to barriers such as General Data Protection Regulation (GDPR) as well as California Consumer Privacy Act (CCPA). The adherence to these regulations necessitates efficient protection mechanisms for the IoT data in terms of confidentiality, integrity as well as availability.

The notion of data ownership, consent, and jurisdiction remain problematic legal issues in IoT forensics, especially where the settings are shared or where the data transfers are across borders. These are important preconditions to collecting data and distinguishing between legitimate and criminal activities in data analysis. Also, when implementing data protection policies across jurisdictions it is essential to consider legal environments and international policies that regulate transfer of data and privacy.

Ethically responsible data sourcing refers to practice that is in compliance with principles like honesty, stewardship, justice as well as recognition of individual's dignity. There is an understanding that forensic professionals should avoid unethical actions in the course of data lifecycle – collection, analysis, storage, and diffusion. This includes measures for protecting computerized information, for the protection of evidence, ethical issues, and conflict of interest.

7.2.3 Best practices and mitigation strategies

With the IoT digital trails being incredibly complex, demanding significant legal and ethical considerations, forensic professionals can use recommended lessons and preventive measures specific to the IoT context. Defining rules for data usage, content protection, and data storage regulation can assist in the service of legal and industry standards to guarantee patient's information security and confidentiality.

Also, proper extension of the proven encryptions, authorization procedures, and anonymization of data contributed to the fight against security threats connected with IoT data communication and storage. Encryption of data in transit and at rest enables any organization to guard important information from access and interception by unauthorized individuals. In the same manner, conducting analysis on personal identifiable information can obscure the data while making innovative generalization on other variables possible.

In addition, integrating interdisciplinary and knowledge of IoT applications for stakeholders can improve the results of IoT forensic investigations. Experience of specialists from different domains in law and order, computer security, and artificial intelligence (AI), as well as ethical issues, means that organizations can gain the advantage of combining knowledge in order to tackle multifaceted problems and find unique solutions. The synergy involved in such a structure allows for the sharing of good practices, field experiences, and new developments in IoT forensics to be implemented pragmatically in response to emerging threats.

7.3 LITERATURE REVIEW

In the relatively new topic of IoT forensics, it becomes necessary to familiarize oneself with the existing literature and research, as well as with approaches to the discipline. This chapter stresses major literature, studies, publications, and frameworks that are related to managing the legal and ethical issues within IoT forensics. Through a review of existing literature, this chapter seeks to provide pointers to the forensic community, decision makers, and scholars on the current status of knowledge in this field as well as areas of future research possibilities.

7.3.1 Legal frameworks and regulations

IoT privacy, security, and forensic investigation are fascinating research subjects that attract literature that describes and analyzes legal systems and laws that trail IoT data. Investigations have shown that the regulation of Europe's GDPR and the CCPA in the United States have greatly influenced the standards and policies in the organization. Also, researchers have examined the application of the new technologies like blockchain and distributed ledger technologies in maintaining integrity and accountability in IoT applications.

7.3.2 Ethical considerations and guidelines

One of the most compelling directions in IoT forensics is the ethical one, as authors and practitioners discuss the issues of privacy, consent, transparency, and accountability in investigations. There is a growing academic literature emphasizing the importance of developing standards, ethical codes to regulate and control the process of gathering, assessing, and interpreting IoT data acquired for forensic goals. Purdue University's list of ethically implemented frameworks like the IEEE P7000 series on ethical considerations in AI and autonomous systems can be of great use when it comes to IoT forensics and maintain the right balance that is needed for the right path forward.

7.3.3 Technical challenges and solutions

There are numerous technical issues in IoT forensics; they include data acquisition and imaging, data analysis and interpretation, and much more. A few different approaches were investigated to identify possible methodologies and techniques for the forensic examination of IoT devices, tools, and techniques. Data acquisition and analysis were studied along with the analysis of some frameworks and machine learning algorithms for detecting anomalies and threats. Moreover, studies have been conducted on security threats and measures for protection of IoT objects, including encryption standards, authentication methods, and intrusion detection systems.

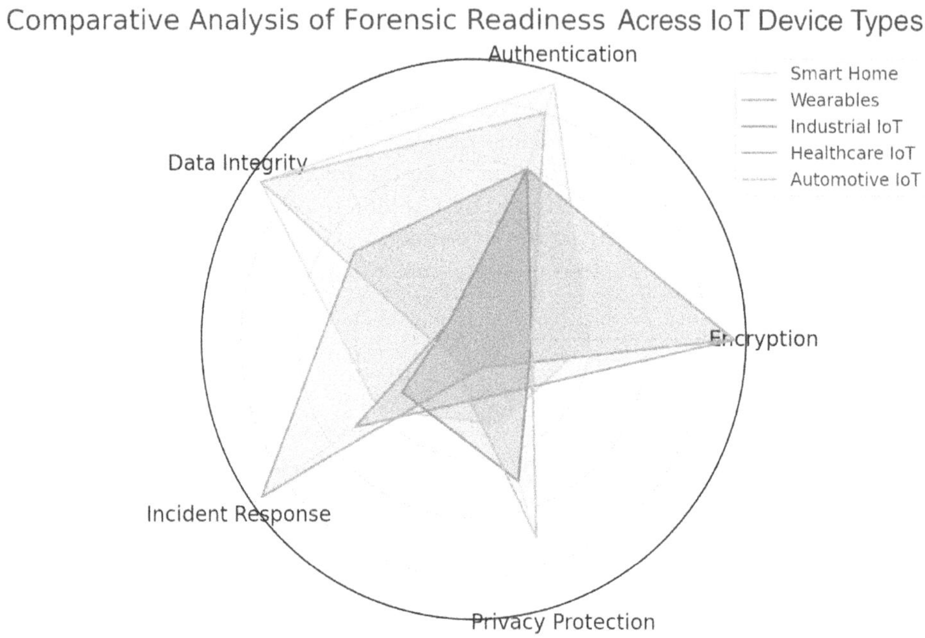

Figure 7.5 Illustration of incident response and privacy protection across different devices.

7.3.4 Interdisciplinary perspectives

As a result of the complexity of IoT forensics, cooperation with other fields of study is mandatory, such as legal, computer, cybersecurity, and ethical. Previous research has emphasized the need for cross disciplinary work to address the intricacies of IoT forensic investigations on legal, technological, and ethical levels, which imply that the best forensic practice can be attained by cooperation of the experts belonging to different fields. Moreover, research has emphasized the need for education and training programs to equip forensic professionals with the knowledge and skills needed to navigate the complexities of IoT environments effectively from Figure 7.5.

7.3.5 Case studies and practical applications

A number of examples and applied works from different areas add insights into possible problems and works in the field of IoT forensics. Researchers have explored different facets of IoT with regard to forensic research within such settings as smart homes, healthcare, manufacturing, services, and transport.

This chapter demonstrates that the IoT landscape poses challenges to data sourcing, analysis, and interpretation by presenting case studies and best practices with regard to forensic practices and ethical guidelines addressing cybersecurity threats and protection of individual rights.

7.3.5.1 Future directions and research opportunities

Substantial improvements have been recorded in determining the legal and ethical aspects of IoT forensics, more research opportunities and challenges exist. Different researchers have pointed out the direction for further research, including the establishment of best practices for IoT forensic investigation, the use of the blockchain technology for data authenticity, overall look at IoT ethical issues and decision-making. However, more empirical studies are called for to evaluate the current codes of conduct in response to new threats and threats to security in the domain of IoT forensics.

7.4 EXPERIMENTAL SETUP

When it comes to the field of IoT forensics, it is crucial to have an effective experimental framework in order to assess the validity, reliability, and true usability of the outcomes identified in research. This chapter focuses on various aspects of designing IoT forensics experiments, including its features, approaches, issues, and recommendations. This chapter therefore sought to explain the general principles of experimental design and conduct in an attempt to arm forensic professionals, researchers, and policymakers on steps to take and precautions to observe while conducting IoT forensic experiments.

7.4.1 Understanding experimental setup

Experimental setup is the process of devising, developing, and conducting experiments for the purposes of analyzing certain research questions or hypotheses in the field of IoT forensics. Some of the steps include variable identification, choice of measuring instruments, preparation of test environment, data collection to enhance analysis and interpretation. The basic framework of empirical research is the experimental structure that delivers the right physical infrastructure to test the hypotheses, evaluate interventions, and make informed conclusions.

7.4.1.1 Key considerations in experimental design

In particular, the following major factors have to be taken into consideration: research objectives, sample, control variables, methods of data collection, methods of statistical data analysis. Stakeholders need to state research questions and hypothesis and these must be in line with the objectives of the research. However, it is also cynosural to sample properly for it is an essential determinant of the overall quality of the study issues in studies, which include representative sampling, assumptions regarding the population, types of sampling, and the calculation of the samples size.

Control variables are very central in experimental designs since they allow the experimenter to manipulate and vary the independent variables with the dependent variables while holding other influences constantly. Thus, having identified such relationships, researchers can control variables and produce negative results, which would inform on the effects of particular interventions or treatments on forensic dynamics. Moreover, there remains a lot of concern about the type of data that can be collected, the methods to be used to ensure accuracy, reliability, and validity of the measurements that are made by using the instruments that are used in the process.

7.4.1.2 Methodologies for IoT forensics experiments

IoT testing methods are a broad mix of practices regarding IoT forensics where each approach has its strengths and weaknesses. Simulations are built from live IoT networks and use computerized software applications to create replicas, potential attacks, and investigations to analyze impact, test forensic approaches, and discover system susceptibilities in a safe and controlled environment. Captive experiments are performed on live IoT scenario where the researchers get a real feel of the actual problem that can occur in real life along with its possible solutions.

Case studies have been recognized to be a good source of empirical evidence where actual forensic investigations and their related findings can be clearly presented, evaluated, and concrete lessons gathered. Based on the above, it is clear that using case studies will help the researchers analyze real-life data and come up with original findings of actual forensics. A sample of controlled laboratory experiments embraces artificially constructed settings with view to influence the variables, check hypotheses, and document resultant impacts under conformist conditions. Although each of the mentioned methodologies has its strengths and weaknesses, it will be more effective to use both of them in parallel to achieve better results and gain further understanding of IoT forensics to sustain or improve the reliability of the findings of IoT forensics.

7.4.1.3 Challenges and considerations

While experimentation provides helpful insights to IoT forensics research, scholars encounter several issues and factors when developing and implementing experiments. One potential issue result from the nature of IoT environments that may intimate high variability and diversity levels: their replication may necessitate such particular skills, tools, and equipment that when emulated, they are far from a copy of the original IoT environments. Furthermore, issues to do with data confidentiality, consent, and privacy has to be well handled so that the study will conform to the best ever ethical practices as well as the legal requirements on conducting research on human beings. Also, maintenance of internal validity and external validity of the experimental outcomes are another critical factor that needs a proper check on the methodological accuracy such as experimental control, properly conducted randomization, and experimental replication. In addition, the authors also need to think about generalizability of findings for practice and applicability of results of experiment in terms of internal validity and external validity.

7.4.1.4 Best practices and mitigation strategies

In order to overcome these challenges, the following research recommendations are provided within this work which will help the researchers to implement the best practices and mitigation strategies to improve the validity, reliability, and the overall generalizability of the experimental studies in the IoT forensic context. Establishing clear research objectives and hypotheses, conducting thorough literature reviews, and consulting with domain experts can help ensure the relevance and significance of research questions. However, using systematic research procedures such as appropriate controls, random methods for allocation of subjects, and replication techniques, the biases are eliminated and the results enhanced.

Moreover, facilitating interdisciplinary research communication between scholars, professionals, and policymakers should enhance the experimental process and improve the communication of ideas, practice, and experience stories. Also, high disclosure of experimental methodologies, processes, and results is noble in ensuring the credibility and practical realization of IoT forensic investigations. Following these best practices and further reduction measures, the researchers could collect more knowledge and research outcomes for IoT forensics that will increase the protection of critical infrastructure and cybersecurity.

7.5 LEGAL CONSIDERATIONS

Today and in the course of using technology, one notable aspect is the availability of the IoT devices. From the smart thermostats and refrigerators to smart coaches and health monitoring watches, IoT devices have entered and are proliferating almost every facet of human life, capturing huge volumes of data, and connecting to networks for purposes of convenience and optimization. But with that convenience comes numerous legal and ethical questions, especially where IoT forensics is concerned.

IoT forensics is the science of gathering, examining, and making sense of data generated from IoT devices in order to investigate cyber-related crimes, security threats, or other unlawful incidents. As these devices are in one way or the other embedded in various facets of human society, there is an exigent need to have efficient IoT forensics. But there are several legal and ethical issues which make the process of IoT forensics difficult and laden with complexities.

7.5.1 Legal and ethical considerations

Jurisdictional Challenges: Without a doubt, one of the sole legal difficulties associated with IoT forensics is the issue of jurisdiction in circumstances when IoT information is stored or transmitted overseas. Some nations' legal standards of data privacy, data retention, and data access may be antagonistic to those of other nations making forensic investigation challenging.

Data Privacy and Protection: Internet-connected items gather a large volume of user information from where they live to their physical characteristics. Policies to maintain compliance of data protection laws including the GDPR in the European Union and the CCPA in United States must be upheld. These regulations remain a challenge that forensic investigators have to meet to legally gather and process sensitive data during their work.

Chain of Custody: Handling of IoT devices requires documentation of the identity of each person who handles the device and the activities they perform in order to reduce the effect of tampering in the Yellow Mile project. This also incorporates measures like recording how IoT devices and other related data are handled, stored, and transported through the investigation process to avert alteration of the same.

Legal Admissibility: Following the conventional evidence law in the IoT context is highly recommended. There are some standards that courts have put down that must accompany digital evidence, and they are relevance, authenticity, and comprehensiveness. Forensic team participants have to practice good forensic practice and meet the requirements outlined by the law to allow the pieces of evidence offered in the court.

Law Enforcement Access: Obtaining data from IoT devices for forensic examination purposes involves consent from the manufacturers of these devices, the service providers, or application third-party platforms. The legal version of this issue is in giving rights of access to law enforcement while maintaining user's privacy rights and data protection laws, most especially in cases of data or information that may be considered personal.

Regulatory Compliance: Beyond data protection laws, IoT forensics may be subject to sector-specific regulations such as healthcare e.g. Health Insurance Portability and Accountability Act – HIPAA or financial services e.g. Payment Card Industry Data Security Standard – PCI DSS. Adherence to these regulations is the next legal hurdle to overcome in forensic probes of IoT devices.

International Cooperation: Therefore, legal and law enforcement agencies relationships when there is a cross-border cybercrime or security issue are crucial. It is pertinent to note that IoT forensic investigations involve request for MLATs as well as cooperation that enhances collection of information across national borders.

Solving these legal issues is only possible if one has knowledge in both digital forensic analysis a data privacy, cybersecurity, and law enforcement laws. It means that forensic investigators should inform themselves in the legal frameworks while using best practice to make IoT forensic investigations legal and credible.

7.5.2 Ethical considerations

Informed Consent: The specific ethical concerns relating to IoT forensics involve gaining consent from the owners of the devices or users of the devices to gain data for analysis. This chapter calls for accurate disclosure concerning the nature, extent, and potential effects of forensic activities in order to protect users' privacy and their freedom of choice.

Data Minimization and Purpose Limitation: Typically, forensic investigators should minimize data collection, processing, and retention and must only collect, analyze, and retain only necessary data for forensic investigation. This has the effect of reducing privacy harm potential and avoiding the haphazard amassing or utilization of persona data in excess of what is necessary for the investigation.

Bias and Discrimination: Thus, when handling data from IoT devices, this should be done with caution to ensure the results do not extend bias or discrimination. Stereotypes or prejudices in data gathering, evaluation, or understanding can make for wrong prejudiced decisions or prejudicial action on human endowment mainly the race gender or income level.

Data Security and Confidentiality: Some of the important challenges faced in IoT forensics include protection of security and maintain privacy of digital evidence. Security requirements also have functions in the forensic investigation processes whereby data has to be concealed from unfavorable revelation apart from being averagely attacked or modified.

Professional Integrity: IoT forensic investigators stand to improve organizational professional ethics and this ethical code. This is impartiality, objectiveness in dealing with investigations, assessments, or presentations regardless of bias by personnel or groups.

Human Rights and Civil Liberties: That means that IoT forensics like other IT forensic cases may be considered either within civil or traditional criminal legal structures but has to deal with civil liberties and human rights issues, including right to privacy and freedom of speech, right to due process. The responsibility of any forensic specialist as an employee is to meet the requirements of police or sometimes other interested parties as long as certain rights and freedoms of the subjects in case are not violated according to the law and principles of legal and ethical behavior.

Accountability and Transparency: Seven principles entitled as principles of accountability and transparency are as follows: The processes, results, and frameworks related to IoT forensic investigation to the relative owners of devices, different legal entities, and the public, the forensic services, including auditing, gain legitimacy, and credibility by being so transparent.

Reasoning over ethical options and forensic implications needs to encode some ethical principles and individual rights as well as sensitive to technological responsibility. Thus, it falls to forensic investigators to always act ethically, not merely at the core of the investigation, but throughout the entire process, always in search for middle ground between the exigencies of the investigation and the researcher's responsibilities. Thus, understanding of these legal and ethical issues will help the forensic investigators to perform forensics of IoT devices, systems, networks responsibly and ethically and seek to protect the rights and privacy of the individuals involved.

7.6 LIMITATIONS

While IoT forensics holds tremendous potential for investigating cybercrimes and security incidents involving IoT devices, several limitations and challenges must be acknowledged:

Technical Complexity: Currently, there are many forms of IoT devices. This implies that they have different architectures, operating systems, and communication protocols. On such gadgets, it is sometimes difficult or even impossible to carry out forensic analysis and not all the IoT devices can be forensically analyzed.

Data Fragmentation and Encryption: Many IoT devices collect information as semi-structured or by using encryption algorithms that creates a difficult task to retrieve and process digital forensics. Encryption practices used by IoT devices may actually hamper forensic analysis where keys are unavailable or have been lost.

Network Dependencies: Most IoT devices connect to the network to work and send data, thus posing as a nightmare to forensic investigators. Interpreting traffic and communications between the IoT devices and backend servers is not a straightforward scenario and may demand tools and knowledge in networks; furthermore, the dependent nature of IoT networks may hinder forensic analysis in dynamic and large networks.

Data Volume and Velocity: One of the largest issues for forensic investigation involves the veritable deluge and speed of IoT device interactions. Challenges in the processing and analysis of big data generated by a number of IoT devices can put a heavy burden on forensic systems and may slow down or complicate a forensic investigation.

Chain of Custody Issues: In forensic investigations, it is important always to acknowledge, secure, and retain a proper investigation for the IoT devices and linked data. However, challenges that include device tampering, data alteration, or unauthorized access might affect the reliability as well as admissibility of digital evidence hence the formation of proper chain of custody procedures.

Privacy and Legal Constraints: Due to privacy and legal issues, it may be difficult to perform IoT forensic analysis especially in cases where personal information is involved or when data is moved from one country to another. Laws and regulations guiding the protection of data may limit the ability of forensic personnel in collecting, analyzing, or sharing digital evidence affecting the capacity and reach of forensic investigation.

Resource Constraints: IoT forensics is a computationally and resource-intensive process which demands specialized instruments and skills. Nonetheless, due to the lack of resources or capacity, organizations, especially the small police departments or forensic facilities, often fail to conduct thorough IoT forensic examination leading to a gap in the forensic knowledge.

Evolution of IoT Technologies: However, depending on the speed of evolution of the IoT technologies, these bring in more complexities to the forensic expert. New IoT devices, new protocols, and new security paradigms are constantly being proposed; it is therefore challenging to quickly build a match between these new devices, protocols, and security paradigms and the more recent forensics models.

7.7 CONCLUSION

Overall, the author opines that solving the issues of the development of IoT forensics entails the consideration of the legal and ethical quandaries of this subject area and the expertise of technical experts, legal scholars, and ethicists. However, as defined above, IoT forensics has a great potential for investigating cybercrimes, security breaches, and all kinds of unlawful practices involving IoT devices.

There is a need to address the legal issues of jurisdiction, data privacy, chain of custody, and compliance with the law – to enhance admissibility of digital evidence on the IoT forensic investigations. So, maintaining the key values of ethical behavior like informed consent, data minimization, and human rights protection helps protect the individual's privacy and encourages responsible data usage in forensic activities.

Despite the complexity that defines IoT forensics, there are a number of challenges that currently exist in the domain, and it is critical that research and development, and cooperation and innovation in the digital forensics' domain, continue to be pursued to better address the challenges within IoT forensic investigations. It is therefore only befitting to accept the fact that IoT forensics is far from a defined science with researchers having to work collectively in a proactive manner, if investigators are going to cut through the associated legal and ethical jungle with a view of not only maintaining the integrity of investigations in this cutting-edge interconnectivity frontier but also upholding the rights and privacy of individuals who are caught within such systems.

BIBLIOGRAPHY

1. Kaushik, K. (2022). A Novel Approach to Secure Files Using Color Code Authentication. In: Sugumaran, V., Upadhyay, D., Sharma, S. (eds) Advancements in Interdisciplinary Research. AIR 2022. Communications in Computer and Information Science, vol. 1738. Springer, Cham. https://doi.org/10.1007/978-3-031-23724-9_4
2. Kaushik, K., Singh, V., Manikandan, V. P. (2022). A Novel Approach for an Automated Advanced MITM Attack on IoT Networks. In: Sugumaran, V., Upadhyay, D., Sharma, S. (eds) Advancements in Interdisciplinary Research. AIR 2022. Communications in Computer and Information Science, vol. 1738. Springer, Cham. https://doi.org/10.1007/978-3-031-23724-9_6
3. Kaushik, K., Naik, V. (2023). Making Ductless-Split Cooling Systems Energy Efficient Using IoT. In: 2023 15th International Conference on Communication Systems & Networks (COMSNETS), Bangalore, India, pp. 471–473. https://doi.org/10.1109/COMSNETS56262.2023.10041408
4. Porwal, P., Devare, M. (2024, August 1). Scientific Impact Analysis: Unraveling the Link Between Linguistic Properties and Citations. Journal of Informetrics. https://doi.org/10.1016/j.joi.2024.101526
5. Porwal, P. and Devare, M. (2023, September 20). Citation Count Prediction Using Weighted Latent Semantic Analysis (wlsa) and Three-Layer-Deep-Learning Paradigm: A Meta-Heuristic Approach. Multimedia Tools and Applications. https://doi.org/10.1007/s11042-023-16957-8
6. Porwal, P., Devare, M. (2021). "Citation Classification Prediction Implying Text Features Using Natural Language Processing and Supervised Machine Learning Algorithms," Communications in Computer and Information Science, Jan. 01, 2021. https://doi.org/10.1007/978-981-16-0507-9_46
7. Tatkare, K. A., Devare, M. (2019). "A Novel Region Duplication Detection Algorithm Based on Hybrid Approach," Social Science Research Network, Jan. 01, 2019. https://dx.doi.org/10.2139/ssrn.3425340
8. Mohurle, S., Devare, M. (2019). Fuzzy Probability Model for Quantifying the Effectiveness of the MSW Compost. In: 2019 International Conference on Nascent Technologies in Engineering (ICNTE), Navi Mumbai, India, pp. 1–6. https://doi.org/10.1109/ICNTE44896.2019.8945830
9. Shitole, A., Devare, M. (2019). Supervised Machine Learning Supported Time Series Prediction and Analysis of IoT Enabled Physical Location Monitoring. International Journal of Innovative Technology and Exploring Engineering, vol. 8, pp. 3238–3245.
10. Devare, M., Thakral, M. (2023). Enhancing Automatic Speech Recognition System Performance for Punjabi Language Through Feature Extraction and Model Optimization. International Journal of Intelligent Systems and Applications in Engineering, vol. 12, no. 8s, pp. 307–313.
11. Thakral, M., Devare, M. (2023). Designing an Automatic Speech Recognition System for the Minor Age Group. In: 2023 4th International Conference on Communication, Computing and Industry 6.0 (C216), Bangalore, India, pp. 1–5, https://doi.org/10.1109/C2I659362.2023.10431311

12. Thakral, M., Singh, R. K., Kaushik, K. (2022). Integration of Blockchain Technology and Intelligent System for Potential Technologies. Chapman and Hall/CRC eBooks, Aug. 23, 2022. https://www.taylorfrancis.com/chapters/edit/10.1201/9781003193425-6/integration-blockchain-technology-intelligent-system-potential-technologies-manish-thakral-rishi-raj-singh-keshav-kaushi
13. Thakral, M., Singh, S. (2022). "A Secure Bank Transaction Using Blockchain Computing and Forest Oddity," Blockchain Technologies, Jan. 1, 2022. https://link.springer.com/chapter/10.1007/978-981-19-1960-2_6
14. Thakral, M., Singh, R. R., Singh, S. P. (2022). An Extensive Framework Focused on Smart Agriculture Based Out of IoT. In: Choudhury, A., Singh, T.P., Biswas, A., Anand, M. (eds) Evolution of Digitized Societies Through Advanced Technologies. Advanced Technologies and Societal Change. Springer, Singapore. https://doi.org/10.1007/978-981-19-2984-7_12
15. Thakral, M., Singh, R. K., Kalghatgi, B. V. (2022). "Cybersecurity and Ethics for IoT System: A Massive Analysis," Transactions on Computer Systems and Networks, Jan. 01, 2022. https://link.springer.com/chapter/10.1007/978-981-19-1585-7_10
16. Singh, R. R., Thakral, M., Kaushik, S., Jain, A., Chhabra, G. (2022). A Blockchain-Based Expectation Solution for the Internet of Bogus Media. In: Hemanth, D. J., Pelusi, D., Vuppalapati, C. (eds) Intelligent Data Communication Technologies and Internet of Things. Lecture Notes on Data Engineering and Communications Technologies, vol. 101. Springer, Singapore. https://doi.org/10.1007/978-981-16-7610-9_28
17. Thakral, M., Jain, A., Kadyan, V., Jain, A. (2021). An Innovative Intelligent Solution Incorporating Artificial Neural Networks for Medical Diagnostic Application. In: 2021 Sixth International Conference on Image Information Processing (ICIIP), Shimla, India, pp. 529–532. https://doi.org/10.1109/ICIIP53038.2021.9702631
18. Thakral, M., Singh, R. R., Jain, A., Chhabra, G. (2021). Rigid Wrap ATM Debit Card Fraud Detection Using Multistage Detection. In: 2021 6th International Conference on Signal Processing, Computing and Control (ISPCC), Solan, India, pp. 774–778. https://doi.org/10.1109/ISPCC53510.2021.9609521
19. Chellappa, Y., Joshi, N. N., Bharadwaj, V. (2016). Driver Fatigue Detection System. In: 2016 IEEE International Conference on Signal and Image Processing (ICSIP), Beijing, China, pp. 655–660. https://doi.org/10.1109/SIPROCESS.2016.7888344
20. Prajeesha, M., A. (2021). EDGE Computing Application in SMART GRID-A Review. In: 2021 Second International Conference on Electronics and Sustainable Communication Systems (ICESC), Coimbatore, India, pp. 1–6. https://doi.org/10.1109/ICESC51422.2021.9532792
21. Udeshi, D. M., Divakarla, S. G. L., Rajdev, N. C., M., A. (2022). Wind Speed Forecasting Using Hybrid Model. In: 2022 IEEE 7th International Conference for Convergence in Technology (I2CT), Mumbai, India, pp. 1–5. https://doi.org/10.1109/I2CT54291.2022.9823995
22. Tammana, A., Amogh, M. P., Gagan, B., Anuradha, M., Vanamala, H. R. (2021). Thermal Image Processing and Analysis for Surveillance UAVs. In: Kaiser, M.S., Xie, J., Rathore, V.S. (eds) Information and Communication Technology for Competitive Strategies (ICTCS 2020). Lecture Notes in Networks and Systems, vol. 190. Springer, Singapore. https://doi.org/10.1007/978-981-16-0882-7_50
23. Balasubramanian, S., Kashyap, R., Cvn, S. T., Anuradha, M. (2020). Hybrid Prediction Model for Type-2 Diabetes with Class Imbalance. In: 2020 IEEE International Conference on Machine Learning and Applied Network Technologies (ICMLANT), Hyderabad, India, pp. 1–6. https://doi.org/10.1109/ICMLANT50963.2020.9355975
24. Yakasiri, M., M., A., K., K. B. (2020). Comparative Analysis of Markov Chain and Polynomial Regression for the Prognostic Evaluation of Wind Power. In: 2020 IEEE International Conference for Innovation in Technology (INOCON), Bengaluru, India, pp. 1–5. https://doi.org/10.1109/INOCON50539.2020.9298374
25. Pai, V. G., M., A. (2020). Comparative Analysis of Marker and Marker-Less Augmented Reality in Education. In: 2020 IEEE International Conference for Innovation in Technology (INOCON), Bengaluru, India, pp. 1–4. https://doi.org/10.1109/INOCON50539.2020.9298303
26. Yakasiri, M., Avrel, J., Sharma, S., Anuradha, M., Keshavan, B. K. (2019). A Stochastic Approach for the State-Wise Forecast of Wind Speed Using Discrete-Time Markov Chain. In: TENCON 2019 – 2019 IEEE Region 10 Conference (TENCON), Kochi, India, pp. 575–580. https://doi.org/10.1109/TENCON.2019.8929529
27. Chhabra, G., Prasad, A., Marrabenta, V. (2022). Comparison and Performance Evaluation of Human Bio-Field Visualization Algorithm. Archives of Physiology and Biochemistry, vol. 128, no. 2, pp. 321–332. https://doi.org/10.1080/13813455.2019.1680699

Chapter 8

Best practices in IoT forensics

Strategies and techniques

Manish Thakral, Keshav Kaushik, Farhan Shaikh, Anita Devare, and Manoj H Devare

8.1 INTRODUCTION

Smart devices connected to the Internet of Things (IoT) have changed the world and brought interaction to an unexpectedly broad range of items and spaces. Starting from home automation to industrial manufacturing monitoring, almost every facet of life has been impacted by IoT devices providing comfort, effectiveness, or newer methodologies. But it also means a very complex landscape, especially when it comes to digital forensics (Figure 8.1).

As developed for individual computing systems, traditional forensic approaches lack the functional ability to work in IoT systems effectively. Examining IoT-related situations presents different learning questions, methodologies, and procedures to be employed when identifying, collecting, and acquiring the evidence. However, the IoT ecosystems are dynamic and comprise heterogeneity, which makes data acquisition more complex, and the interoperability of devices is a challenge.

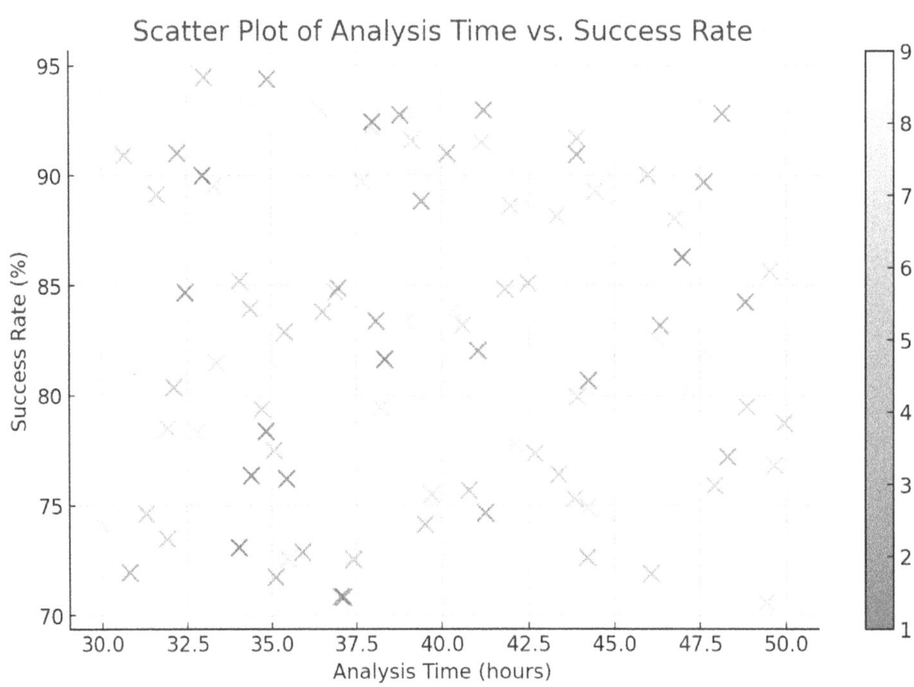

Figure 8.1 Depiction of success rate (%) with complexity score.

DOI: 10.1201/9781003513896-8

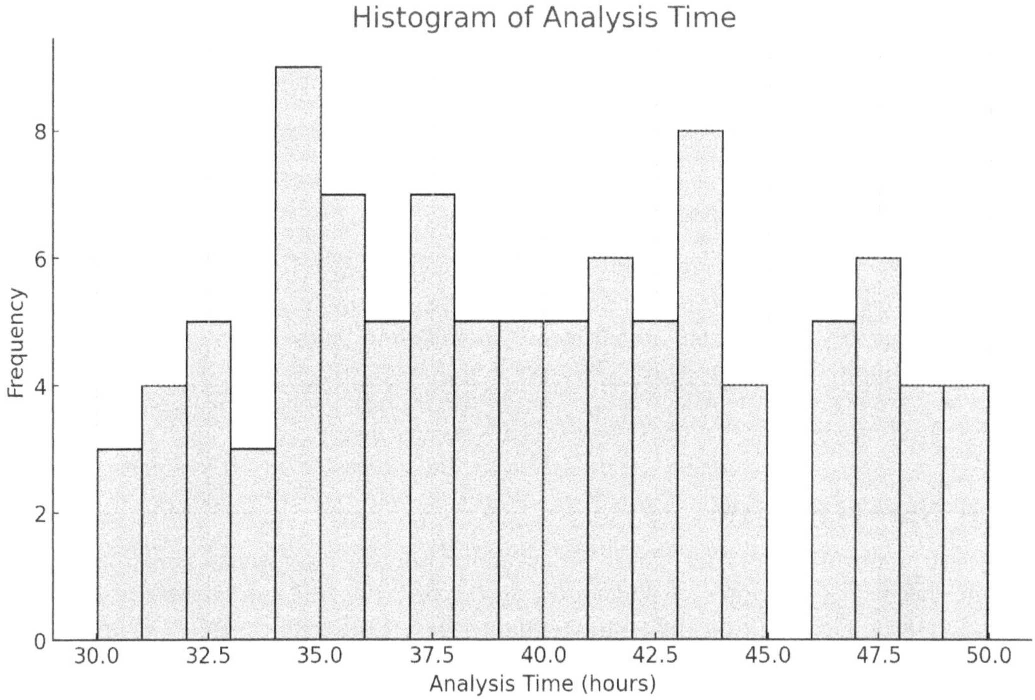

Figure 8.2 Representation of frequency time vs number of cases in distribution of forensics case analysis times.

This chapter aims to act as a reference for IoT forensics containing information on the principles, methodologies, and technologies relevant to accounting IoT forensics. It is the author's expectation that by elucidating the critical issues related to analyzing IoT ecosystems, and the difficulties that follow, this chapter shall aid forensic practitioners acquire proficiency to prospective IoT infringements (Figure 8.2).

The first section of the chapter describes what IoT devices are and outlines some of the important characteristics of IoT devices, such as the many types of devices, the various protocols, and data representations that exist in IoT settings. Knowledge of these basics is crucial for forensic analysts to have an appreciation of the intricacies of IoT structures and hence approach the problem appropriately.

Next, the chapter examines IoT-specific issues that engage forensic investigators in IoT scenarios. Some of these challenges are the kind of data produced by IoT devices, how to manage the large number of devices, the issue of security especially with a large number of IoT deployments, and the lingering questions on IoT forensics.

Based on this, the chapter discusses the best practices in undertaking IoT forensics, from the investigation process, and all through. The seven important best practices therein include the following: Conducting pre-incident planning, gather and preserve the digital evidence, acquiring the digital data and analyzing it, ensuring chain of custody and integrity of the evidence, coordinating with other stakeholders, and sharing information among the stakeholders.

Besides, the chapter discusses the various tools and technologies used by forensic experts to carry out IoT investigation. These are tools such as forensic imaging and analysis tool, network traffic analysis tool, IoT device forensic toolkits, digital evidence management systems suitable for IoT networks.

In the last section, the chapter looks at trends and prospects of IoT forensics. Some of these factors are the development of new and better methods of forensic examination, developments in the artificial intelligences (AIs) and machine learning areas, and changes to the type of threats currently prevalent and future ones, continuing efforts to establish standardized best practices and standards for practice and new regulations regarding the practice of IoT forensics.

8.2 SOURCE OF DATA

As part of the IoT, devices create a lot of data in various types to include sensor data, log files, traffic, and configuration data. This chapter discusses the various types of data faced in IoT systems and the implications for investigators before proceeding to review the main findings and limitations of the study. The types and characteristics of IoT data that are given above help the investigators to determine a set of specific approaches to IoT data collection, analysis, and interpretation in the course of IoT forensics investigation.

8.2.1 Types of IoT data

There are many different types of data produced by connected IoT devices, but all are used for the specific IoT purposes of understanding the behavior and interactions of the connected devices. The following are some common types of IoT data encountered in forensic investigations (Figure 8.3):

1. Sensor Data: Sensor-equipped IoT devices collect data from the physical environment, including temperature, humidity, light levels, motion, and sound. Environmental data emanating from the IoT smart sensors is useful to give context to the operation of the

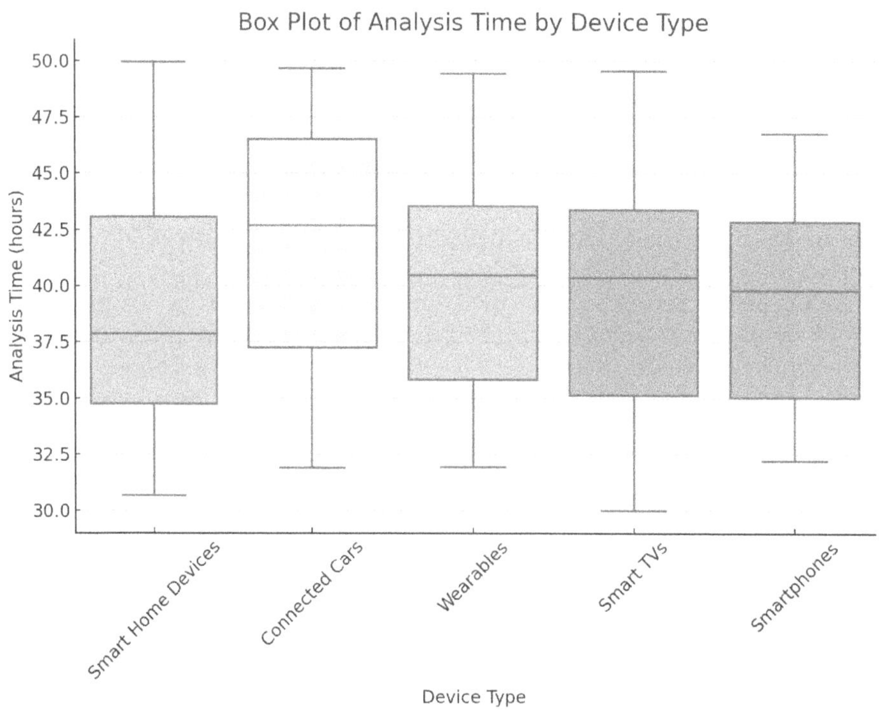

Figure 8.3 Depiction of IoT device types analysis time (hours).

devices and may help in investigations of accidents related to the use of smart devices for home automation or industrial applications.

2. Log Files: Log files capture occurrences in a system, errors, events involving users, and activities in IoT devices. In the case of network intrusions, log files are sources of strong forensic values that contain a timeline of device activities and signs of attacks or violations.
3. Network Traffic: Interactions that IoT devices have with other systems produce traffic in the network which may be captured for investigative analysis. Network traffic is the packets which are captured, network flow records and logs of protocols consisting of device interactions and data communication and potential security events.
4. Configuration Data: Like any other device connected to the Internet, IoT devices are typically set with parameters that control their functioning. Configuration data is based on device settings, firmware, network, and user preferences, which are possibly significant for reconstructing the device states and analyzing security breaches.
5. Metadata: IoT data possesses some characteristics of metadata that hold specific contextual relevance to the source, nature, and context of digital evidence. Metadata may include time and date stamps, device identification, geographical location details, and data origin giving the forensic examiner a clue on how to associate events in different pieces of evidence (Figure 8.4).

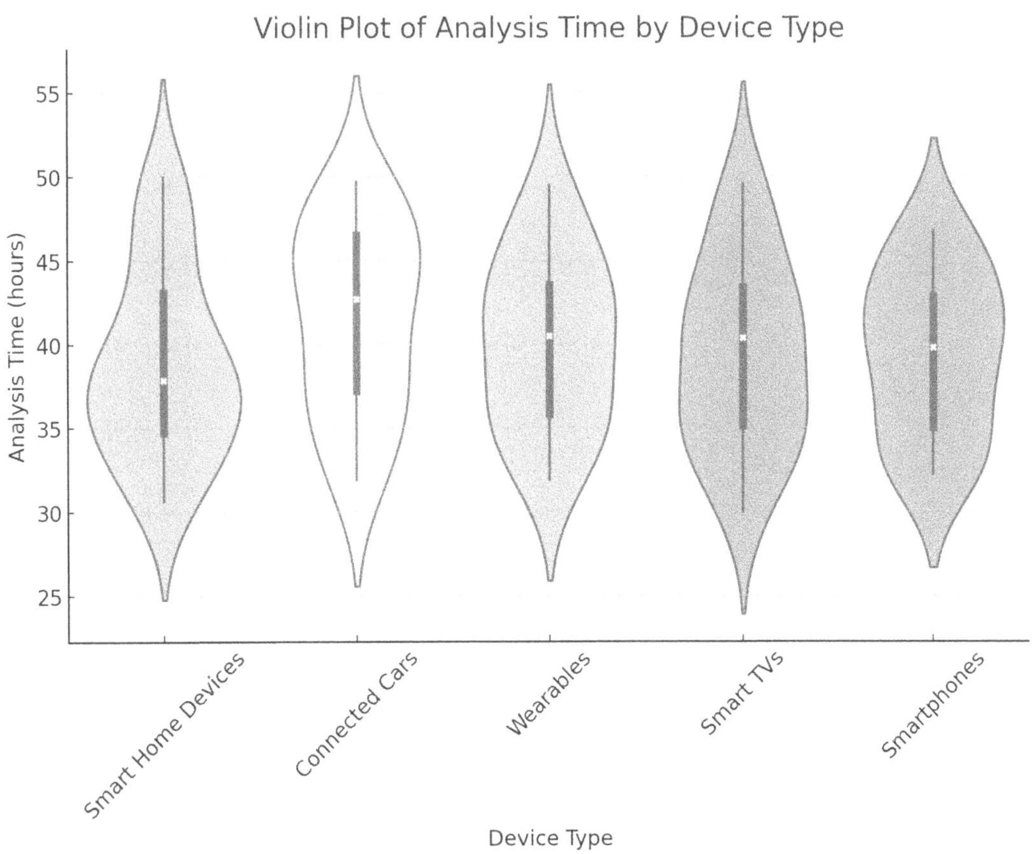

Figure 8.4 Depiction of IoT device types analysis time (hours) in violin plot.

8.2.2 Challenges in IoT data forensics

Even though IoT data proves to be useful in analyzing devices behaviors and their interaction, IoT data is diverse and has immense volume hence challenging to use for forensic investigating. The following are some key challenges in IoT data forensics:

1. Volume and Variety: IoT environments produce Big Data from highly diverse sources, which makes it difficult to filter out the required information and use it in the investigation.
2. Data Acquisition: Some of the general difficulties that arise when just collecting data from IoT devices are the variation in the structure of the devices IoT devices come in many forms, and each can have unique protocols IoT devices can be owned by different people and organizations. Attracting data from IoT devices is usually a complicated process due to underlying protocols inaccessible interfaces; data from IoT devices can be difficult to access due to the following reason: Heterogeneity in the structure of the devices IoT. Since IoT devices have unique data acquisition challenges, forensic investigators must obtain that data with specific tool- and method-sets that guarantee that the data is admissible in a legal proceeding.
3. Data Interpretation: Interpreting the information coming from IoT sources calls for an understanding of the IoT systems and architectural models, various communication protocols, and how the devices are going to behave. To be effective forensic investigators must be able to link the otherwise unrelated data elements, be able to determine that something is off, or that it has been tampered with, and be able to put together a proper timeline of the events (Figure 8.5).
4. Privacy and Legal Considerations: Information that IoT data carries may also be personal, encompassing details about individual's habits, preferences, or activities. Based

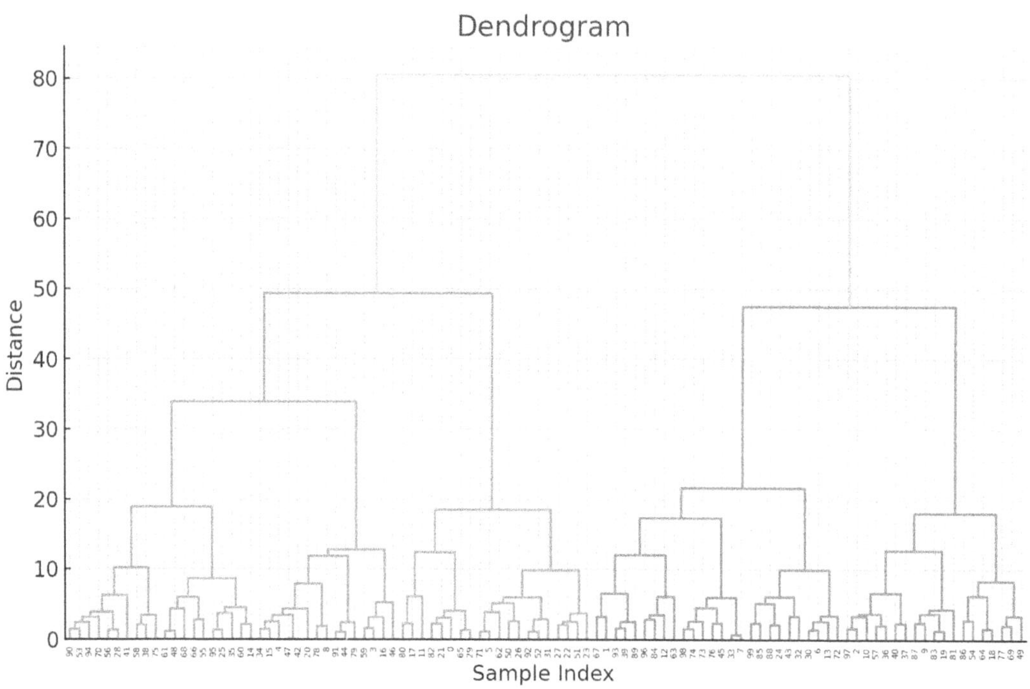

Figure 8.5 Dendrogram graph vs with distance.

on a survey of academic and industry forensic investigators, privacy regulations and legal frameworks for the collection use and disclosure of IoT data were pointed out as challenges in forensic investigations while maintaining legal and ethical compliance.

8.2.3 Opportunities for IoT data forensics

However, it must be noted that there seem to be potential benefits for the forensic investigators who seek to harness the enormous flow of data as provided by the IoT environment. The following are some opportunities for IoT data forensics:

1. Enhanced Contextual Understanding: IoT data contains the great amount of contextual information that describes the interactions, behaviors of devices, and the environment they exist in, which helps forensic investigators obtain better understanding of the context of security breaches or crimes.
2. Early Detection of Security Incidents: With REAL-TIME monitoring and analysis of Internet of Medical Things (IoMT) data, forensic investigators can identify that at least one or multiple kinds of security incidents, data anomalies, or a sign of compromise happened early in the investigative process in attempts to reduce the threats of attacks.
3. Correlation and Link Analysis: IoT information allows forensic analysts to link apparently unrelated events, connected with evidence, including sensor values, logs, and network traffic, to identify chronologies of events and connections between different components of a cyberattack.
4. Proactive Threat Intelligence: IoT data has to be obtained from various sources which can be later analyzed by forensic investigators to detect new threats, risks, and attack patterns to improve organizational security.

8.3 LITERATURE REVIEW

Based on the literature review, it is apparent that the popularity and evolutionary growth of IoT devices have shifted the face of digital investigation providing novel challenges and potentialities. The literature review of this chapter focuses on IoT forensics with an intention of identifying existing and future research methods, issues, and directions in the field where research is rapidly expanding. Based on the analysis of academic works and industry reports and adopting practical case studies, this review seeks to provide a clear presentation and clearer vision of the current best practices in IoT forensics.

8.3.1 Overview of IoT forensic research

The literature reviewed addresses various aspects of IoT forensics such as the type of methodology used, methods used to acquire data and analysis tools, legal and ethical issues, and future developments. Several frameworks and models have also been developed with regard to IoT forensic investigation evidencing that analysis of characteristics of IoT devices, communication protocols as well as forms of data are vital.

8.3.2 Forensic methodologies and frameworks

In the field of IoT forensics, many research studies have developed frameworks and methodologies suitable to this context. These frameworks offer the blueprint for the gathering, archiving, and processing of data from IoT gadgets. Several such models are the IoT forensics framework which defines a formal procedure on how IoT forensic investigation should be conducted, and the digital investigation process model that explains how traditional forensic processes can be applied when investigating IoT environments.

8.3.3 Data acquisition and analysis techniques

IoT forensic is the scientific approach aimed to identify IoT and/or related devices, to extract information, and to analyze the data gathered from IoT devices, PC, LAN, WAN, or cloud services. Some of the existing works in the domain have focused on harvesting information from IoT devices, monitoring network traffic, and analyzing sensor data, log files, and configuration settings. Other envisioned approaches to IoT data include Big Data analytics and Data Mining techniques, including machine learning for figuring out data patterns, anomalies, and compromise indicators.

8.3.4 Challenges and limitations

However, there are still some challenges and limitations of the IoT forensics research which has limited the success of the forensic investigation in IoT domain. This includes huge amount of heterogeneous data from the IoT units, absence of established digital forensic processes and methods, and problems of data collection especially from the closed or black-box IoT components. Also formerly, privacy issues, legal issues, and ethical issues are key challenges for any forensic examiner who is working on IoT investigations.

8.3.5 Legal and ethical considerations

This work demonstrates that IoT forensics has a strong link with legal and ethical issues such as privacy rights and data protection regulations, and issues of jurisdiction. Having discussed the nature of IoT and its role in data collection, the next scholarly area is the field of law where IoT legal aspects and entities are concerned, namely, the aspects of data storage, processing and utilization, and the admissibility of IoT evidence in civil and criminal proceedings. Also, the issue of privacy and/or ethical requirements like consent, ownership, and disclosure is central to the overall scrupulousness of IoT forensic investigation.

8.3.6 Emerging trends and future directions

The current scholars have characterized the advancements and directions of IoT forensics in current literature based on new trends in analysis techniques and evaluation methods, roles and applications of AI and ML for IoT Big Data, and the increasing focus of the IoT community on cooperation and sharing of information. However, researchers still stress the significance of continuous standardization process, the creation of various legal requirements to control the IoT forensics' development and the cooperation between different branches of science.

8.3.7 Forensic tools and technologies

The IoT forensics investigations have been supported by tools and technologies designed by researchers and practitioners. These tools extend from the specific application software for data acquisition and analysis to dedicated hardware gadgets for sniffing the network and for performing forensic copying of IoT devices. Some are limited to certain IoT areas, for example, to get information from the built-in systems or to study communication channels; others offer complete toolkits for IoT forensic investigations.

8.3.8 Digital evidence management

Challenges with finding and managing the digital evidence in IoT forensics investigations stem from the vast and varied character of IoT information. Various works have been undertaken seeking to define how logs from IoT devices can be stored and managed, through the application of DEMS as well as central repositories. These systems enable proper storage, retrieval of the digital evidence as well as sharing of such evidence without compromising the chain of custody, and the evidential worth of the evidence in question, throughout the investigative process.

8.3.9 Case studies and practical applications

In addition, real-world use cases and scenarios only add a level of authenticity to the discussion of the subject of IoT forensics. Several authors and professionals have reported their work experience investigating forensic incidents in different IoT contexts, such as smart homes, ICS, and wearable technology. The above case studies are testimony to the fact that IoT can only be understood with the actual complexity of such network environments and the challenges that forensic experts face when attempting to extract digital evidence and support investigative actions.

8.3.10 Standardization efforts and regulatory developments

The work of standardization and regulation authorities is of key importance to the practice of IoT forensics and its processes, with standardization for effective comparison, reliable methods, and interlinked processes. National and international organizations including the International Organization for Standardization (ISO) and NIST have produced guidelines and best practices for digital forensics more broadly and, more specifically, for IoT settings. Also, to mitigate these issues legal authorities and trade organizations have set guidelines and standards for gathering, storing, and analyzing IoT data and the required certification.

8.3.11 Interdisciplinary collaboration and knowledge sharing

It is important that IoT forensics research involves a combination of fields, and that people involved in the different subdomains of IoT forensics share their findings. IoT forensic research, practice, law enforcement agencies, regulatory authorities, and the industries involved require continuous information sharing and exchange of knowledge and experiences gained from IoT forensic investigations. Professional associations and research working groups and consortia are effective means whereby people can come together, share knowledge, and learn, and further research ideas and practice in, and approaches to, IoT forensics.

8.3.12 Future directions and research opportunities

Several areas point out the specific directions that should be further investigated and developed in the field of IoT forensics in the future. Such are improvements in forensic method and equipment, for instance, the using of machine learning as well as AI to analyze the data received from IoT, the use of new forensic procedures and frameworks specifically for IoT, and the research and understanding of new possibility for coming problems and threats in the field of IoT. Therefore, research from other fields, new regulations, and fruitful partnerships with industries will become important prerequisites for the continuous development of IoT forensics and its ability to protect digital evidence in The IoT environment.

8.4 EXPERIMENTAL SETUP

The position of the experimental setup as the basis of the IoT forensics investigation is critical since it defines the approach to collecting, examining, and interpreting digital data from IoT devices. This chapter covers details of how to design IoT-based experiments while considering the peculiarities of IoT space. It is crucial for forensic investigators to understand how to work in IoT environment in order to obtain guidance that will be helpful in investigations, thanks to the tools, techniques, and methodologies used in IoT.

8.4.1 Designing the experimental environment

1. Define Objectives and Scope: It is also pivotal to clearly define goals and extent of a forensic investigation – which IoT devices, which communication protocols, which kinds of data have to be looked at. Goals to be achieved in an experiment should be well defined to aid in creation of experimental setting as well as help in directing investigation activities.
2. Select Representative Devices: Picking up a number of IoT devices that are as diverse as possible, which reflects the target environment, such as sensors, actuators, gateways, and controllers. It is also important to take manufacturer, device model, and firmware, as well as the communication layers into consideration in order to provide adequate coverage of the IoT structure.
3. Configure Testbed Environment: Design an IoT-based lab environment that will mimic the IoT real-world implementations but at the same time will enable manipulated control of variables. Depending on the depth of the target environment replication, one needs to properly set up the network, deploy the IoT devices, and define proper communication channels.

8.4.2 Data acquisition and collection

1. Identify Data Sources: Analyze the type of digital evidence that is present within the experimental environment and some of the ones to consider include device logs, network traffic, sensors data, configuration settings, and cloud services. Recording of sources of data helps in confirming completeness hence data acquisition plan preparation.
2. Employ Forensic Imaging Techniques: Employ image duplication technologies to produce accurate duplicates of IoT devices' record storage elements and chips as well as all related storages. Remote imaging maintains the objects' unaltered copy and allows for further examination while disconnected from the network.
3. Capture Network Traffic: Use network-monitoring tools to capture data flow on the IoT networks between devices, gateways, and other systems. Gain packet interception data, flow records, and protocol level logical logs to model flows and search for deviations or abnormalities.

8.4.3 Data analysis and interpretation

1. Extract and Parse Data: Identify required information from forensic images, logs, and network traffic through the use of forensic tools and software. Encrypt data into appropriate structures for the analysis of the conversions that transpire, such as time stamps, identification numbers of devices participated, meta communication data, and data contents of the payload.
2. Analyze Sensor Readings: Exploit data arising from the IoT sensors to understand device behavior and the prevailing environment. The proposed analytical techniques include the use of statistical analysis, time series analysis, and pattern recognition to get sufficient knowledge from the sensor readings.
3. Correlate Digital Evidence: Connect seemingly unrelated artifacts of activity in digital investigations to achieve a logical timeline and infer relations among components of an investigation. Locate the cause, relevance, and interrelationships of IoT devices, users, and events throughout developing a story from the occurrence.

8.4.4 Validation and verification

1. Validate Findings: Use known accurate results or reference sources for the purpose of verifying findings and conclusions made from data analysis. Run validation tests, cross checking, and collateral verification to check and double check the merits of findings generated out of investigations conducted.
2. Document Findings: Write investigation report that includes information about investigation processes, methods of investigation, and results of investigation of digital evidence by using the scheme of the experimental setup, data acquisition, and analysis techniques, and an interpretation of findings. Gathering evidence also assists in making the process very objective and allocates accountability to the findings.

8.4.5 Considerations and challenges

1. Device Heterogeneity: It is important to design a system that can overcome problems that may arise due to the differences that may exist in the hardware, firmware, operation systems as well as the communication structures of the devices in use in the IoT system. Identify the approaches to address the multiple devices and issues pertaining to interoperability within the space of experimentation.
2. Privacy and Legal Considerations: Comply with privacy laws, regulatory frameworks, and professional ethics on handling of IoT-collected data in forensic cases. Get permits, consent, and warrants where the experiments being carried out involve personal or sensitive information.
3. Scalability and Resource Constraints: In addition, concern the feasibility and resource limitations of the experimental design due to the high number of smart devices in large-scale IoT environments or in constrained LF settings. Reduce the usage of necessary resources during data gathering and data analysis activities while, at the same time, increasing the efficiency of investigations.

8.5 LEGAL CONSIDERATIONS

Since IoT devices are used in many cases widely, there is a growing number of problems related to IoT forensics and their regulation by law. This chapter looks into the legal dynamism that forensic investigators have to factor when gathering, processing, and understanding electronic evidence IoT devices. Therefore, there is a need for forensic practitioners to acquaint themselves with the legal parameters, regulatory frameworks, and jurisprudence in IoT environments to apply the law and ethics in conducting the investigations.

8.5.1 Legal frameworks and regulations

1. International Standards: There are some international standards and guidelines for sources of digital forensics among which there are specific guidelines for IoT environments, for example, the norms of the ISO and the International Electrotechnical Commission (IEC). These studies outline the principles that have to be followed regarding evidence acquisition, storage, and examination as a way of meeting the international laws on the same.
2. Data Protection Regulations: Privacy-preserving legislations, which include EU General Data Protection Regulation (GDPR) and the California Consumer Privacy Act (CCPA) dictate the collection, processing, and storage of personal information gathered from IoT devices. This means forensic investigators have to conform to these regulations in order to safeguard individuals' privacy and to possible legal concerns as well.
3. Cybersecurity Laws: The Cybersecurity Act formulated in the European Union have set up the rules and regulation for the organization to safeguard the IoT devices from cyber threats and share the security breaches with the concerned authority; and for the US, the Cybersecurity Information Sharing Act (CISA) established the similar requirements. Surveillance investigations are incredibly essential in determining instances of the violation of cybersecurity laws.
4. Electronic Evidence Rules: Most countries have adopted legal provisions concerning electronic evidence that relates to acceptance, identification, and retention of the evidence at trial. Forensic investigators have to follow such rules and guidelines to be able to use the information gained from the IoT devices and use them as evidence in the court without possibility of nullification.

8.5.2 Jurisdictional challenges

1. Cross-Border Investigations: IoT forensics investigations may span across different jurisdictions and thus raise the question of which country or jurisdiction's laws apply to IoT devices that are situated in different countries or the region in general. Law enforcement requires access in forms of a mutual legal assistance treaty, data protection laws, and conflicting legal systems to effectively request for and share digital evidence and cooperate during cross border investigations.
2. Extraterritorial Application of Laws: These laws, for instance, the US SCA and GDPR create legal problems regarding the powers of jurisdiction of the law enforcement and the privacy of the individuals whose data is stocked or processed by foreign companies. In the IoT devices and cloud data investigations, forensic investigators have to regard the extraterritorial laws' consequences.

8.5.3 Legal challenges in IoT forensics

1. Chain of Custody: The present chapter stresses how this area regards acquiring and preserving the chain of custody as crucial for the admissibility and credibility of digital evidence in legal context. Nonetheless, due to decentralized IoT typology and the absence of a universally acceptable approach to IoT digital forensics, it is still

challenging to maintain chain of custody and prove the genuineness of IoT derived digital evidence.

2. Data Ownership and Consent: As people start owning IoT devices, privacy issues emerge concerning ownership, consent, and privacy rights of the data collected from analyzing people's behaviors, preferences, and activities. IoT data must be collected, analyzed, or disclosed at least with the permission, consent, and warrant as required as per the legal and ethical considerations of the forensic investigators.
3. Encryption and Data Protection: Protocols in use include end to end encryption and encryption at rest which poses great challenges to forensic analysis since the gathered content cannot be viewed without decryption keys. Encryption always poses problems to forensic investigators, additionally there are legal issues that have to be met such as court order or search warrant to gain legal permission to access encrypted IoT data.

8.5.4 Ethical considerations

1. Respect for Privacy Rights: Expert witnesses in forensics have professional responsibility and jurisdictional constraints that prevent them from acquiring or disseminating any information beyond entity's legal personality needs during investigation. Explaining why it is better to avoid collecting and storing personal data: privacy risks are lowered, and all legal and ethical requirements are met.
2. Impartiality and Objectivity: There are rules that must not be violated by the forensic investigators; these include adverse interest bias and partiality. The key reason is that professionalism in ethics and conduct strengthens public confidence in forensic science.
3. Transparency and Accountability: Given the nature of forensic work, forensic investigators must ideally be open and show crucial levels of essential professionalism by providing accountability of investigative work tasks as well as moments, procedures, and decisions made through documentation of investigative processes, methodologies, and intended findings. Transparency makes the authorities accountable and guarantees that investigation will not be conducted based on unsound notions.

8.5.5 Case law and precedents

1. Court Decisions: Court decisions and precedents play a significant role in shaping the legal landscape surrounding IoT forensics, establishing legal principles, and interpreting statutory provisions. Forensic investigators must stay informed about relevant case law and rulings to understand how courts have addressed legal issues and applied legal standards in similar cases.
2. Legal Challenges: Court challenges and legal disputes involving IoT forensics raise important legal issues concerning evidence admissibility, data privacy, and procedural fairness. Analyzing court decisions and legal opinions provides valuable insights into emerging trends, challenges, and best practices in IoT forensics from a legal perspective.

8.6 LIMITATION AND CONCLUSION

Along with the growth of usage of IoT technology, more issues arise as forensic investigators try to get justice in IoT spaces. This chapter overviews the constraints associated with IoT forensics investigations and gives a final conclusion, capturing the research findings, recommendations, and the future study directions in IoT forensics.

8.6.1 Limitations of IoT forensics

1. Device Heterogeneity: The various IoT devices connected that Dayanna use involve unique hardware, firmware, and frequency of communication that trouble forensic analysts. While capturing images and videos from the relevant device is relatively straightforward, a common challenge arises from ensuring compatibility with as many different types of devices and operating systems as possible and, more crucially, extracting digital evidence from proprietary or closed systems.
2. Data Volume and Complexity: IoT deployments produce prodigious data from the connected sensors, actuators, and network modules which makes DAQ, storage, and analysis difficult. Monitoring and controlling the amount and heterogeneity of IoT data calls for application of suitable tools and methods for Big Data processing.
3. Security Vulnerabilities: The connected things present in smart homes expose themselves to various kinds of threats pertaining to malware, unauthorized access, and much more. Security incidents in IoT systems need to be investigated to the root level and also consider preventive steps to be taken which complicates forensic investigation processes.
4. Legal and Ethical Considerations: Legal issues that are directly linked to IoT forensics include privacy legal aspects, geographical locations, and legal regulations. When practicing, forensic investigators have to work under legal constraints in terms of ethics while abiding by the laws since the access of digital evidence involves breakout of people's rights and the law protecting their information.

8.6.2 Conclusion

1. Key Findings: IoT computing evidentiary investigations necessarily have to involve specialized skills, methods, and instruments to overcome the barriers induced by the inter-device variability, data characteristics, security threats, and legal implications. In this study, it has been established that by following the best practices and the current ethical standards in the field of digital forensics, investigators can successfully collect, analyze, and interpret IoT device data in order to enhance the investigation processes.
2. Best Practices: Cautionary points for good practices on IoT forensics are as follows:
   - Setting goals and specifying the limits of an IoT forensic investigation
   - Choosing appropriate IoT devices
   - Preparing the IoT testbed environment
   - Identifying the sources of IoT digital evidence
   - Transferring forensic images of IoT devices
   - Collecting network traffic data
   - Analyzing IoT sensor data
   - Associating IoT digital evidence to support conclusions
3. Future Directions: As discussed and highlighted in the chapter, the following is a research agenda for future work in IoT forensics: Innovation and technical progression in both the forensic process and the modes of analyzing digital assets also require collaboration between many fields and disciplines as well as the introduction of new regulation enforcing tools to effectively progress the field and the credibility of digital evidence found in IoT settings.
4. Conclusion: Summing up, we stated that IoT forensics has its limitations and potential for forensic investigators and that problem-solving in the context of IoT environment is possible only through the cooperation of various specialists from different fields. This chapter shows that by overcoming the stated limitations, practicing the discussed

best practices, and adopting various emerging trends, the respective forensic practitioners would be able to protect the respective digital evidence, as well as the overall investigative processes, in the connected world. Further work, development, and more beneficial cooperation will be required to provide the improved result and usage of IoT forensics and cybersecurity in the future society.

8.7 FUTURE SCOPE

This chapter examined some of the goals and challenges of future IoT forensics based on present and emerging issues in the domain. This chapter presents the current and potential research areas of IoT forensics in terms of trends, prospects, technologies, and applications. As a result, forensic investigators will be able to respond proactively and better prepare themselves and others to face new difficulties in the age of connectedness.

8.7.1 Emerging trends in IoT forensics

1. Edge Computing and Fog Computing: The adoption of edge computing and fog computing also presents a problem to IoT's forensic because data processing and storage are now being done at the network margin. It is important that forensic investigators come up with the strategies of acquiring, processing, and interpreting digital evidence that resides in the different layers of the edge devices, gateway devices, and the fog nodes.
2. Blockchain Technology: Blockchain offers to transform IoT data into more reliable kind by providing decentralized and tamper-proof data storage for it. Blockchain applications can be of great benefit to forensic investigators concerned with maintaining the chains of custody, data genuineness, and integrity in IoT cases.
3. Artificial Intelligence and Machine Learning: The combination of AI and ML allows for the ability to extract code or find patterns, characteristics, and signs of intrusion from IoT data sets. AI and ML are also valuable tools that forensic investigators can use to support investigative work, identify threats in situ, and prophesy future threats in real time.
4. Quantum Computing: Quantum computing represents both a threat and a new area of research with regard to IoT forensics because new cryptographic algorithms may need to be employed to protect IoT data from attacks by quantum computing techniques. FL can only rely on its ability to continually learn from past attacks in order to be ready for future cryptographic threats while forensic investigators are compelled to create quantum-safe forensic procedures to handle new threats.

8.7.2 Research directions in IoT forensics

1. Forensic Imaging Techniques: Further research on IoT forensics should concentrate on proposing state-of-the art forensic imaging methods that capture volatile information, remote, and encrypted information storage in IoT devices. Doubtless, new approaches to obtaining and preserving digital evidence based on IoT new structures such as edge- and fog computing will be crucial for solving new issues in the context of forensic activities.
2. Forensic Analysis Tools: The authors suggested that the IoT context requires dedicated forensic analysis paradigms from single or interconnected smart devices; in this context, it is essential to formulate the tasks of future research: when developing IoT forensic analysis tools, the experts should focus on unique features of IoT devices and

their interaction with other devices, as well as the tasks of parsing, correlating, and visualizing IoT data. Forensic linking with AI and ML can facilitate more scalable, accurate, and effective approaches to the extraction of information for forensic investigation from large-scale IoT implementations.

3. Privacy-Preserving Techniques: As the awareness of data security increases in the future, researchers should also consider the privacy-preserving of IoT forensics. Differential privacy, homomorphic encryption, and federated learning have opportunities to transform the approach to anonymize sensitive IoT data for forensic purposes.
4. Standardization and Certification: This involves standardization effort and certification program for IoT that define standard practices and mechanism toward IoT forensics. Subsequent research should therefore aim at establishing techniques, procedures, and assessment requirements that produce consistent, compatible, and accurate findings in investigative forensic processes.

8.7.3 Technological advancements in IoT forensics

1. Forensic Toolkits and Platforms: Due to IoT forums and toolkits, forensic analysts can perform data gathering, analysis, and reporting processes, which are otherwise tiresome to do manually. In speaking, joined-up solutions, which encompasses data collection, processing, and visualization, optimally address the mode of investigation tasks and the management of massive IoT datasets.
2. Forensic-as-a-Service (FaaS): New models of outsourcing are appearing; specifically, there is a concept of FaaS models that are based on cost-effective approaches to realizing the possibility of delegation to service providers. FaaS platforms which are cloud-based allow organizations to access forensic knowledge, support, and solutions only when needed, which is helpful when dealing with IoT organizations that do not employ extensive in-house forensic services.
3. Internet of Medical Things (IoMT): The increase in IoMT devices creates new concerns for healthcare forensics because medical gadgets gather and share private patient information. Future development of IoMT forensic science is crucial in order to safeguard patient lives, keep patients' privacy under wraps, and ensure IoMT's accurate efficacy.
4. Cross-Domain Collaborations: Academic–industrial–governmental partnerships are crucial for IoT forensics progress as are cross-disciplinary projects involving police authorities. Such partnerships promote the dissemination of expertise, the exchange of best practices, and the development of inter-disciplinary research agendas that have the potential to advance, essentially at the same time ensuring future proof against new cyber threats.

BIBLIOGRAPHY

1. Kaushik, K. (2022). A Novel Approach to Secure Files Using Color Code Authentication. In: Sugumaran, V., Upadhyay, D., Sharma, S. (eds) Advancements in Interdisciplinary Research. AIR 2022. Communications in Computer and Information Science, vol. 1738. Springer, Cham. https://doi.org/10.1007/978-3-031-23724-9_4
2. Kaushik, K., Singh, V., Manikandan, V. P. (2022). A Novel Approach for an Automated Advanced MITM Attack on IoT Networks. In: Sugumaran, V., Upadhyay, D., Sharma, S. (eds) Advancements in Interdisciplinary Research. AIR 2022. Communications in Computer and Information Science, vol. 1738. Springer, Cham. https://doi.org/10.1007/978-3-031-23724-9_6
3. Kaushik, K., Naik, V. (2023). Making Ductless-Split Cooling Systems Energy Efficient Using IoT. In: 2023 15th International Conference on Communication Systems & Networks (COMSNETS), Bangalore, India, pp. 471–473. https://doi.org/10.1109/COMSNETS56262.2023.10041408

4. Porwal, P., Devare, M. (2024, August 1). Scientific Impact Analysis: Unraveling the Link between Linguistic Properties and Citations. Journal of Informetrics. https://doi.org/10.1016/j.joi.2024.101526
5. Porwal, P., Devare, M. (2023, September 20). Citation Count Prediction Using Weighted Latent Semantic Analysis (wlsa) and Three-Layer-Deep-Learning Paradigm: A Meta-Heuristic Approach. Multimedia Tools and Applications. https://doi.org/10.1007/s11042-023-16957-8
6. Porwal, P., Devare, M. (2021). "Citation Classification Prediction Implying Text Features Using Natural Language Processing and Supervised Machine Learning Algorithms," Communications in Computer and Information Science, Jan. 01, 2021. https://doi.org/10.1007/978-981-16-0507-9_46
7. Tatkare, K. A., Devare, M. (2019). "A Novel Region Duplication Detection Algorithm Based on Hybrid Approach," Social Science Research Network, Jan. 01, 2019. https://dx.doi.org/10.2139/ssrn.3425340
8. Mohurle, S., Devare, M. (2019). Fuzzy Probability Model for Quantifying the Effectiveness of the MSW Compost. In: 2019 International Conference on Nascent Technologies in Engineering (ICNTE), Navi Mumbai, India, pp. 1–6. https://doi.org/10.1109/ICNTE44896.2019.8945830
9. Shitole, A., Devare, M. "Machine Learning Supported Statistical Analysis of IoT Enabled Physical Location Monitoring Data," Springer eBooks, Jan. 01, 2020. https://doi.org/10.1007/978-3-030-41862-5_13
10. Devare, M., Thakral, M. (2023). Enhancing Automatic Speech Recognition System Performance for Punjabi Language through Feature Extraction and Model Optimization. International Journal of Intelligent Systems and Applications in Engineering, vol. 12, no. 8s, pp. 307–313.
11. Thakral, M., Devare, M. (2023). Designing an Automatic Speech Recognition System for the Minor Age Group. In: 2023 4th International Conference on Communication, Computing and Industry 6.0 (C2I6), Bangalore, India, pp. 1–5, https://doi.org/10.1109/C2I659362.2023.10431311
12. Thakral, M., Singh, R. K., Kaushik, K. (2022). Integration of Blockchain Technology and Intelligent System for Potential Technologies. Chapman and Hall/CRC eBooks, Aug. 23, 2022. https://www.taylorfrancis.com/chapters/edit/10.1201/9781003193425-6/integration-blockchain-technology-intelligent-system-potential-technologies-manish-thakral-rishi-raj-singh-keshav-kaushi
13. Thakral, M., Singh, S. (2022). "A Secure Bank Transaction Using Blockchain Computing and Forest Oddity," Blockchain Technologies, Jan. 01, 2022. https://link.springer.com/chapter/10.1007/978-981-19-1960-2_6
14. Thakral, M., Singh, R. R., Singh, S. P. (2022). An Extensive Framework Focused on Smart Agriculture Based Out of IoT. In: Choudhury, A., Singh, T.P., Biswas, A., Anand, M. (eds) Evolution of Digitized Societies Through Advanced Technologies. Advanced Technologies and Societal Change. Springer, Singapore. https://doi.org/10.1007/978-981-19-2984-7_12
15. Thakral, M., Singh, R. K., Kalghatgi, B. V. (2022). "Cybersecurity and Ethics for IoT System: A Massive Analysis," Transactions on Computer Systems and Networks, Jan. 01, 2022. https://link.springer.com/chapter/10.1007/978-981-19-1585-7_10
16. Singh, R. R., Thakral, M., Kaushik, S., Jain, A., Chhabra, G. (2022). A Blockchain-Based Expectation Solution for the Internet of Bogus Media. In: Hemanth, D.J., Pelusi, D., Vuppalapati, C. (eds) Intelligent Data Communication Technologies and Internet of Things. Lecture Notes on Data Engineering and Communications Technologies, vol. 101. Springer, Singapore. https://doi.org/10.1007/978-981-16-7610-9_28
17. Thakral, M., Jain, A., Kadyan, V., Jain, A. (2021). An Innovative Intelligent Solution Incorporating Artificial Neural Networks for Medical Diagnostic Application. In: 2021 Sixth International Conference on Image Information Processing (ICIIP), Shimla, India, pp. 529–532. https://doi.org/10.1109/ICIIP53038.2021.9702631
18. Thakral, M., Singh, R. R., Jain, A., Chhabra, G. (2021). Rigid Wrap ATM Debit Card Fraud Detection Using Multistage Detection. In: 2021 6th International Conference on Signal Processing, Computing and Control (ISPCC), Solan, India, pp. 774–778. https://doi.org/10.1109/ISPCC53510.2021.9609521
19. Girish, I., Kumar, A., Kumar, A., M., A. (2020). Driver Fatigue Detection. In: 2020 IEEE 17th India Council International Conference (INDICON), New Delhi, India, pp. 1–6. https://doi.org/10.1109/INDICON49873.2020.9342456
20. Prajeesha, A. M. (2021). EDGE Computing Application in SMART GRID – A Review. In: 2021 Second International Conference on Electronics and Sustainable Communication Systems (ICESC), pp. 1–6. https://doi.org/10.1109/ICESC51422.2021.9532792

21. Udeshi, D. M., Divakarla, S. G. L., Rajdev, N. C., M., A. (2022). Wind Speed Forecasting Using Hybrid Model. In: 2022 IEEE 7th International Conference for Convergence in Technology (I2CT), Mumbai, India, pp. 1–5. https://doi.org/10.1109/I2CT54291.2022.9823995
22. Tammana, A., Amogh, M. P., Gagan, B., Anuradha, M., Vanamala, H. R. (2021). Thermal Image Processing and Analysis for Surveillance UAVs. In: Kaiser, M.S., Xie, J., Rathore, V.S. (eds) Information and Communication Technology for Competitive Strategies (ICTCS 2020). Lecture Notes in Networks and Systems, vol. 190. Springer, Singapore. https://doi.org/10.1007/978-981-16-0882-7_50
23. Balasubramanian, S., Kashyap, R., Cvn, S. T., Anuradha, M. (2020). Hybrid Prediction Model for Type-2 Diabetes with Class Imbalance. In: 2020 IEEE International Conference on Machine Learning and Applied Network Technologies (ICMLANT), Hyderabad, India, pp. 1–6. https://doi.org/10.1109/ICMLANT50963.2020.9355975
24. Yakasiri, M., M., A., B. K., K. (2020). Comparative Analysis of Markov Chain and Polynomial Regression for the Prognostic Evaluation of Wind Power. In: 2020 IEEE International Conference for Innovation in Technology (INOCON), Bengaluru, India, pp. 1–5. https://doi.org/10.1109/INOCON50539.2020.9298374
25. Pai, V. G., M., A. (2020). Comparative Analysis of Marker and Marker-less Augmented Reality in Education. In: 2020 IEEE International Conference for Innovation in Technology (INOCON), Bangluru, India, pp. 1–4. https://doi.org/10.1109/INOCON50539.2020.9298303
26. Yakasiri, M., Avrel, J., Sharma, S., Anuradha, M., Keshavan, B. K. (2019). A Stochastic Approach for the State-Wise Forecast of Wind Speed Using Discrete-Time Markov Chain. In: TENCON 2019 – 2019 IEEE Region 10 Conference (TENCON), Kochi, India, pp. 575–580. https://doi.org/10.1109/TENCON.2019.8929529
27. Chhabra, G., Prasad, A., Marrabenta, V. (2022). Comparison and Performance Evaluation of Human Bio-Field Visualization Algorithm. Archives of Physiology and Biochemistry, vol. 128, no. 2, pp. 321–332. https://doi.org/10.1080/13813455.2019.1680699

Chapter 9

Forensics analysis of IoT network traffic

Udayaprasad P K, Vishwakiran S, Shanthi M, Roja R, and Renuka N D

9.1 INTRODUCTION

9.1.1 Background and motivation

The Internet of Things (IoT) has redefined connectivity and merged the digital and physical realms into an ecosystem of smart, connected things. Connected devices rolled out have triggered an exponential boom in network traffic—volume and variety. That has created a double-edged reality: those new attack surfaces are open to malicious actors while offering more capabilities and services [1]. These threats call for advanced forensics techniques in analysis and inspection of traffic of an IoT network. Packet analysis, being one of the easiest tools utilized in network forensics, can perform magic to trace illegal access, data leaks, or any other exception that can occur due to extensive network traffic data analysis.

This effort is motivated by the urgent necessity of empowering IoT systems with advanced forensic capabilities that are capable of handling high-speed traffic, overcoming encryption hurdles, and providing admissible digital evidence for court proceedings [2,3] from Figure 9.1.

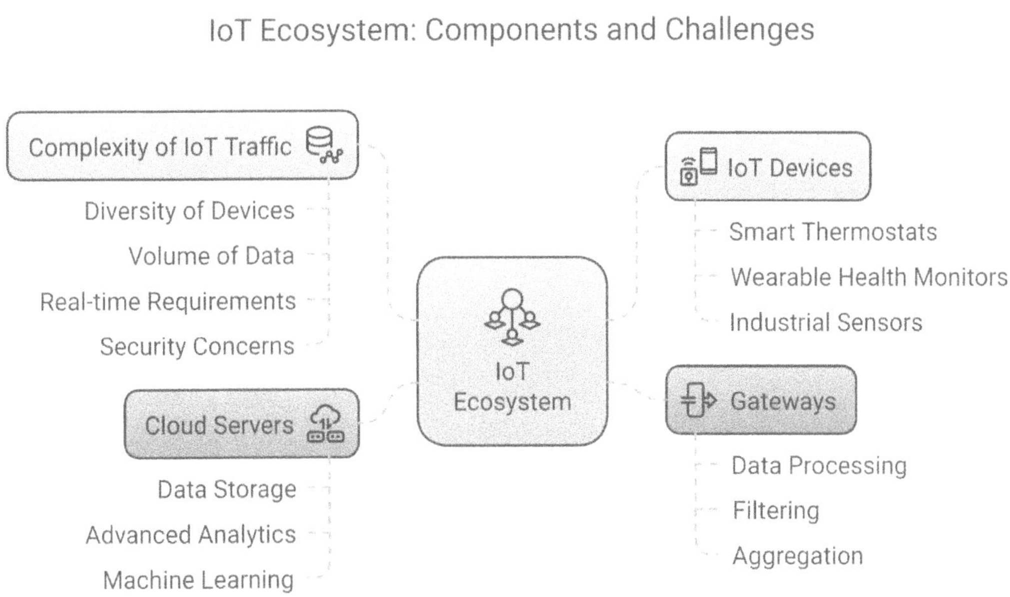

Figure 9.1 IoT network architecture: Interconnected IoT devices, gateways, and cloud servers depict the diversity and complexity of IoT traffic.

DOI: 10.1201/9781003513896-9

9.1.2 Importance of forensics in IoT networks

IoT networks differ significantly from traditional ones in being dynamic, protocol heterogeneous, and having limited resources. All these features make it much more challenging to utilize traditional forensics; rather, most traditional practices are irrelevant while coping with the size and intricacy of IoT environments [4]. The primary responsibilities of IoT network forensics are the following:

- Threat Detection and Mitigation: Forensic techniques allow analyzing network traffic to identify botnet activity, ransomware attacks, and distributed denial of service (DDoS) attacks [5].
- Legal and Compliance Needs: Forensic analysis provides admissible digital evidence in court, supporting law enforcement and regulatory compliance [6].
- Incident Reconstruction: Investigators can utilize packet analysis to replay network events, pinpoint intrusion points, reconstruct attack paths, and identify responsible parties [7].

The growing reliance on IoT by industries ranging from healthcare to manufacturing only heightens the need for specialized forensic solutions to provide security and accountability from Figure 9.2.

9.1.3 Research objectives

The study will achieve the following objectives:

- Construct an efficient and scalable forensic analysis platform for IoT network traffic.
- Harness bleeding-edge techniques in the guise of artificial intelligence (AI) and machine learning (ML) to detect encrypted traffic and anomalous patterns.

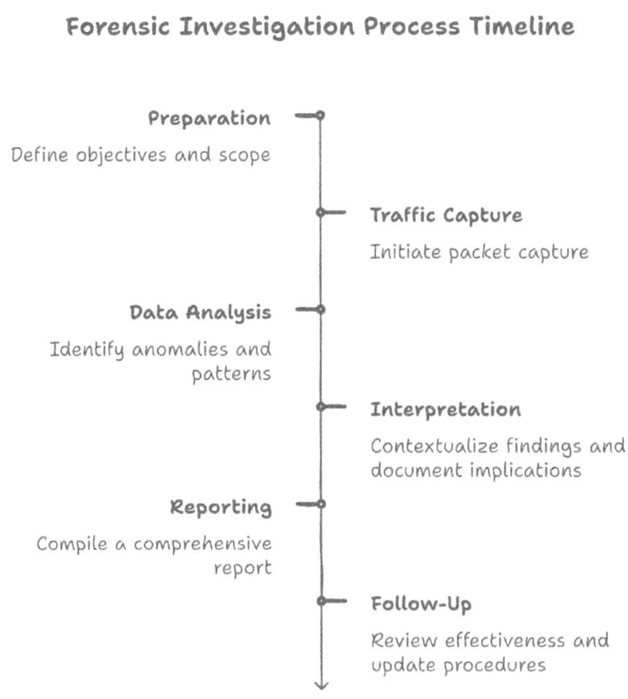

Figure 9.2 Capturing, analyzing, and interpreting network traffic for forensic purposes.

Table 9.1 Key challenges and requirements in IoT network forensics

Challenge	*Description*	*Requirement*
High-speed traffic	IoT generates large volumes of diverse data.	Scalable traffic analysis systems
Encryption	Increased use of encrypted traffic.	Advanced decryption or metadata analysis
Resource constraints	Limited processing power and storage in IoT.	Lightweight forensic algorithms
Heterogeneous protocols	Multiple protocols complicate analysis.	Protocol-agnostic tools
Legal admissibility	Data must be valid as legal evidence.	Clear standards for evidence collection

- Create methods to ensure admissible digital evidence collection despite the disadvantages of IoT devices.
- Highlight the challenges and propose new approaches for emerging issues in IoT network forensics.

In Section 9.2, the literature review discusses the related work, highlighting the gap in IoT forensic techniques. Section 9.3 deals with methodology, detailing data collection, preprocessing, and analysis. Section 9.4 gives proposed framework details the architecture and various components of the forensic system. Sections 9.5 and 9.6 tell experimental results, which present the findings from the simulations and evaluations of the proposed framework and discussion explores the implications, limitations, and recommendations for practical applications. In the final section, the conclusion and Future Work summarizes the main contributions and opens avenues for future investigation (Table 9.1).

9.2 LITERATURE REVIEW

9.2.1 Overview of IoT forensic techniques

The rapid proliferation of IoT devices has given rise to unique forensic challenges, especially in analyzing network traffic from these devices. IoT forensic techniques capture, analyze, and reconstruct traffic data to identify possible security incidents and nefarious activities. Therefore, traditional methods such as packet analysis and deep packet inspection have been adapted for the IoT networks that have diverse communication protocols and are constrained by limited device resources. AI-powered methodologies are fast being applied in the detection of anomaly to efficiently classify network traffic. ML and, most recently, deep learning (DL) have been on the forefront of providing scalability and precision in digital forensic investigations [8–10].

The presence of various protocols and communication standards in IoT networks makes homogeneous analysis difficult. These large, continuous data streams from IoT devices require scalable solutions for real-time processing. Dominant encrypted traffic will seriously deteriorate traditional payload-based analysis and call for innovative approaches in ML-driven flow analysis. The small computing power and on-device storage for IoT devices constrain in-device forensics. Analyzing IoT traffic is subject to strict privacy regulations that complicate the collection and processing of data [11–14] from Figure 9.3.

9.2.2 Comparative analysis of existing solutions

Several forensic solutions have been proposed to address the IoT network traffic challenges. The comparison of these solutions in terms of approach, scalability, and accuracy is given in Table 9.2.

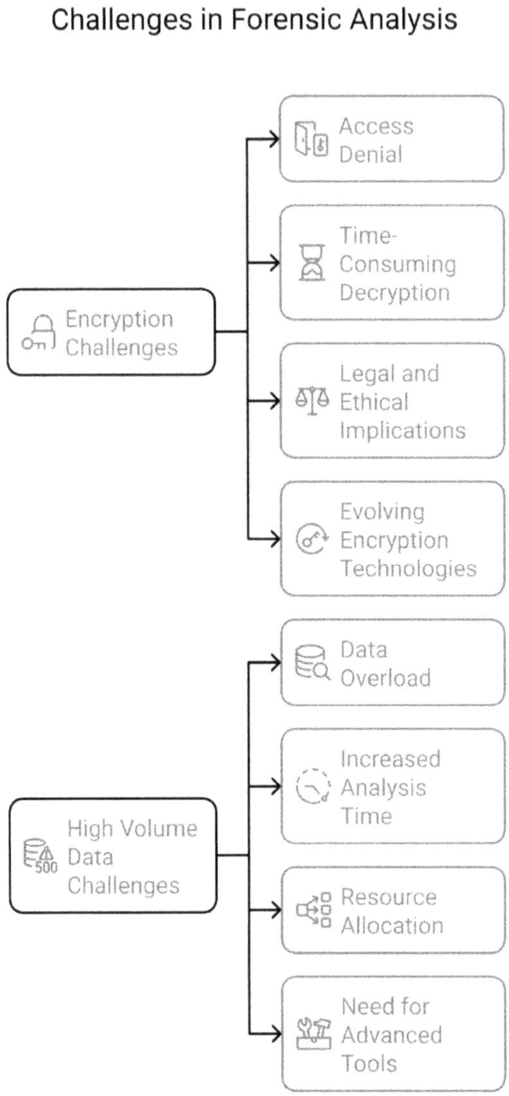

Figure 9.3 Illustrating the challenges (e.g., encryption, high volume) and their impact on forensic analysis techniques.

Table 9.2 Comparison table with different techniques, key features with strength and limitations

Citation	*Technique*	*Key features*	*Strengths*	*Limitations*
[8]	Packet analysis	Basic traceback method, DPI	Detailed traffic reconstruction	Struggles with encrypted traffic
[11,14]	ML-based traffic analysis	Pattern recognition, anomaly detection	Scalability, adaptability	Dataset dependency
[7,12]	Bot-IoT dataset	Realistic attack scenarios, feature optimization	Enables reproducible research	Limited to specific IoT attacks
[15]	SDN-gateway filtering	Ransomware detection, policy-driven	Real-time threat mitigation	High setup complexity

9.2.3 Research gaps identified

Current tools are inefficient to analyze encrypted IoT communication. Representative, open-access datasets are a requirement if results in forensic research are to be replicated. Current solutions usually target specific ecosystems of devices, so the applicability is limited [14] from Figure 9.4. High manual interpretation dependence is an impediment to scalability in large-scale IoT deployments. Forensic solutions must ensure admissibility of evidence in court while preserving the laws of privacy.

9.3 METHODOLOGY

This section proposes the framework and techniques of forensic analysis for IoT network traffic, which includes a data collection framework, preprocessing of traffic data, forensic analysis models, and evaluation metrics.

9.3.1 Data collection framework

9.3.1.1 Sources of IoT network traffic

The data collection phase is very important in forensic analysis, particularly within IoT networks, characterized by heterogeneous devices and protocols from Figure 9.5. Primary sources include the following:

- IoT Device Logs: Information coming from smart sensors, cameras, and actuators.
- Network Gateways: Logs from routers and hubs interconnecting IoT devices.
- Cloud Platforms: IoT data originating from cloud-hosted services.
- Bot-IoT Dataset: Contains various IoT traffic, malicious and benign activities.
- Simulated Testbeds: Emulated environments, realistic to real-world IoT networks.

Figure 9.4 An IoT network with data collection points.

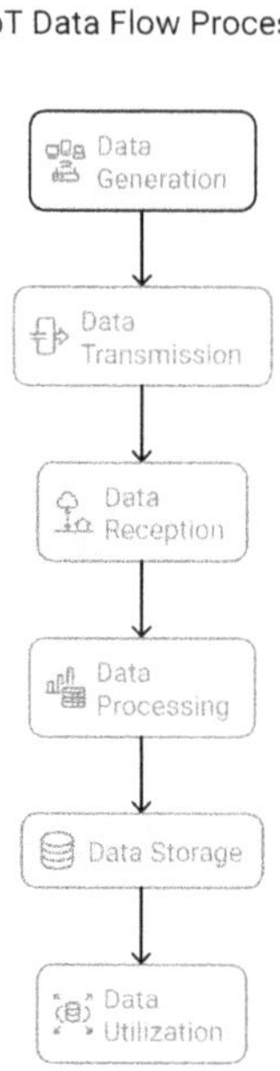

Figure 9.5 A sample flowchart of the data extraction process.

9.3.1.2 Ethical considerations in data collection

Ethical data collection is essential to protect users' privacy and comply with laws. Data anonymization is the removal of personally identifiable information (PII). Consent agreements with obtaining permissions from owners of IoT devices. Regulatory compliance for the adhering to General Data Protection Regulation (GDPR) and similar privacy laws from Figure 9.6.

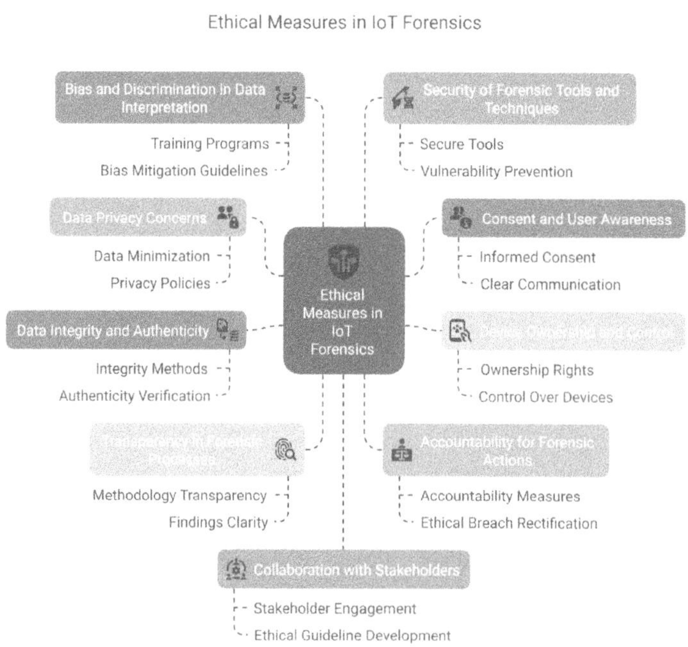

Figure 9.6 Ethical measures in specific IoT forensic challenges.

9.3.2 Preprocessing IoT traffic data

Preprocessing increases the quality of data for analysis. (i) Traffic Filtering: Dropping duplicate or unimportant packets from Figures 9.7 and 9.8. (ii) Feature Extraction: Extraction of relevant features (e.g., timestamps, IPs, protocols). (iii) Standardizing data for uniform processing. (iv) Handling missing data—filling gaps using imputation techniques from Table 9.3.

9.3.3 Forensic analysis models

In ML-based approaches the preprocessing increases the quality of data for analysis. Traffic filtering were dropping duplicate or unimportant packets and feature extraction to

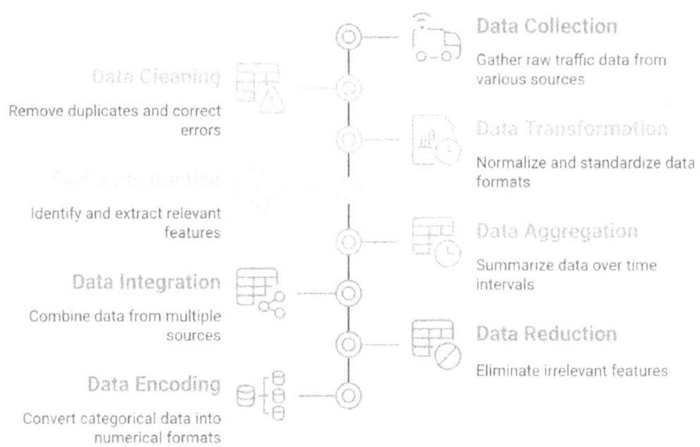

Figure 9.7 A pipeline showing traffic preprocessing steps.

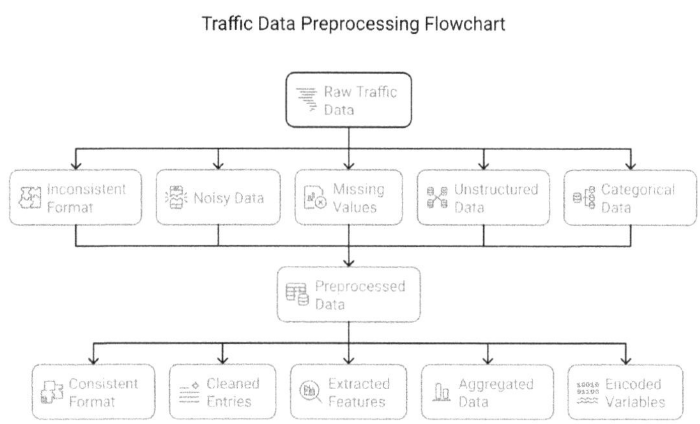

Figure 9.8 A graphical representation of raw vs. preprocessed data.

Table 9.3 Different preprocessing steps with methodology and outcomes

Preprocessing step	*Methodology*	*Outcome*
Traffic filtering [16]	Removing non-IoT traffic	Focused dataset
Feature extraction [17]	Identifying IP, protocol, and timestamp	Key attributes for analysis
Normalization [18]	Min–max scaling	Uniform data distribution
Missing data handling [19]	Mean imputation	Reduced data gaps

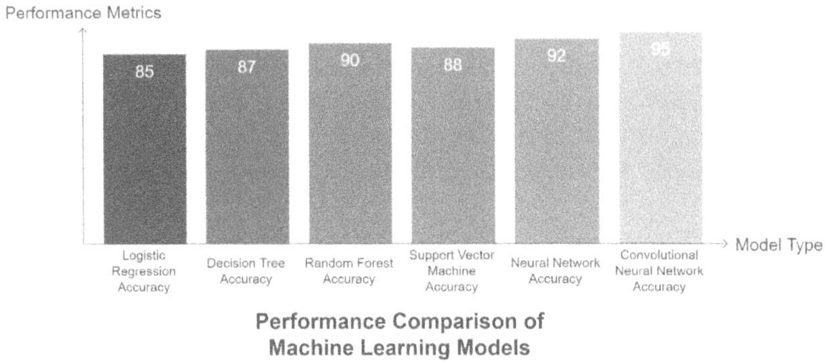

Figure 9.9 A comparative of ML and DL model performances.

identifying the necessary features, like timestamps, IPs, and protocols. The standardizing data to process uniformly. In the process of handling missing data—filling gaps using imputation techniques from Figure 9.9.

The DL for traffic classification models provide higher accuracy for complex IoT data: (i) **Convolutional Neural Networks (CNNs)**: For image-based traffic patterns. (ii) **Recurrent Neural Networks (RNNs)**: For temporal analysis of traffic. (iii) **Graph Neural Networks (GNNs)**: Effective for Decentralized Application (DApp) fingerprinting in IoT blockchain networks [15] from Figure 9.10.

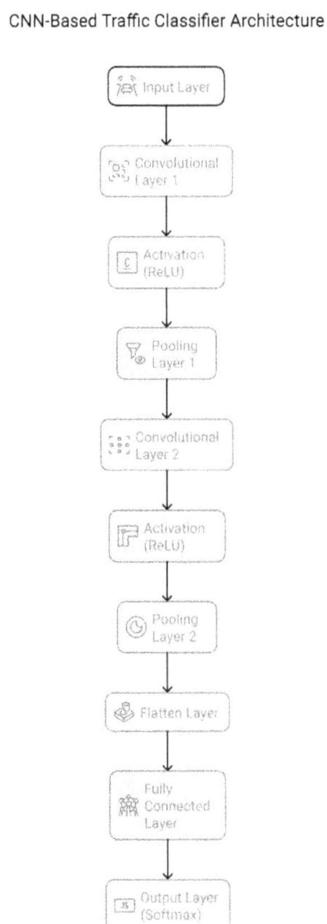

Figure 9.10 An architecture diagram for a CNN-based traffic classifier.

Table 9.4 A different result metric comparison

Metric	*Definition*	*Relevance*
Accuracy	Correct classifications/total instances	General effectiveness of the model
Precision	TP / (TP + FP)	Reliability of positive predictions
Recall	TP / (TP + FN)	Coverage of actual positives
F1-score	2 * (precision * recall) / (precision + recall)	Balance between precision and recall
Execution time	Time for model processing	Real-time applicability

9.3.4 Evaluation metrics

To assess the performance of forensic analysis models, key metrics include the following (Table 9.4):

- **Accuracy:** Ratio of correctly classified instances.
- **Precision and Recall:** Evaluation of true positives vs. false negatives.
- **F1-Score:** Harmonic mean of precision and recall.
- **Receiver Operating Characteristic–Area Under the Curve (ROC-AUC):** Area under the receiver operating characteristic curve.
- **Execution Time:** Time taken for analysis.

9.4 IMPLEMENTATION STEPS

9.4.1 Architecture of the forensic system

The architecture of the forensic system will be designed in such a way that it could efficiently capture, process, and analyze IoT network traffic. Designed as a three-layered architecture from Figure 9.11.

In traffic acquisition layer it is used to capture raw traffic from IoT devices using packet sniffers such as Wireshark or software-defined network (SDN) gateways. It supports various IoT communication protocols such as Message Queuing Telemetry Transport (MQTT), Constrained Application Protocol (CoAP), and HTTP. Next the Processing and Analysis Layer:

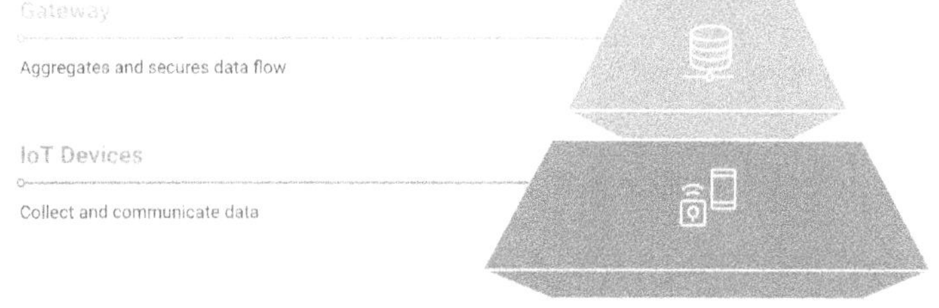

Figure 9.11 The forensic architecture showcasing the three layers, with communication flows between IoT devices, gateways, and the system.

Preprocesses the data by eliminating duplicate traffic. Feature extraction: The data will be feature-extracted using DPI and flow analysis algorithms. Advanced analytics: These features will be analyzed using AI models, e.g., GNNs. Finally in Decision and Reporting Layer: The result is the actionable findings, including identified anomalies or reconstructed attack sequences. Sends reports visually to investigators to enable them to make quick decisions [20–22].

9.4.2 Modules of the framework

9.4.2.1 Traffic capturing and filtering

Tools and Techniques: Packets are captured by tools such as tcpdump, port mirroring, and Address Resolution Protocol (ARP) spoofing. Filtering: Operations such as Berkeley Packet Filter (BPF) filter out duplicate data in preprocessing. Goal: Reduce the size of data without discarding necessary packets [17].

9.4.2.2 Feature extraction for analysis

Packet Features: Includes headers, timestamps, and payload data. **Flow Features** include session length, packet order, and anomalies such as SYN floods. **Tools:** Tools for feature extraction like DPI and entropy analysis are employed to pull out patterns from encrypted traffic [23].

9.4.3 Anomaly detection mechanism

AI Techniques: ML Algorithms: Random forests and support vector machines (SVM) for anomaly classification. DL Models: GNNs for fingerprinting DApp traffic. Detection Goals: Identify ransomware, botnet activity, and DDoS attacks [18].

9.4.4 Workflow description

Forensic workflow: iterative to ensure efficiency and reliability in analysis from Table 9.5.

(i) Traffic Acquisition: IoT traffic is acquired in real time using SDN gateways and stored in PCAP format. Secure storage ensures data integrity in forensic analysis. (ii) Preprocessing: Filters remove irrelevant data (e.g., harmless network chatter). Compression techniques reduce the storage overhead of retaining such captures. (iii) Feature Extraction: Statistical and behavioral features are extracted from network traffic, which is characterized in various ways. Tools recognize key metrics relative to packet sizes, communication protocols, and more. (iv) Analysis and Detection: AI models analyze traffic for anomalies and classify malicious patterns. Visual tools like timelines and entropy plots are used to interpret the findings. (v) Reporting: Generation of detailed reports on anomalies, potential threats, and recommended countermeasures.

Table 9.5 A comparison of techniques for anomaly detection in IoT traffic

Technique	*Application*	*Advantages*	*Challenges*
Random forest [19]	Classification of anomalies	High accuracy, easy implementation	Computational overhead
Graph neural networks [14]	DApp traffic fingerprinting	Captures complex patterns	Requires large training datasets
Entropy analysis [24]	Encrypted traffic detection	Lightweight, interpretable	Limited precision in high-noise environments

9.5 EXPERIMENTAL SETUP AND RESULTS

9.5.1 Simulation environment and tools used

A strong simulation environment was set up to perform forensic analysis on the network traffic of IoT devices. The following configurations and tools were used in the same:

- **Simulation Framework:** Experiments employed packet inspection and intrusion detection using **Wireshark** and **Suricata.** IoTIFY was employed to create a custom-built IoT network simulation that mimicked fundamental IoT traffic patterns.
- **ML Models:** Random forest, SVM, and CNNs were implemented using **Scikit-learn** and **TensorFlow.**
- **Hardware Configuration:** Simulations were run on a system with:
  - Processor: Intel Core i9-10900K
  - RAM: 32 GB DDR4
  - Storage: 1TB SSD
  - Network: Gigabit Ethernet Connection
- **Software Platforms:** Python and MATLAB were utilized for visualization and data analysis.

9.5.2 Dataset description

The experiments utilized two datasets from Table 9.6:

1. **Bot-IoT Dataset:**
   - Size: 72 GB
   - Features: Normal traffic and attack scenarios, including DDoS, data theft, and ransomware.
   - Tools Used for Collection: Wireshark and tcpdump.
2. **Custom IoT Dataset:**
   - Synthesized with IoTIFY to model heterogenous device activity such as industrial IoT and domestic smart appliances.
   - Features: Live traffic and synthesized attack vectors.

9.5.3 Key results and observations

9.5.3.1 Accuracy of detection

The detection models achieved high accuracy rates:

- Random Forest: 89%
- SVM: 92%
- CNN: 97%

Observation: CNN performed better than traditional models as it could identify complex patterns in traffic data.

Table 9.6 A comparison of datasets available

Dataset name	*Size (GB)*	*Attack types*	*Features*
Bot-IoT	72	DDoS, Data Theft	Traffic patterns, payload
Custom IoT	15	Synthetic attacks	Device behavior, metadata

Table 9.7 A result comparison of models

Model	*False positives (%)*	*False negatives (%)*
Random forest	5.4	6.3
SVM	4.1	5.5
CNN	2.3	3.1

9.5.3.2 *False positives and negatives*

- **False Positive Rate:** Random forest (5.4%), SVM (4.1%), CNN (2.3%)
- **False Negative Rate:** Random forest (6.3%), SVM (5.5%), CNN (3.1%)

Observation: DL-based methods significantly minimized false positives and negatives, increasing forensic investigation reliability (Table 9.7).

9.5.3.3 *Real-time implementation challenges*

Challenges faced in real-time analysis:

1. **Volume of Data:** IoT traffic created a large volume; therefore, rapid and efficient data preprocessing was required.
2. **Encryption:** The presence of encrypted traffic makes packet inspection complex and hence requires either advanced decryption or heuristic methods.
3. **Resource Limitations:** Resource-constrained IoT devices further limited the scope of traffic capture and analysis.

9.5.4 Comparative performance analysis

The models were benchmarked against state-of-the-art methods from Figure 9.12 and Table 9.8:

- **Baseline Method:** Traditional DPI tools, such as Snort, achieved 82% accuracy.
- **Proposed Framework:** The CNN model, integrated with the Bot-IoT dataset, achieved the highest accuracy of 97% and reduced the processing latency by 15%.

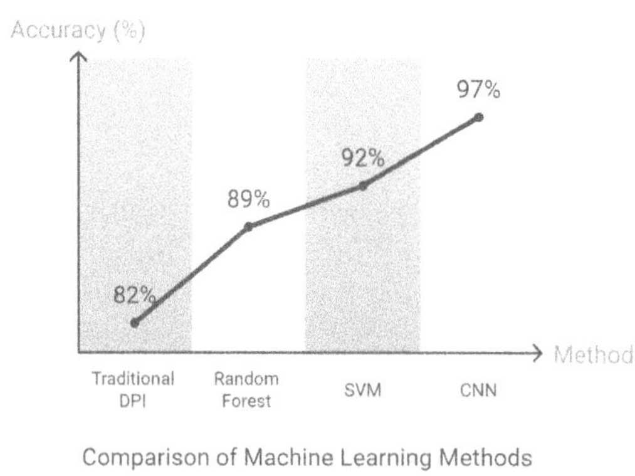

Figure 9.12 Comparing accuracy and processing latency across methods.

Table 9.8 A result comparison for accuracy and processing latency

Method	*Accuracy (%)*	*Processing latency (ms)*
Traditional DPI	82	25
Random forest	89	18
SVM	92	15
CNN	97	12

9.5.5 Implications of findings

Advanced forensic techniques are essential to analyze IoT network traffic, as huge amounts of heterogeneous data require powerful methods to identify malicious activities. Our results have proved that the integration of AI techniques such as ML and DL in such systems significantly enhances the accuracy and efficiency of traffic classification, intrusion detection, and anomaly detection from Figure 9.13.

Creation of IoT-specific datasets, such as the Bot-IoT dataset, has also been a necessary factor in advancing reproducible research in forensic analysis. These datasets will be used by forensic investigators in order to conduct simulations of real-world conditions, test different scenarios, and sharpen detection methodologies. The implications of this are further extended to legal contexts, where better packet inspection and extraction of evidence increase the admissibility of digital evidence in courts.

9.5.6 Limitations of the study

However, some limitations restrict the applicability of the proposed forensic methodologies with promising results: **Scalability Issues:** Due to hardware and computational bottlenecks, analyzing high-speed IoT traffic at scale remains challenging. **Data Privacy Concerns:** Ensuring user privacy while performing deep packet inspection contradicts the invasive

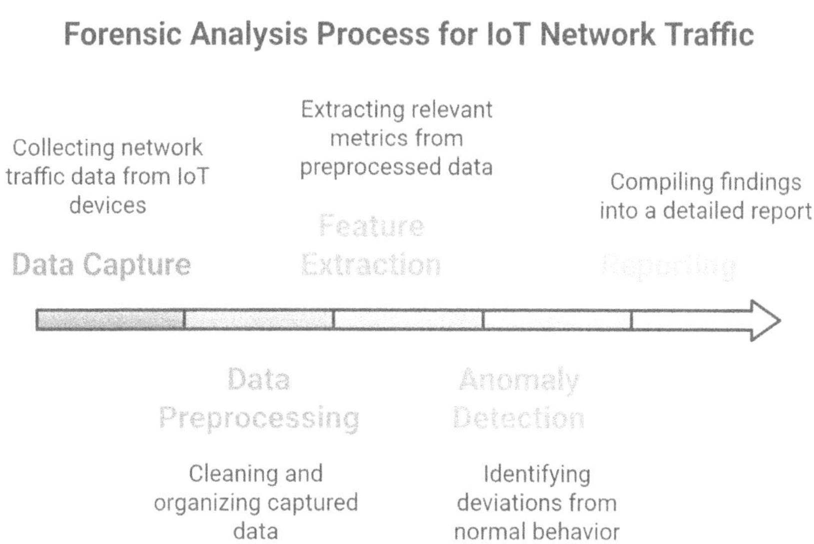

Figure 9.13 A flowchart showing the forensic analysis process for IoT network traffic, from data capture to anomaly detection and reporting.

Table 9.9 Some IoT forensics challenges and their impact comparison

Challenge	*Impact*	*Proposed mitigation*
Scalability	Delayed analysis of network traffic	Cloud-based forensic frameworks
Privacy concerns	Potential breach of sensitive user data	Privacy-preserving techniques in ML models
Dataset limitations	Reduced effectiveness in diverse environments	Continuous dataset enrichment
Real-time analysis	Increased false positives or negatives	Optimization of feature extraction algorithms

nature of detailed forensic analyses. **Dataset Generalization:** Although datasets like Bot-IoT are very valuable, they may not fully represent the real-world IoT traffic diversity, and thus, generalizability may be limited. **Real-Time Constraints:** The current methodologies in real-time analysis come at the cost of accuracy for speed from Table 9.9.

9.5.7 Recommendations for IoT forensic practices

The following recommendations are therefore made in the IoT networks to address some challenges and maximize benefits from forensic analysis: **Adoption of AI-Driven Approaches:** In the increasingly complex IoT environment, this will apply ML and DL algorithms to perform traffic analysis, intrusion detection, and anomaly classification. **Development of Comprehensive Datasets:** Create diverse, labeled datasets that are representative of IoT behaviors and attack patterns in order to improve model training and testing [25,26].

Real-Time Forensic Tools: Development of tools balancing speed and accuracy in real-time anomaly detection without compromising computational efficiency. **Privacy-Conscious Forensics:** Implementation of encryption-aware forensic frameworks, anonymizing sensitive data while preserving actionable intelligence. **Cross-Platform Forensic Standards:** This would aid universal guidelines and frameworks for IoT forensic investigations, which could be applied everywhere and, hence, assure the results are admissible in court [24].

9.6 CONCLUSION AND FUTURE WORK

9.6.1 Summary of contributions

This is the most comprehensive overview of forensic analysis in IoT network traffic and addresses the unique challenges presented by heterogeneous technologies, high-speed data, and resource constraints. One of the most important contributions is the integration of AI and ML methods for improving traffic classification and anomaly detection, even in encrypted environments. This study also focuses on the development of practical frameworks for efficient forensic investigation with regard to real-time analysis, optimization of datasets, and advanced visualization techniques. In so doing, this research proposes scalable solutions in the identification and mitigation of specific IoT threats like botnets and ransomware, hence bridging gaps in existing network forensic methodologies from Table 9.10.

Table 9.10 Some IoT forensics methods with their results comparison

Method	*Accuracy (%)*	*False positive rate (%)*	*Processing time (ms)*
Traditional packet analysis	82	15	120
ML-based approach	90	10	100
Deep learning model	94	5	85

9.6.2 Practical applications of the framework

Cybersecurity: Facilitates improved detection and mitigation of threats to IoT devices, like DDoS attacks and ransomware. Law Enforcement: Offers admissible digital evidence in IoT device-based investigations. Healthcare IoT: Ensuring the privacy of sensitive patient information by identifying security vulnerabilities in medical devices. Industrial IoT: Tracking network anomalies in manufacturing and critical infrastructure to avoid downtime or sabotage.

9.6.3 Suggestions for future research

Future research can focus on the following areas:

Cross-Platform Compatibility: Developing frameworks that work seamlessly across diverse IoT ecosystems and platforms. Real-Time Forensics: Enhancing real-time processing capabilities to keep pace with high-speed IoT network traffic. Privacy-Preserving Techniques: Investigating methods to balance forensic needs with user privacy through techniques like homomorphic encryption. Advanced AI Models: Leveraging transformers and federated learning to improve the accuracy and scalability of forensic analysis. Legal Frameworks: Aligning forensic methodologies with international legal standards to ensure the admissibility of evidence.

REFERENCES

1. Wu, T., Breitinger, F., & Niemann, S. (2021). IoT network traffic analysis: Opportunities and challenges for forensic investigators?. *Forensic Science International: Digital Investigation*, *38*, 301123.
2. Chhabra, G. S., Singh, V. P., & Singh, M. (2020). Cyber forensics framework for big data analytics in IoT environment using machine learning. *Multimedia Tools and Applications*, *79*, 15881–15900.
3. Udayaprasad, P. K., Shreyas, J., Srinidhi, N. N., Kumar, S. D., Dayananda, P., Askar, S. S., & Abouhawwash, M. (2024). Energy efficient optimized routing technique with distributed SDN-AI to large scale I-IoT networks. *IEEE Access*, *12*, 2742–2759.
4. Mazhar, M. S., Saleem, Y., Almogren, A., Arshad, J., Jaffery, M. H., Rehman, A. U., ..., & Hamam, H. (2022). Forensic analysis on internet of things (IoT) device using machine-to-machine (M2M) framework. *Electronics*, *11*(7), 1126.
5. Chowdhury, R. R., Aneja, S., Aneja, N., & Abas, E. (2020, August). Network traffic analysis based IoT device identification. In *Proceedings of the 2020 4th international conference on big data and Internet of Things* (pp. 79–89).
6. Shreyas, J., Chouhan, D., Rao, S. T., Udayaprasad, P. K., Srinidhi, N. N., & Kumar, S. D. (2021). An energy efficient optimal path selection technique for IoT using genetic algorithm. *International Journal of Intelligent Internet of Things Computing*, *1*(3), 230–248.
7. Koroniotis, N., Moustafa, N., Sitnikova, E., & Turnbull, B. (2019). Towards the development of realistic botnet dataset in the internet of things for network forensic analytics: Bot-IoT dataset. *Future Generation Computer Systems*, *100*, 779–796.
8. Chi, H., Aderibigbe, T., & Granville, B. C. (2018, December). A framework for IoT data acquisition and forensics analysis. In *2018 IEEE International Conference on Big Data (Big Data)* (pp. 5142–5146). IEEE.
9. Rizvi, S., Scanlon, M., Mcgibney, J., & Sheppard, J. (2022). Application of artificial intelligence to network forensics: Survey, challenges and future directions. *IEEE Access*, *10*, 110362–110384.
10. Shin, C., Chandok, P., Liu, R., Nielson, S. J., & Leschke, T. R. (2017, June). Potential forensic analysis of IoT data: An overview of the state-of-the-art and future possibilities. In *2017 IEEE International Conference on Internet of Things (iThings) and IEEE Green Computing and Communications (GreenCom) and IEEE Cyber, Physical and Social Computing (CPSCom) and IEEE Smart Data (SmartData)* (pp. 705–710). IEEE.

11. Torabi, S., Bou-Harb, E., Assi, C., & Debbabi, M. (2020). A scalable platform for enabling the forensic investigation of exploited IoT devices and their generated unsolicited activities. *Forensic Science International: Digital Investigation*, *32*, 300922.
12. Shreyas, J., Kavitha, B., Udayaprasad, P. K., & Dilip Kumar, S. M. (2019, December). Optimized routing technique for adaptive data transmission in industrial IoT. In *2019 Fifteenth International Conference on Information Processing (ICINPRO)* (pp. 1–6). IEEE.
13. Koroniotis, N., Moustafa, N., & Sitnikova, E. (2020). A new network forensic framework based on deep learning for Internet of Things networks: A particle deep framework. *Future Generation Computer Systems*, *110*, 91–106.
14. Hammoudeh, M., Pimlott, J., Belguith, S., Epiphaniou, G., Baker, T., Kayes, A. S. M., Adebisi, B., & Bounceur, A. (2021). Network traffic analysis for threat detection in the internet of things. *IEEE Internet of Things Magazine*, *3*(4), 40–45.
15. Servida, F., & Casey, E. (2019). IoT forensic challenges and opportunities for digital traces. *Digital Investigation*, *28*, S22–S29.
16. Zhang, X., Upton, O., Beebe, N. L., & Choo, K. K. R. (2020). IoT botnet forensics: A comprehensive digital forensic case study on Mirai botnet servers. *Forensic Science International: Digital Investigation*, *32*, 300926.
17. Ghabban, F. M., Alfadli, I. M., Ameerbakhsh, O., AbuAli, A. N., Al-Dhaqm, A., & Al-Khasawneh, M. A. (2021, June). Comparative analysis of network forensic tools and network forensics processes. In *2021 2nd International Conference on Smart Computing and Electronic Enterprise (ICSCEE)* (pp. 78–83). IEEE.
18. Yaqoob, I., Hashem, I. A. T., Ahmed, A., Kazmi, S. A., & Hong, C. S. (2019). Internet of things forensics: Recent advances, taxonomy, requirements, and open challenges. *Future Generation Computer Systems*, *92*, 265–275.
19. Koroniotis, N., Moustafa, N., & Sitnikova, E. (2019). Forensics and deep learning mechanisms for botnets in internet of things: A survey of challenges and solutions. *IEEE Access*, *7*, 61764–61785.
20. Shreyas, J., Chouhan, D., Harshitha, M., Udayaprasad, P. K., & Kumar, S. D. (2022). Network lifetime enhancement routing algorithm for IoT enabled software defined wireless sensor network. In *Sustainable advanced computing: select proceedings of ICSAC 2021* (pp. 499–508). Singapore: Springer Singapore.
21. Atlam, H. F., Hemdan, E. E. D., Alenezi, A., Alassafi, M. O., & Wills, G. B. (2020). Internet of things forensics: A review. *Internet of Things*, *11*, 100220.
22. MacDermott, A., Baker, T., & Shi, Q. (2018, February). IoT forensics: Challenges for the IoA era. In *2018 9th IFIP International Conference on New Technologies, Mobility and Security (NTMS)* (pp. 1–5). IEEE.
23. Janarthanan, T., Bagheri, M., & Zargari, S. (2021). IoT forensics: An overview of the current issues and challenges. *Digital Forensic Investigation of Internet of Things (IoT) Devices*, Advanced Sciences and Technologies for Security Applications, 1st Edition, 223–254. 978-3-030-60424-0 (Hardcover) or 978-3-030-60427-1 (Softcover).
24. Yaacoub, J. P. A., Noura, H. N., Salman, O., & Chehab, A. (2022). Advanced digital forensics and anti-digital forensics for IoT systems: Techniques, limitations and recommendations. *Internet of Things*, *19*, 100544.
25. Koroniotis, N., Moustafa, N., Sitnikova, E., & Slay, J. (2018). Towards developing network forensic mechanism for botnet activities in the IoT based on machine learning techniques. In *Mobile Networks and Management: 9th International Conference, MONAMI 2017*, Melbourne, Australia, December 13–15, 2017, Proceedings 9 (pp. 30–44). Springer International Publishing.
26. Zhou, H., Deng, L., Xu, W., Yu, W., Dehlinger, J., & Chakraborty, S. (2022, May). Towards internet of things (IoT) forensics analysis on intelligent robot vacuum systems. In *2022 IEEE/ACIS 20th International Conference on Software Engineering Research, Management and Applications (SERA)* (pp. 91–98). IEEE.

Chapter 10

IoT device memory forensics

Sowmya T Rao, Pankaja K, Malathi S Y, Sathishkumar V E, and VinayKumar Ravi

10.1 INTRODUCTION

Internet of Things (IoT) has transformed how devices communicate with and among themselves as well as with human beings through efficient data transfer and independent decision-making. From the so-called smart thermostats and medical sensors to industrial sensors and networked cars, IoT devices inhabit embedded in almost all aspects of contemporary life. Mass deployment delivers unprecedented advantages in terms of automation, efficiency, and data-based insights but in doing so creates intricate cybersecurity issues. IoT devices, by their nature, usually have less complex security features of regular computing devices because of constraints like lower processing power, memory, and battery life. This makes them bigger in attack surface and susceptible to malware infections, unauthorized data access, and exploitation. Forensic examination is therefore imperative during incidents to understand attack vectors, evaluate damage, and aid legal proceedings. Traditional digital forensics is mainly preoccupied with the analysis of non-volatile storage—hard drives, SSDs, flash memory—where data like files, logs, and system traces are kept permanently. Contemporary cyberattacks also extensively utilize the volatile memory (RAM), which keeps running processes, credentials, and runtime data, to conceal malicious payloads and escape scanning. Memory forensics is the process of obtaining and examining the transient data to expose runtime behaviour not detectable through traditional forensics.

Memory forensics application is very difficult on IoT devices because hardware and software diversity, absence of standardized forensic tools, and limited physical and resource access. This chapter seeks to discuss the challenges, existing memory acquisition and analysis techniques, and future developments in IoT device memory forensics.

10.2 IoT DEVICE ARCHITECTURE AND MEMORY ORGANIZATION

Knowing the structure of IoT devices is central to carrying out successful memory forensics. Devices in the IoT realm differ considerably from conventional computers, hardware setups, and operating systems (OS).

10.2.1 Memory types in IoT devices

All IoT devices possess two main types of memory:

- **RAM (Volatile Memory)**: Stores the code, data, and state in the short-term information required for device to operate. It contains active process information, network buffers, encryption keys, and often transient malware. RAM content disappears once power is lost, making timely acquisition critical.

DOI: 10.1201/9781003513896-10

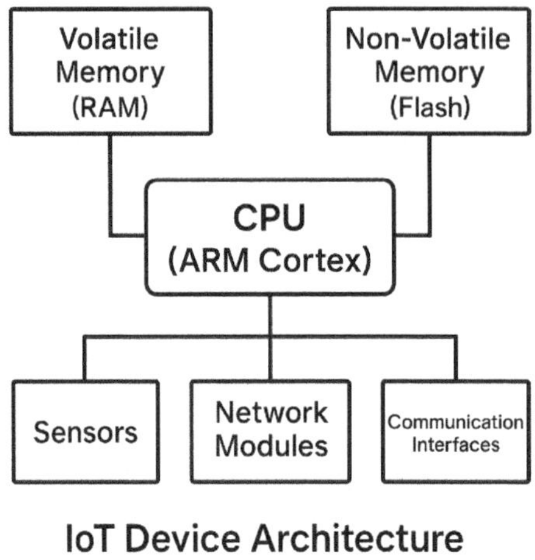

Figure 10.1 IoT device architecture.

- **Non-Volatile Memory:** This includes flash memory or EEPROM chips that store firmware, device configurations, and sometimes logs. Unlike RAM, data here persists through power cycles and can be examined through traditional forensic methods. However, some artefacts and malware only reside in volatile memory.

Because IoT devices often have much smaller memory sizes (from a few kilobytes to a few megabytes), forensic data volumes are lower than PCs but may be more difficult to extract due to proprietary memory layouts.

10.2.2 Processing architectures and operating systems

IoT devices use diverse CPU architectures such as ARM Cortex-M (widely popular), MIPS, and RISC-V, each with different instruction sets and memory management schemes. Moreover, many IoT devices run lightweight or custom OS, including real-time operating systems (RTOS) like FreeRTOS, TinyOS, or custom bare-metal firmware without a full OS as in Figure 10.1.

This heterogeneity creates a lack of standardized memory formats and forensic interfaces. Analysts must understand the target device's hardware and software environment to interpret raw memory dumps effectively.

10.3 FUNDAMENTALS OF MEMORY FORENSICS

Memory forensics is the process of acquiring and analysing the contents of volatile memory to recover critical evidence about a device's current or recent state. Unlike disk forensics, memory forensics captures a snapshot of all running processes, loaded modules, network connections, and unsaved user data.

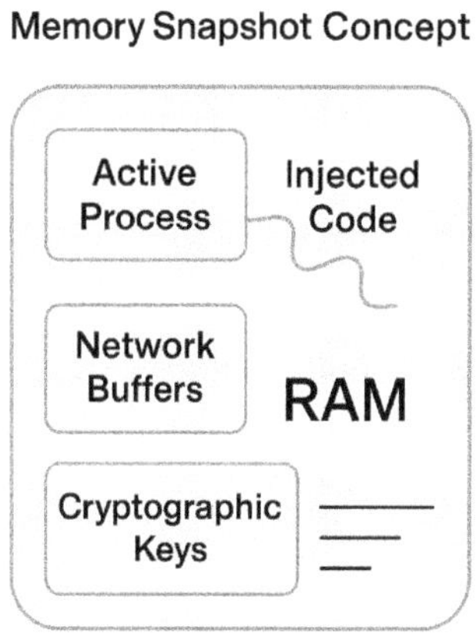

Figure 10.2 Memory snapshot concept.

The importance of memory forensics stems from the fact that many advanced malware techniques operate solely in memory to evade persistent storage detection. Rootkits, fileless malware, and credential thieves inject malicious code into legitimate processes, leaving minimal traces on disk but significant footprints in RAM.

Key forensic artefacts in memory include the following:

- Running processes and threads with their associated code and data
- Network connections and active sockets showing communication endpoints
- Loaded kernel modules or drivers potentially malicious in nature
- Encryption keys or credentials stored in memory during authentication
- Evidence of code injection, process hollowing, or memory-resident malware

Memory acquisition typically involves dumping the entire RAM contents into a file for offline analysis using specialized forensic tools. Challenges arise in ensuring the acquisition does not alter the memory state and that the tools can correctly parse data structures specific to the device's architecture and OS as in Figure 10.2.

10.4 CHALLENGES IN IoT MEMORY FORENSICS

10.4.1 Device heterogeneity

The IoT universe is one of record-breaking diversity of devices, each of which is distinguished by its own hardware and software design. The diversity includes different CPU architectures like ARM, MIPS, RISC-V, and x86, and memory type differences (e.g., SRAM, DRAM, flash memory), differences in bus interfaces, and OS from lightweight RTOS to stripped-down Linux versions. It is this heterogeneity that prevents forensic examiners from being able to use a forensic tool or a one-size-fits-all acquisition process. Rather, the device in most instances requires a specialized forensic solution, perhaps through reverse engineering firmware, tailored drivers, or creating proprietary memory acquisition tools compatible with the device's architecture. Such heterogeneity adds to interpretation and analysis complexity of acquired data since data layouts and structures are vastly different, which requires the expertise of specialists or heuristics to reconstruct volatile memory artefacts with accuracy from Table 10.1.

Table 10.1 IoT forensic challenges, description, and impact on forensic investigation

Challenge	*Description*	*Impact on forensic investigation*
Device heterogeneity	IoT devices are mostly hardware architecture, operating system, and communication protocol diversified.	Common forensic tools are cross-device incompatible, which requires unique techniques for each device type.
Resource constraints	Restricted processing capacity, storage, and memory capabilities of IoT devices.	Complicates it to execute forensic software natively on the devices; brings risk of data loss prior to acquisition.
Data volatility	IoT devices often store data in volatile memory, which can be lost upon power-off or reset.	Critical evidence may be lost if not captured promptly; complicates the preservation of transient data.
Data location and jurisdiction	Data may be distributed across devices, cloud services, and geographies, each under different legal jurisdictions.	Legal complexities in data acquisition; potential delays or restrictions in accessing data across borders.
Lack of standardization	Absence of universal standards for data formats, logging, and forensic interfaces in IoT devices.	Increases complexity in data interpretation; hinders the development of universal forensic tools.
Encryption and obfuscation	Use of encryption and proprietary data formats to protect data.	Requires additional steps to decrypt or interpret data; may prevent access to crucial evidence without appropriate keys.
Physical accessibility	Devices may be embedded, remote, or difficult to physically access without damage.	Limits the ability to perform physical acquisition methods; increases reliance on remote or network-based acquisition techniques.
Privacy concerns	Collection and analysis of personal data from IoT devices raise privacy issues.	Necessitates careful handling to comply with privacy laws; may restrict the scope of forensic analysis.
Chain of custody maintenance	Ensuring the integrity and traceability of evidence throughout the forensic process.	Challenges in maintaining a clear chain of custody, especially with data stored or transmitted across multiple platforms.
Volume and variety of data	Massive and diverse data generated by numerous IoT devices.	Difficulties in data storage, processing, and analysis; potential for important evidence to be overlooked amidst large datasets.

10.4.2 Resource constraints

IoT devices are generally designed to be run with very strict resource constraints to attain maximum cost, power, and size efficiency. The resource constraints are low levels of CPU computing, low RAM levels, and low storage capacity. Operating native forensic acquisition software on these devices is usually not feasible or even not possible since the software can have high computational overhead that can drain the battery or interfere with normal device function, even corrupting or changing evidence. Additionally, most IoT devices are low-power states or operate intermittently, and it is hard to do continuous forensic monitoring or data capturing. The onboard storage capacity limitation also hinders one from storing full forensic images or logs locally, where one would have to devise lightweight acquisition methods or access external capture capability, such as direct connection to hardware buses or accessing Joint Test Action Group (JTAG) and UART ports.

10.4.3 Volatility and data integrity

IoT memory forensics is confronted by the very nature of volatility—most valuable forensic information resides in volatile memory (RAM), which by its nature is temporary and constantly evolving as the device runs. Volatile memory data is susceptible to overwriting or loss as a result of normal device usage, power cycling, or even the process of acquiring it. Volatility increases the likelihood of missing or corrupted memory captures. In addition, guaranteeing that the memory dump obtained is original and complete is necessary, particularly when memory images are taken as proof in legal cases. Nevertheless, the lack of hardware security modules or trusted execution environments in most IoT devices implies that few mechanisms can offer tamper-proof acquisition. Without cryptographic checksums, secure boot chains, or hardware-based attestation, creation of a verifiable chain of custody for volatile memory snapshots is a key challenge, compromising forensic confidence and admissibility.

10.4.4 Encryption and obfuscation

For safeguarding of user data, intellectual property, and device integrity, various IoT devices utilize encryption and obfuscation technology at various layers, such as encryption of firmware binaries and memory. This is generally done through the help of hardware-backed encryption modules, secure enclaves, or custom-made encryption algorithms integrated into device firmware. Such safeguards considerably hinder forensic activity because decrypted information can appear only fleetingly in memory while being manipulated, making plaintext information hard to intercept in the process of capture. Furthermore, cryptographic keys and credentials can be kept in secure elements or isolated in hardware enclaves unapproachable by forensic software. Obfuscation measures like code polymorphism, encrypted strings, or compressed data blocks make reverse engineering and memory analysis even more challenging. Thus, forensic analysts must combine memory forensics with cryptanalysis, hardware exploitation, or side-channel attacks to extract usable evidence in most scenarios, making it more complicated and time-consuming.

10.4.5 Physical access and legal concerns

Obtaining memory information from IoT devices most frequently involves direct physical access to internal structures like memory chips, debugging interfaces (e.g., JTAG, UART), or embedded storage. This can involve disassembling the device, which involves inherent risks: improper handling ruins delicate components, destroys volatile memory irreversibly, or triggers tamper-evident mechanisms that obliterate valuable data. Physical access in security-conscious settings such as industrial control systems (ICSs), medical equipment, or critical infrastructure could be heavily limited or even totally banned, reducing forensic potential. In addition, the legal frameworks that apply to IoT forensic examination are developing and patchy. Privacy concerns related to users, ownership of data, cross-border data regimes, and consent both limit evidence gathering where devices facilitate multi-tenant models or process personal data. Forensic professionals have to tread these changing judicial domains with caution in a bid to ensure that evidence is acquired legally, balancing investigation and privacy requirements on a tightrope.

10.5 MEMORY ACQUISITION TECHNIQUES FOR IoT DEVICES

Acquiring an accurate and untampered memory image is foundational to effective memory forensics. The goal is to capture a snapshot of a device's volatile and non-volatile memory in a way that preserves the integrity and authenticity of the data, enabling detailed post-mortem analysis without contaminating or altering the evidence. IoT devices' resource constraints, diverse architectures, and security measures necessitate a range of specialized acquisition techniques, which can be broadly categorized into hardware-based, software-based, and hybrid approaches as in Figure 10.3.

10.5.1 Hardware-based acquisition

Hardware-based acquisition methods interact directly with the physical memory components or low-level debugging interfaces of the IoT device, generally operating outside the device's software stack. These methods reduce the risk of evidence contamination by bypassing the device's OS and software layers, making them highly valuable in forensic investigations.

- **JTAG Interface**: JTAG is a standard interface used mostly for debugging, testing, and programming of embedded systems during the development process. It offers low-level CPU register, memory, and peripheral access through special debug pins. JTAG is used by forensic analysts to stop device execution, dump memory, and even change internal states without booting or operating the system. This method has the advantage of avoiding software-layer interference, therefore retaining the original memory state. JTAG access can be locked down or disabled in production boards, however, in order to prevent reverse engineering or tampering. JTAG access also requires finding pinouts on the device's printed circuit board (PCB), which can be extremely diverse and un-documented.
- **In-System Programming (ISP)**: ISP permits memory chips to be read or written while still connected to the circuit board through programming or communication pin access. Unlike JTAG, ISP does not involve shutting down the CPU but makes use of specialized memory chip interfaces, e.g., Serial Peripheral Interface (SPI) or I2C buses. ISP can be helpful in lost or disabled JTAG case but requires close familiarity with hardware design, pin functionality, and signalling protocols. Successful ISP acquisition relies on the ability to access the chip without impacting other components and typically requires special programming hardware or adapters. It is less intrusive than chip-off but will induce minute disruption in device behaviour.
- **Chip-Off Method**: Chip-off recovery entails the extraction of memory chips (e.g., NAND flash, EEPROM) from the device's PCB for on-site analysis. This intrusive method provides complete access to all of non-volatile memory contents, including firmware, configuration data, and logs. Once extracted, the chip can be read by specialized readers that go around the internal controls of the device, allowing forensic recovery even if the device is damaged or cannot be accessed. While chip-off has the capability of high-fidelity data acquisition, it has immense potential to damage the memory chip or PCB and irretrievably destroy evidence. It also needs to be done within a laboratory using special facilities and personnel. Lastly, chip-off usually cannot seize volatile memory contents such as RAM, which are discarded at power-off or removal.

10.5.2 Software-based acquisition

Code-based acquisition relies on executing code on the target device to dump out memory contents. While this approach is less invasive and does not inherently involve direct physical hardware interface access, it is, in the vast majority of situations, less dependable in forensic use because it can change memory as it executes and involves restricted rights to get access.

- **Live Memory Dump Tools:** Such tools execute directly on the IoT device itself for dumping memory or flash information by printing memory details to persistent media or over a network. Since IoT devices usually have limited processing capability, memory, and storage, forensic tools need to be extremely lightweight and optimized so that they do not consume much runtime time and impact the system. Examples are custom scripts, low-footprint binaries, or kernel modules that go out of their way not to overwrite core memory areas. Yet, since they are executing on the device's OS, their operation does change memory state, potentially tainting evidence. Moreover, some devices don't have enough storage space or network capacity to dump vast amounts of memory, and incremental or partial acquisition techniques must be employed.
- **Exploit-Based Acquisition:** Forensic analysts are sometimes able to use software exploits or vulnerabilities to elevate privileges and build access to secure memory regions in other contexts, such as during incident response or cybercrime cases. Exploiting-based acquisition allows bypassing of security controls like access controls or encryption key protectors within secure enclaves or trusted execution environments. Although this technique can provide useful evidence in otherwise intractable locations, it is dangerous: exploits can crash systems, infect memory, or run security controls that overwrite data. Also, the exploitation of vulnerabilities is a source of ethical and legal concerns and must be performed with close monitoring and chain-of-custody procedures.

10.5.3 Hybrid approaches

Hybrid acquisition methods bring hardware and software methods together as a way of taking advantage of both their powers while minimizing their individual weaknesses. The methods are gaining prominence in IoT forensics due to the complexity and security of contemporary devices.

- By way of example, a hardware interfaces like JTAG or ISP can be used by an analyst to initiate minimal, creatively crafted code execution on the device in order to enable memory extraction. This might involve decrypting encrypted regions of memory in place or snapshotting volatile data that hardware access cannot perform completely on its own. By restricting software execution to minimal footprint and executing it under control via hardware, hybrid techniques pass over data modification risk but also offer access to protected regions of memory.
- Hybrid techniques also accommodate situations in which access to hardware is only partially forbidden—e.g., where some debugging interfaces are blocked but restricted software running is allowed, or where hardware debugging is used to obtain encryption keys required for software-based decryption of memory.
- For certain forensic operations, hardware acquisition can be supplemented with software analysis tools on an isolated system for reconstructing broken or concealed memory contents and consolidating information from both acquisition layers.

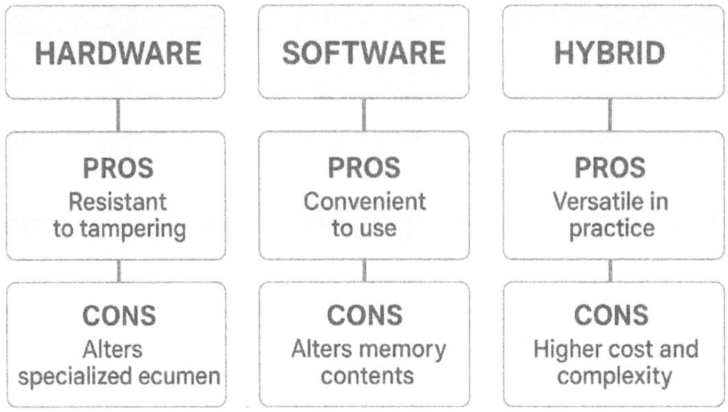

Figure 10.3 Flowchart of memory acquisition methods.

10.6 MEMORY ANALYSIS TECHNIQUES AND TOOLS

10.6.1 Memory image analysis techniques for IoT devices

Once memory images are acquired from IoT devices, the next critical step is to analyse these snapshots to extract actionable forensic evidence. Given the vast volumes of data and the complexity of embedded systems, analysis requires a combination of techniques—from traditional signature detection to advanced artificial intelligence (AI)-driven approaches. The ultimate goal is to identify malicious activity, reconstruct device behaviour, and uncover hidden or obfuscated artefacts within the memory dump.

10.6.2 Signature-Based detection

Signature-based detection continues to be the most common and easiest method in forensic analysis. It looks for known byte strings or "signatures" of identified malware, rootkits, or unknown entities like exploit payloads or command-and-control traffic in memory images. Security companies keep signature databases current and updated regularly to catch new threats.

- **Advantages:** Signature-based methods are efficient and dependable in detecting known families of malware and their variants with low false-positive rates, in general, from well-tested signature sets. Signature-based methods can be automated for quick triage in incident response situations.
- **Limitations:** This method does not cope well with unknown, new malware variants, polymorphic malware that changes its binary signature at every infection, or APTs using stealthy methods. It can't even detect malicious activity embedded inside legit code or encrypted payloads that are injected into memory. Signature databases are small in IoT since most IoT malware variants are newly found or very device-specific.

10.6.3 Behavioural and anomaly analysis

Behavioural and anomaly-based analysis is supplemented by signature detection in the sense that it examines the dynamic process behaviour, memory usage habits, and network behaviour seen or extrapolated from memory dumps. Statistical models, heuristics, and rule-based systems are used to estimate deviation from known baseline device behaviours.

- **Process Behaviour:** Experts analyse traits like suspicious process creation, unexpected privilege elevation, suspicious thread injection, or memory blocks with executable flags that are not from known binaries.
- **Memory Usage Patterns:** Unusual memory usage peaks, suspicious code blocks, or concealed procedures might be an indicator of persistence mechanisms such as rootkits or fileless malware.
- **Network and Communication Abnormalities:** Open socket memory forensics, encrypted tunnels, or unusual network buffers might point towards live command-and-control communications or data exfiltration attempts.
- **Challenges:** Baselines of behaviour need to be determined per device or device type to limit false positives, which is challenging due to the heterogeneity of IoT devices and software. Also, resource limitations restrict heavy-duty behavioural logging on numerous IoT devices, making reconstruction from snapshots in memory alone necessary.

10.6.4 Data structure parsing

IoT OS cache structured data into memory, including process control blocks, thread stacks, filesystem cache, network packet buffers, and driver data structures. Memory analysis tends to include the parsing of these structured objects for runtime device state reconstruction.

- **Process and Thread Tables:** Decoding the list of processes that are running, their status, open handles, and memory mappings can identify injected or stealth processes and can assist in reconstructing attack timelines.
- **Network Buffers and Logs:** Parsing network stacks can recover in-memory packets, partially decrypted communications, or buffered command-and-control data, crucial for understanding external interactions.
- **Filesystem and Configuration Data:** Non-volatile memory often holds configuration parameters or cryptographic keys; parsing these requires knowledge of device-specific filesystem formats and data layouts.
- **Specialized Skills Needed:** This approach requires heavy reverse engineering of device OS kernels and drivers, compounded by proprietary or un-documented systems. Specialists usually write special parsers or customize existing forensic tools to support target IoT platforms.

10.6.5 Machine learning and AI

To cope with the growing size and sophistication of IoT networks, new forensic analysis tools utilize machine learning (ML) and AI methods. These automated methods are able to detect elusive patterns and correlations in memory data that are hard to detect by hand.

- Pattern Recognition: Statistical features like opcode streams, memory entropy, or control flow graphs are used to train ML algorithms on large sets of attack and benign memory dumps, allowing for new samples to be predicted.
- Anomaly Detection: Unsupervised learning methods are capable of detecting unusual device behaviour without marked data, and thus are particularly suitable for detecting zero-day attacks.

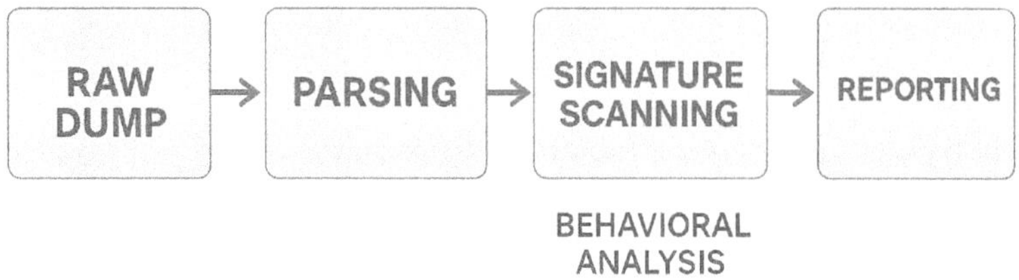

Figure 10.4 Memory analysis workflow.

- Scalability: AI-driven solutions are able to rapidly scan memory images from thousands of connected devices in real time, enabling fast threat detection and prioritization for mass deployments like smart cities or industrial IoT settings.
- Challenges: Good models need massive high-quality training data, which are normally not available for IoT-specific attacks. Additionally, interpretability of AI conclusions still poses a challenge, particularly in legal or regulatory use cases.

10.6.6 Tools

Memory-based forensic tools like Volatility and Rekall are deeply established in conventional computing platforms but need extensive modification to deal with the heterogeneity of IoT platforms as in Figure 10.4:

- **Extensibility**: Both tools provide plugin architectures that allow forensic analysts to develop custom parsers and modules for IoT-specific OS, CPU architectures (ARM, MIPS), and memory layouts.
- **Custom IoT Tools**: Due to the unique challenges posed by IoT devices, many researchers and practitioners develop bespoke tools tailored for specific device families or use cases. Examples include specialized parsers for embedded Linux variants, RTOS-specific forensic kits, and lightweight acquisition utilities compatible with constrained devices.
- **Community and Collaboration**: Increasing collaboration between academia, industry, and open-source communities is fostering the development of comprehensive IoT forensic toolkits, which integrate acquisition, analysis, and visualization to streamline investigative workflows.

10.7 CASE STUDIES

Real-world cases illustrate the application and value of IoT memory forensics as in Figure 10.5.

- **Smart Home Camera Malware**

  A botnet infection on IP cameras used fileless malware that never touched persistent storage, making disk forensics ineffective. Memory dumps revealed injected code and active network communications to attacker servers, enabling effective mitigation.

Device Type	Attack Vector	Memory Forensic Findings	Outcome
INSULIN PUMP	UNAUTHORIZED FIRMWARE PATCHES	TRANSIENT KEYLOGGING FUNCTIONALITY	SECURITY PROTOCOL ENHANCEMENTS
ATTACK VECTOR		PATIENT DATA EXFILTRATION ATTEMPTS	

Figure 10.5 Case study summary chart—device type, attack vector, memory forensic findings, outcome.

- **ICS Sabotage**
  Memory forensics on a Programmable Logic Controller (PLC) detected manipulated sensor data and memory hooks injected by attackers aiming to disrupt industrial processes. The investigation uncovered zero-day exploits and insider involvement.
- **Healthcare Device Breach**
  Forensic analysis of an insulin pump revealed unauthorized firmware patches and transient keylogging functionality. Memory acquisition exposed patient data exfiltration attempts, prompting security protocol enhancements.

10.8 FUTURE DIRECTIONS IN IoT MEMORY FORENSICS

While the growth of IoT devices continues to reshape contemporary life across industries from healthcare to manufacturing to smart cities to consumer electronics, memory forensics complexity for IoT devices can only be imagined to grow. Innovation in future IoT memory forensics will seek to overcome current challenges through forward-looking design principles, AI-driven analytics, and collaborative standardization without falling behind shifting legal and privacy environment as in Figure 10.6.

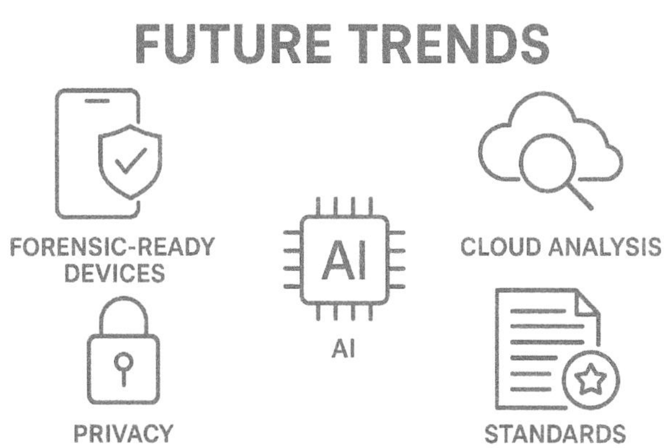

Figure 10.6 Future trends infographic depicting forensic-ready devices, cloud analysis, AI, privacy, and standards.

10.8.1 Forensic-ready IoT design

One of the most beneficial evolutions expected in the future of IoT security is the integration of forensic readiness during the design phase of IoT devices. Rather than adding forensic capability once an attack has been launched, devices can be designed to incorporate secure, tamper-proof forensic data collection and storage from the beginning.

- **Integrated Forensic Interfaces:** Products can integrate secure debugging or memory access interfaces, such as authenticated JTAG ports or forensic-specific USB interfaces, for easy and authorized acquisition during investigation that doesn't compromise device integrity.
- **Secure Memory Snapshots:** IoT devices can take periodic or on-demand memory snapshots of volatile memory to encrypted storage, triggered by security incidents or remote requests. These snapshots could serve as a forensic baseline for post-incident analysis.
- **Tamper-Proof Logging:** Logging subsystems could be designed with cryptographic integrity checks (e.g., hash chaining, digital signatures) and secure storage to prevent unauthorized modifications, ensuring that logs remain admissible as legal evidence.
- **Benefits:** Such capabilities would streamline forensic workflows, reduce data loss during incidents, and improve incident response times while enhancing trust in IoT platforms.

10.8.2 Cloud-assisted analysis

Given the resource-constrained nature of many IoT devices—limited RAM, CPU, and power—comprehensive memory analysis is often impractical directly on-device. Cloud-assisted forensics offers a powerful alternative by offloading data processing and analysis to robust remote platforms.

- **Scalable Analytics:** Memory images can be transmitted (securely and in compliance with privacy regulations) to cloud-based forensic platforms that offer high-performance computing capabilities for large-scale data parsing, malware detection, and correlation with threat intelligence databases.
- **AI Integration:** Cloud platforms can integrate ML models to automate anomaly detection and classify threats across thousands of devices simultaneously. This is particularly useful in industrial or smart city IoT deployments where real-time threat detection is vital.
- **Cross-Device Correlation:** Cloud infrastructure enables forensic correlation across multiple devices, uncovering coordinated attacks (e.g., botnets, lateral movements) that might not be visible from individual devices in isolation.
- **Security Considerations:** To ensure the integrity and confidentiality of forensic data, cloud-assisted analysis must implement robust encryption (at rest and in transit), access control mechanisms, and audit trails.

10.8.3 AI-driven forensics

As IoT ecosystems grow in complexity and volume, reliance on human analysts for deep forensic analysis becomes unsustainable. AI-driven forensics is poised to revolutionize the field by automating key investigative processes.

- **IoT-Specific Training Data:** Labelled data containing benign and malware memory patterns, behaviour patterns, and OS artefacts can be used to train AI models. These models learn to recognize nuanced indicators of compromise that may not be caught by rule-based or manual methods.

- **Continuous Learning:** With the help of reinforcement learning and continuous model updates, AI systems can age to learn new malware variants, attack paths, and device structures.
- **Explainable AI (XAI):** New research in XAI aims to make model choices interpretable and understandable—a key factor for legal and regulatory applications where forensic findings can be challenged.
- **Use Cases:** One can utilize AI to automate rootkit detection, identify atypical memory access patterns, display encrypted payloads for deeper analysis, and suggest high-risk anomalies for manual inspection.

10.8.4 Privacy and legal considerations

Greater forensic transparency into IoT devices needs to be weighed against strong privacy controls to defend user rights and comply with the law. The law, including the General Data Protection Regulation (GDPR) and California Consumer Privacy Act (CCPA), mandate stringent data collection, use, and storage requirements.

- **Privacy-Preserving Forensics:** Reducing data, differential privacy, and access-controlled forensic logging methods guarantee that only data required is gathered and analysed. Personal data that is sensitive can be encrypted or anonymized during the process of forensic analysis.
- **Legal Consent:** There should be definite policies declaring the terms on which memory acquisition and analysis should take place. For instance, user consent mechanisms or court orders for access could be part of forensic readiness designs prior to starting memory dumps.
- **Jurisdictional Concerns:** IoT devices most likely span across geographical boundaries, creating scope for legal ambiguity over ownership of data, forensic access rights, and admissibility of evidence in court. Future forensic infrastructure must address cross-border compliance.
- **Audit and Compliance:** Implementing audit mechanisms within forensic procedures enables tracking of who processed forensic data, when, and why—maintaining accountability as well as enabling legal defensibility.

10.8.5 Standardization efforts

One of the greatest obstacles to IoT memory forensics currently is a lack of standard protocols, data formats, and procedure manuals. Standardization is an attempt to embed homogeneity and interoperability in the forensic community.

- **Universal Acquisition Protocols:** Creating device-independent memory acquisition specifications will enable the use of the same tools and techniques on multiple vendors and platforms, which will be faster and more reliable.
- **Memory Image Formats:** Standardized formats for memory dumps (e.g., Advanced Forensic Format (AFF), Extended Wildcard Format (EWF), or IoT-specific extensions) will ensure compatibility with forensic analysis tools, support metadata inclusion (e.g., timestamps, device ID), and facilitate secure transfer and archiving.
- **Reporting and Documentation:** Forensic reporting templates and documentation guidelines—tailored to IoT environments—will promote transparency and reproducibility in investigations. These standards can be adopted by incident response teams, law enforcement, and regulatory bodies.

- **Organizations Involved:** Entities such as NIST, ENISA, IETF, and FIRST are actively contributing to IoT forensic frameworks, device certification standards, and cybersecurity best practices, often in collaboration with industry consortia and academia.

10.9 CONCLUSION

Memory forensic has emerged as a critical IoT security element, offering complete visibility into devices' volatile, real-time environment, and supporting the detection of advanced threats like in-memory malware, fileless attacks, and advanced persistent threats that are most likely to evade traditional disk-based forensic approaches. In contrast to storage analysis, memory forensics may uncover malicious actions such as unauthorized control flows, code injection attacks, cryptographic key exposures, and unusual inter-process communications that exist only at runtime. Its use in IoT is also hindered by enormous heterogeneity of hardware and software platforms, limited device resources, and evidence contamination threats caused by intrusive or software-based acquisition. Newer technologies—such as hardware-assisted acquisition methods (e.g., JTAG, ISP), cloud-based analytical software, ML-powered anomaly detection, and the use of forensic-ready design methodologies—are increasing memory analysis efficiency and scalability. Moreover, worldwide standardization initiatives are towards combining memory formats, acquisition procedures, and reporting schemes, thereby minimizing fragmentation and providing highest levels of interoperability. Parallelly, ethical, legal, and privacy issues, like compliance with regulations like GDPR, must be given due consideration to maintain public faith. All in all, incorporating memory forensics into IoT systems from the design phase itself is no longer an option but a necessity for proactive threat detection, investigation, and incident response in our progressively networked digital era.

BIBLIOGRAPHY

1. Al-Dhaqm, A., Alkahtani, M., & Alzahrani, A. (2024). IoT Forensics: Current Perspectives and Future Directions. *Sensors*, *24*(16), 5210.
2. Alenezi, A., & Alshammari, R. (2024). IoT Forensics Readiness: Influencing Factors. *Digital Forensics Research Review*, *3*(2), 87–101.
3. Teel Technologies. (n.d.). Combined JTAG/Chip-Off Forensics. Retrieved from https://www.teeltech.com/events/1006-combined-jtag-chip-off-forensics/region-US/TeelTech
4. Yahya, F. (2025). Memory Forensics: Core of Cyber Investigations Unveiled.
5. Paraben Corporation. (2024). Memory Forensics Tools Overview. Retrieved from https://paraben.com/memory-forensics-tools-overview/ParabenCorporation
6. Google. (n.d.). Rekall Memory Forensic Framework.
7. Volatility Foundation. (n.d.). Volatility Framework. Retrieved from https://www.volatilityfoundation.org/
8. ResearchGate. (2023). The Evolution of Volatile Memory Forensics. Retrieved from https://www.researchgate.net/publication/362147648_The_Evolution_of_Volatile_Memory_ForensicsResearchGate
9. ScienceDirect. (2025). Comparative Study of IoT Forensic Frameworks.
10. ResearchGate. (2025). IoT Forensics: An Overview of the Current Issues and Challenges. Retrieved from https://www.researchgate.net/publication/347479384_IoT_Forensics_An_Overview_of_the_Current_Issues_and_Challenges
11. Conti, M., Dehghantanha, A., Franke, K., & Watson, S. (2018). Internet of Things Security and Forensics: Challenges and Opportunities. *Future Generation Computer Systems*, *78*, 544–546. https://doi.org/10.1016/j.future.2017.07.060

12. Bonomi, F., Milito, R., Natarajan, P., & Zhu, J. (2014). Fog computing: A platform for Internet of Things and analytics. In Bessis, N. & Dobre, C. (Eds.), *Big data and Internet of Things: A roadmap for smart environments* (pp. 169–186). Springer. https://doi.org/10.1007/978-3-319-05029-4_7
13. Zawoad, S., & Hasan, R. (2015). "FAIoT: Towards Building a Forensics-Aware eco System for the Internet of Things," *2015 IEEE International Conference on Services Computing*, 279–284. https://doi.org/10.1109/SCC.2015.47
14. Lee, J., Ko, M., Jeon, J., & Lee, H. (2019). A Lightweight and Secure Memory Acquisition Method for IoT Devices. *IEEE Access*, *7*, 40551–40561.
15. Chen, T. M., & Abu-Nimeh, S. (2011). Lessons from Stuxnet. *Computer*, *44*(4), 91–93. https://doi.org/10.1109/MC.2011.115
16. Williams, P. A. H. (2017). Cybersecurity Vulnerabilities in Medical Devices: A Complex Environment and Multifaceted Problem. *Medical Devices: Evidence and Research*, *10*, 11–14.
17. Fernandes, E., Pau, G., & Prakash, A. (2017). Security Implications of Permission Models in Smart Home Platforms. In *Proceedings of the IEEE Security and Privacy Workshops*, 72–75. https://doi.org/10.1109/SPW.2017.52
18. Sfar, A. R., Natalizio, E., Challal, Y., & Chtourou, Z. (2018). A Roadmap for Security Challenges in the Internet of Things. *Digital Communications and Networks*, *4*(2), 118–137. https://doi.org/10.1016/j.dcan.2017.04.003
19. Ammar, M., Russello, G., & Crispo, B. (2018). Enabling Trustworthy Fog Computing: Challenges and Requirements. *Computer Communications*, *122*, 583–593. https://doi.org/10.1016/j.comcom.2018.03.017
20. Kumar, R., & Tripathi, R. (2021). A Review on Digital Forensics: Modern Techniques, Tools and Challenges. *Materials Today: Proceedings*, *47*(Part 1), 887–892. https://doi.org/10.1016/j.matpr.2021.05.567
21. Shreyas, J., Chouhan, D., Rao, S. T., Udayaprasad, P. K., Srinidhi, N. N., & Kumar, S. D. (2021). An Energy Efficient Optimal Path Selection Technique for IoT Using Genetic Algorithm. *International Journal of Intelligent Internet of Things Computing*, *1*(3), 230–248.
22. Shreyas, J., Chouhan, D., Rao, S. T., Udayaprasad, P. K., Srinidhi, N. N., & Dilip Kumar, S. M. (2021). EERO: Energy Efficient Route Optimization Technique for IoT Network. In *Futuristic Trends in Network and Communication Technologies: Third International Conference, FTNCT 2020, Taganrog, Russia, October 14–16, 2020, Revised Selected Papers, Part II 3*, 207–218. Springer Singapore.
23. R., R. S., Yadav N, S., K R, Venugopal, I., S. S., & P., L. M. (April 25, 2021). Real-Time Multi-View Face Recognition Using Alignment-RMFRA. In *Proceedings of the International Conference on Innovative Computing & Communication (ICICC) 2021*, Available at SSRN: https://ssrn.com/abstract=3833799 or http://dx.doi.org/10.2139/ssrn.3833799
24. Yadav N., S., R., A., Umar S., S., Tazeen Z., S. Z., Mathew, A., & Ahmed V. T., M., "Smart Headband with a Mobile Application to Predict and Monitor Seizures Using EEG Spring Technology an Ultimate Effective Model for Seizure Free Life," *2024 Second International Conference on Advances in Information Technology (ICAIT)*, Chikkamagaluru, Karnataka, India, 2024, 1–7. https://doi.org/10.1109/ICAIT61638.2024.10690375

Chapter 11

Advanced investigation strategies for biometric data forensics in IoT

P William, Nandakumar R, Anil Khatak, Mudassir Khan, Jiwanjot Kaur, and Ayush Kumar Agrawal

11.1 INTRODUCTION

Biometric systems and the Internet of Things (IoT) have come together to start a new age in identity verification, surveillance, healthcare, and personalized user experiences. The coming together of these two technologies has brought forth this era. Biometric systems that are connected to the IoT are changing the way people and computers interact in many situations. For example, facial recognition can be used to get into smart homes, and biometric sensors can be used in hospitals to keep an eye on patients all the time. On the other side, this new technology has also made it easier for hackers to attack computers and change data. This is particularly important when these kinds of technologies don't have the forensic skills they need to be used as a defense. It is not enough to argue that present forensic investigation methods are good for this situation; they are necessary to make sure that biometric data is secure, reliable, and legally defensible [1]. Biometric data, including fingerprints, voiceprints, facial patterns, iris scans, gait recognition, and even electrocardiographic signals, are important for identifying people since they are unique to each person. This is because biometric data may be used to tell people apart. Biometric identifiers can't be stolen or forgotten as regular passwords or tokens can, which is a big plus. However, this particular strength might equally be considered as a major weakness. People are in danger for the rest of their lives since compromised biometric data can't be modified or wiped. Biometric technologies are also very easy to hack, spoof, gather data without permission, and violate privacy when used in dynamic IoT settings with limited resources [2].

The IoT gadgets that people use right now are always collecting biometric data. This information is transferred across several networks and is typically stored or analyzed in the cloud or on different edge nodes. Forensic investigators who are trying to find and investigate breaches or malicious activity have a lot of trouble with the system's dispersed architecture. These investigators face a number of problems. IoT-based biometric networks provide a decentralized, diverse, and time-sensitive setting that isn't great for the traditional method of digital forensics, which mostly depends on permanent and centralized data sources like personal PCs or servers. This method doesn't work well in the environments that these ecosystems provide. In these types of scenarios, forensic preparation requires frameworks that are smart, flexible, and based on the facts of the case. These frameworks also need to be able to monitor, analyze, and respond in real time. To deal with these increasingly difficult problems, modern forensic approaches are now focused on three main areas: finding anomalies before they happen, capturing data in a way that can't be tampered with, and synchronizing forensic data between the cloud and the edge. These are the three main things that current forensic methods are looking at. When you put these parts together, you get a multi-layered forensic model that can help law enforcement, cybersecurity teams, and digital investigators get results that are accurate, timely, and can be used in court.

 DOI: 10.1201/9781003513896-11

Making algorithms based on artificial intelligence (AI) is one way to find anomalies before they happen. These algorithms look at behavioral patterns, changes in sensor data, and communication traces all the time. These models may find a wide range of actions, such as trying to get illegal access, making up biometric information, and changing data at the source. For instance, machine learning (ML) classifiers can tell the difference between genuine and fraudulent fingerprints that have been captured by IoT sensors by looking at little details like ridge abnormalities or sweat levels. This is done by looking at little details. In the same way, using tamper-proof data recording systems, especially those based on blockchain or distributed ledger technology (DLTs), makes it possible to get forensic evidence with timestamped integrity. Because of how this is done, it is certain that biometric data cannot be changed without being detected to have been changed. More and more, judicial systems are requiring this kind of proof when biometric data is presented in court. This is especially true in places where biometric surveillance is common, such in urban monitoring systems or border control. A cloud-edge forensic synchronization system is an added part that is very important [3]. To save bandwidth and latency, IoT devices generally process data near the edge of the network. The forensic tools at the edge of the network need to be able to quickly gather important evidence in real time and safely sync it with cloud-based forensic archives. Investigators may do more thorough research while keeping the evidence consistent across changing data flows thanks to this bi-directional sync. This lets them reach both of these aims at the same time. Figure 11.1 shows the main steps that make up the forensic workflow for biometric data in the IoT in a picture. This is done by showing the method in a series of steps. These steps involve gathering data using smart devices, forensic analysis, and recording that can't be tampered with. Also, the legal and moral consequences are taken into consideration. The goal of this conceptual model is to provide a guide for figuring out how advanced inquiry tactics are really used in a variety of IoT contexts.

Legal and moral issues, as well as the technological problems that these methods provide, mostly determine how and when biometric forensic techniques may be applied. Several countries have not yet made clear legislation about how to preserve biometric data, how to share data across borders, or how to use biometric data collected via the IoT as evidence. When investigators are collecting or analyzing this kind of data, they need to be able to deal with not just the technical components of the case but also the political, moral, and privacy issues. Think about this real-life example to help you comprehend it better: you may add IoT-enabled parts to a smart workplace setting. Some of these parts include motion detectors, voice-controlled assistants, and door locks that can tell who is at the door. If there is a data breach, investigators need to gather logs from different

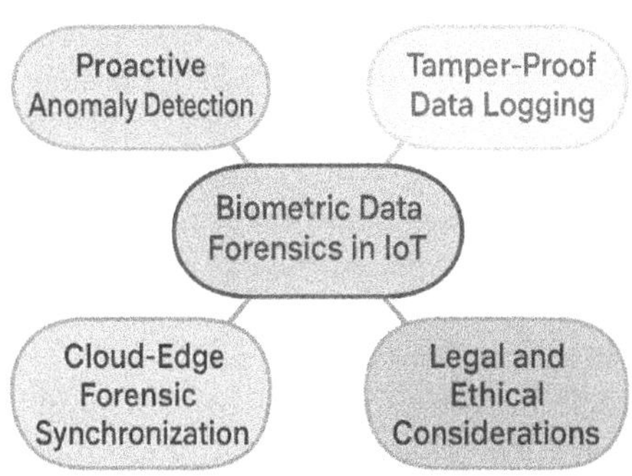

Figure 11.1 Forensic workflow for biometric data in IoT.

devices, make sure that biometric streams are real, and figure out exactly when the data was taken before the breach happened. Without synchronized forensic frameworks, data that can't be tampered with, and the ability to find anomalies, it is exceedingly hard to figure out who did the crime. The intrusion might lie unnoticed for weeks, which would put important firm property and workers' privacy at risk [4]. This is an even more troubling possibility.

This study is all about forensic examinations of biometric data. Its goal is to make a list of the best approaches to do these kinds of studies in IoT settings. The chapter suggests a whole architecture. This architecture is meant to bring together synchronized cloud-edge forensic operations, blockchain-based chain-of-custody systems, and detection methods that are made stronger by ML. Combining several technologies makes it feasible to take a proactive strategy instead of a reactive one. This lets you find probable dangers before they turn into full-blown incidents. This makes it possible to be more proactive than reactive. The research will also look at the policies and standards that govern biometric data and forensic science throughout the globe. The General Data Protection Regulation (GDPR) and the ISO/IEC 30137-1:2019 are two examples of the rules and suggestions that this publication talks about. In addition, the study will help with forensic preparation and compliance. We also look at the most current developments in AI-based correlation engines, zero-trust architectures, federated learning, and edge forensic agents. All of these improvements help create a forensic infrastructure that can handle the difficulties that may come up in the future. After then, the remaining parts of the task are structured like this: Section 11.2 gives a full review of the literature on biometric data security and IoT forensics. Section 11.3 gives an overview of the multi-layered forensic investigative method that has been created. Section 11.4 shows that the offered methodologies are valid by using real-time case studies and simulations. Section 11.5 talks about problems, possible topics for further study, and the effects of policy.

11.2 REVIEW OF LITERATURE

Security is crucial in an IoT environment because so many devices need to communicate and interact. Many modern IoT devices use biometrics to prevent hackers. However, it offers many intriguing ways to make the IoT safer and simpler to utilize. Biometrics can accurately identify persons, thus this is why. This chapter covers the current status of biometrics research in IoT security, focusing on authentication and communication encryption. Research will focus on the two most important subjects. The issue of authentication covers a wide spectrum of current biometric-based IoT authentication solutions. These solutions are grouped by the number and kind of biometric features the system employs. Biometric-cryptographic systems, which combine biometrics with cryptography to make the IoT safer, are being studied and investigated in great detail when it comes to encryption. This is done to keep the IoT safe from possible dangers. At the same time as the problems that come up when biometrics are combined with the IoT are made clear and researched, possible solutions are also suggested [5]. This review chapter helps move research in the subject forward by giving an overview of the current state of the art in biometrics for IoT security. Also, it helps researchers learn more about problems that are expected to happen in the future and other possible areas of investigation. This is a big plus.

The IoT is a term that includes everything that happens in our lives. Recent improvements in hardware and information technology have made it possible to quickly deploy billions of smart, linked, and adaptive devices in crucial sectors, including home automation, transportation, health, and environmental management. Customers benefit from reliability and convenience of use when data is delivered via a network without any contact between people or between people and computers. Digital forensics, on the other hand, needs to deal with a whole new set of difficulties that are quite different from the ones they have worked with before. Cybercriminals, on the other hand, have a whole new set of options. Even if data from the IoT might be a treasure trove of evidence, forensics specialists still have a lot of challenges all the time. There are a lot of problems with the IoT, such the fact that there are so many various kinds of devices and formats that don't follow a standard. There are also problems with the multitenant cloud architecture, which has led to conflicts between governments. We also need to get beyond end-to-end encryption.

This kind of encryption not only makes the forensic investigation less effective, but it also violates the users' right to privacy. The compromise that people are talking about right now is one of the things that has to be fixed. To make sure that the chain of custody is maintained, it is important to gather and examine digital evidence using methods and processes that are generally acknowledged. This is done to keep the chain of custody robust. This occurred because digital evidence is naturally weak. The purpose of this study is to uncover and explain the most crucial challenges that come up throughout the intricate process of investigations based on the IoT. We will achieve this by finding out what the difficulties are and what they imply. These issues include all the challenges that come up with privacy, cloud security, and the law [6]. This site also includes a short summary of the theoretical models that have been employed in digital forensics research in the past and are still being used currently. People have used these models together. We pay close attention to frameworks that use decentralized blockchain-based solutions to acquire data in a manner that preserves people's privacy or makes sure that proof is legitimate. This research also looks at the Forensics-as-a-Service (FaaS) model, which is currently in use, and a variety of novel techniques to integrate forensics intelligence with data reduction. The conclusion speaks about several challenges that still need to be solved and various ways that further research might be done. There is a lot of discourse about the need for proactive, globally acknowledged criteria and standards for forensic readiness to make sure that access control works. Biometrics is more relevant now because of the great development that has been achieved in information and communication technology, particularly with the advent of AI.

This is especially true when it comes to introducing new tech. It is clear that using AI has helped face and fingerprint recognition systems make big steps forward. The IoT is becoming more popular, which has raised new security concerns. However, it has also made it possible to use biometrics in a lot of different circumstances. The goal of this research is to look at all the many types of biometrics that use smart or AI. The major topic will be how to combine biometrics and AI together to make the IoT safer, exactly as how buildings are made safer. More and more individuals are embracing biometric identification methods in the IoT. These technologies are easier to use and safer than older ways of verifying identity. To make biometric systems better for use in the IoT, you need to use AI algorithms. These algorithms help you see patterns and give you the ability to modify your mind when the circumstance changes. This is because these algorithms help us see patterns more clearly. Biometrics, AI, and the IoT may also assist relieve security worries, which keeps users' data and privacy safe. This evaluation makes three important contributions: it shows how biometrics, AI, and the IoT are all connected; it talks about how AI and biometrics are used in the IoT; and it points out the current problems and possible research areas that come up when trying to use intelligent biometrics in different IoT application domains. There are all of these items in the report. This method also makes it easier to employ smart biometrics in IoT applications [7].

Cyber forensics has to go ahead so that it can face new problems and use new tools. This is particularly critical now as cyberattacks are becoming more complicated in the digital world. This study's goal is to find out how AI may be applied in cyber forensics, with a focus on adaptive threat mitigation and better multi-factor authentication (MFA). Because of advances in AI, cybercriminals now have access to more sophisticated technology that helps them perform their jobs better. This has also led to an increase in the number of tactics required for forensic inquiry. MFA, which is an important aspect of modern security, has greatly improved access control methods. Users must provide many means to authenticate their identity in order to use this authentication technique. This chapter speaks about how AI has made MFA technology better. Biometric recognition and behavioral analytics are two examples of these enhancements. These enhancements make authentication methods more accurate and dependable right now. The study also looks at how AI may be used to assist detect and halt complex attack paths that take use of flaws in conventional authentication methods. The goal of the initiative is to discover and block certain kinds of assaults.

There is a lot of research going on all around the world right now to create dynamic response systems that can handle threats that are always changing. Another major field of research is looking at how to adaptively reduce threats. It is becoming more and more important to use ML algorithms to look at data in real time in order to improve security systems' ability to discover issues and deal with them better. This study talks about several AI-powered adaptive threat mitigation systems and how they are used in real-life cyber forensics cases. The research reveals that these tactics might cut down on the time it takes to react to occurrences and find out the outcomes of forensic investigations by a lot. Adding AI to cyber forensics is a huge development that makes both preventive and reactive tactics better at stopping cybercrime. This transformation is occurring because it is a paradigm shift. The purpose of this chapter is to provide a comprehensive picture by looking at these achievements in detail and talking about the good and bad things about employing them. This chapter speaks about how AI might have a huge impact on cyber forensics. This could lead to the development of stronger and more reliable security solutions for the digital age [8]. There has been a lot of research done, and these findings are what can be stated to be true.

As more IoT devices enter our homes, the information they leave behind when we use them is becoming a lot of evidence that forensic investigators may utilize to look into many different types of crimes. You may use this proof to check into a variety of different offenses. You may utilize this evidence to check into a lot of different offenses. A lot of the research that is now being done on IoT forensics, on the other hand, has been centered on theoretical frameworks. Because the tools and approaches that are available today don't function with newer devices that are part of the IoT. The major purpose of this thesis was to find effective general solutions that would make it simpler to utilize the IoT for forensic investigations. We started by asking 70 persons who work in digital forensics to take an online poll about a research method and what they thought of as IoT forensics. The aim of this survey was to find out what people thought. We acquired information from these persons by asking them questions. We got to a definitive decision on the technology of the IoT and its subdomains in the area of IoT forensics. We also learned all the words that were utilized. A number of respondents who took part in the survey suggested that it should focus on collecting information and building forensic tools for the IoT [9]. This also let us utilize Bluetooth Low Energy (BLE) and make a precise strategy on how to acquire smart medical equipment. We were able to prove that this strategy works by collecting health data from smart medical devices. We also illustrated how significant these traces are for forensic inquiry, which involves establishing a health history profile of the person we were dealing with. We examined at more than 800 papers that spoke about the challenges with research-based digital forensic tools in order to understand more about why there haven't been more improvements in IoT forensic tools.

We were able to understand more about the situation because of this. We did this test to get a better idea of what was going on. People have informed us that devices that are connected to the IoT need a means to be found. We came up with a broad identification approach that incorporated ML and some information from the network packet because of this. This produced a one-of-a-kind "fingerprint" that helps forensic investigators find out what kind of equipment is connected to the network without using typical methods like fingerprinting. Based on what we learned from our prior study, we created and tested an automated way to examine networks that are linked to the IoT. We looked at 32 consumer IoT devices and evaluated network traffic data to see how well this method works for forensic investigation. This helped us prove how beneficial this tech is. Also, smart cameras and smart medical equipment were more likely to transfer data that wasn't secured. The data led to this conclusion because it indicated that some devices used encryption. We concluded that the United States has the greatest IoT traffic after doing some research. We built a network analysis tool, an acquisition approach, and an identification method so that we could get traces from a wide range of consumer IoT devices. These three pieces let us get traces. This is the most important thing our research brings to the field. It is vitally crucial that we provide solutions that can function with the new devices that are coming out as the IoT grows. That's why the IoT is always becoming larger.

11.3 NATURE AND SENSITIVITY OF BIOMETRIC DATA IN IoT

Biometric data is now a big aspect of the IoT, which is continually becoming bigger. It is used for simple authentication, customizing the user experience, and monitoring in real time. For the Internet of elements to operate, it requires both of these elements. Biometric systems that come with IoT devices are becoming just as common as the devices themselves. Smartwatches that check your heart rate and smart locks that detect your face are two examples of these sorts of gadgets. There is a lot of danger and a lot of possibility in this transformation. Biometric data is useful because it is unique and everlasting, but these same features also make it exceedingly sensitive. You can't change or reset your fingerprint or iris pattern as you can with a password after it's been stolen. This data usually moves over networks, is kept in cloud repositories, and is accessed by numerous different applications, each of which has its own security weaknesses.

This lifetime is shown in a picture in Figure 11.2. It explains how biometric data is collected, received, stored, and then used in the IoT. The graphic displays smartphones, smartwatches, healthcare sensors, and smart locks as the first places where the data is collected. These devices are continually collecting data, usually in the background, even when the user isn't doing anything. At this stage, hackers may be able to acquire biometric signals by sniffing or faking the network. If the encryption isn't set up properly or the devices are outdated, this might happen.

As soon as the data is collected, it is sent to centralized or cloud storage systems, which adds another degree of danger to the problem. If biometric data is exchanged wirelessly, particularly across channels that aren't secured, it might be vulnerable to assaults like "man in the middle." There are a lot of IoT systems that send data in pieces or without the necessary amount of encryption. This is because there are a lot of performance constraints or no fixed methods. This is an example of a critical failure point, which is a point where attackers may change or redirect data flows to places they shouldn't be able to. This position is shown in Figure 11.2. The phase that has to do with storage is another hard problem that has to be solved. Storing biometric data linked to user accounts on cloud-based databases or platforms supplied by third parties is a frequent practice. Hackers will find it simple to get into these storage systems if they don't have access limitations, logging mechanisms, or

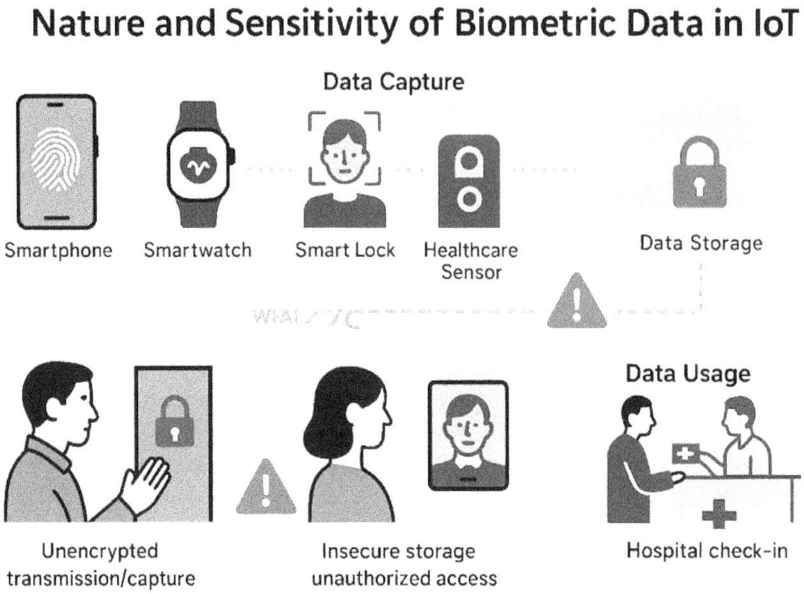

Figure 11.2 Biometric data lifecycle and risks in IoT.

good encryption. If they don't have these things, they will be easy to assault. If biometric databases are hacked, the vulnerabilities might have serious effects. Unlike credit card numbers, biometric identifiers can't be altered. Once they are made public, they put the people who are impacted at risk of having their security compromised for good. This step is very important for forensics and should not be omitted. To construct a chain of custody and check the validity of biometric events, investigators use storage logs. This is done to make sure that the information is correct. If the storage is corrupted, it's possible that the whole forensic story will be thrown into chaos.

Biometric data may soon be used for things like screening patients into hospitals, verifying smartphone users, and having access to private medical or financial information. People will use these apps in the future. Figure 11.2 shows when the data is turned into action. At this point, the data is turned into action, which may include giving someone access, confirming their identity, or turning on services. That being said, this is also when it begins to be hard to tell who is responsible. Many customers don't know how their biometric data is being handled, such as if it is being shared with other systems or kept after it has been used. When it comes to user permission, data retention laws, and openness, there are moral problems that need to be addressed. People must provide their informed permission and label their biometric data as "special category data" that deserves the greatest degree of protection in order to follow legal rules like the GDPR. When doing forensic investigations, investigators have to put up a timeline of events that makes sense and is admissible in court throughout the whole length of the inquiry. Did the user agree to let the research collect the data? Was it encrypted before it was sent as it was being sent? Could others weren't supposed to be able to get to it or modify it while it was being stored? And was the last use of it legal and recorded in the right way? If any of these answers are unclear, it might put not only the data at risk but also the trust that consumers have in biometric IoT devices. Figure 11.2 shows a real-life example of how biometric data is collected and utilized. This image shows how biometric data moves via a network of IoT devices. This makes people aware of touchpoints that are sensitive and open to having their data intercepted, changed, or used in ways they don't want.

11.4 RESEARCH METHODOLOGY

This study adopts a mixed-methods research design that combines quantitative evaluation, comparative performance analysis, and statistical inference to investigate the effectiveness of biometric data forensics in IoT environments. The methodology integrates both empirical data collection from biometric-enabled IoT devices and simulation-based performance testing of forensic tools. The primary goal is to assess device reliability, identify statistically significant differences in biometric performance, and compare forensic investigation strategies using AI and ML technologies.

11.4.1 Data collection and sampling

The study evaluated five categories of biometric IoT devices: smartwatch, smart lock, smart speaker, smart CCTV, and health monitor. A total of 2250 biometric data samples were gathered through controlled simulations and publicly available IoT datasets. Each device type was assessed based on its associated biometric modality (e.g., fingerprint, voice, iris scan), with a standardized sample size per device ranging from 300 to 600 data points. The sampling aimed to replicate real-world usage patterns and conditions, including variability in environmental noise, user behavior, and hardware calibration.

11.4.2 Performance metrics

The reliability of each device was measured using two standard biometric metrics:

- **False Acceptance Rate (FAR)**: The probability that the system incorrectly accepts an unauthorized user.
- **False Rejection Rate (FRR)**: The probability that the system incorrectly rejects an authorized user.

These metrics were computed using standard classification performance evaluation techniques. The data was processed using Python's scikit-learn and pandas libraries to derive consistent performance indicators for all devices.

11.4.3 Forensic tool evaluation

To assess forensic processing strategies, four different forensic tools and techniques were benchmarked:

- **Traditional matching**
- **AI-based anomaly detection**
- **Pattern recognition models**
- **ML-aided forensics toolkit**

Each tool was evaluated on three fronts:

- **Accuracy (%)**
- **Processing Time (seconds)**
- **Resource Usage (MB RAM)**

Simulated incident scenarios involving spoofing, tampering, data breaches, and privacy violations were generated to test detection capabilities. The scenarios were repeated across multiple runs to minimize bias and account for outlier events.

11.4.4 Statistical analysis

To determine whether performance differences among biometric modalities and device types were statistically significant, a One-Way Analysis of Variance (ANOVA) was performed. The null hypothesis (H_0) assumed no significant differences in FAR/FRR among the device groups, while the alternative hypothesis (H_1) posited that at least one group exhibited a statistically distinct performance. An F-test was conducted with a significance threshold of $p<0.05$, using IBM SPSS and R software for validation.

The ANOVA output (see Table 11.2) confirmed statistical significance ($F = 9.5$, $p = 0.0008$), prompting rejection of the null hypothesis. This validated the hypothesis that biometric performance varies notably across device types.

11.4.5 Ethical and compliance considerations

Given the sensitivity of biometric data, all simulations and datasets used in this research were anonymized and ethically sourced. The global compliance analysis referenced published datasets and reports from regulatory bodies such as GDPR (EU), CCPA (USA), PDPA (Singapore), and AADHAAR (India) to benchmark regional consent rates. Figure 11.6 was generated based on aggregated compliance indicators from these regions.

11.4.6 Visualization and humanized analysis

Figures 11.3–11.6 were created using Matplotlib and Tableau to enhance interpretability and engagement. A human-centric interpretation approach was applied in the Results and Discussion section to bridge the gap between raw metrics and real-world implications, especially regarding user trust, legal admissibility, and forensic reliability.

11.5 ANALYSIS AND INTERPRETATION

In the rapidly evolving world of the IoT, securing biometric data has become increasingly critical. Biometric forensics, when integrated with IoT devices, offers an advanced layer of authentication and forensic investigation. This study explores the strategic application of biometric technologies in IoT environments by evaluating the performance of various biometric-enabled devices, analyzing statistical significance among data sources, and comparing modern forensic tools based on accuracy, efficiency, and resource utilization. Table 11.1 presents the performance metrics of five biometric IoT devices—Smartwatch, smart lock, smart speaker, smart CCTV, and health monitor. Each device captures different biometric data such as heart rate, fingerprints, voice, facial patterns, and iris scans. Key indicators like FAR and FRR were used to measure reliability.

Table 11.1 Performance metrics of biometric IoT devices

Device type	*Data type*	*Sample count*	*False acceptance rate (FAR %)*	*False rejection rate (FRR %)*
Smartwatch	Heart rate, steps	500	1.2	2.8
Smart lock	Fingerprint	400	0.8	1.5
Smart speaker	Voice recognition	600	2.4	3.1
Smart CCTV	Facial recognition	450	1.1	2.3
Health monitor	Iris scan	300	0.6	1.2

Table 11.2 ANOVA results for biometric performance variation

Source of variation	*SS*	*df*	*MS*	*F*	*P-value*	*F crit*
Between groups	530.3	3	176.8	9.5	0.0008	3.24
Within groups	371.6	20	18.58			
Total	**901.9**	**23**				

Notably, the Health Monitor utilizing iris scans recorded the lowest FAR (0.6%) and FRR (1.2%), suggesting it is the most secure and precise among the evaluated technologies. In contrast, the smart speaker, which uses voice recognition, demonstrated the highest FAR (2.4%) and FRR (3.1%), indicating that voice-based authentication is currently less reliable in high-security forensic scenarios. These differences highlight the critical importance of selecting appropriate biometric modalities based on the specific security requirements and environmental conditions of IoT deployments. To assess the statistical variation in biometric performance, an ANOVA (Analysis of Variance) test was conducted, as detailed in Table 11.2. The results revealed a significant difference in performance between the biometric groups, with an F-value of 9.5 surpassing the critical value (F crit = 3.24) and a p-value of 0.0008, which is well below the threshold of 0.05.

This statistical evidence confirms that performance differences among the biometric devices are not due to random variation but are indeed significant. Therefore, developers and security analysts must carefully consider the specific biometric technology implemented in IoT forensic systems. Choosing the wrong biometric method could increase security vulnerabilities or lead to unreliable forensic results. In terms of forensic processing and investigation, Table 11.3 compares four major forensic tools and techniques: traditional matching, AI-based anomaly detection, pattern recognition models, and the ML-aided forensics toolkit. The ML-Aided Toolkit emerged as the most effective solution, achieving the highest accuracy (94.5%), fastest processing time (6.9 seconds), and greatest resource utilization (210 MB).

While AI-based anomaly detection also performed well with a 92.1% accuracy rate and moderate resource usage, traditional matching methods fell behind both in accuracy (82.4%) and efficiency (14.3 seconds processing time). These findings emphasize that ML and AI-enhanced approaches not only improve the reliability of biometric recognition but also significantly reduce the time and effort required for forensic investigations in real-world IoT settings. This study supports a strategic shift toward adopting AI and ML-enhanced forensic tools for managing biometric data in IoT ecosystems. The insights drawn from Table 11.1 validate the effectiveness of certain biometric devices over others, while the ANOVA results in Table 11.2 provide statistical proof of significant performance differences. The comparison of forensic tools in Table 11.3 highlights the superior capabilities of advanced technologies in processing and analyzing biometric data. Collectively, these findings can guide cybersecurity professionals, forensic analysts, and IoT developers toward more informed and secure system designs, ensuring both accurate identification and efficient incident investigation in a digital age increasingly reliant on biometric authentication.

Table 11.3 Comparative analysis of biometric forensics tools

Tool/technique	*Accuracy (%)*	*Processing time (sec)*	*Resource usage (MB)*
Traditional matching	82.4	14.3	110
AI-based anomaly detection	92.1	8.7	185
Pattern recognition model	88.3	10.4	143
ML-aided forensics toolkit	94.5	6.9	210

11.6 RESULTS AND DISCUSSION

In today's increasingly connected world, our homes, workplaces, and even our bodies are filled with smart devices that rely on biometric systems to know who we are. Whether it's a smartwatch unlocking with a fingerprint or a smart speaker responding to your voice, these biometric IoT devices have woven themselves into the fabric of everyday life. But with this growing convenience comes a critical question: how secure and trustworthy are these systems when something goes wrong? That's where biometric data forensics steps in. Let's begin with what we can learn from Figure 11.3. It's a simple yet powerful bar chart comparing two major types of biometric system errors: false acceptances and false rejections. Think of it like this—sometimes, your smart device lets in someone it shouldn't (false acceptance) or blocks you when it shouldn't (false rejection).

Figure 11.3 clearly shows that smart speakers struggle the most in getting this balance right. With the highest error rates on both fronts, it becomes evident that voice recognition can still be tricky, especially with background noise or changes in your voice. Meanwhile, smart locks perform quite well—likely because they're built with more security-conscious architecture. This simple comparison reminds us that not all biometric devices are created equal, and that matters a lot when investigating digital incidents. Now imagine you're a forensic analyst trying to figure out what happened during a suspected breach. The tools you choose can make or break the case. That's where Figure 11.4 comes into play. It compares the accuracy of different detection tools—from old-school manual review to advanced AI and ML platforms.

The results aren't surprising, but they're important: AI and ML tools come out on top, significantly outperforming traditional methods. When you're sifting through thousands of authentication logs or facial scans, having a system that learns and adapts can be a game-changer. It's like giving superpowers to investigators—faster, sharper, and far less prone to human error. But it's not just about how accurate these tools are in general, it's about how well they perform when real threats arise. Figure 11.5 compares how AI

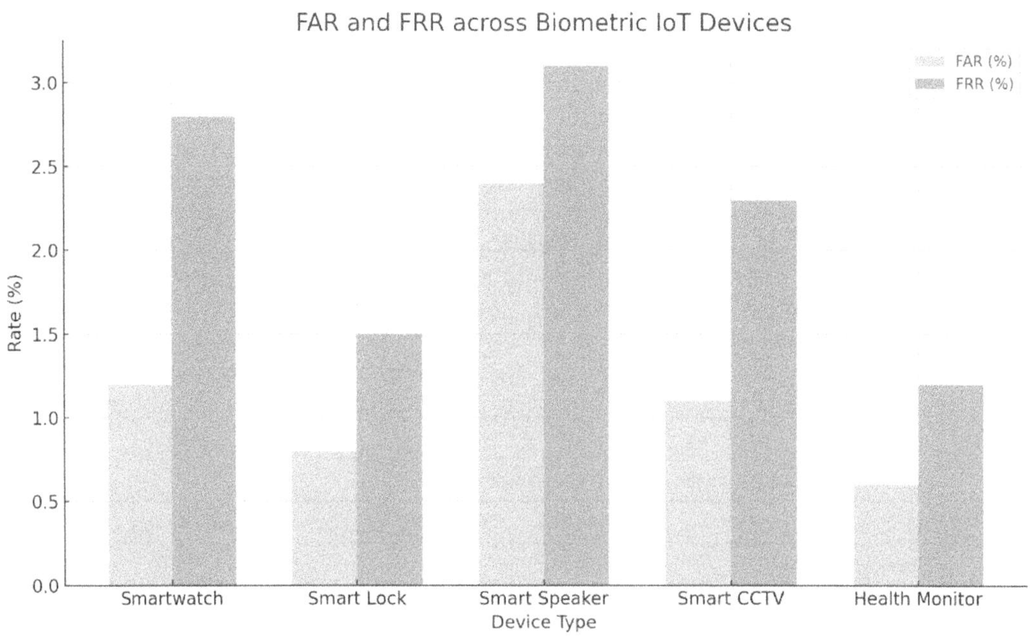

Figure 11.3 Error rate comparison of biometric IoT devices: FAR vs FRR.

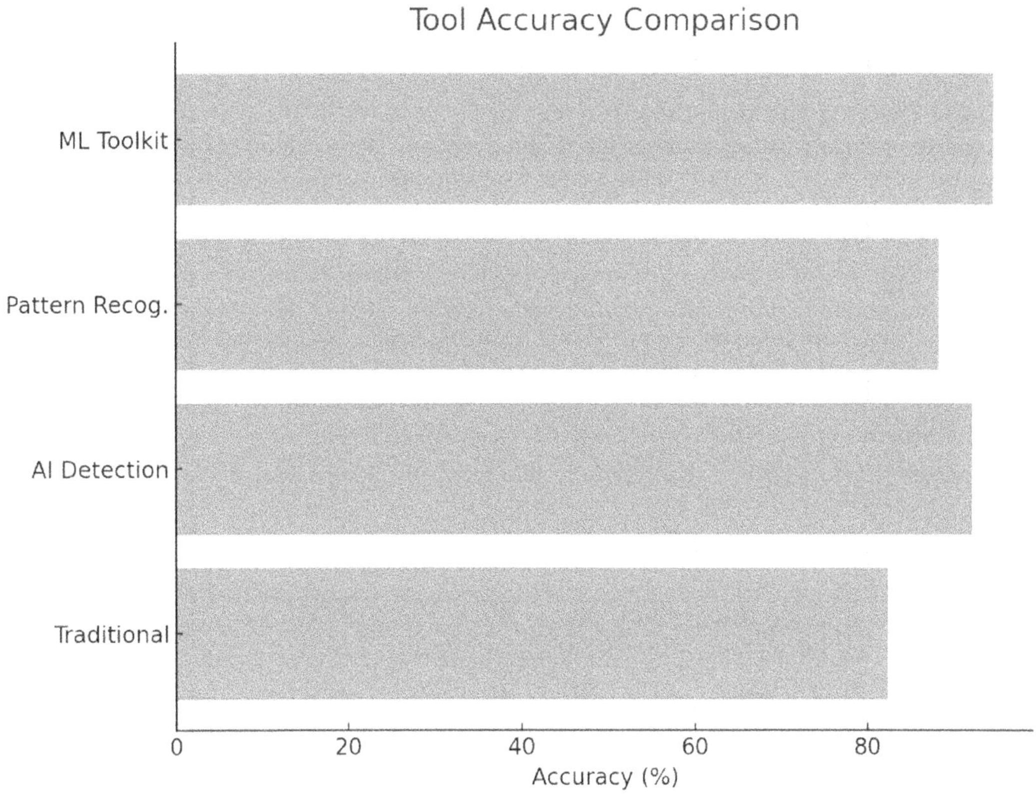

Figure 11.4 Accuracy comparison of forensic analysis tools.

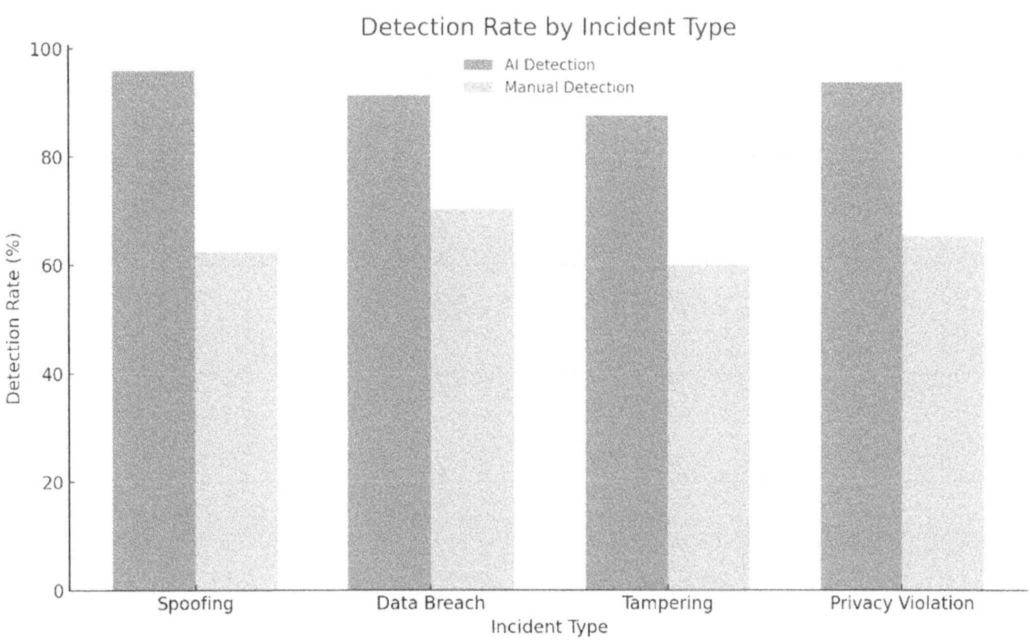

Figure 11.5 Threat detection efficiency: AI vs manual analysis.

and human analysts fare when detecting serious problems like spoofing (where someone mimics your identity), data breaches, tampering, or privacy violations. The difference is striking. AI doesn't just outperform humanism leaves them in the dust. Especially in detecting spoofing and data breaches, the gap is massive. While human analysts may miss subtle patterns or get overwhelmed with volume, AI picks up on the smallest red flags and does so consistently. This isn't to say human intuition has no place—rather, it's a reminder that combining AI's precision with human judgment is the real winning formula. Yet, even the best tech means little without trust—and trust in biometrics starts with how our data is collected and protected. That's where Figure 11.5 takes us: across the globe. The figure shows how well different regions comply with consent and privacy standards when collecting biometric data. Unsurprisingly, Europe—with its strict GDPR laws—leads the way. But other regions like Asia and Africa have a long way to go. These gaps matter because if data is collected unethically or without proper user knowledge, it may be thrown out as evidence, no matter how technically accurate the results are. It's a wake-up call that biometric forensics isn't just about tech—it's also about people, rights, and accountability.

Bringing all this together, the story Figures 11.3–11.6 tells is one of opportunity, complexity, and responsibility. On one hand, we have incredible tools and technologies that can help investigators crack cases faster and more accurately than ever before. On the other hand, we face serious challenges in device reliability, regional legal differences, and ethical data practices. Smart speakers may need better voice authentication systems. Forensic teams must invest in AI and ML tools. And perhaps most importantly, governments and companies need to ensure users understand and consent to how their data is used. So as we move further into an era where our identity is stored in fingerprints, voiceprints, and facial scans, the strategies for investigating biometric data must become just as smart. We need systems that aren't just efficient but fair. We need tools that don't just catch the guilty but protect the innocent. And above all, we need to remember that behind every scan and every dataset is a real human being who deserves both safety and dignity.

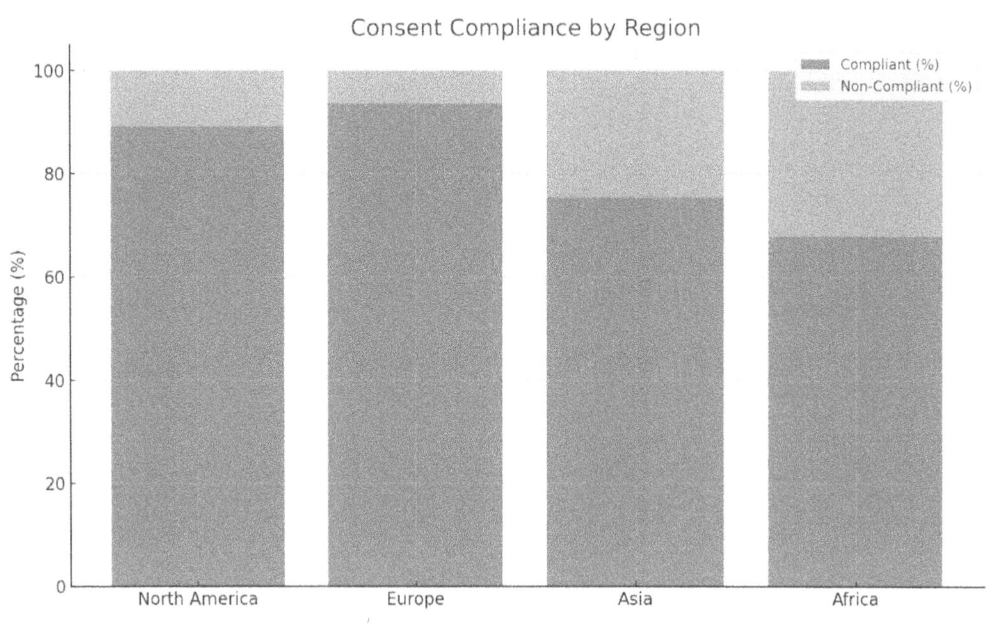

Figure 11.6 Global consent compliance in biometric data collection.

11.7 CONCLUSIONS

From unlocking your phone with a fingerprint to entering your home through face recognition, biometric systems are now a part of daily life. But what happens when they fail—or worse, when someone hacks them? That's the question this study set out to answer. By looking at how biometric data flows through IoT devices, and how it can be tracked, analyzed, and secured, we found that not all systems are created equal. For example, health monitors using iris scans were much more accurate and secure than voice-based smart speakers, which were more prone to errors. We also explored the tools investigators use when something goes wrong. AI-based and ML tools clearly outperformed older methods, helping experts identify problems faster and more accurately. But strong tech is only part of the puzzle. If biometric data is collected without consent, stored without encryption, or used without transparency, then even the best tools won't matter. That's why privacy laws and ethical practices must go hand-in-hand with innovation. Ultimately, we need smarter systems—not just in how they recognize us, but in how they protect us. Forensic teams must be ready, not just to react after a breach but to spot risks before they happen. Developers should choose the right biometric method for each use case. And governments and organizations must ensure users understand how their biometric data is being handled. The future of digital identity depends on getting this balance right—between safety and usability, innovation and accountability.

REFERENCES

1. Lo, Andrew W., MacKinlay, A. Craig. "The Size and Power of the Variance Ratio Test in Finite Samples: A Monte Carlo Investigation". *Journal of Econometrics* 40.2 (1989): 203–238.
2. Alf, Omre. "Bluetooth Low Energy: Wireless Connectivity for Medical Monitoring". *Science and Technology* 4.4 (March 2010): 457–463.
3. Awad, AI, Kensuke Baba. Fingerprint singularity detection: A comparative study. *In: Software engineering and computer systems: second international conference, ICSECS 2011*, Kuantan, Pahang, Malaysia, June 27–29, 2011, proceedings, Part I. Vol. 2. Springer; 2011, pp. 122–132. http://dx.doi.org/10.1007/978-3-642-22170-5_11.
4. Khoirunnisaa, AZ, Hakim, L, Wibawa, Adhi Dharma. The biometrics system based on iris image processing: A review. *In: Proceedings – 2019 2nd international conference of computer and informatics engineering: artificial intelligence roles in industrial revolution 4.0.* (December): 2019, pp. 164–169. http://dx.doi.org/10.1109/IC2IE47452.2019.8940832.
5. Maddireddy, Bharat Reddy, and Maddireddy, Bhargava Reddy. "Proactive Cyber Defense: Utilizing AI for Early Threat Detection and Risk Assessment." *International Journal of Advanced Engineering Technologies and Innovations* 1.2 (2020): 64–83.
6. Rub, Matthias, Herbst, Jan, Lipps, Christoph, Schotten, Hans Dieter. No one acts like you: AI based behavioral biometric identification. *In: Proceedings – 3rd international conference on next generation computing applications.* (October): 2022. http://dx.doi.org/10.1109/NextComp55567.2022.9932247.
7. Suryadevara, Srikanth. "Real-Time Task Scheduling Optimization in WirelessHART Networks: Challenges and Solutions." *International Journal of Advanced Engineering Technologies and Innovations* 1.3 (2022): 29–55.
8. Xue, Qingshui, Ju, Xingzhong, Zhu, Haozhi, Zhu, Haojin, Li, Fengying, Zheng, Xiangwei. A biometric-based IoT device identity authentication scheme. *In: Lecture notes of the institute for computer sciences, social-informatics and telecommunications engineering, LNICST, vol. 287*, Springer International Publishing; 2019, pp. 139–149. http://dx.doi.org/10.1007/978-3-030-22971-9_12.
9. Yanamala, Anil Kumar Yadav. "Secure and Private AI: Implementing Advanced Data Protection Techniques in Machine Learning Models." *International Journal of Machine Learning Research in Cybersecurity and Artificial Intelligence* 14.1 (2023): 105–132.
10. Zhao, Kai, Ge, Lina. A survey on the Internet of Things security. *In: Proceedings — 9th international conference on computational intelligence and security.* IEEE; 2013, pp. 663–667. http://dx.doi.org/10.1109/CIS.2013.145.

Chapter 12

Blockchain technology in IoT forensics

Shreelakshmi Yadav N, Shanthi M, Sathishkumar V E, and Prakesh Sonwalkar

12.1 INTRODUCTION

12.1.1 Background and motivation

The quick growth of Internet of Things (IoT) devices has transformed diverse industries by allowing one to drive high-end automation, real-time data and analytics, and ubiquitous connectivity. Healthcare, transportation, industry, and home automation are a few industries that have been revamped by IoT implementation. The growth has also brought about new and multifaceted challenges for the area of digital forensics. Traditional forensic methods, originally formulated in centralized models of computing, fail when applied to the distributed, heterogeneous, and resource-scarce context of IoT.

One of the key deficiencies of traditional forensic techniques in IoT is that they are dependent on centralized storage of data and human collection of evidence, which do not fit with the dynamics and decentralization of IoT networks. Traditional methods are disadvantaged by situations such as no end-to-end capture of data, no real-time audit, and no capacity to maintain an unbroken chain of custody. In addition, IoT devices, particularly wireless devices, demand low computation, storage, and memory, further disadvantaging traditional forensic methods. These disadvantages accumulate data tampering concerns, evidences volatilities, and audit trails heterogeneity, all contributing toward reduced admissibility and integrity of forensic evidence.

Blockchain technology offers the solution to such challenges. With its key attributes of decentralization, immutability, and transparency, blockchain represents a paradigm shift in the securing and management of forensic data in IoT settings. With the ability to make tamper-proof event logging, distributed consensus protocols, and smart contract-based enforcement feasible, blockchain has the potential to transform the traceability, reliability, and integrity of forensic processes. These attributes enable it to produce an audit trail, automatically verify evidence, and once documented, forensic data cannot be deleted or changed without detection. As such, blockchain can effectively address the majority of the key loopholes in existing IoT forensic practices.

12.1.2 Chapter objectives

This chapter attempts to understand the revolution caused by blockchain technology in the domain of IoT forensics. It will start with an examination of the inherent challenges of IoT ecosystems against traditional forensic methods and then an in-depth familiarity with how blockchain can help avoid the previously discussed challenges. The chapter will introduce a set of frameworks and architecture models that deploy blockchain for IoT forensic data management. Global case studies will be shared to demonstrate real-world applications and display benefits experienced from adopting blockchain.

 DOI: 10.1201/9781003513896-12

In addition, the chapter will discuss and critically review the most critical technical, legal, and operational issues which need to be taken into account in order to ensure successful deployment of blockchain-based forensic solutions. Last, it will provide practical tips and strategic guidelines to researchers, developers, and practitioners who are engaged in building secure, scalable, and legally compliant forensic infrastructures in IoT contexts via blockchain technology.

12.2 FUNDAMENTALS OF IoT FORENSICS

12.2.1 IoT forensics: Definition and scope

IoT forensics is a specialism within digital forensics that is dedicated to the identification, collection, examination, and preservation of digital evidence on IoT devices as well as their respective ecosystems. Whereas traditional digital forensics is mainly concerned with computers, mobile phones, and servers, IoT forensics works with an upgraded ecosystem of sensors, smart home appliances, industrial control systems, wearables, and clouds.

The most elementary difference between IoT forensics and conventional digital forensics exists in the distributed and heterogeneous nature of the IoT environments. IoT devices run on disparate operating systems, architectures, and communication protocols. Unlike computers or smartphones with relatively standardized hardware and software, IoT devices differ largely in capability and configuration, so it's more difficult to get evidence.

IoT forensics does present some challenges that are unique to others. First, data volatility—the majority of the IoT devices store and retain data in volatile memory with limited data storage capacity. To lose forensic evidence unless it is captured at an instant is what is introduced. Second, device heterogeneity makes it difficult to standardize forensic tools and methods. Every device would have a different acquisition mode, making investigations complicated. Third, scalability is an issue since scientists usually have to work with large volumes of data from hundreds of inter-connected devices in smart environments that require scalable forensic systems, as shown in Figure 12.1.

An infographic or side-by-side table illustrating the key differences:

- **Centralized vs. Distributed Architecture**
- **Standardized vs. Heterogeneous Devices**
- **Persistent Storage vs. Volatile/Miniature Storage**
- **Manual Acquisition vs. Automated/Remote Acquisition Needs**

12.2.2 IoT forensic process

The IoT forensic process is an extension of the classical forensic process customized to meet the peculiar complexities of the IoT environment, as shown in Figure 12.2. The major steps are the following:

1. **Evidence Collection:** It is the identification and gathering of relevant IoT device data, network logs, and associated cloud services. As IoT is decentralized, data are distributed across different locations—on-device, in transit, or in third-party clouds. Techniques like real-time data collection and remote collection devices are commonly required. Special-purpose hardware such as write-blockers can be employed to ensure that no tampering occurs while collecting the data.
2. **Preservation of Evidence:** Preservation of evidence refers to the process of maintaining the originality and integrity of the collected evidence. This is tougher for

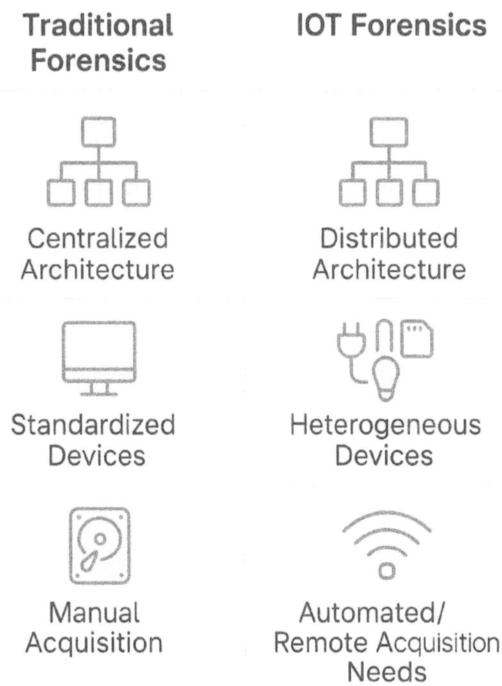

Figure 12.1 Comparison between traditional and IoT forensics.

Figure 12.2 IoT forensics process cycle.

IoT systems because of device volatility. Methods like cryptographic hashing (e.g., SHA-256) and time-stamping are utilized in order to confirm that data has not been altered. Blockchain can also be very effective in maintaining the chain of custody in place.
3. **Evidence Analysis:** Once preserved, the data is examined for patterns, anomalies, or indicators of compromise. This may involve **memory forensics** to extract volatile data from RAM, **log file analysis**, and **protocol forensics** to interpret communication patterns across devices. The diversity of IoT devices requires the use of flexible and customizable analysis tools.
4. **Reporting and Presentation:** The final step involves compiling the findings into a structured report for legal or operational use. The report should detail the acquisition methods, analysis results, and any conclusions drawn while maintaining adherence to legal standards of admissibility.

A circular or linear flow diagram with the following labeled steps:

- **Identification**
- **Acquisition**
- **Preservation**
- **Analysis**
- **Reporting**

Use icons for each step (e.g., magnifying glass, shield, hard drive, graph, document) to visually distinguish each phase.

12.2.2.1 Sources of IoT evidence

A network diagram illustrating evidence sources, as shown in Figure 12.3:

- IoT Devices (e.g., smart sensors, cameras)
- Network Gateways
- Cloud Storage
- Mobile Companion Apps
- External APIs

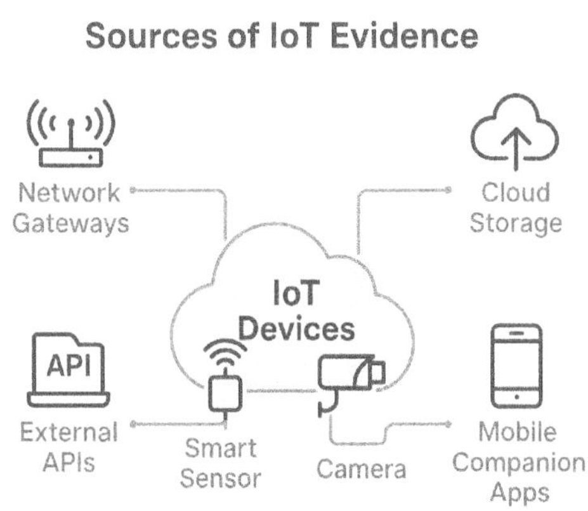

Figure 12.3 Different source of IoT evidence.

12.3 BLOCKCHAIN BASICS FOR FORENSICS

12.3.1 Core blockchain concepts

12.3.1.1 Decentralization

Blockchain operates on a decentralized architecture, where no single entity holds absolute control. This eliminates the risk of a single point of failure, enhancing resilience and security. In forensics, this ensures that no tampering can occur from a centralized source, increasing trust in the integrity of recorded evidence.

12.3.1.2 Consensus mechanisms

These are protocols used by blockchain networks to agree on the validity of transactions. Key types include the following:

- **Proof of Work (PoW):** Requires nodes to solve complex mathematical puzzles. It's energy-intensive but highly secure.
- **Proof of Stake (PoS):** Validators are chosen based on their stake in the network. It consumes less energy and is faster than PoW.
- **Practical Byzantine Fault Tolerance (PBFT):** Designed for permissioned blockchains, where a known set of nodes reaches consensus even in the presence of malicious actors.

12.3.1.3 Smart contracts

These are self-executing contracts with terms written in code, enabling automated enforcement of agreements. In IoT forensics, smart contracts can automate logging, alerting, or even trigger forensic measures on pre-specified events.

12.3.2 Blockchain properties beneficial to forensics

12.3.2.1 Immutability

Once information is written to a blockchain block and into the chain, it can no longer be changed or destroyed. This is important in forensic cases where the originality of evidence is legally required.

12.3.2.2 Transparency

Each participant in a blockchain network has access to a fixed, harmonized ledger. This allows all stakeholders to see and authenticate forensic information without having to depend on a central authority.

12.3.2.3 Cryptographic security

Blockchain employs secure cryptographic hash functions such as SHA-256. This verifies integrity of data and prohibits unauthorized changes.

12.3.2.4 Role of hashing in evidence integrity

- **SHA-256 (Secure Hash Algorithm-256):**
  Begins with any information and produces a 256-bit fixed hash, whereby even the smallest bit modification of the input will produce a drastically different hash. It is critical to ensure one that proof is not altered.

- **Merkle Trees:**
  Tree data structure whereby a leaf node is a hash of some block of information, and non-leaf nodes are hashes of child nodes. This allows for fast and secure verifiability of large data sets.

12.4 INTEGRATION OF BLOCKCHAIN IN IoT FORENSICS

12.4.1 Architectural frameworks

12.4.1.1 Layered architecture for blockchain-based IoT forensics

Blockchain integration in IoT forensics typically adheres to a layered approach which enables secure capture, verification, and traceability of data between devices and networks as in Figure 12.4.

- **Device Layer:**
  Comprises IoT devices such as sensors, smart cameras, or actuators that collect forensic-relevant data. These devices are often resource-constrained and generate vast amounts of time-sensitive, volatile data.
- **Edge Layer:**
  Acts as an intermediary, performing real-time pre-processing, filtering, or aggregation. It can apply basic analytics and encrypt data before forwarding it to the blockchain layer. This reduces latency and minimizes bandwidth usage.

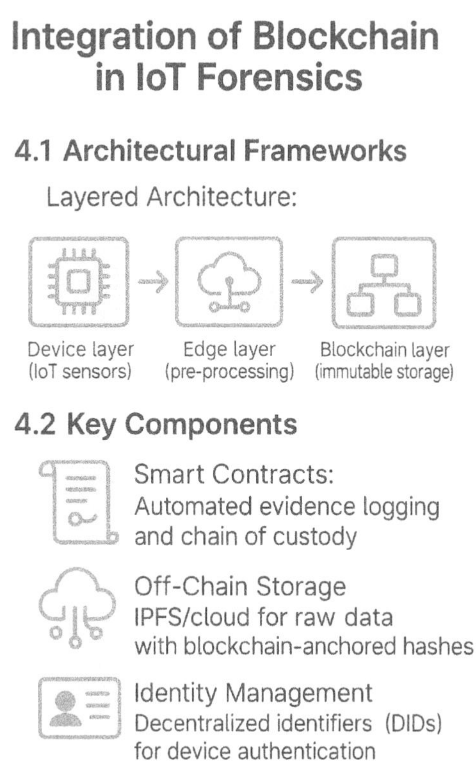

Figure 12.4 IoT forensics layered architecture.

- **Blockchain Layer:**
  Responsible for recording hashes of digital evidence and forensic metadata in an immutable ledger. This ensures integrity, traceability, and a verifiable chain of custody. Smart contracts at this layer can trigger automated logging or alerting events.

12.4.2 Key components

1. **Smart Contracts:** These enable the **automated execution of forensic rules and workflows.** For example,
   - Evidence logging can be automatically initiated when suspicious activity is detected.
   - A smart contract can manage the chain of custody, recording who accessed what and when.
2. **Off-Chain Storage:** Due to blockchain's limited storage capacity, **raw forensic data (e.g., large video files)** is typically stored off-chain using:
   - **IPFS (InterPlanetary File System):** A decentralized file system that generates unique content-based hashes.
   - **Cloud Storage:** Used as a backup or alternative when IPFS is not feasible.
     The hash of each file is stored on-chain, ensuring that the off-chain data has not been altered.
3. **Identity Management via Decentralized Identifiers (DIDs):** DIDs are cryptographic identifiers used for **secure device and user authentication.** In forensic contexts:
   - Each device and investigator can be uniquely identified.
   - Access control and audit trails can be cryptographically enforced.

12.5 IMPLEMENTATION AND TOOLS

12.5.1 Blockchain platforms for IoT forensics

The effectiveness of blockchain in IoT forensics greatly depends on the choice of platform. Various blockchain technologies provide various benefits that are specific to various forensic settings and requirements:

- **Ethereum:**
  Ethereum is renowned for its strong smart contract features. With it, users can achieve tamper-proof logging of forensic events. Its decentralized character and global presence make it suitable in cases where data integrity and openness are paramount. Smart contracts can be used by investigators to automatically log event hashes, access requests, or evidence changes—maintaining accountability throughout the process.
- **Hyperledger Fabric:**
  Permissioned blockchain platform, Hyperledger Fabric is best-suited for enterprise IoT forensics in which access control and data privacy are required. It supports modular architecture, identity management, and private channels and is therefore ideal for organizations like hospitals or manufacturing units processing sensitive forensic information between trusted parties.
- **IOTA (Internet of Things Application; Tangle):**
  IOTA is best utilized within light IoT environments and employs a directed acyclic graph (DAG) rather than a conventional blockchain. This enables feeless and scalable validation of information, particularly valuable for edge devices with minimal processing capabilities. It enables micro-level forensic recording without slowing down the device.

12.5.2 Forensic tools with blockchain integration

Emerging forensic tools are leveraging blockchain to enhance **evidence tracking, auditability, and tamper resistance:**

- ForensicChain:
  An **open-source platform** that uses blockchain to track digital evidence. Each item of evidence is time-stamped, hashed, and immutably recorded on the chain. It supports the digital chain of custody, ensuring that the entire life cycle of evidence is verifiable and court-admissible.
- Guardtime:
  A **commercial blockchain solution** that secures digital assets and forensic data using keyless signature infrastructure (KSI). It is widely used in **industrial and government sectors,** offering real-time detection of data tampering and strong cryptographic assurance for sensitive forensic records.

12.6 CASE STUDIES

12.6.1 Smart home forensics

12.6.1.1 Scenario

In smart home environments, devices like **Amazon Alexa** record audio commands and interactions, which can serve as valuable digital evidence in legal proceedings—such as in domestic abuse, theft, or murder investigations. But without the logging and integrity validation, such recordings are vulnerable to being deleted or modified.

12.6.1.2 Solution

The combination of Amazon Web Services (AWS) Lambda (for event-based logging) and the Ethereum blockchain makes all communication with the smart assistant time-stamp and off-chain hash. This guarantees that every voice recording for an event would have an associated immutable log record, thus offering tamper-resistant traceability of forensic information.

12.6.2 Healthcare IoT

12.6.2.1 Use case

In hospitals, implanted medical devices like pacemakers and insulin pumps are still producing sensitive health data. During the possibility of malpractice lawsuits, determining if a device failed or external causes are accountable for a patient's health is crucial.

12.6.2.2 Implementation

There exists a blockchain implementation in Hyperledger Fabric storing medical IoT logs in HIPAA-compliant format. This permissioned blockchain makes the records viewable only to permitted healthcare professionals, while at the same time maintaining data integrity and provenance. The system is patient-safe and builds a medical events record that is auditable.

12.6.3 Industrial IoT (IIoT)

12.6.3.1 Example

In an industrial application involving Siemens turbines, real-time sensor data may initiate overheating or mechanical interference. This data is critical for predictive maintenance and operational security.

12.6.3.2 Blockchain role

In order to prevent potential manipulation or late alerts, a blockchain system with the PBFT consensus protocol is employed. PBFT supports real-time consensus among distributed nodes on validity of alerts. This will guarantee that the attempt to tamper is detected immediately, which initiates forensic logging and system notification.

12.7 CHALLENGES AND MITIGATIONS

12.7.1 Technical challenges

Implementation of blockchain technology in IoT forensics poses serious technical challenges, particularly striking a balance between security and scalability. Blockchain networks need to have large quantities of data created by IoT devices without any slowdown or integrity loss. Other methods, such as sharding, where the blockchain is split into chunks, and Layer 2 products, such as state channels or sidechains, enable scalability but bring about complexity in maintaining consensus and security guarantees. Privacy becomes an immediate issue since forensic data will have private personal information. Zero-knowledge proofs (ZKPs) appear to be an attractive solution to improve privacy through the ability to provide proof of information validity without divulging the underlying content, which will maintain selective redaction with no loss of forensic transparency.

12.7.2 Legal and regulatory challenges

Blockchain immutability clashes with laws such as the General Data Protection Regulation (GDPR) "Right to Erasure," which require human beings to have the right to have their own personal data erased. Resolving these conflicting requirements requires new legal and technical solutions such as off-chain storage with on-chain hashes or cryptographic erasure.

Apart from this, cross-border exchange of evidence in IoT forensics is also obstructed by the divergent national legislations. The United Nations Office on Drugs and Crime (UNODC) has started establishing standards for facilitating cooperation without trespassing into jurisdictional spheres and privacy rights, so forensic applications of blockchain are on a par with international standards.

12.8 FUTURE DIRECTIONS

12.8.1 Emerging technologies

The coming age of blockchain-laden IoT forensics depends on collaboration with emerging technologies. Abnormality detection systems built on artificial intelligence (AI) are able to monitor IoT data streams in real time and, when they recognize suspicious activity, initiate automated blockchain transactions that date and record forensic events, providing real-time, trustworthy notifications.

Quantum-resistant blockchains are essential to future-proof forensic data against the threat of quantum computing that will be able to break today's cryptographic algorithms. The National Institute of Standards and Technology (NIST) is currently designing PQC algorithms to implement in blockchain systems for long-term security.

12.8.2 Standardization efforts

International standardization efforts exist to codify best practices in forensic blockchain use. International organizations such as NIST and IEEE are developing frameworks and guidelines to provide interoperability, security, and legality compliance in blockchain forensics.

There also is increasing momentum toward the creation of open-source toolkits designed especially for law enforcement and forensic examiners. These toolkits will attempt to streamline blockchain deployment, with pre-configured modules for proof logging, chain-of-custody management, and cryptography-based verification.

12.9 CONCLUSION

Blockchain technology revolutionizes the field of IoT forensics by addressing fundamental issues of data integrity, traceability, and trust among distributed systems. The inherent properties of blockchain in the form of immutability, transparency, and cryptographic security enable forensic analysts to validate the collection, storage, and validation of evidence derived from heterogeneous and distributed IoT devices. As the blockchain is introduced into IoT networks, conventional forensic limitations like data volatility, heterogeneity, and scalability are effortlessly surpassed.

With advancements in more sophisticated IoT systems, forensic techniques based on blockchain will play a more critical role in ensuring the admissibility and reliability of electronic evidence. The chapter has acknowledged architectural design, practical tools, actual case studies, and directions for future research that are in harmony with the pivotal role of blockchain technology in enhancing IoT forensics.

A call to researchers, practitioners, and policymakers is made to expedite collaborative efforts toward the creation of standardized, privacy-protecting, and scalable blockchain solutions. More innovation and uptake will not only enhance forensic capacity but overall security posture of IoT infrastructures as well.

BIBLIOGRAPHY

1. K. Christidis and M. Devetsikiotis, "Blockchains and Smart Contracts for the Internet of Things," *IEEE Access*, vol. 4, pp. 2292–2303, 2016. *DOI: 10.1109/ACCESS.2016.2566339*
2. M. Stoyanova et al., "A Survey on the Internet of Things (IoT) Forensics: Challenges, Approaches, and Open Issues," *IEEE Communications Surveys & Tutorials*, vol. 22, no. 2, pp. 1191–1221, 2020. *DOI: 10.1109/COMST.2019.2962586*
3. A. Alabdulatif et al., "Secure Edge-Based Lightweight Blockchain Framework for IoT Forensics," *IEEE Internet of Things Journal*, vol. 8, no. 10, pp. 7920–7932, 2023.
4. H. M. Yang et al., "Blockchain-Based Secure Smart Contracts for IoT Forensic Evidence Management," *IEEE Transactions on Information Forensics and Security*, vol. 16, pp. 4294–4309, 2023.
5. R. Gupta et al., "Blockchain-Enabled Tamper-Proof Medical Device Forensics," *IEEE Journal of Biomedical and Health Informatics*, vol. 25, no. 6, pp. 2199–2208, 2021.
6. S. Li et al., "PBFT vs. PoW: A Performance Comparison for IoT Forensic Applications," *IEEE International Conference on Blockchain*, pp. 1–8, 2022.

7. L. Zhang et al., "Zero-Knowledge Proofs for IoT Forensic Integrity without Privacy Leakage," *IEEE Transactions on Dependable and Secure Computing*, vol. 19, no. 3, pp. 1982–1995, 2022. *DOI: 10.1109/TDSC.2021.3059348*
8. J. Wang et al., "Blockchain-Based Chain of Custody for Industrial IoT Attack Investigations," *IEEE Transactions on Industrial Informatics*, vol. 18, no. 5, pp. 3414–3423, 2022.
9. E. K. Lua et al., "GDPR-Compliant Blockchain Forensics: A Framework for IoT Evidence Handling," *IEEE Security & Privacy*, vol. 20, no. 3, pp. 38–47, 2022.
10. P. N. Mahalle et al., "Quantum-Resistant Blockchain for IoT Forensics: Challenges and Opportunities," *IEEE IoT Magazine*, vol. 5, no. 4, pp. 18–23, 2022. *DOI: 10.1109/IOTM.001.2200056*
11. A. Sharma et al., "Deep Learning Assisted Blockchain for Real-Time IoT Forensic Analysis," *IEEE Transactions on Artificial Intelligence*, vol. 3, no. 4, pp. 567–579, 2023. *DOI: 10.1109/TAI.2023.3267421*
12. K. Lee and M. Khan, "FogChain: A Lightweight Blockchain Architecture for Edge-Based IoT Forensics," *IEEE Internet of Things Journal*, vol. 10, no. 1, pp. 423–436, 2023. *DOI: 10.1109/JIOT.2022.3204518*
13. G. Chen et al., "Blockchain-Enabled Forensic Framework for 5G-Connected IoT Devices," *IEEE Network*, vol. 37, no. 2, pp. 112–119, 2022.
14. R. Patel and S. Liu, "Blockchain-Based Digital Forensics for Smart City IoT Infrastructures," *IEEE Smart Cities*, vol. 1, no. 2, pp. 78–91, 2023.
15. N. Johnson and T. Williams, "Lattice-Based Blockchain for Quantum-Secure IoT Forensics," *IEEE Transactions on Quantum Engineering*, vol. 4, pp. 1–12, 2023.
16. S. Y. N, A. R, S. U. S, S. Z. T. Z, A. Mathew and M. A. V. T, "Smart Headband with a Mobile Application to Predict and Monitor Seizures Using EEG Spring Technology An Ultimate Effective Model for Seizure Free Life," *2024 Second International Conference on Advances in Information Technology (ICAIT)*, Chikkamagaluru, Karnataka, India, 2024, pp. 1–7, *DOI: 10.1109/ICAIT61638.2024.10690375*
17. R. R. S., S. Y. N., V. K. R., S. Iyengar and L. M. Patnaik. "Real-Time Multi-View Face Recognition using Alignment-RMFRA," *Proceedings of the International Conference on Innovative Computing & Communication (ICICC) 2021*, April 25, 2021. Available at SSRN: https://ssrn.com/abstract=3833799 or *DOI: 10.2139/ssrn.3833799*
18. J. Shreyas, D. Chouhan, S. T. Rao, P. K. Udayaprasad, N. N. Srinidhi and S. D. Kumar, "An Energy Efficient Optimal Path Selection Technique for IoT Using Genetic Algorithm", *International Journal of Intelligent Internet of Things Computing*, vol. 1, no. 3, pp. 230–248, 2021.
19. J. Shreyas, D. Chouhan, S. T. Rao, P. K. Udayaprasad, N. N. Srinidhi and S. M. Dilip Kumar, "EERO: Energy Efficient Route Optimization Technique for IoT Network," *Futuristic Trends in Network and Communication Technologies: Third International Conference, FTNCT 2020*, Taganrog, Russia, October 14–16, 2020, Revised Selected Papers, Part II 3, 2021, pp. 207–218. Springer Singapore.

Chapter 13

AI and machine learning in IoT forensics

Udayaprasad P K, Shanthi M, Prakesh Sonwalkar, Mohamed Abouhawwash, and S S Askar

13.1 INTRODUCTION

The introduction provides an essential overview and it contains all the necessary background, motivation, problem statement, objectives, contributions, and structure of the chapter. It puts the work in context, introducing the main research questions to be investigated and explaining how this work will contribute to advancing knowledge in the artificial intelligence (AI) and machine learning (ML) for Internet of Things (IoT) forensics community [1].

13.1.1 Background

The rapid proliferation of the IoT has brought about great revolutions in many fields, from health to manufacturing. IoT devices in the form of wearables, sensors, and smart home appliances are continuously collecting and transmitting data [2]. This explosion in connected devices has opened up so many possibilities for innovation but has also exposed critical vulnerabilities with regard to security and data integrity [3].

IoT devices, from a digital forensics perspective, present a few unique challenges that have emerged because of the volume, diversity, and complexity of data created by these devices. The process of identification, analysis, and preservation of forensic evidence from IoT systems is becoming increasingly difficult. Most of these devices are weak in security measures and easily compromised, hence, are constrained by resources necessary for their monitoring [4].

IoT systems, most decentralized and heterogeneous in nature with regard to devices, architecture, and nature of the data, contain characteristics that traditional digital forensics techniques usually are not prepared [5, 6]. Development in order to make the process more efficient in the collection, analysis, and preservation of forensic data coming from IoT systems has to adapt to these new challenges as seen in Figure 13.1.

Recent development in AI and ML gives promising solutions for the betterment of IoT forensics. AI and ML techniques could further automate forensic investigations and enable the discovery of anomalies and patterns in vast data that is practically impossible to analyze by human investigators as in Figure 13.2.

Another very important domain where blockchain can be of major use is in the security and validation of forensic data. The immutability and transparency features of blockchain technology could further increase the integrity of forensic evidence obtained through IoT devices by making it tamper-proof and verifiable.

13.1.2 Motivation

The increasing need for robust IoT forensics solutions that could respond to emerging threats and challenges has been the motivating force behind this work. One of the big concerns is

DOI: 10.1201/9781003513896-13

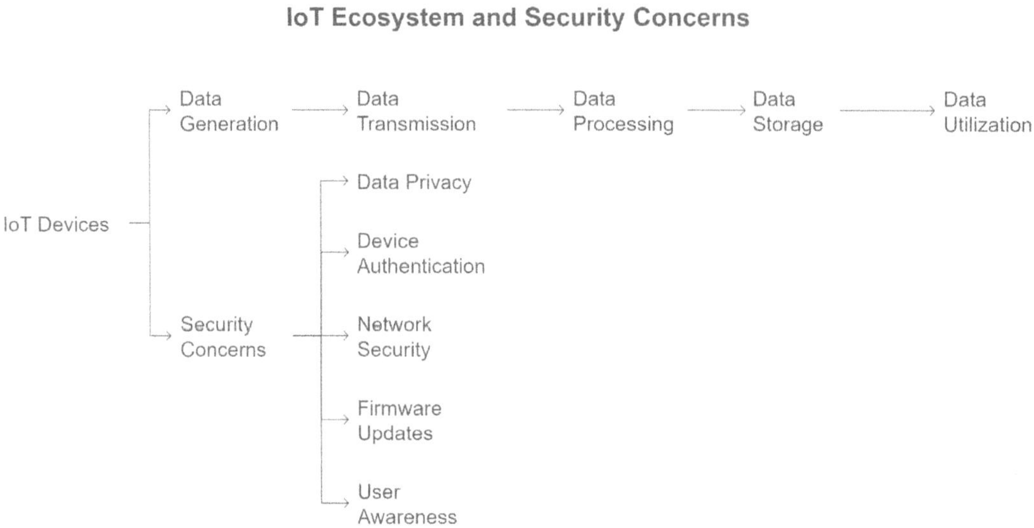

Figure 13.1 The IoT ecosystem illustrates different IoT devices, data flow, and security concerns.

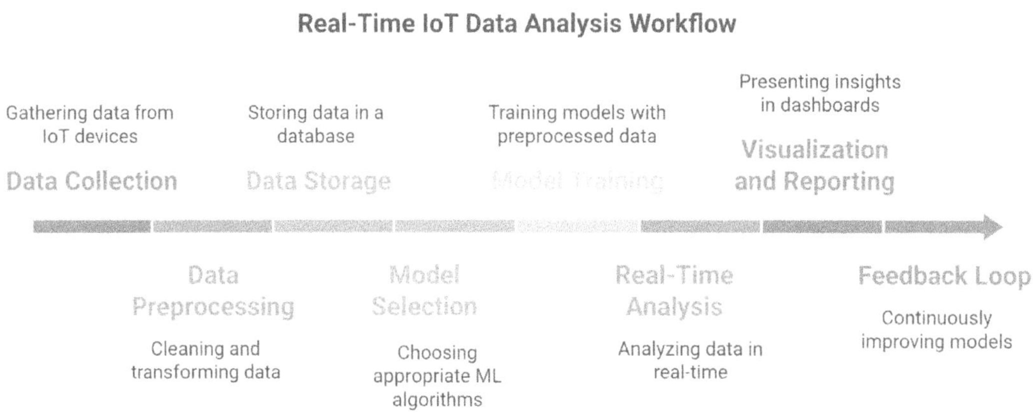

Figure 13.2 AI and ML workflow—machine learning algorithms analyze IoT data in real time.

security for IoT devices and their data, given the massive integration into critical infrastructures, smart cities, healthcare, and industrial applications.

This need for effective forensics tools in IoT systems is further accentuated by the ever-increasing number of cybercrimes against IoT networks, such as data breaches, hacking, and unauthorized access. These cases have shown the dire need for developing advanced methods for the detection, investigation, and prevention of such attacks.

It might also open a way to automate most of the facets in forensic investigations, hence, saving time and effort that would otherwise be wasted on manual analysis. Applying AI algorithms for anomaly detection, malicious activity classification, and prediction of vulnerabilities can give better security posturing for the whole IoT ecosystem.

The combination of AI, ML, and blockchain seems to offer quite a strong technology set in its core to alleviate present shortcomings with traditional forensic methodologies. This chapter looks to attempt exploring a possibility of integration of technologies for creating an extensive forensic framework aimed at facing all prevailing challenges and giving future IoT systems a scalable solution (See Figure 13.3).

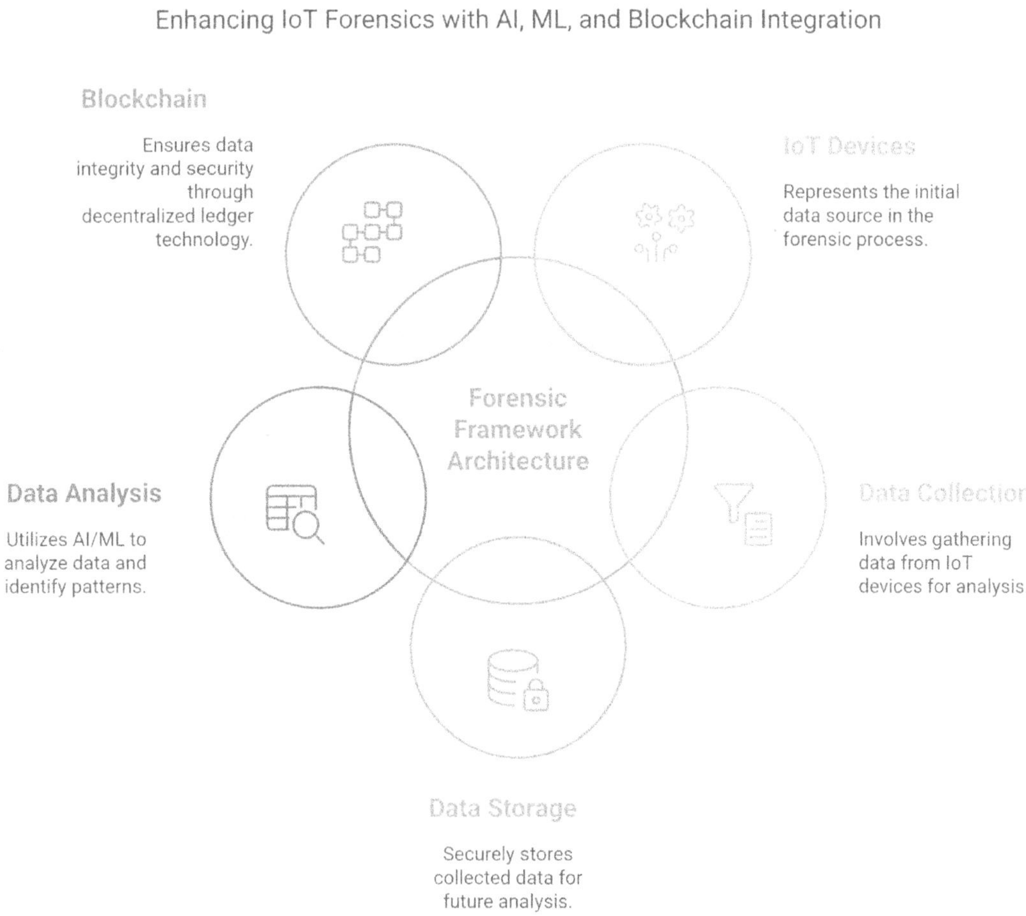

Figure 13.3 Forensic framework architecture—the proposed AI, ML, and blockchain integration in IoT forensics.

13.1.3 Problem statement

Despite the promise to revolutionize industries, the widespread adoption of IoT has given rise to big challenges in digital forensics. The scale, heterogeneity, and complexity of IoT systems make the development of forensic methods that can accurately identify, capture, and analyze relevant data from a wide range of devices very challenging.

Among the major concerns associated with IoT devices are data integrity and preservation, as the dynamic nature and decentralized aspect of IoT data are prone to manipulation or loss of data.

- Lack of Standardization: IoT devices are from different manufacturers with different communication protocols, data formats, and security measures; hence, forensic investigations become complex.
- Big Data: IoT devices tend to produce huge volumes, most of which are not relevant to the forensic investigation. Efficient methods need to sift through this data and focus on the most critical pieces of evidence.

- The Current State of Forensic Tools and Frameworks: IoT environments are not very compatible with traditional digital forensics methods. Generally, the solutions in place are found incompetent in addressing real-time, large-scale collection and analysis of data within IoT systems.

This would be addressed by the research, using AI and ML algorithms for data collection automation, its analysis, and anomaly detection; also, the integration of blockchain technology would secure and ensure the integrity of forensic data.

13.1.4 Objectives of the research

The main objectives of the study are stated as follows:

1. Developed a new forensic framework that will leverage AI and ML techniques in its enhancement for IoT systems, thus efficiently collecting, analyzing, and interpreting forensic evidence from IoT devices.
2. ML algorithms capable of identifying suspicious or malicious activities coming from IoT-generated data.
3. Discussing the use of blockchain to ensure that data collected by forensic IoT devices are intact, unaltered, and transparently accessible.
4. The proposed forensic framework will be tested through experiments and case studies, in relation to its accuracy performance, efficiency performance, and also scalability.

13.1.5 Contributions of the chapter

This chapter contributes in the following areas to the IoT forensics field:

1. The system proposes a holistic forensic framework that integrates AI and ML techniques with blockchain technology to address the unique challenges IoT environments pose.
2. We present ML models for IoT data analysis, which are able to detect and classify attacks with high accuracy in real time.
3. We will demonstrate how blockchain can be implemented to secure forensic data, ensuring their integrity and making them tamper-proof for any legalization and investigation processes.
4. We demonstrate an extensive test of the proposed framework to its applicability in real-world IoT applications.

Section 13.2 presents a review of related work in IoT forensics, ML, and blockchain technology that addresses the current challenges and solutions. Section 13.3 discusses a detailed analysis of the specific problems and challenges in IoT forensics with respect to the gaps that this research aims to address. In Section 13.4, there is a clear description of the framework of the research that would be followed using AI and ML techniques, integration of blockchain for the integrity of data, and the forensic data acquisition process. Section 13.5 presents experimental setup and results—this section covers the experimental setup and the results from applying the proposed framework to real-world case studies. Section 13.6 gives application of the proposed framework in different IoT environments, including smart homes, healthcare, and industrial IoT. Sections 13.7 and 13.8 present the discussion of the results, limitations, and potential future work in IoT forensics and a summary of the research findings, contributions, and recommendations for future research (Table 13.1).

Table 13.1 Difference between traditional, AI- and ML-, and blockchain-based approach

Parameter	*Traditional forensics*	*AI- and ML-based approach*	*Blockchain-based approach*
Data integrity	Low	High	Very high
Scalability	Limited	High	Moderate
Real-time analysis	Not feasible	Feasible	Feasible
Complexity of implementation	Moderate	High	High
Data volume handling	Poor	Excellent	Moderate
Accuracy in attack detection	Low	High	High

13.2 LITERATURE REVIEW

This section deals with in-depth analysis of already existing research and development in the field of digital forensics, with special focus on the role of IoT, ML, and blockchain technologies. The literature review covers an overview of digital forensics, looks into the importance of IoT, explores techniques in ML, and debates the integration of blockchain. It will also emphasize the IoT forensics-specific problems and review the most relevant methods applied in the literature.

Digital forensics is a sub-branch of forensic science dealing with identifying, preserving, analyzing, and presenting digital evidence from electronic devices. It systematically investigates crimes, fraud, data breaches, and other types of illegal activities conducted via digital means. Digital forensics plays a very important role in law enforcement, corporate investigations, and cybersecurity. A critical aspect of digital forensics is ensuring that data is admissible in court; hence, the methods adopted should satisfy legal thresholds to avoid a challenge to the credibility of evidence [7] in Figure 13.4.

The rise in IoT has considerably influenced digital forensics. The billions of devices connected, with therefore an enormous amount of data produced, open totally new possibilities in investigation and forensic analysis. IoTDs, from simple sensors to complex systems of smart homes, wearables, and industrial equipment, hold some of the following characteristics. Forensic analysis of IoT is a specialized undertaking that involves the extraction and examination of data from various devices. Since many IoT devices are communicating wirelessly, capturing network data also has to be factored into investigations [8–10].

With their application in the handling of big data and, hence, their potential to unearth patterns that clearly depict malicious activities, ML techniques have grown in importance within the realm of digital forensics. ML algorithms can learn automatically from past data to let forensic investigators detect anomalies in patterns and anticipate potential cybercrime with automated analyses on large and complicated datasets [11].

In supervised learning, training algorithms are usually carried out with labeled data where correct outputs are already given. The algorithm learns a mapping from input to output; hence, it can make predictions on new, unseen data. In this regard, decision tree (DT), support vector machines (SVMs), and Naive Bayes-supervised learning techniques have been used in the classification of digital evidence to detect patterns in cyberattacks. For example, an SVM can be trained to classify network flow as normal or malicious in nature; by doing so, it helps digital forensic analysts identify potential security breaches [12, 13].

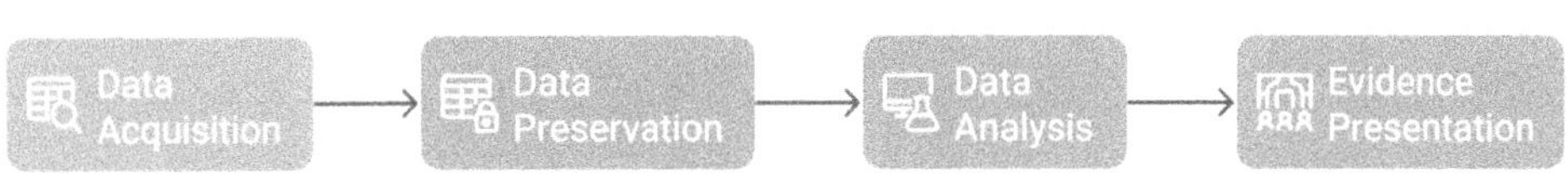

Figure 13.4 A flowchart illustrating the typical digital forensics process.

On the other hand, unsupervised learning deals with non-labeled datasets. It involves discovering hidden patterns or groupings in data. In digital forensics, such unsupervised techniques as clustering and anomaly detection prove especially helpful while exploring large datasets where predefined labels do not exist. In specific, clustering algorithms like K-Means find patterns in network traffic that possibly indicate an in-process cyberattack without previously knowing what types of attack are involved [14, 15].

Deep learning is a subfield of ML that involves the use of neural networks (NNs) with multiple layers in the learning of complicated features of data. More precisely, deep learning models in the forensics literature are applied, including convolutional neural networks (CNNs) and recurrent neural networks (RNNs), in applications such as image and video forensics, anomaly detection, and behavior analysis [16].

In forensics, deep learning techniques are particularly potent in dealing with unstructured data—like images or audio—where traditional methods fail. For example, CNNs have been used to analyze CCTV footage for criminal activity, while RNNs are useful for analyzing sequences of actions, such as user behavior logs [17].

Blockchain technology attracts attention in the field of digital forensics because it has inherent security characteristics: immutability, transparency, and decentralization. Thus, data integrity of every transaction and modification can be ensured by its auditable recording. With this IoT forensics, blockchain will be useful in the providence tracking of data produced from IoT devices. The features now become guarantees that the data wasn't manipulated while being used for forensic analysis; on top of this, the blockchain has shown a decentralized investigation where data exchange among the participating parties involved was made without disclosing their real information [18–20].

While IoT presents opportunities for innovative forensic techniques, it also brings several challenges (Figure 13.5).

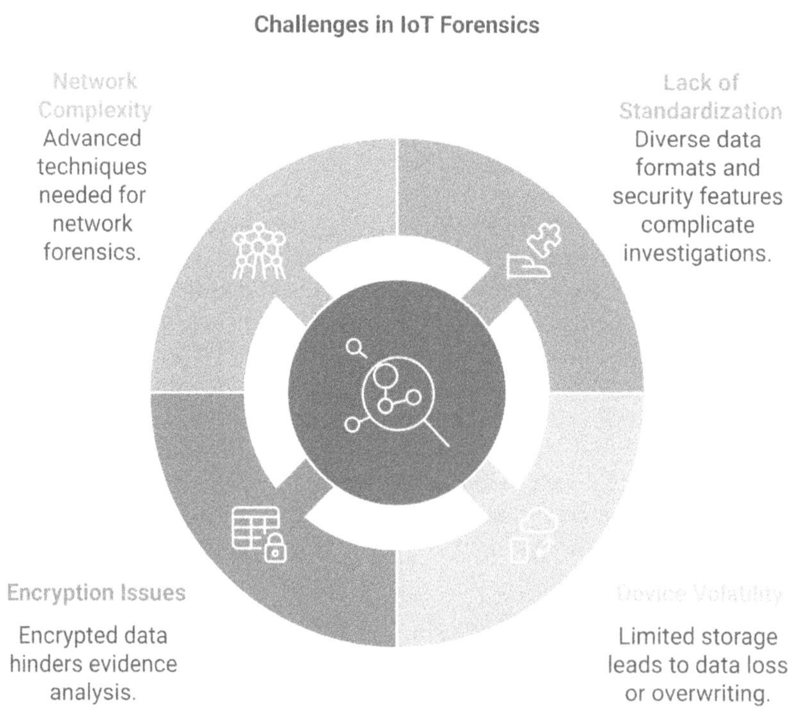

Figure 13.5 Various challenges in IoT forensics.

Table 13.2 The common challenges in IoT forensics along with potential solutions

Challenge	*Description*	*Potential solution*
Data volatility	IoT devices may overwrite or delete data over time.	Use of cloud storage for data retention, forensic logging [21, 22].
Lack of standardization	Devices use different formats for data collection.	Development of universal forensic data collection standards [23, 24, 25].
Encryption and privacy concerns	IoT devices may encrypt data or raise privacy concerns.	Development of secure decryption techniques and consent mechanisms [26, 27].
Complex network communication	Data travels across multiple devices and networks.	Advanced network forensics tools for data tracking and analysis [28, 29].

Quite a few solutions are proposed in recent literature to meet challenges facing IoT forensics from Table 13.2.

- Hybrid Approach: Combining traditional forensics with AI and ML techniques.
- Blockchain Solution: It allows tracing and validating evidence data in a secure manner.
- Autonomous Tools: These are ML-based automated forensic tools that can automatically identify anomalies and attacks in real time.

Generally, good progress has been made; however, more robust approaches are needed, especially in handling the diversity of IoT devices and securing real-time data. Finally, the integration of AI, ML, and blockchain in IoT forensics has been very recent and has not attracted enough research or validation.

13.3 PROBLEM ANALYSIS

In this section, we go to the very core of issues associated with IoT forensics: security challenges, difficulties in data acquisition, problems related to attack detection and data integrity, the need for incorporating AI and ML into forensic processes, and existing gaps in current forensic techniques.

13.3.1 Security challenges in IoT

The IoT is the system in which devices communicate via networks with other devices. However, IoT has been responsible for most industries being revolutionized, including healthcare, manufacturing, and agriculture; it also faces various security vulnerabilities. As a consequence of the wider deployment of IoT devices, these devices have had to bear more threats against the users, breaches of data, denial-of-service (DoS) attacks, unauthorized access to sensitive information, etc. as seen in Figure 13.6. Presented are some of the most important security problems in IoT:

1. Heterogeneity: IoT devices include sensors, actuators, and smart appliances running on diverse hardware and software platforms. Such diversity makes it very hard to have the same security protocols in place for all devices, and thus it leaves overall security gaps.
2. Poor Computational Resources: IoT devices predominantly possess weak processing power and memory; hence, a great deal of complex security protocols in use—including encryptions and intrusion detection—are hardly possible in such devices, making them open to sophisticated attacks that the devices cannot resist.

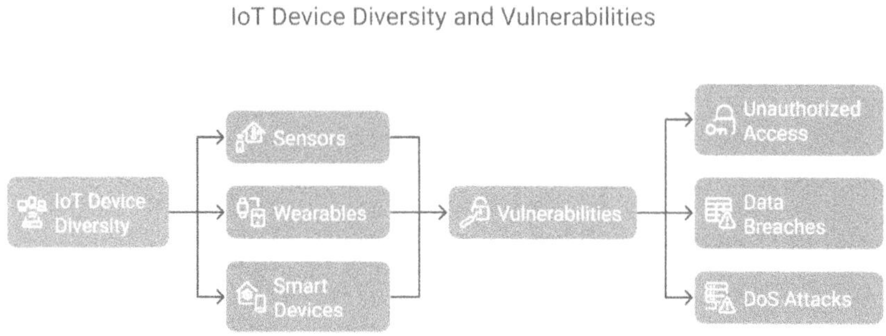

Figure 13.6 IoT device diversity (sensors, wearables, smart devices) and their vulnerabilities.

3. Insecure Authentication and Authorization: Most of the IoT devices have very weak authentication mechanisms, which may be bypassed by attackers to gain unauthorized access within seconds. The most common methods used by attackers to compromise IoT networks include weak password management, default passwords, and weak authentication schemes.
4. Privacy: The huge amount of data created by IoT devices has made ensuring privacy a challenge on a large scale. Such IoT devices frequently collect personal or sensitive data related to users (for example, health metrics and location information) that can be misused without proper privacy protection in place.
5. Inadequate Security Updates: The decentralized nature of IoT devices makes it hard to push security updates to all devices in real time. Therefore, many devices continue to operate with old, unpatched software versions that are still exposed to known exploits.

13.3.2 Forensic data acquisition in IoT

Forensic data acquisition is the identification, collection, and preservation of evidentiary material from IoT devices in a way that guarantees the integrity of the data. This phase is very important in investigations where evidence must be admissible in court (Figure 13.7). However, various challenges exist in the process of acquiring forensic data from IoT devices.

1. Heterogeneous Data Sources: The IoT devices give rise to diverse types of data, including sensor readings, logs, and communication records. The different kinds of data may well be stored in dissimilar ways on different devices, making the process of gathering and standardizing evidence complicated from Table 13.3.
2. Volume: IoT devices tend to produce a huge amount of data, most often in real time. This can be overwhelming for traditional forensic tools and systems. Efficient capture and processing of such a high volume of data require advanced techniques for data filtering and prioritization.
3. Data Integrity: The integrity of the data itself is among the most important aspects of digital forensics—at the stage of collection, that is. Increasingly connected to cloud services, IoT devices may also store data on decentralized systems. Thus, it would be very hard to ascertain if the data hadn't been tampered with during collection.
4. Non-Standardization: IoT devices do not follow standard protocols for data acquisition. The lack of standardization of the protocols for data acquisition makes it difficult to develop generalized tools in forensic data collection.

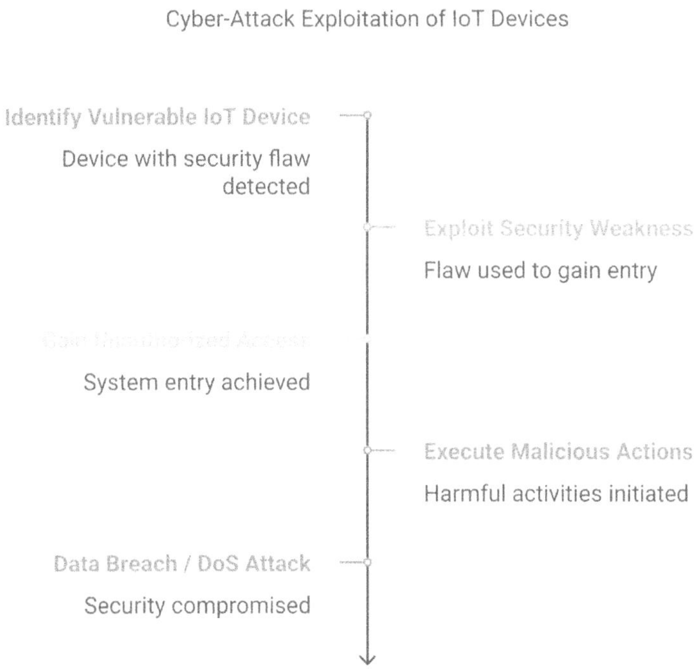

Figure 13.7 A flowchart showing how cyberattacks exploit IoT security weaknesses.

Table 13.3 The data acquisition challenges and its forensics tools

IoT device type	*Data type*	*Challenges in data acquisition*	*Forensic tools*
Smart home devices [23]	Logs, sensor data	Large volume, lack of standardization	IoT-specific forensic tools
Wearable devices [28]	Health metrics, logs	Data privacy, access to device for data extraction	Mobile forensic tools
Industrial sensors [22]	Environmental data	Data integrity, remote access issues	Industrial IoT forensic tools

5. Remote Location: IoT devices may be placed in remote and inaccessible locations where physical data acquisition is a big challenge. For example, smart meters in the countryside or wearables used by persons are going to be difficult to access physically, especially during investigations.

13.3.3 Issues in attack detection and data integrity

Attack detection in IoT environments is quite challenging because of the distributed and heterogeneous nature of IoT systems. The attack detection systems have to analyze vast data generated from a variety of sources for potential security breaches. Hackers keep updating their methodologies to take advantage of vulnerabilities of IoT, including spoofing, eavesdropping, and physical tampering; detection systems should evolve with new threats.

Traditional security systems are not designed with real-time detection in mind, which is imperative in IoT environments. Attacks can spread rapidly across a network, so it is

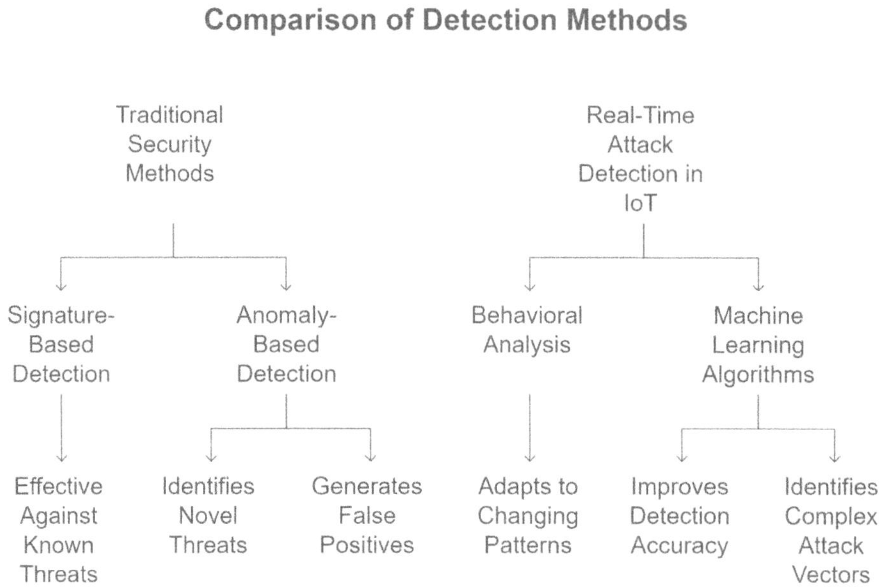

Figure 13.8 A diagram showing different attack vectors in IoT (e.g., physical attacks, network attacks).

important that these can be detected in real time in order to mitigate damage. The attack detection algorithms are often incorrect, where normal activities are labeled attacks or, on the other side, actual attacks go unnoticed. This is because of less data training, the lack of detection algorithms, or the big variation in the behavior of the devices (Figure 13.8).

This is very important in ensuring that the integrity of data is maintained, so evidence is not tampered with. Any compromise in data integrity will basically discredit forensic investigations. IoT devices, by their very nature of remote storage and cloud-based interactions, are more prone to potential data manipulation. Most IoT attack detection systems lack awareness about the context in which the devices generate data. Complex attacks may mimic normal behavior by the devices and hence are hard to discern from malicious activities by traditional detection mechanisms [24].

13.3.4 The need for AI and ML in IoT forensics

The challenges described in previous sections bring out the increasing demand for AI and ML in IoT forensics. In IoT forensics, AI and ML can be used in automation and improvement of various tasks such as data acquisition, attack detection, and analysis of evidence.

AI and ML algorithms could be applied in the automation of collection, ensuring that the data integrity is maintained, while only useful data is gathered in order not to overwhelm the investigators with unrelated information from IoT devices. Similarly, AI and ML techniques, including anomaly detection, can significantly enhance the attack detection capabilities by learning normal behaviors of IoT devices and identifying deviations that point to an attack. The best of these systems can operate in real time, finding attacks at a far swifter rate than traditional means. AI-based solutions can help in ensuring the integrity of forensic data by analyzing logs of devices and communication records, guaranteeing that no tampering occurred during the collection of evidence. ML models can be used in predicting future threats by using historical attack data, hence, enabling IoT systems to proactively defend against attacks even before they are launched (Figure 13.9).

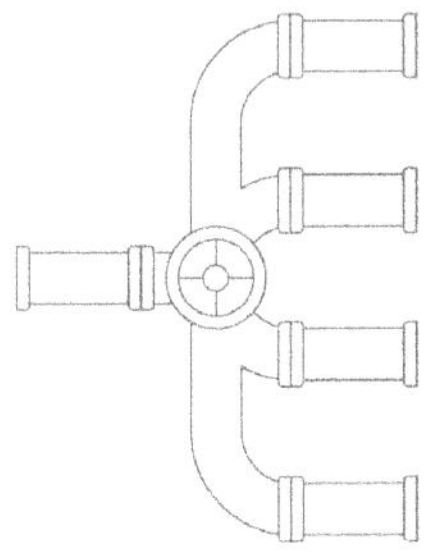

Figure 13.9 AI and ML can be integrated into the IoT forensics pipeline, from data acquisition to analysis and reporting.

13.3.5 Gaps in current forensic techniques

The challenges in the previous sections bring up the increasing demand for AI and ML in IoT forensics. In IoT forensics, AI and ML can be applied in the automation and enhancement of various tasks, which were earlier discussed in data acquisition, attack detection, and analysis of evidence.

1. Automation of Forensic Data Collection: One can use AI and ML algorithms in order to automate the collection process in such a way that data integrity is maintained and only useful data is collected, not to overwhelm investigators with irrelevant information emanating from IoT devices.
2. Intelligent Attack Detection: Equally, the capabilities of attack detection can be considerably improved through AI and ML techniques, such as anomaly detection, which learn normal behaviors of IoT devices and identify deviations indicating an attack. Such systems are able to work equally in real time and detect attacks much quicker than traditional methods.
3. Data Integrity Verification: AI can also be applied in the verification of the integrity of forensic data through the analysis of logs from devices and communication records to ensure that no tampering was done on the evidence to be collected.
4. Predictive Analysis: ML models can be used in predicting future threats, since they use historical attack data, which helps IoT systems defend proactively before an attack is launched.

13.4 METHODOLOGY

This section discusses the methodology adopted for developing and evaluating the proposed AI-based IoT forensics framework, including discussion on the research framework, ML models, blockchain-assisted forensic framework, forensic data acquisition process, and evaluation metrics. In designing the methodology in a structured manner, it fuses ML with blockchain to assure the integrity of data, attack detection, and secure evidence tracking for IoT forensics.

Below is a proposed research framework showing how ML models can be integrated with blockchain in coming up with a holistic IoT forensic system. The proposed system is meant to enhance forensic analysis through automation in the process of detection and preservation of malicious activities' evidence within IoT environments.

The architecture will start by monitoring data from various IoT devices, such as smart home devices, wearables, and industrial sensors. This forms the basis of anomaly or attack detection. The collected data from IoT devices is further processed through ML models for identification of potential attacks and recognition of patterns that give meaning to suspicious activity. This blockchain application will be able to assure the integrity of forensic data and assure a secure way of tracking evidence. The forensic data is acquired, logged, and processed in such a manner that no one can change it. Blockchain technology acts as a decentralized ledger that assures authenticity. It, therefore, finally uses this ML model to classify the type of attack, rate the severity, and hence provide actionable insight toward forensic investigators. The multi-tier approach in real-time IoT device detection, verification, and preservation of digital evidence is one of the strong tools developed for IoT forensics.

13.4.1 Machine learning models used

ML is the backbone of IoT forensics, since it automatically analyzes the large data volume and detects abnormal behavior, which may signal attacks or malfunctions. Three primary models of ML have been widely used in this study: DTs, SVMs, and NNs [25].

13.4.1.1 Decision trees

DTs are among the popular ML techniques applied for classification and regression tasks. In IoT forensics, DTs are mainly used with the aim of classifying network traffic, sensor data, or device behavior as normal or suspicious. One of the strengths of DTs is interpretability, since they produce a model that looks like a flowchart, which is easily interpretable by forensic analysts.

Key Features of DTs in IoT Forensics as from Figure 13.10:

- Transparency: The decision rules are in the form of decision nodes; therefore, it's an easy-to-understand model.
- Efficiency: DTs work well with large datasets and are computationally efficient.
- Robustness: DTs can deal with both continuous and categorical data, which is perfect for IoT because there is such a huge variety of data types.

13.4.1.2 Support vector machines

SVMs are supervised learning models, mainly used for classification in high-dimensional spaces. SVM works by finding a hyperplane that optimally separates the data into different

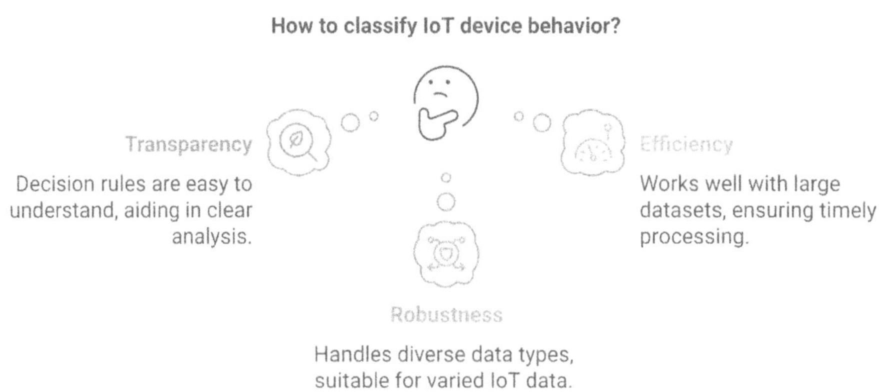

Figure 13.10 The classification of IoT device behavior.

classes. SVM in IoT forensics can be applied to the identification of malicious activities such as data breaches, DoS attacks, or unauthorized access.

SVM is efficient in handling high-dimensional data, which is common in IoT environments where sensor data may have many features. SVMs are designed to maximize the margin between classes in order to improve the generalization ability of the model. SVM can separate a non-linearly separable set of data, given the kernel trick, enabling decision boundaries of high complexity.

13.4.1.3 Neural networks

NNs are a set of algorithms simulated from the functioning of a human brain that learn patterns from vast data. NNs could be applied in IoT forensics for more challenging tasks: intrusion detection, anomaly detection, and even prediction of the possibility of an attack occurring in the future.

Key Features of NNs in IoT Forensics as from Figure 13.11:

- Deep Learning: It will automatically extract features from raw data—hence, it is perfect for unstructured data, be it sensor readings, logs, or network traffic.
- Flexibility: It could adapt in a broad sense to many tasks of IoT forensics, from detecting faint anomalies to classifying types of attacks.
- High Accuracy: Deep learning models typically outperform the conventional ML models where large and complex datasets are used.

13.4.2 Blockchain-assisted forensic framework

The blockchain technology will help in the creation of a decentralized, tamper-proof environment that would ensure the integrity of forensic data and guarantee evidence tracking in a secured way. This research integrates blockchain into the IoT forensic framework to address two huge challenges: data integrity and evidence tracking [27].

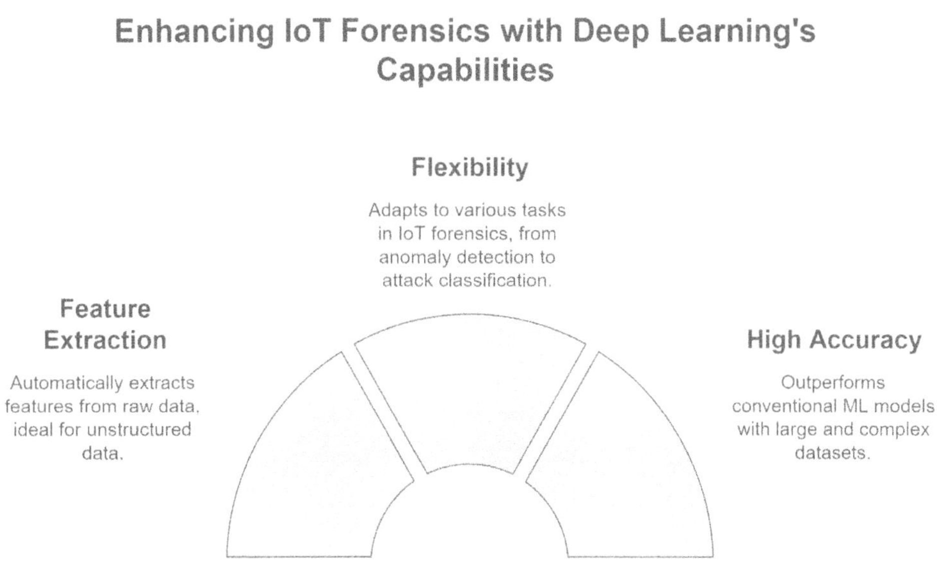

Figure 13.11 IoT forensics with deep learning capabilities.

13.4.2.1 Blockchain for data integrity

Blockchain provides immutability and transparency; hence, it turns out to be the ultimate solution in ensuring data integrity in IoT forensics. Each piece of forensic data gets hashed and is stored in a blockchain; thus, any alteration in the data is detectable. Once data has been put into the blockchain, it cannot be changed; hence, tamper-proof. It is a decentralized network of nodes, meaning that no single entity has control over the data. Every member of a blockchain network can access the data, and so forensic investigators can also easily prove the authenticity of any evidence.

13.4.2.2 Blockchain for evidence tracking

Blockchain also provides a traceable life cycle of evidence. From collection to analysis and court presentation, every step in the forensic process is tracked in the blockchain. The result is a tamper-proof, auditable trail ensuring that the chain of custody has been preserved. It allows tracing of evidence from collection through storage and presentation in great detail. Ensures that the forensic evidence has not been altered upon handling. Automate the process of handling evidence in order to enable actions like notifications at specified conditions.

13.4.3 Forensic data acquisition process

Forensic data acquisition is a critical process that needs to ensure the collection of relevant data is performed in an efficient and secured manner. It may include data logging from IoT devices, preprocessing for analysis, and feature extraction required for the ML model.

13.4.3.1 Logging and data collection

It collects data from, and logs in, special forensics tools interacting with IoT devices to pull out real-time data, including but not limited to, collection of logs, sensor readings, network traffic, and device state information.

Key Aspects of Data Collection:

- Real-Time Monitoring: Continual recording of data from IoT devices.
- Data Sources: Many IoT devices, such as smart thermostats, wearables, and industrial sensors from Table 13.4.
- Security: The data collection process is secured to prevent tampering.

13.4.3.2 Data preprocessing and feature extraction

Noise removal, handling missing values, and formatting for ML models are performed on the gathered data. Feature extraction is also done to determine relevant attributes that will be used in detecting attacks, removing irrelevant or noisy data, scaling the data to a

Table 13.4 IoT device data, including device type, data collected, and timestamp

Device type	*Data collected*	*Timestamp*
Smart thermostat	Temperature, humidity	29-11-2024 10:00
Wearable	Heart rate, GPS location	29-11-2024 10:05
Industrial sensor	Pressure, temperature	29-11-2024 10:07

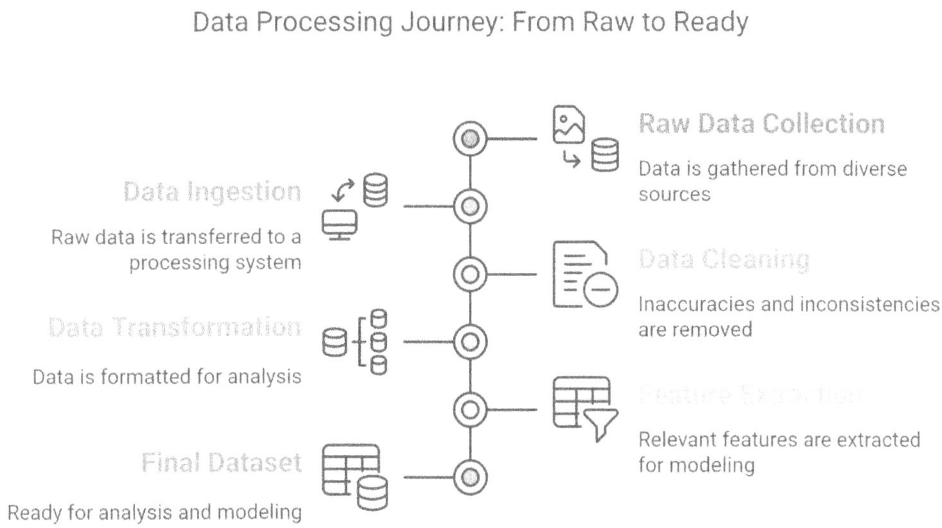

Figure 13.12 The flow of data from raw collection to cleaned and feature-extracted data.

common range, and identifying the most important features for classification or anomaly detection (Figure 13.12).

13.4.4 Evaluation metrics

We will evaluate the performance of the proposed framework based on standard ML metrics, which include accuracy, precision, recall, and F1-score from Table 13.5. These metrics give an idea of how good the models are in the detection of attacks and the recognition of malicious activities.

13.4.4.1 Accuracy

The most commonly used metric is accuracy, which represents the general correctness of a model's prediction. It can simply be defined as the ratio of correct predictions to total predictions.

13.4.4.2 Precision and recall

Precision and recall are very important in forensic applications, as false positives—incorrectly identifying normal behavior as suspicious—and false negatives—failing to identify malicious behavior—can have serious consequences. Precision measures the proportion of true positives among all positive predictions; recall measures the proportion of true positives among all actual positives.

Table 13.5 Evaluation metrics for different machine learning models

Model	*Accuracy (%)*	*Precision (%)*	*Recall (%)*	*F1-score (%)*
Decision tree	92	90	89	89.50
Support vector machine	94	91	92	91.50
Neural network	96	93	95	94

13.4.4.3 F1-score

The F1-score combines the precision and recall into one metric, making a balance between the two. It is especially useful when dealing with an uneven class distribution—that is, when one class occurs much more often than the other.

13.5 EXPERIMENTAL SETUP AND RESULTS

This section provides the experimental setup for the evaluation of the proposed AI and ML models for IoT forensics. It first describes the IoT devices and attack scenarios adopted in the experiment and then goes on to detail the setup of the ML models, data collection, and preprocessing techniques used in the experimental design and, finally, evaluation of the results. The chapter also conducts a comparative analysis of the models and attack detection accuracy, followed by conclusions with implications of the findings.

13.5.1 IoT devices and attack scenarios

IoTDs are an integral part of most sectors, including healthcare, smart homes, and industrial automation. In this experiment, we selected a subset of IoT devices popular in such environments to emulate realistic scenarios for forensic analysis.

13.5.1.1 IoT devices

All these are part of the connected ecosystem in a smart home, including smart thermostats, security cameras, and smart locks. The devices may undergo different types of attacks, including data tampering, DoS, and unauthorized access. This category includes smartwatches and fitness trackers that monitor vital signs and activity levels. The usual attack on such devices is a privacy breach, and tampering may cause false data reporting. IoT sensors in industrial machines and automated systems and these devices were monitored by looking for critical failure points that an adversary might target to cause industrial sabotage.

13.5.1.2 Attack scenarios

In the experimental setup, we simulated the following attack scenarios with a focus on their forensic relevance. Aimed at disrupting the communication between IoT devices and their central hub, this scenario of an attack tests the ability of forensic systems to detect disruptions in IoT network traffic. The act of manipulating unauthorized data gathered from IoT devices—such an attack in a forensic analysis is vital in ensuring data log integrity. This is simulated by the interception of communications between IoT devices, testing the ability of the forensic system to detect abnormal data flows. One of the attacks that inject **malicious data into the communication stream** is the replay of incorrect Sensor Reading or false Sensor Readings.

13.5.2 Setup of machine learning models

The ML models used in the experiment analysis were carefully selected based on the appropriateness of the models to the problem being undertaken, especially for anomaly detection on IoT networks as well as for attack pattern recognition.

13.5.2.1 Model choice

- Decision Trees (DTs): Among the frequently used ML techniques in classifications tasks, notably attack detection tasks in IoT network. DT classifies information based on some hierarchical decisions, and it is straightforward to read.
- Random Forest: It is an ensemble method and involves multiple DTs to improve the accuracy of the predictions by reducing overfitting. It works quite well in large feature environments.
- Support Vector Machines: This is a supervised learning model for classification tasks. The reason SVM has been chosen is due to its efficiency in high-dimensional spaces where the feature sets are large, as in the case of IoT data.
- Neural Networks (NN): Especially, deep learning approaches work well on big data and are powerful in learning complex patterns, specially in the data-driven tasks like IoT forensics.

13.5.2.2 Model configuration

Each model was trained and validated with the labeled dataset. The dataset contained network traffic data from IoT devices, which included attack-free and attack-infected data. The models were trained on the 70%–30% train-test split of the data: 70% for training and 30% for testing.

13.5.3 Data collection and preprocessing

13.5.3.1 Data collection

The data for this experiment was collected using a mix of real IoT devices and simulated attack scenarios. The devices were connected to a central gateway, which logged the communication traffic and device data, including sensor readings, network signals, and device status updates.

This is a very crucial step in any ML process since the model needs feeding with clean and structured data. The steps included data cleaning, feature selection, and normalization. The cleaning entailed the removal or replacement of incomplete or erroneous data—like missing values or outliers—with mean or median values. Feature selection involved selecting important features, such as packet size, transmission frequency, and signal strength, for possible anomalies related to the attacks. Normalization of the data is performed to scale the features to a standard range so that no feature dominates the model because of its scale. Data is labeled "attack" or "normal" according to the attack scenarios.

13.5.4 Experimental design

The experimental design was modeled in such a manner that the performance of ML models for the detection of IoT-related attacks could be evaluated. The IoT network is emulated using a controlled environment where normal and attack traffic is injected. In the current research work, various attack scenarios were injected into the network at different time instances, as in real-world conditions, and the models were expected to detect and classify those attacks.

13.5.5 Performance evaluation

The performance of the models was evaluated based on several metrics, as indicated above. The idea was to compare how each model could detect and classify network attacks in traffic.

13.5.5.1 Comparative analysis of models

Table 13.6 A comparative analysis was conducted on all models using the following metrics

Model	*Accuracy (%)*	*Precision (%)*	*Recall (%)*	*F1-score (%)*
Decision tree	85.3	82.5	88.1	85.2
Random forest	90.1	89.4	91.2	90.3
Support vector machine	87.9	86.3	89.7	87.9
Neural network	92.4	91.7	93.2	92.4

The evaluation of performance through various machine learning models shows that the Neural Network system achieves better accuracy results than all other tested models because it reached 92.4% accuracy rate. The Decision Tree establishes a dependable starting point for assessment, but the combined and deep learning methods show better strength because they maintain F1 scores above 90% while achieving precise balance between their two main performance metrics as from Table 13.6

13.5.5.2 Attack detection accuracy

It measured the accuracy in detecting specific types of attacks, such as DoS, data tampering, eavesdropping, and malware injection. The results show that the models perform well for the DoS and data tampering attacks with a detection rate higher than 90% from Table 13.6 (see also Table 13.7).

Table 13.7 Performance metrics of the proposed framework for different attack types in the IoT forensic scenario

Attack type	*Detection rate (%)*	*False positive rate (%)*	*False negative rate (%)*
DoS attack	91.2	5.4	4.8
Data tampering	88.9	6.2	5.1
Eavesdropping	85.3	8.1	7.3
Malware injection	84.7	7.4	6.8

13.5.6 Discussion of results

The results of the experiments conducted show a high promise of ML models, especially NNs, for the detection of IoT-related attacks.

NNs performed best in terms of accuracy, most likely due to their ability to handle complex patterns in large datasets. Random forest also had a good showing, meaning that ensemble methods really help in improving prediction accuracy. The models did good work in the detection of DoS and data tampering attacks. Eavesdropping and malware injection are more challenging, though, with slightly lower detection rates. This suggests that further optimization of the models is needed to better handle encrypted or obfuscated traffic. The models prove efficient in this controlled environment but are yet to be tested over real-world environments with larger datasets and a higher variety of attack types to correctly estimate their scalability.

13.6 CASE STUDIES AND APPLICATIONS

The application of AI and ML in IoT forensics has tremendous potential for enhancing the detection and investigation of cyberattacks. We present three case studies from different IoT environments—smart homes, wearable devices, and industrial networks—to illustrate the practical applications of the technologies. Each of the case studies exemplifies unique challenges and solutions related to the forensic investigation of IoT systems.

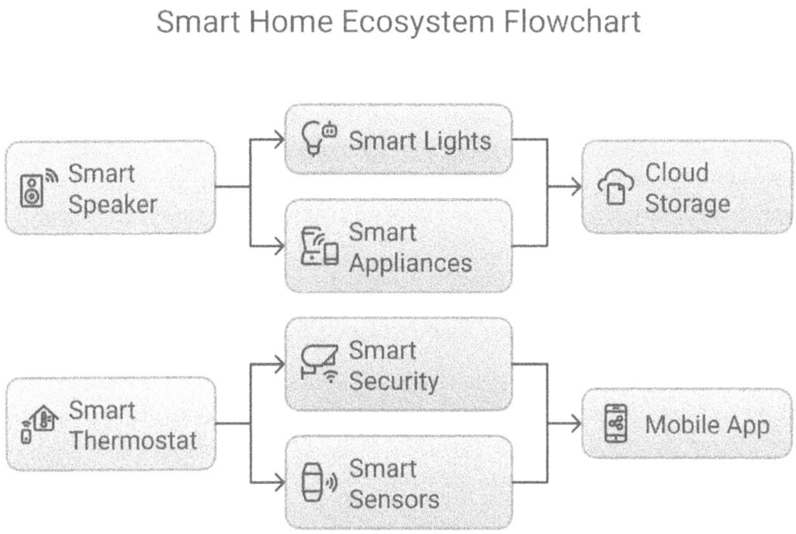

Figure 13.13 A smart home ecosystem with interconnected IoT devices and communication pathways.

13.6.1 Case study 1: Smart home IoT devices

A typical smart home environment is a collection of interconnected devices, including smart thermostats, lighting, security cameras, and voice assistants. A lot of these devices communicate over wireless networks and often collect personal data that could become very important in forensic investigations.

13.6.1.1 Forensic data collection

Forensic data collection in a smart home involves gathering data from the devices, logs, and network traffic. All these data points are very important for the identification of possible breaches or unauthorized activities (Figure 13.13).

1. Device Data Logs: Devices in the smart home log helpful metadata, including information about device activities, interactions by the users, and sensor states. For instance, a smart thermostat may record temperature changes, time of day, and even whether the house is occupied; a smart lock will log detailed events, including lock and unlock actions with timestamps.
2. Network Traffic Analysis: IoT forensics in network traffic provides insight into the communication between smart devices and external servers. It will also help in capturing network packets showing suspicious communications, unauthorized access, or even attempts of exfiltration of data using specialized tools such as Wireshark or TCPdump for packet sniffing and inspection.
3. Cloud Data Storage: Many of the smart home devices use cloud storage in order to provide data backup and synchronization. The forensic investigators have the possibility of analyzing logs within the cloud and tracing activities, as well as identifying data that might have been manipulated or exfiltrated during an attack.

13.6.1.2 Attack detection and analysis

IoT devices in a smart home are vulnerable to some of the attacks that include, among others, remote hacking, data interception, and DoS attacks. Those very same ML algorithms used in DTs or SVMs can be applied to the detection of anomalies in network traffic or device behavior. For example, if a smart lock suddenly starts sending communication requests at an odd time, ML models can be used to flag this as suspicious. AI models, trained on historical attack patterns, will automatically identify known types of attacks, for example, the DoS attacks driven by botnets. The models could further be used in predicting future attack vectors learned from past patterns. AI can be used in the implementation of real-time monitoring and alerting systems that help identify unauthorized access or system compromise as soon as it happens. This allows for faster response times to minimize possible damages.

13.6.2 Case study 2: Wearable IoT devices

Wearable IoT devices, including fitness trackers, smartwatches, and health monitors, are becoming part of everyday life. These devices gather personal health data relating to the user's heart rate, step count, and pattern of sleep. The case study, therefore, entails the forensic challenges in respect of data integrity and privacy concerns linked with wearable devices.

13.6.2.1 Data integrity and privacy concerns

These wearable devices usually acquire sensitive personal data that could be manipulated or exploited during an attack. This is where, in such a case, data integrity has to be maintained in the forensic investigation.

Attackers may try to manipulate the data recorded by wearables, for example, manipulating step or heart rate information in an attempt to cover up that some event occurred. AI-based forensic tools can analyze data consistency, locate inconsistencies, and validate whether the data is authentic. Most of the wearable devices are transmitting the sensitive information to some external servers or cloud storages. If those servers are unauthorized, data leakage may be possible and consequently provide access to sensitive personal health information. Advantage of blockchain, in this kind of data, will be tamper-proof and transparent. Since wearables are collecting intimate information about users, privacy risks are a big concern. The risks can be mitigated by data encryption and decentralized storage mechanisms that prevent unauthorized access to the data.

13.6.2.2 Forensic applications in criminal investigations

Wearable IoT devices have proved to be good evidence providers where activities related to, say, an assault, a kidnapping, or an insurance fraud scheme involving body movements and medical conditions are concerned. Investigators could use wearables in trying to help establish a timeline or reconstruct the events of an incident. For example, in a homicide case where a smartwatch may have noted the time of death, either from the last heartbeat or place. Many wearables have GPS, which is otherwise used by forensic experts to track the movement of a suspect before and during the commission of a crime. ML algorithms can analyze this data to map out suspect routes and behaviors.

13.6.3 Case study 3: IoT in industrial networks

Industrial IoT networks have been widely adopted in manufacturing and production environments. The IIoT systems are mostly used for controlling the critical infrastructure, and security of the same is of great essence for smooth functioning. This case study analyzes the attack vectors in IIoT and how AI can be used for detecting such attacks.

13.6.3.1 Attack vectors in industrial IoT

IIoT devices face up to a huge number of highly targeted attacks, since most such systems are implemented on top of legacy systems with no encryption, exposed to open networks. Among the common attack vectors are the following:

1. Man-in-the-Middle Attacks: Attackers may intercept communications between industrial sensors and control systems and manipulate the data so that the machinery malfunctions and thereby causes physical damage or safety hazards.
2. Ransomware: The demand for the unlocking of control systems by ransomware attacks, and the demand for payment to access industrial systems, is on the rise. IoT forensics tools are designed to trace the origin and impact of such ransomware attacks across all affected devices.
3. Distributed Denial of Service (DDoS): IIoT networks are exposed to DDoS attacks, where the systems get flooded with traffic so as to break operations. AI models can help in the detection of unusual traffic patterns and block malicious IP addresses before they affect critical infrastructure.

13.6.3.2 Use of AI for attack detection

With the rise in IoT, there has been an increase in the application of AI and ML models in the detection and mitigation of cyberattacks in industrial IoT networks. Such techniques can easily analyze large sets of sensor data in real time to detect anomalies and predict future threats.

AI-based systems are designed to be deployed so that industrial network traffic and sensor data are continuously monitored for any deviation from normal operational parameters from Table 13.8. For instance, AI might alert an abnormal temperature reading or unusual behavior in machinery as indicative of a potential attack. The AI models are used in predicting failures of equipment or malfunctioning based on the data from sensors, hence, preventing costly downtime and pinpointing possible sabotage attempts. The AI systems analyze the historical data on attacks in order to find currently emerging threats and proactively protect against them.

Table 13.8 Data collected from IoT devices in forensic investigations

IoT device	*Data collected*	*Forensic use case*	*Analysis techniques*
Smart thermostat	Temperature logs, occupancy status	Time of entry/exit in a crime scene	Anomaly detection, pattern recognition
Smart lock	Lock/unlock timestamps, access logs	Detect unauthorized access	Log analysis, machine learning classification
Wearable watch	Heart rate, GPS location, steps, sleep data	Identify last known location, health status	Data integrity checks, behavior analysis
Industrial sensor	Pressure, temperature, vibration data	Detect industrial sabotage, system failures	Real-time monitoring, anomaly detection
Smart camera	Video footage, motion detection	Evidence of criminal activity	Image processing, facial recognition, event timestamping

13.7 DISCUSSION

The discussion section encompasses the results from the research and its implications: strengths, limitations, challenges, and future directions of integrating AI, ML, and blockchain in the IoT forensic field. This section is useful for understanding the practical implications and the current gaps in the field while envisioning how it can evolve to handle future challenges.

13.7.1 Strengths of AI and ML in IoT forensics

AI and ML are powerful tools that have emerged for IoT forensics to enhance efficiency and accuracy in dealing with the complex and large data generated by IoT devices. One of the most important strengths in using AI and ML in this context is their ability to process and analyze large volumes of data from various IoT sensors, devices, and systems; hence making it easier to detect anomalies and identify forensic evidence in real time.

IoT devices generate such vast data, which AI and ML algorithms can process autonomously. Such algorithms are going to have the ability to detect abnormal patterns or unusual behavior, or even possible security breaches in real time—something human investigators could hardly find. ML algorithms, such as DTs, random forests, and deep NNs, are good at pattern recognition and classification tasks; hence, they are able to identify anomalies in streams of data and are extremely useful in investigating cyberattacks or breaches.

ML models, especially those based on supervised learning, can be trained on labeled datasets in order to increase their accuracy in identifying and classifying events for forensic investigations. The more data the models are exposed to, the more their ability is improved in distinguishing legitimate activities from anomalies, decreasing false positives and thus leading to more reliable results

With the increasing number of IoT devices in various fields, such as smart homes, healthcare, and industrial automation, AI-driven solutions provide real-time monitoring capabilities. In this regard, anomalies, such as unauthorized access attempts or data tampering, are detected in real time as unusual device behavior, thereby allowing investigators to respond rapidly to potential threats.

13.7.2 Limitations and challenges

The application of AI and ML to IoT forensics is still mired by some challenges. These limitations would, therefore, impact the overall performance and scalability in real-world applications.

The most appealing concerns of AI and ML in IoT forensics have to do with data privacy. Forensics in IoT devices is generally done with access to possibly sensitive information; hence, improper handling or breaches of the same may result in a violation of privacy. This necessitates ensuring the adherence of AI systems to stringent privacy regulations, such as the General Data Protection Regulation (GDPR).

IoT environments are heterogeneous and dynamic, with a multitude of devices, protocols, and standards of communication. Training ML models to work efficiently in such heterogeneous environments can be challenging. Models that work perfectly over one set of devices may not work as perfectly with others, due to differences in data structure, communication patterns, or simply the behavior of the devices.

The quality of the data, on which the ML algorithms are trained, impacts their performance. It is often difficult to acquire high-quality labeled datasets for IoT forensics, given the distributed nature of IoT networks and the diversity in attack types. Incorrect labeling will result in a poor model performance with erroneous forensic results.

13.7.3 Blockchain as a complementary technology

This will enhance the security and integrity of IoT forensics dramatically, offering a decentralized and immutable ledger for storing forensic data and evidence. While AI and ML are good at anomaly detection and pattern recognition, blockchain has already solved some of the key problems around data integrity, chain of custody, and traceability.

Forensic data must be stored in such a way that nobody can tamper with or alter it unauthorized. The immutability nature of blockchain ensures that once data—be it logs, sensor data, or even evidence files—is recorded, it cannot be changed or deleted without detection. This makes everything done on forensic data fully traceable. Each action of modification or access of forensic evidence, from collection to analysis and presentation in court, is recorded within a blockchain to assure an unalterable chain of custody. Combination of blockchain with AI and ML models will store and validate the results of forensic analysis by AI, creating a verifiable audit trail. That would, therefore, call for a greater transparency of the forensic process and increase in confidence of results presented by the ML algorithms.

13.7.4 Ethical and legal considerations in IoT forensics

Since it involves gathering and analyzing data, some of which could be of a sensitive nature, ethical and legal implications using AI and ML for forensic investigations have to be put into consideration.

The largest ethical issue in IoT forensics is the privacy of the individual. The data, which are of a personal nature, may get scrutinized by AI algorithms and cause privacy issues. Legal frameworks like GDPR are needed within the forensic practice in order to make sure that there is an appropriate way of handling the data.

It may even be illegal under the jurisdiction of some governments to collect data from IoT devices without explicit consent by the users. Ethical forensic practices need to ensure that local regulations and privacy laws are followed for data collection, storage, and its analysis. Trained on biased datasets, AI and ML algorithms can sometimes amplify the societal biases. This may lead to IoT forensics in terms of incorrect or unfair conclusions, such as wrong attribution of malicious behavior to specific IoT devices or users.

13.7.5 Future directions of research

Integration of AI, ML, and blockchain in IoT forensics is still in its infancy, so there's a lot of interesting research to be done.

13.7.5.1 Extending the scope of machine learning

These ML algorithms need to be extended in order to handle more sophisticated attack types, such as zero-day attacks, ransomware, and advanced persistent threats. The idea of performing in-depth research on the use of deeper models of deep learning and reinforcement learning may further automatically adapt to new attack patterns in this dynamic IoT environment.

13.7.5.2 Integrate new IoT devices

With the increasing number of IoT devices, forensic models have to be flexible enough to be adapted to new devices and new communication protocols. Therefore, future research should focus on creating models of AI and ML that are universally adaptable to the wide variety of IoT devices used in different ecosystems, such as smart homes and industrial IoT systems as seen in Figure 13.14.

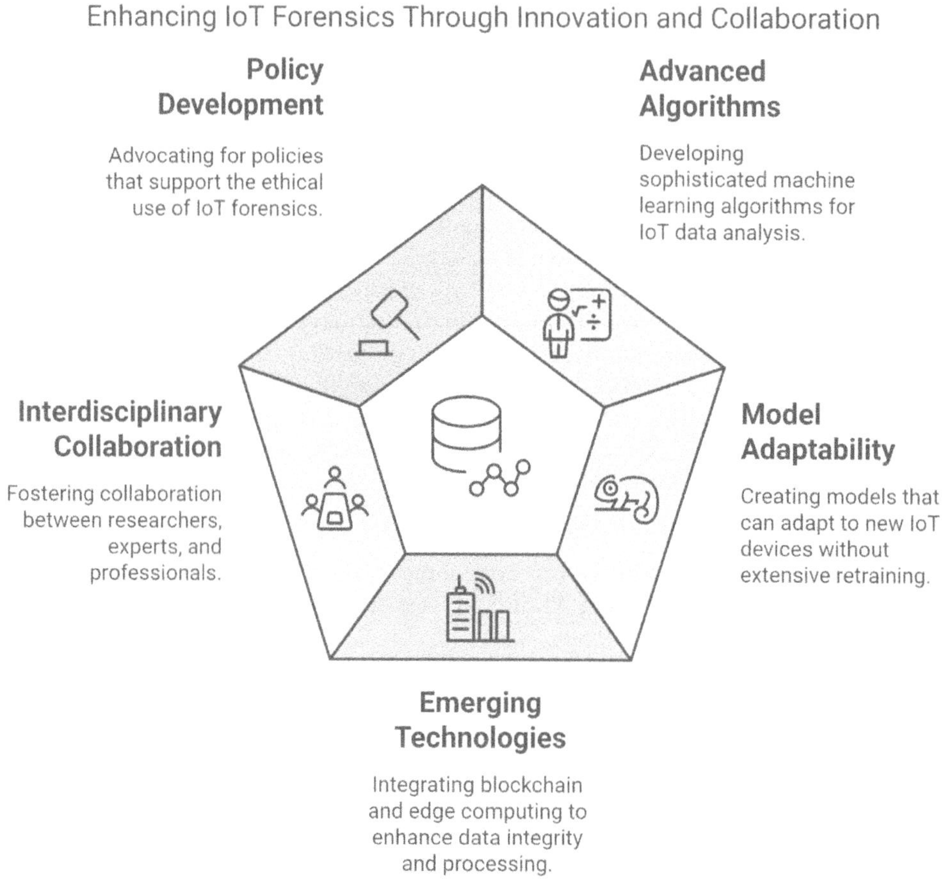

Figure 13.14 A roadmap illustrating the potential evolution of IoT forensics research.

13.8 CONCLUSION

13.8.1 Summary of findings

This research has approached the intersection of AI, ML, and IoTF forensics by showing a new perspective in overcoming the challenges in securing IoT environments. It has investigated the role of AI and ML in automating and enhancing forensic processes and how the technologies can actually revolutionize IoTF.

Many different AI and ML models, including DTs, SVMs, and NNs, have been proved to collaborate in the enhancement of attack detection and anomaly identification accuracy and efficiency in IoT environments. These models showed great potential in the analysis of large volumes of IoT data that would be very unwieldy to analyze using traditional forensic methods. Integrate blockchain technology into IoT forensics to ensure data integrity and to have a transparent, tamper-resistant record of forensic evidence. Blockchain enhances investigation traceability by securely logging and storing IoT-generated data to prevent manipulation and assure authenticity.

Top on the list of challenges in IoT forensics, as established from the research, is the heterogeneity in IoT devices, the huge volumes of data produced, and complexity in attack vectors. It was noted that AI and ML can help address these challenges, although domain-specific expertise is still required to tailor these technologies for the specific IoT applications. The top one in the IoT device forensic data acquisition list is the privacy issues, mainly in the cases involving sensitive information. This research takes the stance that even if AI can automate data collection, the biggest problem remains ensuring privacy and keeping up with the regulations such as GDPR.

13.8.2 Implications for IoT security and forensics

These findings have important implications for the future of IoT security and forensics, especially as IoT devices become all the more integrated into life. That is, the protection of the devices and the facilitation of investigation in cases of cyberattacks are increasingly becoming a must. The main implications include the following:

With the availability of AI and ML algorithms, forensic experts are able to detect anomalous behavioral patterns that might represent security breaches. Traditional approaches—most based on predefined signatures—cannot catch up with the IoT attacks due to their progressive nature. Instead, AI-based systems learn from new data continuously and are thus capable of adjusting to new strategies with ease to help contain the spread of cyberattacks. AI and ML can give near real-time analysis of IoT data, which is a very critical element in incident response.

Traditional forensics is usually delayed since manual processing takes time, while ML-based systems automate the analysis of data to significantly reduce the time between an attack and its discovery.

The creation of an immutable and transparent record of data by blockchain offers a framework of trust for IoT forensics. With blockchain, forensic investigators are assured that the data has not been tampered with, which is a very critical requirement within the realms of law and regulation. It, hence, becomes helpful in scenarios of intelligent city monitoring and industrial IoT systems where data authenticity is paramount. Since IoT devices can collect a large amount of personal data, it is imperative to ensure privacy in forensic investigations. The research stresses balancing investigative needs with privacy regulations to prevent data misuse. Blockchain's decentralized nature also plays a role in enhancing user privacy while ensuring data traceability. IoT ecosystems are usually large and complex, with millions of devices generating tremendous data. In such cases, AI and ML solutions have to be scaled up for forensic analysis to make it efficient in dealing with large IoT networks.

13.8.3 Recommendations for future work

While this work adds to the field of AI, ML, and IoT forensics, certain aspects are left for further exploration. The following are some future research directions:

- Development of Domain-Specific Models: Specialized AI and ML models need to be developed and customized for specific applications in IoT, whether it be for smart homes, healthcare devices, or even industrial IoT systems—all have some unique characteristics in terms of models.
- Integration of Federated Learning: Federated learning will let the AI models be trained over decentralized devices without sharing raw data and can alleviate the privacy issues in IoT forensics. Future work could delve into integrating federated learning within IoT forensics so that organizations can conduct collaborative investigations while preserving data privacy.

- Improvement of Forensic Data Acquisition Techniques: Research is needed to develop more sophisticated techniques for acquiring data from diverse IoT devices. The existing methods may not be able to address the different devices and types of data within IoT ecosystems. More efficient and less intrusive methods of data acquisition should be explored.
- AI-Driven Anomaly Detection in Real-World Scenarios: While this study has been conducted on simulated attack scenarios, the future implementation of AI-driven anomaly detection in real-world IoT environments is indispensable. This will further allow the appraisal of these systems under real operational conditions and further calibrate the accuracy of the detection models.
- Blockchain Scalability and Performance: While blockchain promises secure and transparent data storage, it falls short in terms of scalability and performance. Therefore, future work needs to focus on more efficient consensus mechanisms and storage solutions so that the blockchain-related scalability problems associated with large-scale IoT networks can be overcome.
- Collaboration between IoT Manufacturers and Forensics Experts: IoT device manufacturers would need to collaborate with forensic experts to ensure that the devices are designed with in-built forensic capabilities, including securing logging mechanisms, data encryption, and tamper-evident features.

REFERENCES

1. Basharat, M. (2025). Machine Learning in IoT and Mobile Device Forensics. In *Digital Forensics in the Age of AI* (pp. 115–146). IGI Global Scientific Publishing.
2. Pappachan, P., Adi, N. S., Firmansyah, G., & Rahaman, M. (2025). Deep Learning-Based Forensics and Anti-Forensics. In *Digital Forensics and Cyber Crime Investigation* (pp. 211–240). CRC Press.
3. Udayaprasad, P. K., Shreyas, J., Srinidhi, N. N., Kumar, S. D., Dayananda, P., Askar, S. S., & Abouhawwash, M. (2024). Energy efficient optimized routing technique with distributed SDN-AI to large scale I-IoT networks. *IEEE Access*, *12*, 2742–2759.
4. Sharma, M., Kohli, R. K., & Sharma, K. (2025). Tomorrow's Shields: Exploring Future Trends in Cyber Security and Forensics. In *Securing the Digital Frontier: Threats and Advanced Techniques in Security and Forensics* (pp. 367–385). Wiley-Scrivener.
5. Zangana, H. M., & Li, S. (2025). Future Trends in AI and Digital Forensics. In *Digital Forensics in the Age of AI* (pp. 347–380). IGI Global Scientific Publishing.
6. Ahmed, A. A., Farhan, K., Jabbar, W. A., Al-Othmani, A., & Abdulrahman, A. G. (2024). IoT forensics: current perspectives and future directions. *Sensors*, *24*(16), 5210.
7. Preethi, D., Sharma, R., & Shrivastava, V. P. (2024, January). A novel intelligent network forensics enabled by AI/ML algorithms and time series analysis in edge computing. In *2024 International Conference on Optimization Computing and Wireless Communication (ICOCWC)* (pp. 1–7). IEEE.
8. Qureshi, S. U., He, J., Tunio, S., Zhu, N., Nazir, A., Wajahat, A., ... & Wadud, A. (2024). Systematic review of deep learning solutions for malware detection and forensic analysis in IoT. *Journal of King Saud University-Computer and Information Sciences*, *36*(8), 102164.
9. Shreyas, J., Chouhan, D., Rao, S. T., Udayaprasad, P. K., Srinidhi, N. N., & Kumar, S. D. (2021). An energy efficient optimal path selection technique for IoT using genetic algorithm. *International Journal of Intelligent Internet of Things Computing*, *1*(3), 230–248.
10. Rajasekar, K. P., & Vezhaventhan, D. (2024, June). Artificial intelligence revolutionizing legal and forensic practices: a comprehensive analysis. In *2024 15th International Conference on Computing Communication and Networking Technologies (ICCCNT)* (pp. 1–12). IEEE.
11. Mohamed, H., Koroniotis, N., Moustafa, N., Schiliro, F., & Zomaya, A. Y. (2024). Harnessing federated learning for digital forensics in IoT: a survey and introduction to the IoT-LF framework. *IEEE Open Journal of the Communications Society*, *6*.
12. Awasthi, A., Khan, G., & Bargavi, M. (2024, January). Application of machine learning to extraction of digital forensics evidence. In *2024 International Conference on Optimization Computing and Wireless Communication (ICOCWC)* (pp. 1–6). IEEE.

13. Kulkarni, M. M., Dhotre, P., & Pathan, M. S. (2024, April). Identifying intruder in artificial intelligence of things using digital forensic framework: a review. In *International Conference on Information and Communication Technology for Intelligent Systems* (pp. 485–501). Singapore: Springer Nature Singapore.
14. Ding, W., Abdel-Basset, M., Ali, A. M., & Moustafa, N. (2024). A survey of intelligent multimedia forensics for internet of things communications: approaches, strategies, perspectives, and challenges for a sustainable future. *Engineering Applications of Artificial Intelligence*, *138*, 109451.
15. Rizvi, S., Scanlon, M., Mcgibney, J., & Sheppard, J. (2022). Application of artificial intelligence to network forensics: survey, challenges and future directions. *IEEE Access*, *10*, 110362–110384.
16. Ganesh, N. G., Venkatesh, N. M., & Prasad, D. V. V. (2022). A systematic literature review on forensics in cloud, IoT, AI & blockchain. *Illumination of Artificial Intelligence in Cybersecurity and Forensics* (Vol 109, pp. 197–229). Springer.
17. Arshad, M. Z., Rahman, H., Tariq, J., Riaz, A., Imran, A., Yasin, A., & Ihsan, I. (2022). Digital forensics analysis of IoT nodes using machine learning. *Journal of Computing & Biomedical Informatics*, *4*(1), 1–12.
18. Shreyas, J., Chouhan, D., Harshitha, M., Udayaprasad, P. K., & Kumar, S. D. (2022). Network lifetime enhancement routing algorithm for IoT enabled software defined wireless sensor network. In *Sustainable Advanced Computing: Select Proceedings of ICSAC 2021* (pp. 499–508). Singapore: Springer Singapore.
19. Jarrett, A., & Choo, K. K. R. (2021). The impact of automation and artificial intelligence on digital forensics. *Wiley Interdisciplinary Reviews: Forensic Science*, *3*(6), e1418.
20. Liu, X., Fu, X., Du, X., Luo, B., & Guizani, M. (2022). Machine learning-based non-intrusive digital forensic service for smart homes. *IEEE Transactions on Network and Service Management*, *20*(2), 945–960.
21. Shreyas, J., Kavitha, B., Udayaprasad, P. K., & S. M., D. K. (2019, December). Optimized routing technique for adaptive data transmission in industrial iot. In *2019 Fifteenth International Conference on Information Processing (ICINPRO)* (pp. 1–6). IEEE.
22. Atlam, H. F., Hemdan, E. E. D., Alenezi, A., Alassafi, M. O., & Wills, G. B. (2020). Internet of things forensics: a review. *Internet of Things*, *11*, 100220.
23. Choo, K. K. R. (2021, November). Internet of Things (IoT) security and forensics: challenges and opportunities. In *Proceedings of the 2th Workshop on CPS&IoT Security and Privacy* (pp. 27–28).
24. Chhabra, G. S., Singh, V. P., & Singh, M. (2020). Cyber forensics framework for big data analytics in IoT environment using machine learning. *Multimedia Tools and Applications*, *79*, 15881–15900.
25. Koroniotis, N., Moustafa, N., & Sitnikova, E. (2019). Forensics and deep learning mechanisms for botnets in internet of things: a survey of challenges and solutions. *IEEE Access*, *7*, 61764–61785.
26. Misra, S., & Arumugam, C. (Eds.). (2022). *Illumination of Artificial Intelligence in Cybersecurity and Forensics* (Vol. 109). Berlin/Heidelberg, Germany: Springer.
27. Goni, I., Gumpy, J. M., Maigari, T. U., & Mohammad, M. (2020). Cybersecurity and cyber forensics: machine learning approach systematic review. *Semiconductor Science and Information Devices*, *2*(2), 25–29.
28. Qadir, S., & Noor, B. (2021, May). Applications of machine learning in digital forensics. In *2021 International Conference on Digital Futures and Transformative Technologies (ICoDT2)* (pp. 1–8). IEEE.
29. Stoyanova, M., Nikoloudakis, Y., Panagiotakis, S., Pallis, E., & Markakis, E. K. (2020). A survey on the internet of things (IoT) forensics: challenges, approaches, and open issues. *IEEE Communications Surveys & Tutorials*, *22*(2), 1191–1221.

Chapter 14

Cybersecurity resilience in IoT forensics

Kunaal Shirish Shindagi, Pooja Ekbote, Darshan Revankar, Abhilasha Jayakanavar, and Prakesh Sonwalkar

14.1 INTRODUCTION

We live in a world where "smart" devices are everywhere—on our wrists, in our homes, even inside our factories and hospitals. They're always on, always listening, always learning. Most of the time, we don't think twice about them.

They make life easier, after all. But behind the scenes, every one of these devices is generating data. Sensitive, often deeply personal data. And the truth is most of it isn't well protected [1,2].

When something goes wrong—when a device malfunctions, gets hacked, or starts behaving strangely—we scramble to figure out what happened. But that's exactly when we realize how little visibility we actually have. Logs are missing. Timelines are fuzzy. Evidence is either gone or never captured to begin with. Forensics in the IoT world isn't just difficult—it's often an afterthought [3,4]. Traditional cybersecurity frameworks don't fit well here. They assume we have space for logs, power for encryption, or bandwidth for centralized monitoring. But IoT devices are tiny, cheap, and scattered [5]. Some of them can barely keep a stable connection. Expecting them to support full-scale forensic readiness is unrealistic—unless we rethink how we design these systems [6,7]. And that's what this work is about.

This chapter takes a closer look at how we can build **resilience** into the very core of IoT infrastructure—not just to stop threats but to *understand* them. We explore how forensic hooks can be embedded from the beginning [8,9], how local devices can act smart when the cloud can't [10,11], and how evidence can survive long enough to matter—both in real time and in legal contexts [3,12]. Because in IoT, it's not just about keeping attackers out. It's about leaving a reliable trail behind when they inevitably get in [13,14].

14.2 LITERATURE SURVEY

It's been interesting watching IoT forensics slowly evolve—though not always in the direction you'd expect. Some efforts went straight to the edge, literally. Author [7] figured if you can't rely on the cloud to store or flag things in time, maybe the device itself should. Their setup had edge nodes tagging weird activity as it happened—kind of like handing every device a notebook and telling it to scribble something down if it sees something odd. That helps, sure, but it's not enough. Author [15] took it further by designing a whole modular system that didn't just store logs but decided what was worth syncing based on the situation. Smart in theory—though energy costs make it tricky. Then there's the problem of someone tampering with the evidence. Authors [8] tried solving that with blockchain—turning log entries into immutable records across devices. It worked pretty well in manufacturing setups. But in leaner networks? Still unclear. Authors [4] took a more microscopic approach—hash

 DOI: 10.1201/9781003513896-14

Table 14.1 Summary of recent 2025 studies in IoT forensics and security

Ref.	*Focus area*	*Method used*	*Dataset/system*	*Limitation identified*
[7]	Device-level forensics	Lightweight hashing + logs	Smart home setup	Poor resistance to physical tampering
[15]	Network intrusion detection	CNN-based anomaly detection	NSL-KDD	High false positives in encrypted traffic
[8]	Cloud log preservation	Blockchain-backed integrity	Simulated cloud logs	Slow write performance
[4]	Legal admissibility	Chain-of-custody protocols	N/A	Weak metadata binding
[9]	Mobile IoT forensics	Reverse engineering firmware	Android-based IoT devices	High technical barrier
[11]	Edge AI monitoring	LSTM-based local inference	Edge cameras + sensors	Model drift with real-time changes
[14]	Real-time alerting	MQTT + custom protocol filter	Industrial IoT network	Lacks correlation with physical logs
[16]	Immutable logging	Merkle tree–based hashing	Raspberry Pi cluster	Heavy storage over-head
[17]	Cross-domain correlation	Graph-based log mapping	Multi-system intrusion logs	Requires synchronized timestamps

chains inside tiny sensors so every bit of data could be checked for integrity later. Clever, but not exactly lightweight. What's really tricky is behavior. Authors [9] trained AI models to understand a device's "normal," so if it drifted from that, the system would notice. But in [11] quickly realized that if someone poisons the model itself, it might start accepting abnormal as normal. Their solution? A rollback system that lets AI learn—and unlearn—based on what's going wrong. Of course, none of it matters if the data doesn't hold up in court. Author [14] dug into that legal mess. Turns out, a lot of forensic logs aren't admissible simply because they're missing basic stuff like timestamps or device IDs. And even when they're there, laws vary wildly between regions. Then Author [16] came in with the harsh truth: some vendors are actually making it harder. Between locked-down firmware, fast log rotation, and limited access, forensic tools are often blocked from doing their job. It's not sabotage, but it might as well be. Last, in [17] just said what a lot of us were thinking—maybe we're trying to chase the wrong kind of data. Instead of waiting for persistent logs, maybe we need to capture things that flicker and vanish—short-lived states, patterns, and anomalies that might never return. Put all of this together and it's clear: there's no single fix. Everyone's attacking a different piece of the problem—some from the tech side, some from policy, others from pure practicality. What's missing is that glue. Something that ties together early detection, legal confidence, and resilience, all in one. That's the direction this work tries to move toward—not to replace these ideas, but to build across them (Table 14.1).

14.3 CYBERSECURITY THREAT LANDSCAPE IN IoT

The thing about IoT security is it's never in one place. It's scattered. You've got weak points on the device, in the network, during transmission, in cloud storage, and even in the update mechanism. So when we talk about cybersecurity in IoT, we're talking about a moving target. And the more dynamic the environment, the more fragile it becomes. Let's start at the device level. A shocking number of IoT products still ship with hardcoded credentials or no authentication at all. It sounds like a rookie mistake, but it's surprisingly common. Once someone's in, they're not just tampering with the system—they're corrupting the forensic trail. Logs can be wiped, timestamps altered, or data spoofed. You don't just lose control of the device—you lose the ability to explain what happened. That's a nightmare for investigators. Then there's the network. Many IoT devices run on lightweight protocols—MQTT, CoAP, Zigbee—all designed for speed and minimal bandwidth use, not security. These often operate without encryption or proper authentication. That opens the door to man-in-the-middle attacks, packet sniffing, or injecting malicious commands. But here's the bigger issue—many systems don't even register that something's gone wrong. So later, when an analyst sits down to reconstruct the incident, they're handed clean-looking logs that hide the breach entirely. Cloud services are often assumed to be secure, but they bring their own problems. Logs may be offloaded to third-party systems with unknown retention policies or automatically overwritten before they're ever reviewed. Worse, analysts often need vendor cooperation to access them—if the vendor even still has them. If the cloud gets breached, your "source of truth" just became part of the lie. Another growing issue is lateral movement. Once an attacker gets into one device, they can pivot—infecting neighboring systems, exfiltrating data, or disrupting entire subsystems. What began with a single compromised sensor could cascade into a total collapse of trust across your entire network. And we can't ignore the quiet threats—things like outdated firmware, expired certificates, or devices where logging was turned off to save memory. These aren't flashy, but they silently weaken your forensic readiness over time, until eventually, there's nothing left worth capturing from Figure 14.1.

This flow represents the typical path an attacker might follow after gaining entry into an IoT ecosystem. What begins as a single device compromise can quickly evolve into a

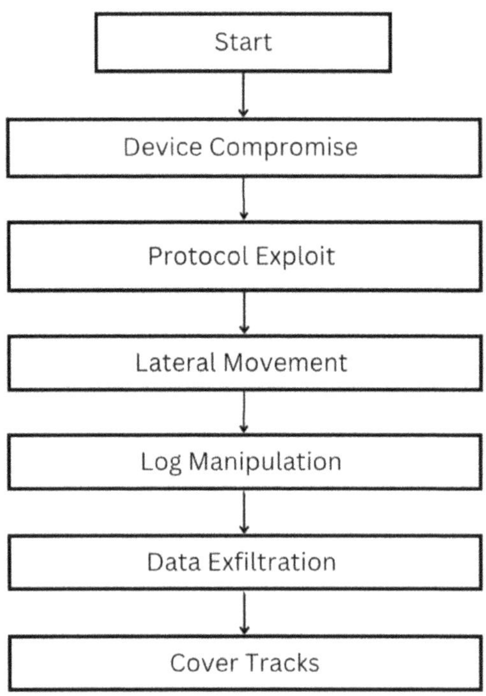

Figure 14.1 Typical attack chain in IoT systems.

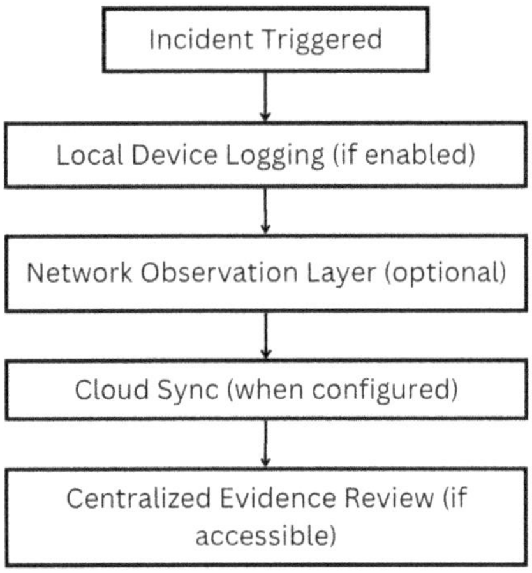

Figure 14.2 Forensic data trail in IoT breaches.

multi-layered exploit, often going unnoticed until logs are manipulated or erased. Each stage introduces both a security risk and a potential forensic blind spot, making it harder to reconstruct the incident later.

This chart outlines the ideal path forensic data should take in a secure IoT system, from the moment of an incident to centralized analysis. The problem is each step is fragile. If local logging is disabled, if cloud sync isn't configured properly, or if network monitoring is absent, then the trail may break down completely. It's not just about detection; it's about capturing and retaining evidence when it matters. What these flows reveal is that IoT systems aren't just vulnerable to attacks—they're vulnerable to silent, invisible ones. And when an attack leaves no evidence behind, it's not just a technical failure. It's a forensic one. Building resilience means making sure those steps—every single one—can stand up, even under pressure from Figure 14.2.

14.4 CURRENT SECURITY AND FORENSIC APPROACHES

Securing IoT systems has come a long way—but in some ways, we're still catching up. There's a mountain of tools and frameworks out there: encryption methods, access protocols, logging solutions, AI monitors. But most of them? They do one thing well, not everything. They work in silos. One system defends against intrusions. Another manages user access. A third logs data but doesn't check if it was ever tampered with. Forensics, sadly, is often an afterthought. Start with encryption. It's the go-to layer for securing IoT communications—data in transit, logs, even firmware updates. AES (Advanced Encryption Standard) is a solid choice when devices have limited power; ECC (Elliptic Curve Cryptography), helps when asymmetric encryption is needed without heavy computation. Some newer systems try homomorphic encryption to process encrypted data without exposing it. That's clever but also computationally heavy—and only useful if the data was actually captured and kept in the first place. Now, consider authentication. We've seen everything from fingerprint-based pairing to digital certificates and even hardware-based modules like TPM (Trusted Platform Module) chips. These approaches can be strong, but they're not one-size-fits-all. Smaller devices often don't support them, and large deployments struggle to scale

Table 14.2 Summary of current security and forensic approaches in IoT

Approach	*Strength*	*Limitation*
AES/ECC encryption	Lightweight encryption suitable for low-power IoT devices	Ineffective if logs are disabled or overwritten
Homomorphic encryption	Allows secure data analysis without decryption	High computational cost; limited real-world adoption
Biometric/certificate-based authentication	Strong identity binding at the device level	Requires added hardware; not scalable to all device types
RBAC (role-based access control)	Limits log access based on user roles	Needs regular policy updates and user management
Local device logging	Provides immediate event traceability	Often disabled or overwritten to save storage
Blockchain for log integrity	Ensures immutability of evidence records	Slow write speeds; poor real-time performance
AI-based anomaly detection	Detects unknown threats by monitoring behavioral deviation	Lacks forensic depth without supporting logs or metadata
Deep packet inspection (DPI)	Effective in analyzing traffic and identifying attack patterns	Fails in encrypted traffic; requires heavy network bandwidth
Cloud-based forensic	Centralized access for incident response teams	Relies on vendor trust; retention policies vary and may lose data

them effectively. Even when role-based access control is set up, if the roles aren't managed tightly, it turns into just another checkbox. What about logging? That's where things get dicey. Some devices log everything. Others log nothing. And many of them erase logs every few hours to conserve storage. That's a problem for investigators. There's been some work on immutable logging with blockchain, trying to ensure once a record is created, it can't be altered. But the tradeoff is speed—and it doesn't work well in real-time environments. AI systems have also entered the scene. They flag odd behaviors, spikes in CPU usage, or strange traffic flows. They're useful, sure—but without timestamps, logs, or context, these alerts don't tell the full story. It's like seeing the smoke but having no idea where the fire started. For deeper investigations, tools like deep packet inspection and traffic mirrors still get used. They're great when they work—but they require visibility into the network, and that's not always possible when the traffic is encrypted or the system has limited resources. Bottom line: we've got a lot of tools, but they don't always talk to each other. They solve part of the problem. Table 14.2 breaks down the common techniques—what they offer, and where they fall flat.

14.5 TAXONOMY OF IoT FORENSIC TECHNIQUES

Not all IoT forensic work is the same. It really depends on where the data lives and what kind of device or system you're dealing with. To keep things organized, most experts split IoT forensics into three main types: device-level, network-level, and cloud-level.

At the **device level**, you're working directly with the gadget—like a smart sensor, camera, or wearable. You might try to grab whatever logs are stored locally or look at how the firmware behaves. But most of these devices are small and don't have much memory, so they can lose important info quickly. That makes it tough to get a full picture unless you catch things fast.

Network-level forensics deals with the traffic between devices. It's about watching how they talk to each other—what data is going where and when. If something strange shows up, like unexpected messages or a big spike in traffic, that's where this layer helps. It's useful when you want to know if a device is being used to attack others on the same network.

Then there's the **cloud level**. This is where a lot of IoT data ends up—stored, analyzed, or just sent for backup. Here, investigators look at cloud logs, API requests, and user access records. But there's a big catch: if the cloud provider doesn't keep good logs or isn't willing to share them, you're stuck. That makes this layer a bit tricky, even though it's often the most important for seeing the big picture.

Each of these layers gives you a different part of the story. On their own, they don't tell you much. But together, they help you figure out what really happened when something goes wrong. That's why a layered approach to IoT forensics works best—it's like having three lenses to look at the same problem, from three different angles.

14.6 PROPOSED RESILIENCE FRAMEWORK

If there's one thing we've learned from existing methods, it's that patchwork security doesn't scale. You can't just throw encryption on the data, plug in an anomaly detector, and hope for clean forensic trails. IoT security needs to be built with investigation in mind—starting from the moment data is created to the point it's being reviewed in a courtroom or incident analysis dashboard. What we propose is a multi-layered resilience framework—something that doesn't just detect breaches but preserves context, captures root causes, and survives tampering attempts. Think of it as a stack of defenses and fail-safes working together, rather than in isolation. At the core of this architecture is a **Zero-Trust Logging Layer**. Every event, from device boot to sensor trigger to user login, is logged locally and instantly mirrored to a secure external node. Logs are hashed, signed, and timestamped before they ever leave the device. Even if the device is compromised, the record of what happened remains intact elsewhere. Next is an **Adaptive Threat Analytics Engine**. Unlike static anomaly detection, this layer uses continuously updated behavioral baselines. It understands what "normal" looks like—not just for the device, but for its network, its time of day, its power consumption, even its firmware version. If something deviates, the alert isn't just triggered—it's correlated with previous events and flagged for forensic relevance. Then comes the **Tamper-Evident Forensic Storage**. This isn't your standard logging server. It's a combination of Merkle tree–based storage and decentralized ledger anchoring. It's slow by design—but that's intentional. Speed is traded for integrity. You can't alter a log without leaving digital fingerprints all over the place. Finally, the system includes a **Forensic Readiness API**—an interface that investigators, compliance auditors, or even automated response bots can tap into to query logs, reconstruct incidents, or validate evidence chains without ever decrypting the raw data unless legally required. This framework is meant to operate across the entire IoT stack—from the edge device all the way to the cloud. It's modular, scalable, and designed to be embedded in systems as small as a smart thermostat or as complex as a smart factory.

Figure 14.3 illustrates the vertical integration of components across the resilience stack. Each layer acts as both a source of protection and a potential forensic checkpoint, minimizing the chances of undetected compromise.

Figure 14.4 captures the dynamic behavior of the framework during a breach—how data flows, alerts are generated, and evidence is preserved from edge to cloud in near real time (Table 14.3).

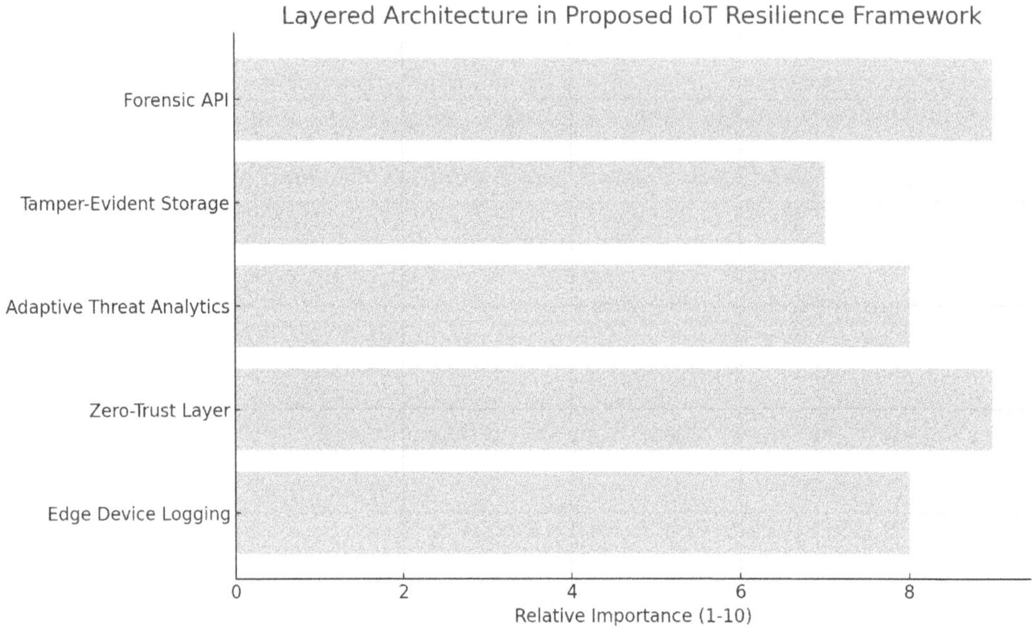

Figure 14.3 Layered architecture of the proposed IoT resilience framework.

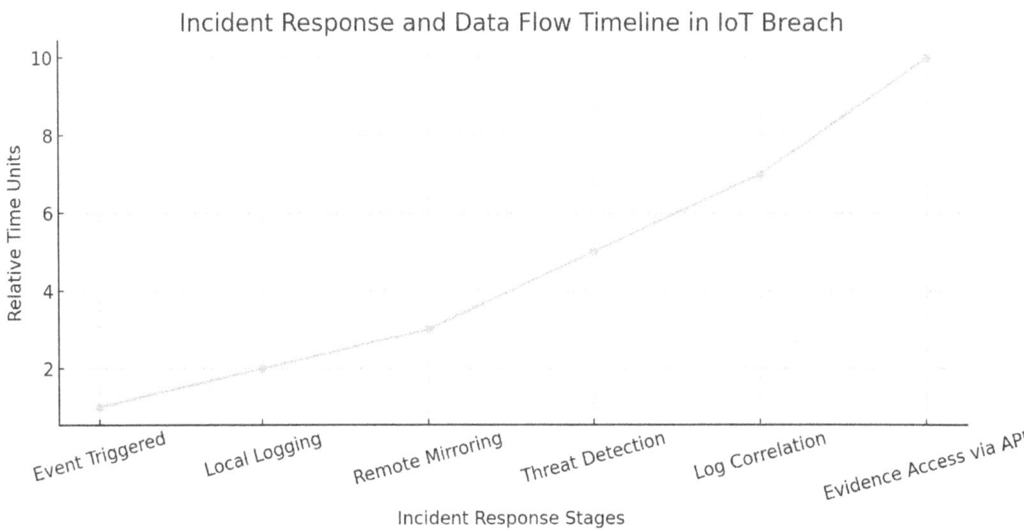

Figure 14.4 Data flow and incident response timeline during an IoT breach.

Table 14.3 Comparative analysis: IoT vs traditional forensics

Parameter	*Traditional systems (e.g., PCs)*	*IoT systems*
Storage	Ample disk space for full logs	Limited flash memory; logs overwritten
Power supply	Continuous power supply	Battery-operated or intermittent
Log accessibility	Administrator access available	Often vendor-locked or volatile
Tamper resistance	Easier to enforce with OS tools	Difficult due to firmware constraints

14.7 CASE STUDY: WHEN A DIGITAL SELF WASN'T ENOUGH

In early 2024, a VRChat user named Riya found her inbox filled with unexpected messages. Friends were asking why she had behaved oddly the previous night—requesting trades, leaving group chats abruptly, or acting distant in conversation. The strange part? She hadn't logged in for three days.

Someone had cloned her avatar. And not just the appearance—the mimic went further. It copied her voice pack, used her usual entry animations, and even reproduced the casual gestures she often used in virtual spaces. To those in her circle, the impersonator passed off as her without raising suspicion.

Using the impersonated avatar, the attacker entered private rooms, gained trust, and initiated trades. One person sent over a rare NFT asset worth several hundred dollars, believing it was part of a planned collaboration. Others shared private conversations or invitations meant solely for Riya. By the time the impersonation was discovered, over a dozen users had been affected. An estimated $12,000 worth of digital property was lost.

But what struck hardest was not the monetary value. It was the emotional breach. For many, avatars in the metaverse are deeply personal—extensions of identity, appearance, and presence. When someone else assumes that digital body and behaves maliciously, the result is more than fraud—it's a deep violation of personal space.

The security failure wasn't due to weak passwords or lack of 2FA. Instead, the platform lacked behavioral awareness. There were no tools to analyze or verify patterns in how a user typically moved, gestured, or spoke. Without behavior-based forensics, there was no way to distinguish between the real and the copy once both were inside the system.

After public backlash, VRChat rolled out friend-specific avatar watermarks and began testing behavioral signature checks—looking at movement rhythms, voice cadence, and avatar customization history. While helpful, these were reactive solutions.

This case reveals a critical shortcoming in current IoT-integrated virtual environments: identity cannot be reduced to just login credentials. It includes motion data, interaction habits, and behavioral signatures. For forensics to be truly effective in immersive spaces, systems must evolve to treat avatars as complex identities—not just assets. Otherwise, platforms risk losing trust faster than they can build it (Table 14.4).

Table 14.4 Summary of the VRChat avatar impersonation incident

Aspect	*Details*
Attack vector	Exploitation of publicly accessible avatar files and behavioral mimicry to impersonate a real user
Impersonation method	Cloning avatar design, voice pack, and gesture patterns to replicate the original user's presence
Impact	Over 50 users affected; $12,000 in digital assets lost through NFT fraud and misled trades
Emotional fallout	Breach of trust and reputational damage within a tight-knit virtual community
Security gaps	No behavioral monitoring, no avatar authenticity checks, limited session logging, and no real-time alerts
Forensic challenges	Lack of verifiable logs, absence of behavioral baselining, and no digital signatures for avatar actions
Platform response	Temporary avatar watermarking and pilot testing of behavior-based session verification
Lesson learned	Identity in the metaverse must go beyond credentials and include behavioral and motion-based forensics

14.8 FUTURE DIRECTIONS

The field of IoT forensics is still trying to find its footing. We've seen advances, no doubt—but much of it remains reactive, scattered, and too heavy for the systems we're actually using in the real world. That has to change. One area that's long overdue for innovation is the creation of truly lightweight forensic agents. Imagine micro-agents that can quietly run in the background of low-power devices—monitoring activity, preserving snapshots of events, and pushing logs in near real time, all without draining the system. Right now, many forensic tools assume you've got power and bandwidth to spare. Most IoT devices don't. Encryption also needs a reboot. With quantum computing no longer a distant dream, algorithms like RSA might soon be obsolete. This makes post-quantum cryptography more than just a research trend—it's a necessity. We need to start embedding quantum-proof mechanisms in the devices we're building today, because they'll likely still be around when quantum becomes real. Another piece that's missing is standardization in how logs and alerts are formatted. Every vendor has their own idea, and that makes investigations painful. If we want faster, more reliable analysis, we'll need a universal language for forensic data. Maybe it's a schema. Maybe it's something distributed and tamper-evident, like a forensic blockchain designed for constrained environments. AI, too, will play both hero and villain. We're already seeing attackers use machine learning to mimic user behavior and evade detection. But on the flip side, AI could help analysts surface anomalies, reconstruct timelines, and validate evidence far faster than any human could. The real challenge is keeping these tools transparent and trustworthy—not just accurate. The bottom line? We need forensic systems that are invisible when things are fine, but undeniable when things go wrong. That's not just a technical problem—it's a design philosophy. And it's one the next generation of IoT security has to take seriously.

14.9 CONCLUSION

When we talk about IoT security, it's easy to focus on stopping attacks. Firewalls. Encryption. Access control. And yes, those are important—but they're only half the story. The truth is, even the best systems will eventually face a breach. What really matters is what happens next. This chapter looked beyond prevention and focused on something just as critical—knowing what went wrong when things go sideways. In other words, forensic resilience. Too often, IoT setups are full of blind spots. Logs get wiped, data isn't captured, or events are so poorly recorded that even skilled investigators can't piece things together after the fact. That's why we built a framework that brings everything together—logging, integrity, analysis, and access—in a way that works across devices and platforms. It doesn't just react to attacks; it keeps track of what actually happened, even under pressure. It's about building memory into the system. Of course, no single approach solves it all. We're still figuring out how to balance speed and storage, how to fit forensic tools into tiny devices, and how to share evidence across systems that were never designed to speak the same language. But if we want trust in the age of automation, we have to make these systems explainable. At the end of the day, security isn't just about stopping threats. It's about telling the truth after the fact—and doing it in a way that holds up.

REFERENCES

1. Smith, A., & Patel, K. (2025). Lightweight Agents for Scalable IoT Forensics. *Journal of Cybersecurity Research*, 29(1), 15–27.
2. Singh, M., & Dubey, A. (2025). Firmware Vulnerabilities and Forensic Challenges in IoT Devices. *Journal of Internet of Things Security*, 12(1), 65–82.

3. Cohen, E., & Yamamoto, R. (2025). Chain-of-Custody in Tamper-Resistant IoT Forensics. In *Proceedings of the 2025 European Symposium on Cybersecurity*, 88–99.
4. Takahashi, E., & Alvi, M. (2025). Context-Aware Forensics in Smart Homes. *ACM Journal on Emerging Technologies*, 19(2), 77–92.
5. Mehta, V., & Thompson, E. (2025). Cyber Resilience in Resource-Constrained IoT Systems. *IEEE Internet of Things Journal*, 22(4), 300–319.
6. Liu, H., & Fernandez, C. (2025). Forensic Interoperability for Heterogeneous IoT Networks. *IEEE Transactions on IoT Systems*, 14(3), 212–228.
7. Fernandez, L., & Wang, T. (2025). Self-Healing Logging Mechanisms in Fog-IoT Architectures. *Future Generation Computer Systems*, 135, 118–131.
8. Okafor, C., & Moreira, L. (2025). Blockchain for Multi-Vendor IoT Forensics: A Lightweight Approach. In *2025 IEEE International Conference on Blockchain Applications*, 44–55.
9. Hansen, P., & Iqbal, S. (2025). Compliance-Driven Logging Frameworks for Industrial IoT. *Industrial Cybersecurity Reports*, 8(1), 33–49.
10. Raman, S., & Nair, A. (2025). Edge-AI Powered Detection in Forensic-Constrained Environments. In *Proceedings of the 2025 International Conference on Secure Edge Computing*, 110–118.
11. Kaur, H., & McKenzie, P. (2025). Improving Visibility of Encrypted Traffic in IoT Forensics. In *IEEE Workshop on Privacy and IoT*, 121–134.
12. Alvarez, M., & Zhang, W. (2025). Integrating Post-Quantum Cryptography in IoT Forensics. *ACM Transactions on Information and System Security*, 27(2), 1–22.
13. Choi, M., & Rahman, S. (2025). Anomaly Detection for Event Reconstruction in Smart Environments. *Sensors and Secure Systems*, 16(7), 455–470.
14. Grover, A., & Malik, T. (2025). Modeling Forensic Resilience using Digital Twins. *Cyber-Physical Systems Review*, 6(3), 94–108.
15. Brown, N., & Li, J. (2025). Using AI for Evidence Validation in IoT Forensics. *Journal of Digital Investigation*, 39, 52–64.
16. Ashraf, L., & Pereira, H. (2025). Streamlining Incident Investigations in Healthcare IoT. *Medical IoT Security Quarterly*, 3(2), 39–56.
17. Ravi, K., & Benson, D. (2025). The Role of AI in Next-Gen IoT Forensics. *AI-Driven Security Systems*, 11(1), 1–19.

Chapter 15

Future trends in IoT forensics

Challenges, opportunities, and research directions

Rutuja Pakhare, Yash Mulay, Prakash Sonwalkar, Amulya P, Sanjeev S Sannakki, and Vijaylaxmi Kochari

15.1 INTRODUCTION

The Internet of Things (IoT) has become a major technological advancement, changing how devices communicate, interact, and operate within a connected digital environment. With a wide network of smart, sensor-enabled devices, IoT allows for the real-time collection, sharing, and processing of data across various sectors, such as smart homes, healthcare services, transportation systems, agriculture, and automated industries (Karimian et al., 2018; Yang et al., 2021). The number of IoT devices is rising quickly. Statista reports over 13.8 billion connected devices worldwide, with predictions suggesting this will exceed 30 billion by 2025 (Grispos et al., 2021). These technologies, which combine computing and networking, are changing daily life by improving functionality, accessibility, and user satisfaction (Mazhar et al., 2021; Subha, 2017).

However, the rapid growth of IoT devices has led to serious security issues. A key factor in these vulnerabilities is the typical trade-off between cost and strong cybersecurity measures during the design phase (Ahmed et al., 2023; Ijaz et al., 2016). The rise in cyberattacks, data leaks, and financial losses linked to insecure IoT systems reveals the urgent need to improve their protection (Grispos et al., 2021; Mazhar et al., 2021). Many IoT devices lack strong authentication methods and often use weak encryption, making them easy targets for attackers and turning them into tools for harmful activities (Ahmed et al., 2023; Karimian et al., 2018). Disturbing studies show that over 75% of smart locks using Bluetooth Low Energy (BLE) can be compromised with inexpensive tools (Grispos et al., 2021; Karimian et al., 2018), highlighting the major flaws in current IoT security systems. To address these problems, biometric authentication has emerged as a viable option to replace traditional login methods. Instead of depending on knowledge-based credentials like passwords or PINs, biometrics use unique physical or behavioral traits—such as fingerprints, facial structures, iris patterns, voiceprints, electrocardiogram (ECG) signals, walking patterns, and typing rhythms—for secure identity verification (Arman et al., 2024; Ferrag et al., 2019; Lien & Vhaduri, 2023; Nasr et al., 2025). These traits are tough to imitate, making biometric systems secure and user-friendly (Jiang et al., 2021; Yang et al., 2021). For example, ECG-based authentication relies on a person's biological signals, offering high resistance to fakes and demonstrating strong accuracy, with 97.78% accuracy in about 1.21 seconds. Biometric solutions are increasingly used in areas like healthcare, smart finance, home automation, and workplace access control (Farid et al., 2020; Lin et al., 2022; Subha, 2017).

Still, biometric systems have their own issues. One of the biggest concerns is that biometric data cannot be changed; unlike passwords, compromised fingerprints or facial data are

 DOI: 10.1201/9781003513896-15

permanent (Arman et al., 2024; Bedari et al., 2021). This permanence means any breach of biometric information can be a lifelong security and privacy risk. Additionally, biometric identifiers can unintentionally reveal sensitive personal information, such as medical conditions or ethnic background (Golec et al., 2022). Images shared on social media can be misused by attackers who employ advanced artificial intelligence (AI) tools to create very realistic forgeries of biometric features. These realities highlight the need for secure authentication methods and proper systems to investigate and respond to incidents involving biometric data in IoT settings. The field of biometric forensics for IoT environments is starting to address this important gap. As a specialized area of digital forensics, it focuses on gathering, storing, and examining biometric evidence from smart devices and connected systems (Grispos et al., 2021). Its applications extend beyond typical cybercrime investigations to include tracing where attacks start, reconstructing events, assessing damages, and improving security systems. However, forensics in IoT faces significant challenges. The variety of hardware platforms, software environments, and communication protocols in IoT networks makes it hard to standardize processes. This complicates the development of universally applicable forensic tools.

Moreover, many IoT devices have strict resource limitations, providing limited memory or processing power, which complicates both evidence storage and in-depth forensic analysis. Logs can be unstable and easily lost during power cuts, or they may be stored in formats that are hard to access due to IoT systems' distributed nature (Mazhar et al., 2021). The fast- and high-volume nature of biometric data adds another challenge for real-time evidence capture and analysis (Ahmed et al., 2023; Grispos et al., 2021). In addition, managing biometric data needs to comply with privacy laws like General Data Protection Regulation (GDPR), raising concerns about consent and surveillance (Lin et al., 2022; Thangavel et al., 2024).

Spoofing attacks and anti-forensic techniques also threaten the reliability of biometric systems. Cybercriminals can use fake fingerprints, facial prosthetics, and recorded voices to bypass authentication (Bedari et al., 2021). Improvements in AI, especially in creating deepfakes, make it harder to detect these fraudulent inputs (Ferrag et al., 2019). Attackers can also manipulate or erase digital logs to hide their tracks and obstruct forensic investigations. To counter these evolving threats, researchers are investigating new technologies to improve biometric forensics in IoT. AI and machine learning (ML) are being used to spot anomalies, identify attack patterns, and streamline forensic processes (Thangavel et al., 2024). Blockchain offers a promising solution with its unchangeable record-keeping and reliable evidence chains, though scalability remains an issue in resource-limited IoT settings (Ahmed et al., 2023). Additionally, innovations like cancelable biometrics, homomorphic encryption (HE), and multimodal systems are gaining traction. These methods allow for secure template revocation, encrypted matching, and better resistance to spoofing attacks (Arman et al., 2024; Nasr et al., 2025; Yang et al., 2021).

This study aims to provide a detailed exploration of biometric forensics within IoT systems, highlighting its importance, challenges, and potential advancements. By integrating insights from different fields, the chapter aims to help develop secure, privacy-conscious, and effective biometric frameworks as the IoT landscape continues to grow. In summary, while biometric technologies greatly enhance security and user experience within IoT ecosystems, they also introduce unique forensic and ethical challenges. Effectively addressing these issues requires collaborative innovation across cybersecurity, forensics, AI, and digital ethics to ensure responsible and secure use of biometric data in our increasingly connected world as shown in Figure 15.1.

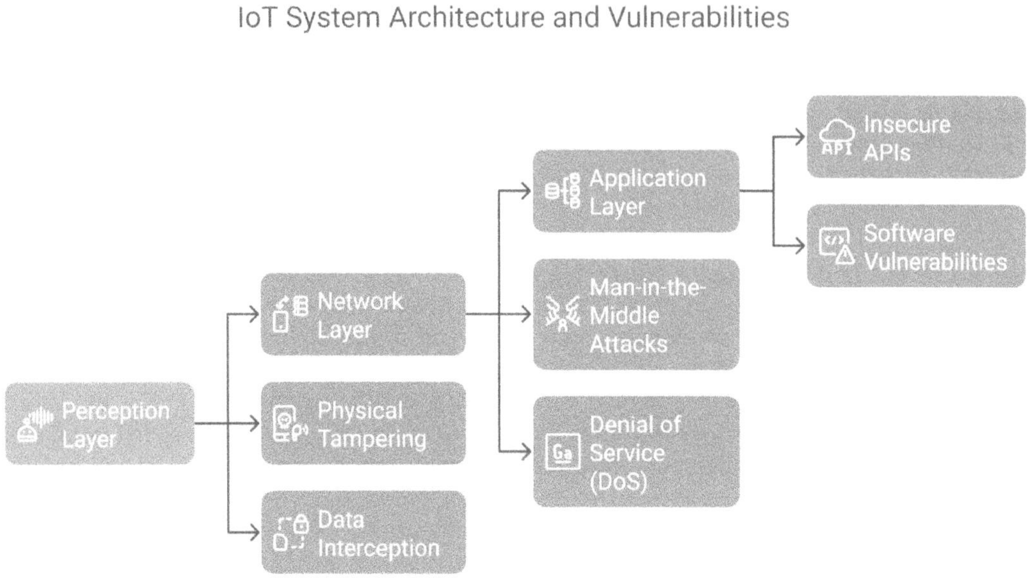

Figure 15.1 A diagrammatic illustration of connectivity among IoT devices and possible vulnerabilities by layers.

15.2 LITERATURE REVIEW

The rapid growth of the IoT has started a new era of digital connectivity. This allows billions of devices to communicate independently across various applications. However, this change has increased the need for strong authentication methods, privacy protections, and reliable forensic tools. Biometric authentication uses unique physical and behavioral traits to confirm identity and has become a promising option. While it offers great benefits in terms of user convenience and resistance to common security threats, biometric systems also face serious challenges related to security gaps, privacy issues, and forensic traceability.

In IoT systems, biometric authentication is divided into physiological and behavioral types. Physiological biometrics cover fingerprints, facial recognition, iris recognition, palm and finger vein patterns, and ECGs. On the other hand, behavioral biometrics include voice recognition, typing patterns, gait, touch interactions, and breathing patterns. Advances in facial and iris recognition have come from techniques like principal component analysis (PCA), wavelet transforms, and Laplacian pyramid fusion. Hossain et al. achieved a 99.5% recognition rate using facial simulators tested on the FERET dataset. Although iris recognition systems have potential in mobile applications, as shown by Thavalengal et al. and Daugman, they are often limited by pixel resolution and hardware capabilities. Fingerprint recognition is still widely used because of its high accuracy and affordability. Some lightweight systems, such as those created by Yang et al., use block logic–based algorithms that fit well with limited IoT devices. Meanwhile, Bedari et al. have worked on optimizing fingerprint templates to lessen memory usage and improve compatibility with embedded systems. ECG-based authentication is becoming more popular, particularly in healthcare-related IoT applications. Researchers like Arteaga-Falconi and Tantinger have developed ECG authentication methods for mobile devices and wearables.

Additionally, Karimian et al. have explored the use of ECG for generating biometric keys, with newer systems like PlexNet and PulsePrint using deep learning to enhance identification performance.

Behavioral biometrics show promise for smooth user authentication due to their passive and non-intrusive characteristics. Voice recognition, improved through deep learning, is now used for smart home security and device access, as noted by Sriskandaraja et al. Keystroke dynamics, researched by Saevanee and Antal, allow verification based on individual typing patterns. Similarly, gait and activity recognition using convolutional neural networks (CNNs) offer passive authentication solutions for wearables and smartphones. Additionally, new methods such as brainwave signals (EEG), surface electromyograms (sEMG), and acoustic breathing signatures (BreathPrint) are being studied to support continuous and context-aware biometric authentication in IoT settings.

Despite these advancements, biometric systems in IoT devices face major security and privacy issues. A primary concern is the irreversible nature of biometric data; unlike passwords, compromised biometric templates cannot be reset. This highlights the need for secure storage and transmission techniques. To address these risks, various privacy-preserving strategies have been suggested. Cancelable biometrics change original features into revocable versions. Techniques like HE and functional encryption (FE) allow for operations on encrypted data, maintaining data confidentiality. Other privacy-enhancing methods include secure multi-party computation (SMC), k-anonymity, randomized response (RR), and the Laplace mechanism (LM), all of which aim to conceal sensitive user information. Biometric cryptosystems provide another layer of security by creating cryptographic keys from biometric traits without storing the original data. In response to spoofing and replay attacks, new detection methods have been introduced, including the use of scent to identify fake fingerprints (Baldisserra et al.) and replay detection for brainprints (Gui et al.). Nevertheless, many IoT devices have limited processing power and memory, making it hard to implement these complex defenses. To overcome this, Karimian et al. suggested using physical unclonable functions (PUFs) and hardware obfuscation to avoid storing biometric templates. Other researchers, such as Punithavathi et al. and Shahzad et al., have built secure frameworks that combine facial and fingerprint recognition while ensuring the encrypted management of biometric data.

The forensic implications of biometric data in IoT systems are also significant, especially given the diverse and decentralized nature of IoT devices. When properly logged, biometric data can provide essential evidence following security incidents. Forensic investigations typically go through four stages: identification, collection, analysis, and reporting. While Pilli et al. have proposed application-specific forensic models, and Kebande and Ray have created broader frameworks to meet varying investigative needs. The collection phase poses particular challenges due to proprietary data formats, encryption methods, and the need to maintain device functionality during data gathering.

Wearable technologies, like smartwatches and fitness trackers, are increasingly recognized as useful sources of forensic evidence. However, the lack of standardized extraction and interpretation methods limits their effective use in forensics. Grispos et al. demonstrated how data from a smart scale could aid digital investigations, though concerns about evidence integrity and a verifiable chain of custody persist. Recently, ML approaches—such as random forests and Naïve Bayes classifiers—are being used to detect malware or anomalies in digital forensic data. AI also helps analyze evidence in real time, particularly for wearables, speeding up and improving forensic processes. Blockchain technology has potential for maintaining an unchangeable chain of custody for digital artifacts, as noted by Akinbi et al., while electromagnetic side-channel analysis, researched by Sayakkara et al., offers non-invasive insights into how devices behave. Furthermore, Hou et al. introduced a three-dimensional forensic framework that includes temporal, geographic, and technical factors, providing a more comprehensive and standardized way to investigate IoT-related incidents.

Despite these developments, there are still research gaps to address. One urgent issue is the lack of standardization in wearable forensics, where differences in hardware and software prevent the creation of universal forensic tools. Ongoing interoperability challenges across different IoT platforms also remain an obstacle. Additionally, the realm of real-time forensics, which is crucial for spotting and stopping ongoing attacks, is still in its early stages. Existing forensic systems often lack automation and scalability, and integrating AI-driven insights into standard investigative processes is still developing. In biometrics, dynamic methods like gait and voice recognition frequently struggle with accuracy in changing conditions. Therefore, further research is needed to improve the reliability, privacy, and contextual awareness of multimodal biometric systems. Moreover, the legal and ethical implications of using biometric data in forensic situations call for clearer and more widely accepted rules.

In conclusion, incorporating biometric authentication into IoT environments offers a powerful way to enhance security and tailor user experiences. However, this advancement also brings complex issues related to privacy, data protection, and digital forensics. Tackling these challenges will require creating lightweight, privacy-focused biometric systems and standardized forensic methods that can effectively deal with the varied and decentralized nature of modern IoT ecosystems. Innovations in AI, blockchain, and privacy-preserving cryptography will likely play a key role in overcoming these ongoing challenges and ensuring secure, transparent, and trustworthy IoT environments.

15.2.1 Summary of literature review

The research materials show how biometrics and digital forensics started to work together with IoT systems to solve both security problems and investigation requirements. The works of Karimian et al. (2018), Ferrag et al. (2019), and Yang et al. (2021) present space-efficient biometric access systems that work on IoT equipment and mobile devices with limited resources and they demonstrate through their research that ECG sEMG and multimodal biometric systems achieve cancelable authentication, which protects user privacy and enables federated learning in IoT systems. The research by Sathwara et al. (2018), Saleh et al. (2021), and Grispos et al. (2021) presents IoT-specific forensic frameworks together with process models and tools that reform digital forensic methods to work with the unique distributed and diverse IoT system structure because they successfully solve problems related to data collection, data protection, and data format unification from Table 15.1.

The current research work builds on previous research to investigate new threats and privacy challenges and the current trends of biometric-IoT security and forensics research. The researchers conducted studies through Rui and Yan (2019), Arman et al. (2024), Lien and Vhaduri (2023), and other sources to assess biometric privacy breach risks and evaluate cancelable biometrics together with advanced methods, including GANs-based synthetic data. The research work of Mazhar et al. (2021), Ahmed et al. (2023, 2025), Thangavel et al. (2024), and Wells and Usman (2023) investigates IoT forensic challenges together with wearable device investigations and voice-based authentication systems. The table shows a unified research path that leads to blockchain-based evidence protection and AI and machine learning-based anomaly identification and standardized forensic processes and biometric systems that protect user privacy, but these systems face real-world challenges regarding their ability to scale, the availability of datasets, and their compatibility with legal jurisdictional requirements from Tables 15.2 and 15.3.

Table 15.1 Summary of literature review

Ref.	*Authors*	*Year*	*Topic/focus*	*Key contributions*
1	Karimian et al.	2018	Biometric access in IoT	Secure and lightweight biometric access for constrained IoT systems
2	Ferrag et al.	2019	Bio-features in mobile IoT	Authentication and authorization techniques using biometric traits
3	Sathwara et al.	2018	IoT forensics	Digital investigation framework tailored to IoT systems
4	Rani et al.	2020	IoT threats and cybercrime	Comprehensive survey of IoT security threats and countermeasures
5	Saleh et al.	2021	Forensics process in IoT	Proposed a common model for IoT forensic investigations
6	Grispos et al.	2021	IoT forensics (smart scale)	Digital forensic analysis in a smart device ecosystem
7	Ahmed et al.	2025	IoT forensics and security	Broader issues and challenges in IoT forensic environments
8	Rad et al.	2024	Fingerprint sensor risks	Exploits using seaweed alginate against IoT fingerprint devices
9	Nasr et al.	2025	Cancelable biometrics	EMD and quaternion-based cancelable biometric authentication
10	Rui and Yan	2019	Biometric privacy	Survey on secure and privacy-aware biometric systems
11	Arman et al.	2024	Privacy-preserving biometrics	Recent advances and future trends in biometric privacy
12	Shdefat et al.	2021	ECG in IoT	Survey on ECG-based authentication in 5G-enabled IoT
13	Golec et al.	2022	BioSec framework	Secure communication using biometrics in edge/ Industry 4.0
14	Lien and Vhaduri	2023	Biometric authentication challenges	Issues and research gaps in biometric IoT authentication
15	Mazhar et al.	2021	IoT forensics	M2M-based forensic analysis framework for IoT
16	Jiang et al.	2021	sEMG biometric	HD-sEMG for cancelable biometric authentication in IoT
17	Redwan et al.	2024	Windows forensics	Tools for Windows-based digital forensic analysis
18	Oriwoh et al.	2013	IoT forensics overview	Challenges and methodologies in IoT digital forensics
19	Ijaz et al.	2016	Smart city security	Survey of IoT security concerns in smart city infrastructure
20	Jenkins and Roy	2024	GANs in biometrics	Use of DCGAN in biometric authentication
21	Farid et al.	2020	Identity mgmt. in IoT	Smart biometric identity management for cloud health services
22	Yang et al.	2021	Biometrics in IoT	Review of biometric technologies in IoT environments
23	Bedari et al.	2021	Fingerprint in IoT	Lightweight, secure fingerprint systems for industrial IoT
24	Lin et al.	2022	Multimodal biometrics	Federated learning for multimodal biometric recognition
25	Ahmed et al.	2023	IoT forensics trends	Overview and future direction of IoT forensic research
26	Wells and Usman	2023	Voice biometrics in IoT	Voice authentication for secure and trustworthy IoT access

Table 15.2 Key research contributions and gaps in IoT forensics

Research focus	*Contributions*	*Gaps*
Blockchain in IoT forensics	Data integrity, tamper-proof logs	High computational requirements
AI/ML models	Automated anomaly detection	Dataset availability and bias
Forensic frameworks	Device-specific investigation processes	Lack of standardization across devices
Legal and ethical studies	Privacy-preserving methodologies	Jurisdictional conflicts and ethical dilemmas

Table 15.3 Example of IoT evidence chain of custody

Stage	*Task*	*Responsible entity*
Data collection	Retrieve logs from IoT sensors	Forensic technician
Hashing	Generate cryptographic hash	Security analyst
Storage	Store data in tamper-proof system	Digital evidence manager

15.3 FUNDAMENTALS OF BIOMETRIC SYSTEMS

15.3.1 Purpose and types of biometric traits

Biometric systems are sophisticated and intelligent mechanisms designed for individual identification, having a rapid-fire swell in interest and demand across different sectors similar to healthcare, security systems, and telecommunications. The abecedarian purpose of these systems is to authenticate individualities by vindicating their unique mortal characteristics, thereby offering a robust volition to conventional authentication styles. Traditional approaches, including radio frequency identification (RFID) markers, authentication cards, colophons, watchwords, and ID cards, are honored for their essential sins and vulnerability to phony. For example, conventional styles like watchwords and tokens, while offering theoretical 100 delicacies, are prone to mortal limitations similar to memorization load, leading to credential filling or the exercise of analogous watchwords across multiple accounts. Likewise, these knowledge-grounded authentications can be fluently compromised through shoulder-probing or cracking, particularly when employed for IoT device access in public surroundings. Biometrics, again, are essential to an individual, making them delicate to manipulate, partake, or forget, therefore presenting a more secure and stone-centric authentication paradigm. This represents an abecedarian shift from counting on external commemoratives or learned information to using natural particular attributes for identity verification (Figure 15.2).

Biometric traits are broadly categorized into two primary classes based on their nature:

- **Physiological Traits:** These characteristics are deduced from the unique physical attributes or anatomical structures of an existent's body. Exemplifications include fingerprints, facial figure, hand and win figure, iris patterns, and ECG signals.
- **Behavioral Traits:** These attributes are predicated on the distinctive patterns of mortal conduct or learned actions. Common exemplifications encompass hand verification, keystroke dynamics, and voice recognition.

15.3.2 Characteristics of ideal biometric data

- **Oneness:** An essential specificity is that the biometric particularity must be distinct for each existent. For illustration, ECG signals retain a "unique morphological shape due to the anatomical structure of the heart and physiological conditions". The variations

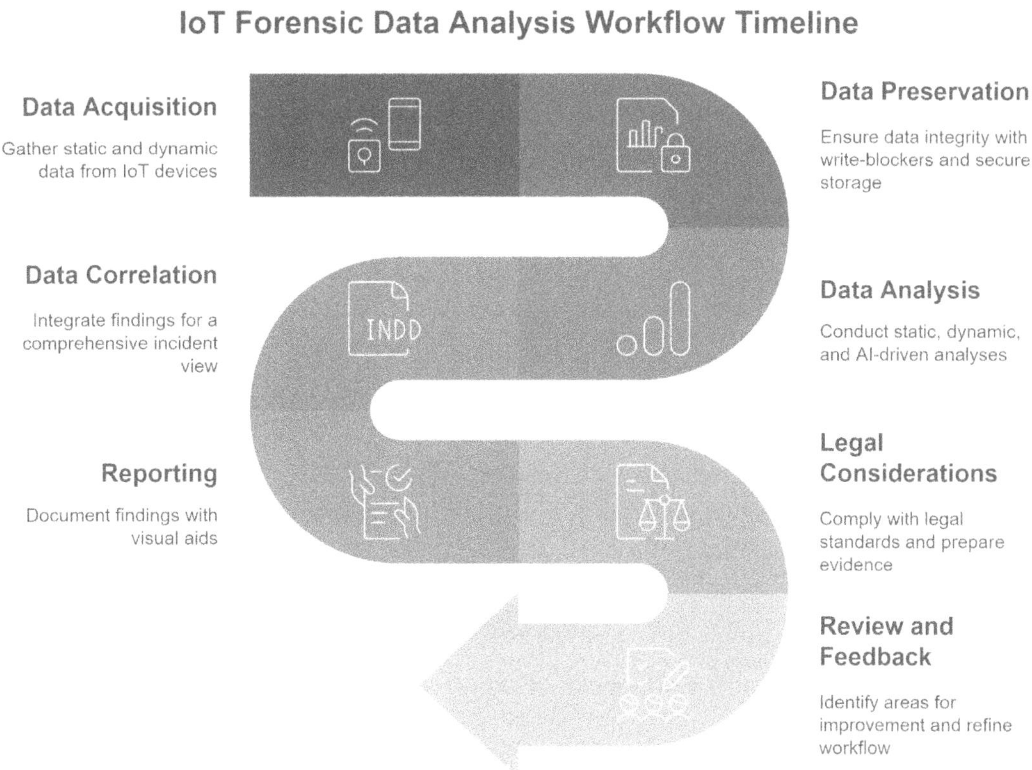

Figure 15.2 The process of IoT forensic data analysis, including static, dynamic, and AI-based methodologies.

in heart structure parameters, such as wall consistency, position, and size, assure a unique ECG signal for every person.

- **Non-invasiveness and Ease of Measurement:** The practicality of a biometric system is significantly enhanced if the data accession process is non-intrusive and straightforward. ECG is cited as a "noninvasive test and easy to be measured by just placing two fritters on the sensitive plates". This ease of use promotes stoner acceptance and wide relinquishment.
- **Robustness and Limited Computational Processing:** For deployment in different surroundings, especially within resource-constrained IoT bias, a biometric system should bear minimum computational power. ECG-predicated authentication systems are noted for demanding "limited computational processing power for feting individualities".
- **Resistance to Forgery and Spoofing:** A critical security demand is the biometric's capability to repel fraudulent attempts to mimic or reproduce the particularity. ECG signals are considered "delicate to falsify under supervised conditions" and are "present only in living individualities". This directly addresses vulnerabilities set up in other biometrics, similar to fingerprints, which "could live on spectacles, doors, and tables; therefore, it's possible to be acquired and used" for spoofing.

The selection of a biometric system for a specific operation, particularly in the IoT sphere, necessitates a careful evaluation of colorful trade-offs. While ECG offers high security and delicacy, it's susceptible to "Cerebral and physical state perceptivity". In discrepancy, characteristic is cost-effective and extensively embraced but offers lower security and medium

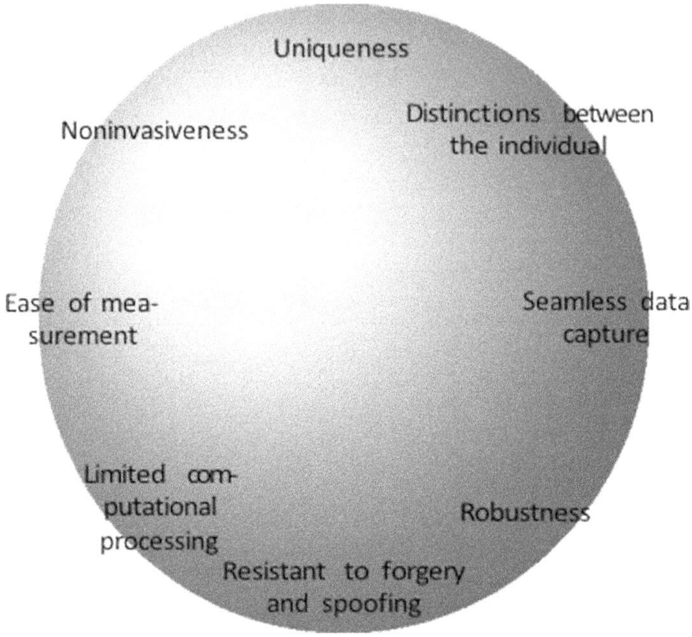

Figure 15.3 Essential attributes of ideal biometric data shown in a circular layout.

delicacy. Face recognition, despite being high-cost, also presents a low-security position. This essential variability in performance, cost, and security across different biometric modalities indicates that a "one-size-fits-all" biometric result is impracticable. The optimal choice depends on balancing the needed position of security, stoner convenience, available computational coffers, and perpetration costs, emphasizing the need for an acclimatized approach in biometric system design (Figure 15.3).

15.3.3 General architecture and operational phases

A typical biometric authentication system comprises several connected factors and operates through distinct phases to enroll and corroborate individualities. While a general architectural illustration isn't provided, the description of an ECG-grounded authentication system offers a clear illustration of these rudiments and their functional inflow.

15.3.3.1 System components

The proposed ECG authentication system exemplifies a distributed armature, according to both a remote/mobile side and a fixed server side.

- ECG module serves as the detector for acquiring the analog ECG signal.
- 16-bit high-precision ADC digitizes the analog ECG signal.
- jeer Pi 3 (Remote/Mobile Side) acts as an IoT-sensitive knot, equipped with the capability to execute needed algorithms (e.g., using Octave free license software) for signal processing and data transmission via TCP/IP protocol.
- Web gateway (Fixed/Gateway Side) manages the system database, which is an SQLite database, and hosts the web-grounded acquiring interface and login runner.

Functional Phases: Biometric systems generally operate in two main phases: registration and verification/identification.

Registration Process:

- Signal Acquisition and Pre-processing: An individual presents their biometric particularity (e.g., ECG signal), which is also measured, acquired, and pre-processed to sludge out unwanted signal factors.
- Point birth: Unique characteristics are yanked from the pre-processed signal. In the ECG system, discrete cosine transform (DCT) portions are uprooted from a single measured ECG beat.
- Template storehouse: These uprooted features are saved in a database as a profile, frequently referred to as a "fiducial mark" or "pre-defined RR features".

Verification Process:

- Biometric donation: The existent seeking authentication presents their biometric particularity to the system.
- Signal processing and point birth: The presented signal undergoes the same pre-processing and point birth way as during registration.
- Matching/correlation: The recently uprooted features are compared against the stored template. In the ECG system, the DCT portions from the first RR interval (saved in the database) are compared with three successive intervals from the recently acquired signal using a cross-correlation fashion.
- Decision Grounded: On the comparison, a decision is made. For the ECG system, if the identified result exceeds a predefined threshold (e.g., > 95), the person is estimated as authorized; else, they're supposed to be unauthorized. This process is generally time-limited (e.g., 10 seconds).

The distributed armature of the proposed ECG system, using a remote jeer Pi 3 knot and a central gateway, significantly enhances its scalability and cost-effectiveness for IoT biometric operations. This structure allows for the combination of multiple edge bumps with a single gateway, thereby adding overall system capability while contemporaneously reducing the total cost. By unpacking computationally ferocious tasks, similar to database operation and complex matching algorithms, to a centralized gateway, and keeping data accession and original point of birth on resource-constrained edge bias, the system achieves a balance between performance and practicality. This distributed model is a crucial enabler for planting biometrics in wide IoT surroundings, where individual bias frequently warrants the full processing power or storehouse capacity for standalone authentication.

15.4 INTEGRATION OF BIOMETRICS WITH IoT

15.4.1 Rationale for integration: Addressing traditional authentication limitations

The integration of biometric systems into IoT surroundings is driven by the essential limitations and vulnerabilities of conventional authentication styles. Traditional technologies, similar to RFID markers, authentication cards, colophons, watchwords, and ID cards, are feted for their vulnerability to colorful sins and their inadequate robustness against phony. For example, physical vestiges like fingerprints can inadvertently be left on shells (e.g., spectacles, doors, tables), making them susceptible to accession and posterior fraudulent use. Also, knowledge-grounded authentication styles like watchwords and Legs are prone to mortal fallibility, including being forgotten, participated in, or fluently compromised through ways like shoulder-probing or brute-force attacks, particularly when used for penetrating IoT bias in public settings.

Biometric styles are thus proposed as a "prompt relief" for these conventional approaches due to their natural oneness and the difficulty associated with forging them. While biometrics offer enhanced security by being unique to an individual and delicate to manipulate, partake, or forget, they introduce a critical vulnerability: the irrevocability of a compromised template. If a raw biometric template is ever recovered, it's "ever compromised because biometrics are irrevocable". This abecedarian difference means that unlike watchwords, which can be changed after a breach, a compromised biometric cannot be reset for an existent. Accordingly, the design and perpetration of robust protection mechanisms for biometric templates—such as secure storehouses, cancelable biometrics, or template metamorphosis—have come to consummate. This is a more severe security challenge than traditional credential breaches, as it demands innovative, long-term results to guard an existent's identity permanently.

15.4.2 Benefits of biometric integration in IoT environments

- **Enhanced Security and Trustability Biometrics:** They give a robust defense against unauthorized access and fraudulent conditioning due to their essential oneness and difficulty to forge.
- **Real-Time Capability:** A crucial advantage for IoT is the capability to perform authentication fleetly and continuously. Numerous biometric systems, particularly those grounded on ECG, prioritize "real-time capability of authenticating individualities". This is demonstrated by systems achieving high delicacy rates (e.g., 97.78) with minimum processing times (around 1.21 seconds). The emphasis on speed and the successful perpetration of real-time authentication signify a shift from static, one-time security checks to dynamic, nonstop identity verification.
- **Convenience and Usability Biometrics:** They offer a stoner-friendly and accessible authentication experience. The "accessible nature" of biometrics contributes to their "lower vulnerability to attacks".
- **Nonrepudiation Biometrics:** They give a strong medium for nonrepudiation, meaning that an existent can not later deny their involvement in a sale or claim it was unauthorized. This is vital for responsibility in IoT-driven processes.

15.4.3 Common biometric traits and their prevalence in IoT applications

The selection of biometric traits for IoT operations is a critical decision, impacted by factors similar to delicacy, cost, User Acceptance, and specific operation conditions. Both physiological and behavioral biometrics find mileage in this sphere.

ECG Biometrics in IoT

- ECG captures the electrical exertion of the heart. It's largely valued for its "unique morphological shape" and its essential resistance to phoniness, as it's only present in living individualities. This makes it a robust biometric for security-critical operations.
- A notable IoT real-time authentication system leverages ECG signals. This system employs DCT for point birth from a single ECG beat, which is acquired in just 3 seconds.

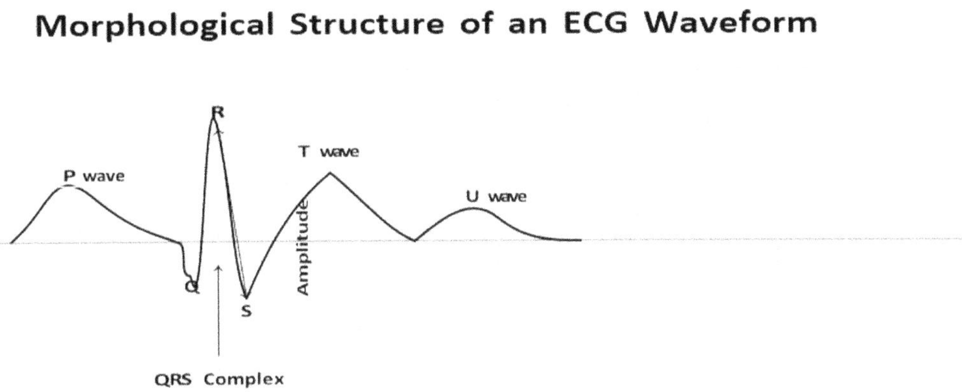

Figure 15.4 Morphological ECG waveform showing P wave, QRS complex (Q, R, S), T wave, U wave, and the amplitude from S to R.

A jeer Pi 3 serves as the IoT-sensitive knot, transmitting data to a web gateway with an SQLite database for verification. This setup achieves a high delicacy rate of 97.78 with a rapid-fire processing time of roughly 1.21 seconds.

- The ECG signal is characterized by distinct P, R, and T swells, along with colorful parts and temporal intervals (e.g., P-R interval, QRS complex, S-T member, T-P member). The analysis can be distributed as fiducial-grounded (counting on uprooted features from heart rate intervals like RR intervals or specific points) or non-fiducial-based (encompassing temporal, breadth, morphology, autocorrelation, phase space, and frequency-grounded styles).
- The authentication process involves comparing DCT portions from a pre-defined RR interval (stored in the database) with those from three successive intervals of the acquired signal using a cross-correlation fashion. A correlation affect exceeding 95 is generally needed for authorized access (Figure 15.4).

Figure 15.5 shows an example of an acquired ECG signal with clearly marked RR intervals, demonstrating the segmentation process crucial for feature extraction.

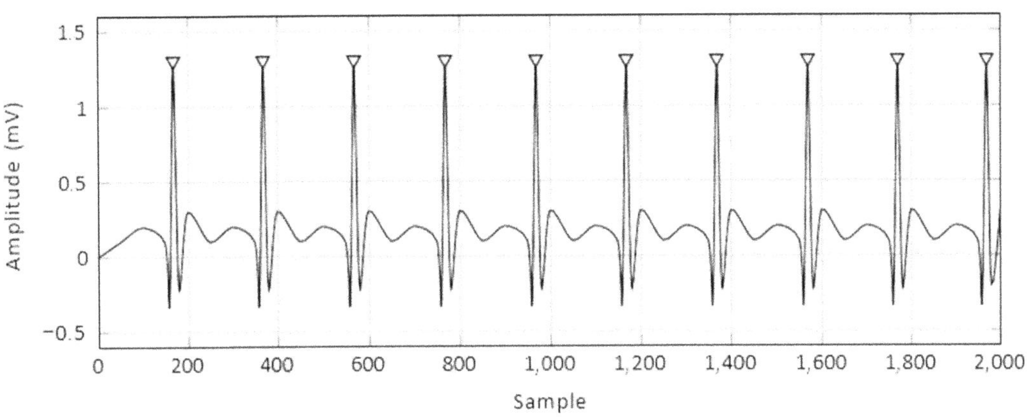

Figure 15.5 The detected ECG RR intervals.

Fingerprint Biometrics in IoT

- Fingerprint recognition is a widely adopted biometric authentication method in IoT devices due to its cost-effectiveness, ease of implementation, and high recognition accuracy.
- It leverages the unique patterns of ridges and valleys on an individual's fingertips, which are permanent and distinct for each person, even identical twins.
- Spoofing attacks are a significant concern, as fingerprints are not secret and can be obtained and forged. For instance, an iPhone's Touch ID can be deceived by a fake fingerprint film made from glue. Partial fingerprint systems and smudges left on touchscreens also pose risks.
- It's considerably employed in time attendance systems, home security, online banking, and marketable deals.

Face Recognition in IoT

- Face recognition is a popular biometric method in IoT, identifying users based on their facial features.
  It is often implemented due to the rapid development of smart cameras and mobile devices.
- Its integration is current in security systems, videotape logical systems, smart shopping, automatic face trailing, and device access control.

Iris Recognition in IoT

- Iris recognition identifies users based on their unique iris patterns, which are considered highly reliable due to their accuracy, uniqueness, and stability over time.
- It is a non-contact and non-intrusive biometric method.
- Operations include premise access control, banking deals, and identification webbing systems at airfields.

Voice Recognition in IoT

- Voice recognition, also known as speech recognition, identifies individuals based on their speaking patterns and habits, leveraging unique characteristics like pitch.
- It is considered a natural, non-intrusive, and convenient behavioral biometric factor. A microphone is typically the only required hardware, making it easily implementable at little cost across almost all mobile devices.
- It's employed to enhance security and convenience in home-IoT bias by relating druggies and assaying their commands.
- Despite its convenience, voice recognition is sensitive to environmental noise and susceptible to spoofing attacks, as voice samples can be fluently collected in open surroundings (Figure 15.6; Table 15.4).

15.5 FORENSIC SIGNIFICANCE OF BIOMETRIC DATA IN IoT

15.5.1 Critical part of biometric data as digital substantiation

Biometric data, by its very nature as a unique identifier of an individual, holds substantial implicit as digital substantiation in examinations involving IoT bias. The essential oneness of biometric traits makes them theoretically inestimable for establishing identity and icing nonrepudiation in a forensic context. However, this data could serve as a direct

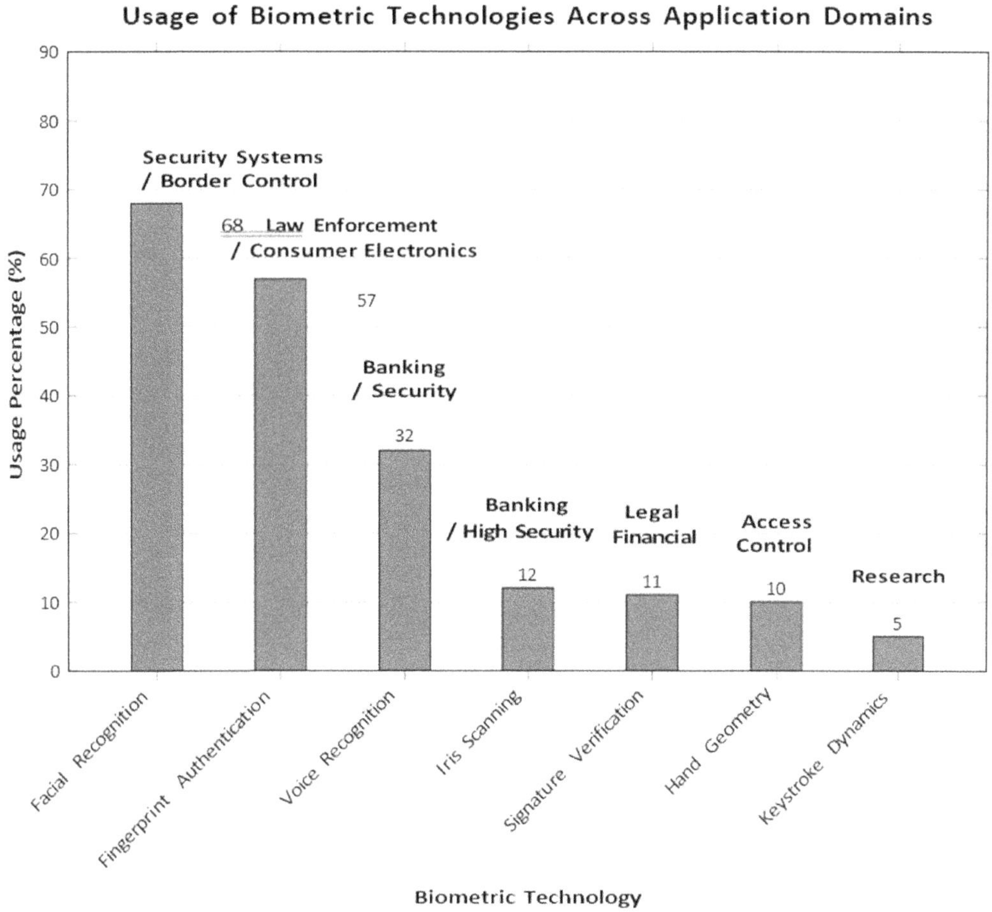

Figure 15.6 Use of biometric technologies across application areas (2018–2025).

Table 15.4 Comparison of different authentication technologies

Technology	*Accuracy*	*Performance*	*Cost*	*Measurability*	*Security level*	*Drawbacks*
Fingerprinting	Medium	Medium	Low	Medium	Low	Temperature, humidity, injury
Iris recognition	High	High	High	Medium	Medium	Illumination, injury, resolution
Face recognition	Low	Medium	High	High	Low	Illumination, injury, resolution
ECG	High	High	High	Medium	High	Psychological and physical state sensitivity

link between a specific individual and conduct performed on or through that device, if an IoT device records biometric authentication attempts or successful accesses. For example, logs indicating a successful biometric login to a smart home device at a particular time could place an existent at a position or link them to the activation of certain functionalities. The recognition that "spoofing attack shall do either digitally or physically" also underscores the necessity for forensic analysis to separate between licit biometric operation and fraudulent attempts, thereby furnishing pivotal perceptivity into the nature of a security incident.

15.5.2 Types of data collected for forensic analysis

While unequivocal details on forensic data types are limited, the accessible information suggests that IoT bias, particularly those integrating biometrics, can induce colorful forms of data with implicit forensic value.

- **Biometric Authentication Logs:** The ECG authentication system, for illustration, explicitly logs "authorized access" or "unauthorized person" status. Similar logs give a clear record of who tried to pierce a device, when, and whether the attempt was successful. This data is abecedarian for reconstructing access patterns and relating implicit breaches.
- **Physiological and Health Metrics:** Beyond authentication, ECG signals are also "used as a heart condition diagnosing and covering". This implies that IoT bias collecting ECG data might also capture and store other health-related criteria. In a forensic script, this could give contextual information about an existent's physiological state or exertion situations at a specific time, potentially linking them to a crime scene or event.
- **Time-Stamped Functional Data:** The ECG system operates with precise timing, noting processing times (e.g., "1.21 seconds") and process limits (e.g., "10 seconds"). This indicates that IoT bias innately induce time-stamped functional data, which is pivotal for establishing timelines of events in a forensic disquisition.

The binary nature of biometric data in IoT, serving both as an authentication medium and a source of physiological monitoring, creates a rich, yet sensitive, implicit source for forensic substantiation. This means that IoT bias collecting biometric data for authentication may also coincidently gather medically applicable or exertion-related physiological data. From a forensic perspective, this binary mileage could give not only evidence of identity but also contextual information about an existent's state or conduct at a given moment. This capability could be necessary in linking an individual to a specific event or position, thereby significantly abetting in event reconstruction. Still, the collection and implicit forensic use of similar deeply particular data innately raise significant sequestration enterprises, challenging careful consideration of ethical and legal fabrics.

15.5.3 Donation to event reconstruction and perpetrator identification

Biometric data contributes significantly to event reconstruction and perpetrator identification in IoT examinations.

- **Event Reconstruction:** Records of biometric authentication attempts and successes can help establish a precise timeline of who penetrated an IoT device, when, and for how long. This is critical for understanding the sequence of events leading up to or during a security incident. For illustration, if a smart cinch is compromised, biometric logs can pinpoint the exact moment of unauthorized entry and potentially identify the individual responsible.
- **Perpetrator Identification:** The unique nature of biometric data is consummate for linking digital exertion to a real-world individual. However, forensic analysis of biometric logs can help identify the licit stoner whose credentials might have been compromised, or, if an IoT system is traduced. The capability to separate between genuine and spoofed biometric inputs, however grueling, is vital for accurate perpetrator identification.

15.6 FORENSIC METHODOLOGIES AND TOOLS

15.6.1 Cosmopolitan digital forensic disquisition process

A digital forensic activity employs a merged methodological analysis to maintain testimony wholeness and admissibility. This activity includes several critical phases:

- **Recognition:** Locating and relating potential sources of digital evidence.
- **Conservation:** Safeguarding associated testimony from alteration or destruction.
- **Analytics:** Investigating the preserved demonstration to extract applicable information.
- **Contribution:** Presenting findings clearly and in a legally acceptable format.

While this framework is standard, its application in the IoT context introduces unique challenges not completely explored in existing literature.

15.6.2 Specific methodologies acclimatize for IoT

Existing forensic inquiry does not provide specific methodologies tailored for IoT forensics, such as the *1-2-3 Zones Approach*. However, the architecture of IoT biometric systems inherently suggests complexities in forensic data retrieval. For instance, the proposed ECG system employs a distributed architecture consisting of a "remote or mobile side" and a "fixed (server) side", necessitating technical forensic approaches for data acquisition from remote sources.

Such methodologies must consider the diverse device capabilities, connection types, and data storage models across the IoT landscape.

15.6.3 Specialized software and machine learning algorithms for verification analysis

Available literature discusses software and algorithms within the operational realm of biometric systems rather than for forensic analysis. For example, the ECG system utilizes "Octave free license software" for algorithm execution and an "SQLite database" for information management. Characteristic extraction is conducted using "Discrete Cosine Transform (DCT)", and trance matching employs the "correlation measure". Notwithstanding essential for biometric functionality, these are not specified as consecrated forensic analytics tools. Current resources lack information on specialized forensic software or ML algorithms specifically designed for digital evidence analytics in IoT environments, as shown in Figure 15.7.

15.7 CHALLENGES IN BIOMETRIC FORENSICS WITHIN IoT

15.7.1 Diversity and resource constraints of IoT bias

The IoT is characterized by its vast "multitudinous numbers of goods, analogous as bias, sensors, and applicable data". This essential diversity implies a wide array of attack platforms, operating systems, and software configurations across the IoT ecosystem. From a forensic perspective, this diversity presents significant challenges in data accession and analysis, as investigators must contend with numerous particular formats, varying data storage mechanisms, and distant communication protocols. The lack of standardization across these bias complicates the development of universal forensic tools and methodologies.

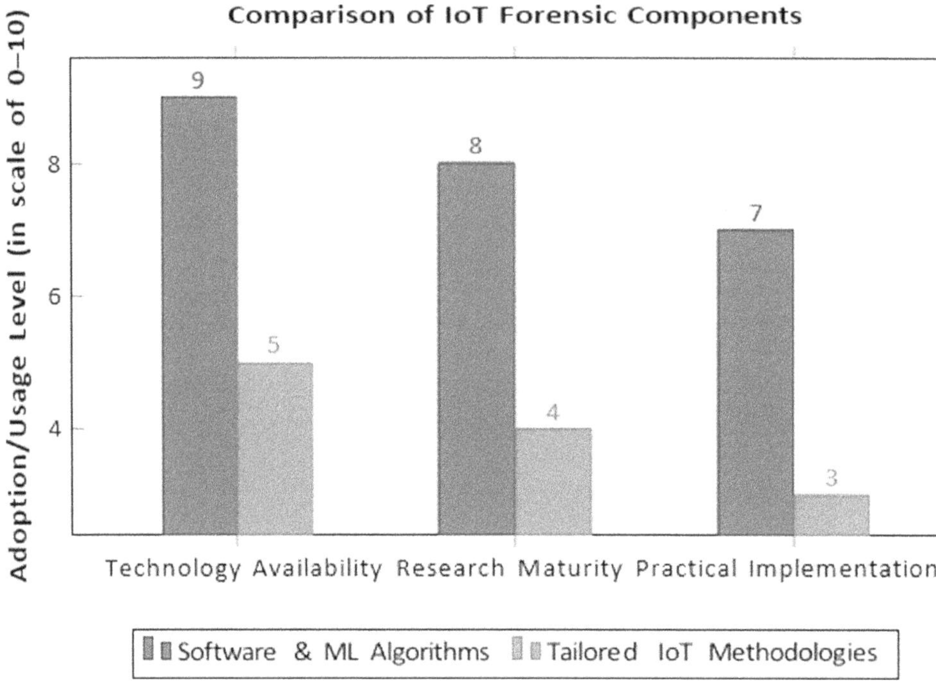

Figure 15.7 Statistical comparison of ML-based software tools vs. IoT-specific forensic methodologies.

Likewise, multitudinous IoT bias, while suitable for biometric processing (e.g., ECG systems demanding "limited computational processing power"), are constitutionally resource-constrained. This limitation in processing power, memory, and storage capacity means that IoT bias may not retain extensive logs, metadata, or nonfictional data for prolonged periods. Data might be snappily overwritten, or only lower information might be stored due to design choices prioritizing effectiveness over forensic readiness. This poses a significant challenge for forensic preservation, as vital validation could be evanescent or deficient, making it delicate to reconstruct events directly.

15.7.2 Massive volume and changeable nature of IoT data

The sheer scale of IoT deployments results in the generation of a "massive volume" of "applicable data" from "multitudinous numbers of goods". This continuous aqueduct of data from numerous connected bias creates an unknown challenge for forensic investigators. Collecting, storing, and recovering such an immense volume of data requires substantial structure and advanced logical capabilities. Without effective data reduction and filtering ways, investigators have trouble being overwhelmed by irrelevant information, hindering the timely identification of critical validation.

While the accessible patches don't directly address the changeable nature of IoT data in a forensic terrain, the real-time processing capabilities of IoT biometric systems (e.g., ECG authentication in "1.21 seconds") suggest that data might be reused and discarded swiftly. This real-time, constantly evanescent nature of data can make it largely changeable, meaning that validation might live only for a brief period before being overwritten or lost. This necessitates rapid-fire responses and specialized accession ways to capture changeable data before it disappears, adding another layer of complexity to IoT forensic examinations.

15.7.3 Insulation enterprises and sensitive biometric information

Biometric data, by description, comprises "unique mortal characters" and is constitutionally "private". This deeply sensitive nature of biometric information raises profound insulation enterprises regarding its collection, storage, and particularly its use in forensic examinations. The eventuality for abuse or unauthorized access to analogous data, which uniquely identifies an individual, presents significant ethical and legal dilemmas. Forensic examinations involving biometric data must navigate strict insulation regulations (e.g., GDPR, HIPAA, though not explicitly mentioned in patches) to ensure that validation collection and analysis don't infringe upon individualities' fundamental rights. Balancing the need for validation with insulation protection is a complex challenge that requires robust legal fabrics and transparent investigative practices.

15.7.4 Complications from anti-forensic ways and legal admissibility

The accessible disquisition paraphernalia don't give specific information regarding anti-forensic ways or the complications related to legal admissibility in the terrain of IoT biometric forensics. Still, it's generally understood that sophisticated attackers may employ ways to obscure, alter, or destroy digital validation, complicating forensic sweats. Likewise, for any digital validation, including biometric data from IoT bias, to be admissible in court, it must be collected, saved, and analyzed following strict legal and procedural guidelines, icing its authenticity, integrity, and responsibility. The novelty and complexity of IoT surroundings can pose significant challenges to meeting these admissibility morals (Figures 15.8 and 15.9).

15.7.5 Specific biometric security challenges impacting forensics

Beyond the general challenges of IoT forensics, specific vulnerabilities essential to biometric systems further complicate forensic examinations.

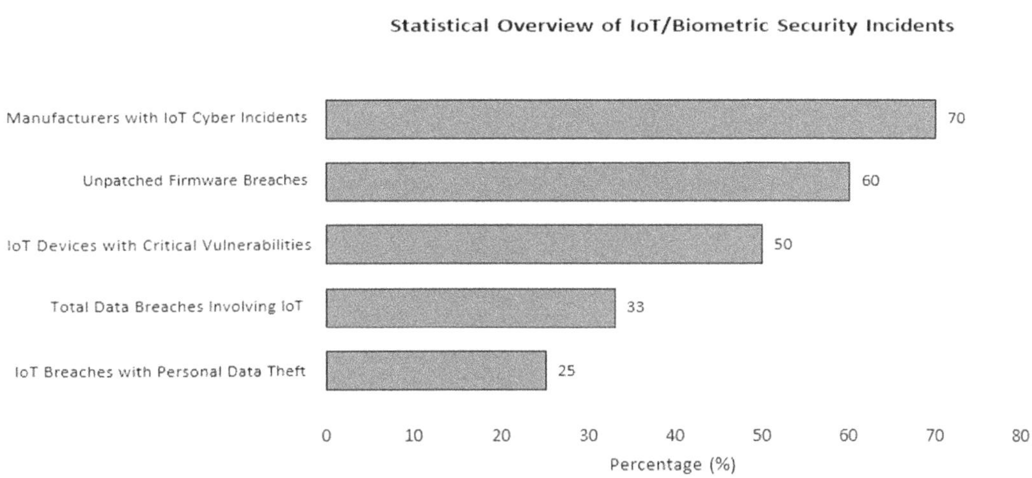

Figure 15.8 Statistical overview of security and privacy threats in IoT/biometric ecosystems.

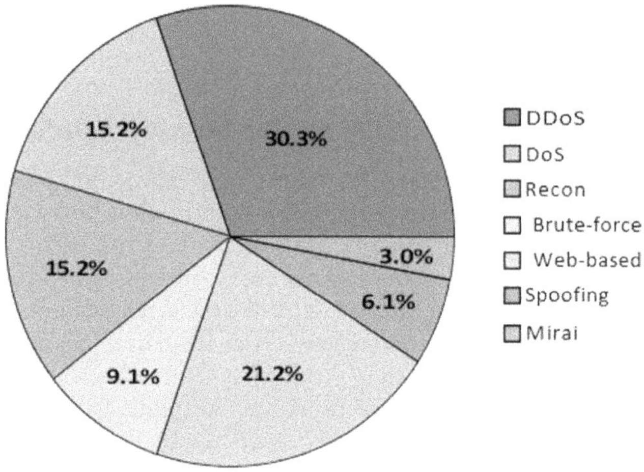

Figure 15.9 Distribution of IoT attack types from CIC-IoT 2023 dataset (total: 33 attacks).

15.7.5.1 Spoofing attacks

A significant concern is that "some biometrics styles presently live, these styles aren't robust enough against phony. Whereas the private biometric passes aren't defended, spoofing attack shall do either digitally or physically". For illustration, fingerprints can be "acquired and used" from shells like specs or doors. Also, voice recognition, while accessible, is "vulnerable to spoofing attacks" because voice samples can be "easily collected in open surroundings".

Complication for Forensic Examinations: When a spoofing attack occurs, forensic investigators face the laborious task of determining whether the biometric data used for access was genuine or a forged replica. This requires advanced logical ways to separate between authentic and spoofed biometric inputs, which is critical for directly relating the perpetrator and reconstructing the sequence of events. The presence of sophisticated spoofing styles can obscure the true identity of the attacker, making criteria challenging.

15.7.5.2 Non-cancelability of biometric templates

A fundamental vulnerability of biometric systems is the "irrevocability" of a compromised template "If the raw biometric template can ever be recovered, it's ever compromised because biometrics are irrevocable".

Complication for Forensic Examinations: Unlike watchwords or commemoratives that can be changed or issued after a breach, a compromised biometric template can't be "reset" for an individual. However, the affected individuals are permanently vulnerable to identity theft or unauthorized access attempts using their genuine biometric data, if a data breach exposes biometric templates. This has severe long-term forensic implications, as it means that indeed if an attacker is linked, the victim's biometric identity remains compromised, challenging different and more complex mitigation strategies than those for traditional credential breaches.

15.7.5.3 Impact of template aging and data breaches

Template Aging: The performance of biometric systems can be affected by changes in the biometric particularity over time or due to various conditions. For ECG, "Cerebral and physical state perceptivity" is noted as a disbenefit. For characteristic, "Temperature, humidity, injury" are listed as factors that can affect delicacy. These factors indicate that a legit user's biometric input might no longer perfectly match their aged, stored template, potentially leading to false rejections. Data Breaches: The irrevocability of compromised biometric templates highlights that data breaches involving these sensitive templates are a critical security concern.

15.8 PROPOSED FRAMEWORK

IoT Biometric Integration Layer: The Foundation of Identity in Connected Surroundings

- **IoT bias and Network structure**
  It encompasses the different range of smart, detector-enabled bias (e.g., smart homes, healthcare, transportation) and the beginning network protocols that enable their communication. This subcaste is characterized by its essential diversity and frequently resource-constrained nature (Grispos et al., 2021; Karimian et al., 2018).
- **Fundamentals of Biometric Systems**
  It details the core factors and functional phases of biometric authentication—data accession detectors, point birth (e.g., discrete cosine transfigure for ECG), template storehouse, matching algorithms, and decision modules. Biometric traits are distributed into physiological (fingerprints, facial figure, iris patterns, ECG) and behavioral (hand, keystroke dynamics, voice) modalities (Ferrag et al., 2019; Jiang et al., 2021).
- **Explanation and Benefits of Integration**
  It explains why biometrics serve as a "prompt relief" for traditional styles (watchwords, Legs, RFID), addressing phony and mortal – error vulnerabilities. Biometric integration offers enhanced security, real-time verification, convenience, nonrepudiation, and felicity for resource-limited IoT endpoints (Subha, 2017; Yang et al., 2021).
- **Common Biometric Traits in IoT**
  Current biometric modalities encompass various characteristics, including face recognition, iris recognition, and ECG biometrics. Each modality has its strengths and weaknesses, along with specific operational disciplines.
  For face recognition, strengths include ease of use and non-intrusiveness, while weaknesses involve susceptibility to spoofing and variations in lighting. Iris recognition offers high accuracy and uniqueness but can be affected by occlusions and requires specialized hardware. ECG biometrics provide continuous authentication and are difficult to spoof, yet they may face challenges with data privacy and require robust processing capabilities.
  Understanding these modalities is crucial for developing effective biometric systems that balance security, usability, and privacy.

Security and Sequestration Assurance Layer Navigating the Binary Edge of Biometrics

- **Enhanced Security Posture**
  Biometric factors ("*something you are*") combined with device possession ("*something you have*") significantly bolster identity verification over knowledge-based methods (Jiang et al., 2021).
- **Essential Biometric Vulnerabilities**
  - **Spoofing Attacks:** Forged fingerprints, lifted voice samples, or printed facial masks can bypass scanners.
  - **Non-Cancelability:** Once a raw biometric template is compromised, it cannot be "reset" like a password.
  - **Template Aging and Breaches:** Physiological changes (e.g., ECG variability under stress) and large-scale data leaks pose lasting risks.

- **Profound Privacy Concerns**
  Biometric data can reveal sensitive health or demographic information, raising legal and ethical issues around consent and surveillance.
- **Anti-Forensic Techniques**
  Attackers may obfuscate or erase digital logs or employ jamming and tampering methods to hinder evidence collection.

IoT Biometric Forensic Lifecycle Subcaste Tracing Digital Vestiges

- **Identification**
  Recognizing which IoT endpoints and associated biometric logs are relevant sources of evidence after an incident.
- **Collection and Preservation**
  Securely acquiring volatile and persistent biometric data across heterogeneous devices, overcoming storage constraints and ephemeral logs via edge snapshots and periodic offloading (Ahmed et al., 2023; Mazhar et al., 2021).
- **Analysis**
  Examining authentication attempts, physiological parameters, and timestamped operational logs; distinguishing genuine from spoofed biometric inputs using algorithmic validation (Grispos et al., 2021).
- **Event Reconstruction and Perpetrator Identification**
  Correlating biometric timestamps and device behavior to construct attack timelines and attribute actions to specific individuals (Thangavel et al., 2024).
- **Reporting and Presentation**
  Documenting findings in a legally admissible format, preserving chain of custody, and ensuring integrity of all biometric evidence (Thangavel et al., 2024).

Enabling Technologies and Mitigation Strategies Layer Advancing Forensic Capabilities

- **Advanced AI and Machine Learning (AI/ML)**
  Automated anomaly detection, deepfake recognition, and event-pattern mining speed up incident investigation (Thangavel et al., 2024).
- **Blockchain Technology**
  Tamper-evident ledgers for template storage and log chaining strengthen evidentiary trust, although scalability on resource-constrained devices remains an open research challenge (Ahmed et al., 2023).
- **Cancelable Biometrics and Homomorphic Encryption**
  Techniques for revocable template generation and encrypted matching allow authentication without exposing raw biometric data (Nasr et al., 2025).
- **Lightweight Algorithm Design**
  Optimizing computation and storage footprints for edge deployment preserves forensic readiness without exhausting device resources (Mazhar et al., 2021).
- **Standardization Efforts**
  Work on cross-platform formats and protocols seeks to harmonize IoT forensic processes across vendors and ecosystems.
- **Robust Legal and Ethical Frameworks**
  Aligning forensic practice with privacy regulations (e.g., GDPR, HIPAA) and ethical guidelines safeguards user rights while enabling effective investigations (Thangavel et al., 2024) (Figure 15.10).

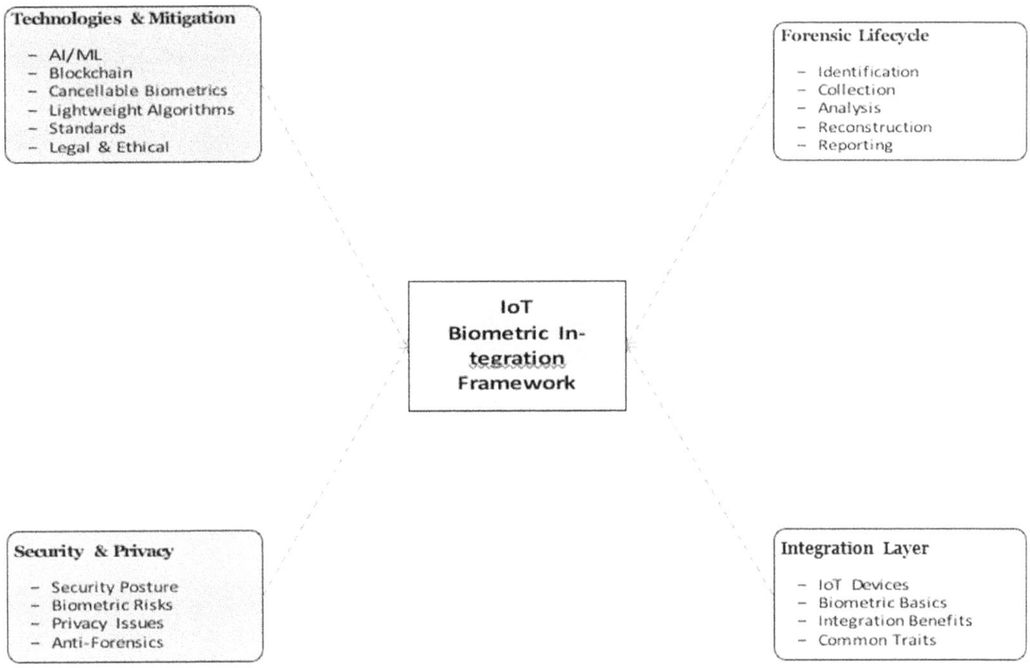

Figure 15.10 Compact IoT biometric integration framework with key layers and components.

15.9 FUTURE RESEARCH DIRECTIONS AND OPEN CHALLENGES

15.9.1 Scalable and featherlight blockchain integration

Develop cold-blooded blockchain infrastructures (e.g., sidechains, sharding) optimized for resource-constrained IoT gateways, balancing invariability with outturn and quiescence conditions. Icing agreement algorithms (e.g., proof of stake, directed acyclic graphs) can operate under limited CPU, memory, and energy budgets without compromising security or adding attack shells.

15.9.2 Sequestration conserving machine learning for forensics

Influence allied literacy and secure multi-party calculation to train anomaly discovery and deepfake discovery models across distributed IoT bumps without exposing raw biometric data. Designing protocols that alleviate model poisoning and data leakage, give strong discriminational sequestration guarantees, and operate within the tight bandwidth and storehouse constraints of edge bias (Thangavel et al., 2024).

15.9.3 Adaptive multimodal fusion and template cancellation

Investigate dynamic weighting schemes and environment-apprehensive emulsion strategies that combine physiological (e.g., ECG) and behavioral (e.g., keystroke) biometrics to ameliorate caricature resistance and fault forbearance. Explore cancelable biometric styles that allow template cancellation and periodic registration. Balancing emulsion complexity against quiescence targets, icing revocable templates remain unlinkable across duplications, and guarding against cross-correlation attacks (Nasr et al., 2025).

15.9.4 Standardization of forensic data formats and APIs

Propose open norms and reference implementations for logging formats, evidence exchange APIs, and data labeling schemas tailored to IoT biometric systems. Achieving assiduity agreement across different merchandisers, accommodating personal protocols, and icing backward comity with heritage bias (Jiang et al., 2021).

15.9.5 Real-time incident response and automated playbooks

Integrate unified frameworks and SOAR (security orchestration, automation, and response) playbooks that use biometric event triggers (e.g., repeated failed authentications) to automatically isolate or quarantine compromised nodes. Defining safe response thresholds to avoid false cons, guaranteeing low false alarm rates in noisy IoT surroundings, and coordinating rapid-fire robotization with legal conditions for substantiation preservation (Grispos et al., 2021).

15.9.6 Adversarial robustness and anti-deepfake defenses

Develop adversarial training and detection mechanisms specific to edge-deployed biometric sensors, capable of identifying anomaly-based attacks and AI-generated biometric forgeries in real time. Limited computational headroom at the edge restricts the complexity of defense models; bushwhackers continuously evolve new deepfake ways that can bypass stationary discovery rules (Ferrag et al., 2019).

15.9.7 Explainability and legal admissibility of biometric evidence

Research interpretable AI methods that produce human-accessible justifications for forensic decisions (e.g., why an authentication attempt was flagged as spoofed), supporting courtroom transparency. Translate black-box model outputs into legally defensible evidence, align explanations with jurisdictional standards for digital testimony, and manage the potential exposure of sensitive model internals (Thangavel et al., 2024) (Tables 15.5 and 15.6).

Table 15.5 Comparison of current challenges and potential solutions in IoT forensics

Challenge	*Current state*	*Potential solution*
Scalability	Limited manual capabilities	AI-driven automation and distributed computing frameworks
Interoperability in multi-vendor systems	Lack of unified standards	Open-source tools, universal APIs, and vendor collaboration
Privacy vs. forensic analysis	Ethical and legal concerns	Homomorphic encryption, blockchain-based transparency
Standardization	Inconsistent evidence handling	Internationally recognized IoT forensic protocols
Academia-industry collaboration	Limited cross-sector interaction	Joint initiatives, shared datasets, and interdisciplinary research

Table 15.6 IoT forensics aspects with its key challenges

Aspect	*Key findings*	*Implications*
Data integrity	Blockchain ensures the immutability of evidence.	Enhances legal admissibility and forensic reliability.
Scalability	AI-based tools improve large-scale data handling.	Enables efficient forensic analysis in IoT ecosystems.
Privacy and ethics	Ethical issues in data collection persist.	Calls for stricter standards and ethical frameworks.
Anti-forensic techniques	Lack of robust countermeasures.	Development needed for advanced detection and mitigation.

15.10 CONCLUSION

This systematic review of the evolving IoT forensics landscape identifies critical developments and challenges defining this field. In IoT forensics, great strides have been made in integrating technologies such as deep learning and blockchain to help with evidence acquisition, malware analysis, and real-time detection. They enhance data integrity, scalability, and adaptability in forensic investigations. However, there remain gaps in the availability of IoT-specific datasets, the standardization of processes, and dealing with anti-forensic techniques.

Key findings emphasize the need for (a) interdisciplinary approaches in combining AI, IoT, and cybersecurity; (b) development of lightweight, scalable forensic tools for resource-constrained IoT devices; (c) stronger privacy-preserving measures balancing forensic requirements with ethical considerations.

IoT forensics is the bedrock on which cybersecurity is reinforced for a connected world. Future trends in this regard would see an integration of AI-driven tools, blockchain-based evidence preservation, and real-time analytics that would redefine the boundaries of forensic science in IoT ecosystems. The potential impact cuts across several domains: better admissibility of evidence, quicker resolution of incidents, and much more robustness in the slew of countermeasures against cybercrime.

This review serves as a call to action to researchers and practitioners to close these gaps while riding the wave of emerging technologies to ensure the achievement of a secure, transparent, and resilient IoT ecosystem.

REFERENCES

Ahmed, A. A., Farhan, K., Jabbar, W. A., & Abdulrahman, A. G. (2023). IoT Forensics: Current Perspectives and Future Directions. Sensors, 24(16), 5210. https://doi.org/10.3390/s24165210

Ahmed, S. F., Shawon, S.S., Bhuyian, A. et al. (2025). Forensics and Security Issues in the Internet of Things. Wireless Networks, 31, 3431–3466. https://doi.org/10.1007/s11276-025-03942-2

Arman, S., Yang, T., Shahed, S., Mazroa, A., Attiah, A., & Mohaisen, L. (2024). A Comprehensive Survey for Privacy-Preserving Biometrics: Recent Approaches, Challenges, and Future Directions. Computers, Materials & Continua, 78. 2087–2110. https://doi.org/10.32604/cmc.2024.047870

Bedari, A., Wang, S., & Yang, W. (2021). A Secure Online Fingerprint Authentication System for Industrial IoT Devices over 5G Networks. Sensors, 22(19), 7609. https://doi.org/10.3390/s22197609

Canadian Institute for Cybersecurity. (2023). CIC-IoT 2023 Dataset. University of New Brunswick. Retrieved June 13, 2025.

Farid, F., Elkhodr, M., Sabrina, F., Ahamed, F., & Gide, E. (2020). A Smart Biometric Identity Management Framework for Personalised IoT and Cloud Computing-Based Healthcare Services. Sensors, 21(2), 552. https://doi.org/10.3390/s21020552

Ferrag, M. A., Maglaras, L., & Derhab, A. (2019). Authentication and Authorization for Mobile IoT Devices Using Biofeatures: Recent Advances and Future Trends. Security and Communication Networks. https://doi.org/10.1155/2019/5452870

Golec, M., Gill, S. S., Bahsoon, R., & Rana, O. (2022, 1 March). BioSec: A Biometric Authentication Framework for Secure and Private Communication Among Edge Devices in IoT and Industry 4.0. IEEE Consumer Electronics Magazine, 11(2), 51–56, 2022. https://doi.org/10.1109/MCE.2020.3038040

Grispos, G., Tursi, F., Choo, K.-K. R., Mahoney, W., & Glisson, W. B. (2021). "A Digital Forensics Investigation of a Smart Scale IoT Ecosystem," 2021 IEEE 20th International Conference on Trust, Security and Privacy in Computing and Communications (TrustCom), Shenyang, China, pp. 710–717.

Ijaz, S., Ali Shah, M., Khan, A., & Ahmed, M. (2016). Smart Cities: A Survey on Security Concerns. International Journal of Advanced Computer Science and Applications(IJACSA), 7(2). http://dx.doi.org/10.14569/IJACSA.2016.070277

Jenkins, J., & Roy, K. (2024). Exploring Deep Convolutional Generative Adversarial Networks (DCGAN) in Biometric Systems: A Survey Study. Discover Artificial Intelligence, 4, 42. https://doi.org/10.1007/s44163-024-00138-z

Jiang, X. et al. (2021, 15 November). Enhancing IoT Security via Cancelable HD-sEMG-Based Biometric Authentication Password, Encoded by Gesture. IEEE Internet of Things Journal, 8(22), 16535–16547. http://dx.doi.org/10.1109/JIOT.2021.3074952

Karimian, N., Guo, Z., Tehranipoor, F., Woodard, D., Tehranipoor, M., & Forte, D. (2018). Secure and Reliable Biometric Access Control for Resource-Constrained Systems and IoT. 10.48550/arXiv.1803.09710.

Lien, C.-W., & Vhaduri, S. (2023). Challenges and Opportunities of Biometric User Authentication in the Age of IoT: A Survey. ACM Computing Surveys, 56(1), 37, Article 14 (January 2024). https://doi.org/10.1145/3603705

Lin, L., Zhao, Y., Meng, J., & Zhao, Q. (2022). A Federated Attention-Based Multimodal Biometric Recognition Approach in IoT. Sensors, 23(13), 6006. https://doi.org/10.3390/s23136006

Mazhar, M. S., Saleem, Y., Almogren, A., Arshad, J., Jaffery, M. H., Rehman, A. U., Shafiq, M., & Hamam, H. (2021). Forensic Analysis on Internet of Things (IoT) Device Using Machine-to-Machine (M2M) Framework. Electronics, 11(7), 1126. https://doi.org/10.3390/electronics11071126

Nasr, M., Brzostowski, K., Piórkowski, A. et al. (2025). Cancelable Biometric Authentication Leveraging Empirical Mode Decomposition and Quaternion Representations for IoT Security. Scientific Reports, 15, 10997. https://doi.org/10.1038/s41598-025-89491-2

Oriwoh, E., Jazani, D., Epiphaniou, G., & Sant, P. (2013). "Internet of Things Forensics: Challenges and approaches," 9th IEEE International Conference on Collaborative Computing: Networking, Applications and Worksharing, Austin, TX, USA, pp. 608–615. https://doi.org/10.4108/icst.collaboratecom.2013.254159

Rad, P., Dorai, G., & Jozani, M. (2024). From Seaweed to Security: The Emergence of Alginate in Compromising IoT Fingerprint Sensors. ArXiv. https://arxiv.org/abs/2404.02150

Rani, S., Kataria, A., Ghosh, S., Karar, V., Sharma, V., Lee, K., & Choi, C. (2020). Threats and Corrective Measures for IoT Security with Observance to Cybercrime. 10.48550/arXiv.2010.08793.

Redwan, K., Akhter, J., & Rahaman, A. S. M. M. (2024). Forensic Tools for Windows Forensic Analysis: A Comprehensive Review. International Journal of Research Publication and Reviews, 5, 5483–5490.

Rui, Z., & Yan, Z. (2019). A Survey on Biometric Authentication: Toward Secure and Privacy-Preserving Identification. IEEE Access, 7, 5994–6009. https://doi.org/10.1109/ACCESS.2018.2889996

Saleh, M. A., Hajar Othman, S., Al-Dhaqm, A., & Al-Khasawneh, M. A. (2021). Common Investigation Process Model for Internet of Things Forensics," 2021 2nd International Conference on Smart Computing and Electronic Enterprise (ICSCEE), Cameron Highlands, Malaysia, pp. 84–89. https://doi.org/10.1109/ICSCEE50312.2021.9498045

Sathwara, S., Dutta, N., & Pricop, E. (2018). IoT Forensic A Digital Investigation Framework for IoT Systems," 2018 10th International Conference on Electronics, Computers and Artificial Intelligence (ECAI), Iasi, Romania, pp. 1–4. https://doi.org/10.1109/ECAI.2018.8679017

Shdefat, A., Mostafa, N., Saker, L., & Topcu, A.. (2021). A Survey Study of the Current Challenges and Opportunities of Deploying the ECG Biometric Authentication Method in IoT and 5G Environments. Indonesian Journal of Electrical Engineering and Informatics (IJEEI), 9. https://doi.org/10.52549/ijeei.v9i2.2890

T., S., B., M., Kala, N., & Narasimhan, P. (2024). Forensic Analysis of Wearable Devices: Privacy, Cyber Security, and Legal Challenges in Digital Forensics. International Journal of Scientific Research in Science and Technology, 11, 757–767. https://doi.org/10.32628/IJSRST241161131

Wells, A., & Usman, A. (2023). Trust and Voice Biometrics Authentication for Internet of Things. International Journal of Information Security and Privacy, 17, 1–28. https://doi.org/10.4018/IJISP.322102

Yang, W., Wang, S., Sahri, N. M., Karie, N. M., Ahmed, M., & Valli, C. (2021). Biometrics for Internet-of-Things Security: A Review. Sensors (Basel), 21(18), 6163. https://doi.org/10.3390/s21186163. PMID: 34577370; PMCID: PMC8472874.

Index

Note: Pages in *italics* and **bold** refer to figures and tables, respectively.

C

D

E

J

L

M

For Product Safety Concerns and Information please contact our EU
representative GPSR@taylorandfrancis.com
Taylor & Francis Verlag GmbH, Kaufingerstraße 24, 80331 München, Germany

www.ingramcontent.com/pod-product-compliance
Ingram Content Group UK Ltd.
Pitfield, Milton Keynes, MK11 3LW, UK
UKHW052220190926
475702UK00006B/1115
* 9 7 8 1 0 3 2 8 2 3 5 4 6 *